# THE
# LIFE AND WITNESS
## OF
# PETER

LARRY R. HELYER

IVP Academic

An imprint of InterVarsity Press
Downers Grove, Illinois

Apollos
Nottingham, England

InterVarsity Press, USA
P.O. Box 1400
Downers Grove, IL 60515-1426, USA
World Wide Web: www.ivpress.com
Email: email@ivpress.com

APOLLOS (an imprint of Inter-Varsity Press, England)
Norton Street
Nottingham NG7 3HR, England
Website: www.ivpbooks.com
Email: ivp@ivpbooks.com

InterVarsity Press®, USA, is the book-publishing division of InterVarsity Christian Fellowship/USA® <www. intervarsity.org> and a member movement of the International Fellowship of Evangelical Students.

Inter-Varsity Press, England, is closely linked with the Universities and Colleges Christian Fellowship, a student movement connecting Christian Unions throughout Great Britain, and a member movement of the International Fellowship of Evangelical Students. Website: www.uccf.org.uk

Cover design: Cindy Kiple
Images: St. Peter, from the Crypt of St. Peter, Byzantine School at St. Peter's, Vatican, Rome, Italy /
         The Bridgeman Art Library
Interior design: Beth Hagenberg

USA ISBN 978-0-8308-3982-7
UK ISBN 978-1-84474-600-2

Printed in the United States of America ∞

**Library of Congress Cataloging-in-Publication Data**

Helyer, Larry R.
   The life and witness of Peter / Larry R. Helyer.
      p. cm.
   Includes bibliographical references and index.
   ISBN 978-8308-3982-7 (pbk. : alk. paper)
   1. Peter, the Apostle, Saint. 2. Bible. N.T. Peter—Criticism,
interpretation, etc. I. Title.
   BS2515.H35 2012
   225.9'2—dc23

2012027651

**British Library Cataloguing in Publication Data**

A catalogue record for this book is available from the British Library.

| P | 20 | 19 | 18 | 17 | 16 | 15 | 14 | 13 | 12 | 11 | 10 | 9 | 8 | 7 | 6 | 5 | 4 | 3 | 2 | 1 |
|---|----|----|----|----|----|----|----|----|----|----|----|---|---|---|---|---|---|---|---|---|
| Y | 29 | 28 | 27 | 26 | 25 | 24 | 23 | 22 | 21 | 20 | 19 | 18 | 17 | 16 | 15 | 14 | 13 | 12 |

# CONTENTS

# ABBREVIATIONS

**Biblical Texts and Versions**

| | |
|---|---|
| ESV | English Standard Version |
| GNB | Good News Bible |
| HCSB | Holman Christian Standard Bible |
| JPS | Jewish Publication Society |
| KJV | King James Version |
| LXX | Septuagint |
| MS(S) | manuscript(s) |
| MT | Masoretic Text |
| NAB | New American Bible |
| NASB | New American Standard Bible |
| NEB | New English Bible |
| NET | New English Translation |
| NIV | New International Version |
| NJB | New Jerusalem Bible |
| NLB | New Living Bible |
| NRSV | New Revised Standard Version |
| NT | New Testament |
| OT | Old Testament |
| TEV | Today's English Version |
| TNIV | Today's New International Version |

**Other Ancient Texts**

| | |
|---|---|
| *1 Clem.* | *1 Clement* |
| *1 En.* | *1 Enoch* |
| 1 Macc | 1 Maccabees |
| 1QHa | *1QHodayot* |
| 1QM | *1QWar Scroll* |
| 1QpHab | *Pesher Habakkuk* |
| 1QS | *1QRule of the Community* |
| *2 Bar.* | *2 Baruch* |
| *2 En.* | *2 Enoch* |

| *2 Esd.* | *2 Esdras* |
|---|---|
| 2 Macc | 2 Macabees |
| 4Q174 | Same as 4QFlorilegium (from Qumran Cave 4) |
| *ʾAbot* | *ʾAbot (Fathers)* |
| *Acts Pet.* | *Acts of Peter* |
| *Acts Pet.12 Apos.* | *VI,1 Acts of Peter and the Twelve Apostles* |
| *Ann.* | Tacitus, *Annales* |
| *Ant.* | Josephus, *Jewish Antiquities* |
| *Apoc. Pet.* | *Apocalypse of Peter* |
| *As. Mos.* | *Assumption of Moses* |
| *Bapt.* | Tertullian, *De baptismo (Baptism)* |
| *Barn.* | *Barnabas* |
| Bar | Baruch |
| *C. Ap.* | Josephus, *Contra Apionem (Against Apion)* |
| *Cels.* | Origen, *Contra Celsum (Against Celsus)* |
| CD | Cairo Genizah copy of the *Damascus Document* |
| *Comm. Mat.* | Origen, *Commentary on Matthew* |
| *Dial.* | Justin Martyr, *Dialogus cum Tryphone (Dialogue with Trypho)* |
| *Dial.* | Seneca, *Dialogi* |
| *Embassy* | Philo, *On the Embassy to Gaius* |
| *Flacc.* | Philo, *Against Flaccus* |
| *Gen. Rab.* | *Genesis Rabbah* |
| *Geogr.* | Strabo, *Geographica (Geography)* |
| *Gos. Mary* | *Gospel of Mary* |
| *Gos. Pet.* | *Gospel of Peter* |
| *Haer.* | Irenaeus, *Adversus haereses (Against Heresies)* |
| *Hist. eccl.* | Eusebius, *Historia ecclesiastica (Ecclesiastical History)* |
| *Hom. Jer.* | Origen, *Homiliae in Jeremiam (Homilies on Jeremiah)* |
| *Hypoth.* | Philo, *Hypothetica* |
| Ign. *Rom.* | Ignatius, *To the Romans* |
| *J. W.* | Josephus, *Jewish War* |
| *Jub.* | *Jubilees* |
| *m.* | Mishnah |
| *Marc.* | Tertullian, *Adversus Marcus (Against Marcion)* |
| *Praesc.* | Tertullian, *De praescriptione haereticorum (Prescription Against Heretics)* |
| *Pss. Sol.* | *Psalms of Solomon* |

| | |
|---|---|
| *Sanh.* | *Sanhedrin* |
| *Scorp.* | *Scorpiace* (*Antidote for the Scorpion's Sting*) |
| Sir | Sirach |
| *Strom.* | Clement of Alexandria, *Stromata* (*Miscellanies*) |
| *T. Jud.* | *Testament of Judah* |
| *Theog.* | Hesiod, *Theogonia* (*Theogony*) |
| *Unit. eccl.* | *De catholicae ecclesiae unitate* (*The Unity of the Catholic Church*) |
| *Vir. ill.* | Jerome, *De viris illustribus* |
| Wis | Wisdom of Solomon |

## Secondary Sources

| | |
|---|---|
| *ABD* | *Anchor Bible Dictionary*. Edited by D. N. Freedman. 6 vols. New York: Doubleday, 1992 |
| ACCS | Ancient Christian Commentary on Scripture |
| AnBib | Analecta biblica |
| *ANET* | *Ancient Near Eastern Texts Relating to the Old Testament*. Edited by J. B. Pritchard. 3rd ed. Princeton: Princeton University Press, 1969 |
| *ANF* | *Ante-Nicene Fathers* |
| ANTC | Abingdon New Testament Commentaries |
| ASNU | Acta seminarii neotestamentici upsaliensis |
| *BAFCS* | *Book of Acts in Its First Century Setting* |
| BAGD | *Greek-English Lexicon of the New Testament and Other Early Christian Literature*. By W. Bauer, W. F. Arndt, F. W. Gingrich and F. W. Danker. 2nd ed. Chicago: University of Chicago Press, 1979 |
| *BAR* | *Biblical Archaeology Review* |
| *BBR* | *Bulletin for Biblical Research* |
| BDAG | *Greek-English Lexicon of the New Testament and Other Early Christian Literature*. By B. W. Bauer, F. W. Danker, W. F. Arndt and F. W. Gingrich. 3rd ed. Chicago: University of Chicago Press, 1999 |
| BECNT | Baker Exegetical Commentary on the New Testament |
| *Bib* | *Biblica* |
| *BRev* | *Bible Review* |
| *BSac* | *Bibliotheca Sacra* |
| *BTB* | *Biblical Theology Bulletin* |

| | |
|---|---|
| *CBQ* | *Catholic Biblical Quarterly* |
| *CTJ* | *Calvin Theological Journal* |
| *DJG* | *Dictionary of Jesus and the Gospel.* Edited by Joel B. Green and Scot McKnight. Downers Grove, Ill.: InterVarsity Press, 1992 |
| *DLNTD* | *Dictionary of the Later New Testament and Its Developments.* Edited by Ralph P. Martin and Peter H. Davids. Downers Grove, Ill.: InterVarsity Press, 1997 |
| *DNTB* | *Dictionary of New Testament Background.* Edited by Craig A. Evans and Stanley E. Porter. Downers Grove, Ill.: InterVarsity Press, 2000 |
| *DPL* | *Dictionary of Paul and His Letters.* Edited by Gerald F. Hawthorne and Ralph P. Martin. Downers Grove, Ill.: InterVarsity Press, 1993 |
| *DTIB* | *Dictionary for Theological Interpretation of the Bible.* Edited by Kevin J. Vanhoozer. Grand Rapids: Baker, 2005 |
| EBC | Expositor's Bible Commentary |
| *EDBT* | *Evangelical Dictionary of Biblical Theology.* Edited by Walter A. Elwell. Grand Rapids: Baker, 1996 |
| *EDEJ* | *The Eerdmans Dictionary of Early Judaism.* Edited by John J. Collins and Daniel C. Harlow. Grand Rapids: Eerdmans, 2010 |
| *EDNT* | *Exegetical Dictionary of the New Testament.* Edited by H. Balz and G. Schneider. 3 vols. Grand Rapids: Eerdmans, 1990-1993 |
| *EDSS* | *Encyclopedia of the Dead Sea Scrolls.* Edited by Lawrence H. Schiffman and James C. VanderKam. 2 vols. Oxford: Oxford University Press, 2000 |
| *ExpTim* | *Expository Times* |
| HNTC | Harper's New Testament Commentaries |
| HUT | Hermeneutische Untersuchungen zur Theologie |
| ICC | International Critical Commentary |
| *IDB* | *The Interpreter's Dictionary of the Bible.* Edited by G. A. Buttrick. 4 vols. Nashville: Abingdon, 1962 |
| *IDBSupp* | *The Interpreter's Dictionary of the Bible: Supplementary Volume.* Edited by K. Crim. Nashville: Abingdon, 1976 |
| *ISBE* | *International Standard Bible Encyclopedia.* Edited by G. W. Bromiley. 4 vols. Grand Rapids: Eerdmans, 1979-1988 |

IVPNTC      InterVarsity Press New Testament Commentaries
*JBL*        *Journal of Biblical Literature*
*JETS*       *Journal of the Evangelical Theological Society*
*JSNT*       *Journal for the Study of the New Testament*
*JSNTSup*    *Journal for the Study of the New Testament: Supplement Series*
KEK         Kritisch-exegetischer Kommentar über das Neue Testament
            (Myer-Kommentar)
MM          Moulton, J. H., and G. Milligan. *The Vocabulary of the Greek Testament*. London, 1930. Reprint. Peabody, Mass., 1997
NAC         New American Commentary
*NBD*        *New Bible Dictionary*. Edited by D. R. W. Wood. 3rd ed. Downers Grove, Ill.: InterVarsity Press, 1996
*NDBT*       *New Dictionary of Biblical Theology*. Edited by T. Desmond Alexander and Brian Rosner. Downers Grove, Ill.: Inter-Varsity Press, 2000
*NDT*        *New Dictionary of Theology*. Edited by Sinclair B. Ferguson and David F. Wright. Downers Grove, Ill.: InterVarsity Press, 1988
*NEAEHL*     *New Encyclopedia of Archaeological Excavations in the Holy Land*. Edited by E. Stern. 4 vols. Jerusalem: Carta, 1993
*NHL*        *Nag Hammadi Library in English*. Edited by J. M. Robinson. 4th rev. ed. Leiden: Brill, 1996
NICNT       New International Commentary on the New Testament
*NIDNTT*     *New International Dictionary of New Testament Theology*. Edited by Colin Brown. 4 vols. Grand Rapids: Zondervan, 1975-1985
*NIDOTTE*    *New International Dictionary of Old Testament Theology and Exegesis*. Edited by Willem A. VanGemeren. 5 vols. Grand Rapids: Zondervan, 1997
NIVAC       NIV Application Commentary
*NTS*        *New Testament Studies*
*OCD*        *Oxford Classical Dictionary*. Edited by S. Hornblower and A. Spawforth. 3rd ed. Oxford: Oxford University Press, 1996
*OTP*        *Old Testament Pseudepigrapha*. Edited by J. H. Charlesworth. 2 vols. New York: Doubleday, 1983
PG          Patrologia graeca. Edited by J.-P. Migne. 162 vols. Paris, 1857-1886

| | |
|---|---|
| *TDNT* | *Theological Dictionary of the New Testament*. Edited by G. Kittel and G. Friedrich. Translated by G. W. Bromiley. 10 vols. Grand Rapids: Eerdmans, 1964-1976 |
| *TLNT* | *Theological Lexicon of the New Testament*. By Ceslas Spicq. Translated and edited by J. D. Ernest. 3 vols. Peabody, Mass.: Hendrickson, 1994 |
| TNTC | Tyndale New Testament Commentaries |
| *TWOT* | *Theological Wordbook of the Old Testament*. Edited by R. L. Harris and G. L. Archer Jr. 2 vols. Chicago: Moody, 1980 |
| *TynBul* | *Tyndale Bulletin* |
| WBC | Word Biblical Commentary |
| *WJT* | *Westminster Theological Journal* |
| WUNT | Wissenschaftliche Untersuchungen zum Neuen Testament |
| *ZPEB* | *Zondervan Pictorial Encyclopedia of the Bible*. Edited by Merrill C. Tenney. 5 vols. Grand Rapids: Zondervan, 1975 |

# PREFACE

BIBLICAL SCHOLARS OFTEN COMMENT on the relative neglect of Peter's theology.[1] Given the shape of the Christian canon, perhaps this is inevitable. The Gospels, foundational documents of the Christian faith, and the letters of the apostle Paul overshadow the Galilean fisherman's contribution. And yet, Martin Luther had the highest regard for Peter's theological contribution to the NT, calling the Gospel of John, Romans and 1 Peter "the true kernel and marrow" of the NT message.[2] This book invites Peter to the table as a major contributor to the theological message of the NT,[3] sharing Martin Hengel's conviction that Saint Peter is "the underestimated Apostle."[4] As F. J. Foakes-Jackson reminds us, "the very fact that Peter was singled out by

---

[1] Whereas J. H. Elliot considered 1 Peter an "exegetical stepchild" ("The Rehabilitation of an Exegetical Step-Child: 1 Peter in Recent Research," *JBL* 95 [1976]: 243-54) and bemoaned its "benign neglect" by the scholarly guild (ibid., p. 243), the situation is somewhat improved in twenty-first-century biblical scholarship. See the review of Robert L. Webb and Betsy Bauman-Martin, eds., *Reading First Peter with New Eyes: Methodological Reassessments of the Letter of First Peter* (Library of New Testament Studies 364; New York: T&T Clark, 2007) by Bonnie Howe, *Review of Biblical Literature* 05 (2009): 3-4: "No longer 'an exegetical step-child,' 1 Peter has not only been adopted by the biblical studies guild; it continues to receive the attention and recognition it deserves." But for the larger Christian community, J. Ramsey Michaels's assessment still holds true: "1 Peter's place in the NT canon has been a humble one. . . . For whatever reason, when Christians spoke of 'the apostle' (especially in connection with the canon) in the early centuries, they almost always meant Paul, not Peter" ("1 Peter," *DLNTD*, pp. 920-21). As to 2 Peter, Peter H. Davids describes it as "one of the 'ugly stepchildren' of the NT," a letter that "has suffered neglect in the modern period" ("2 Peter, Book of," *DTIB*, p. 583).

[2] *Prefaces of the New Testament* (1522) cited by J. H. Elliot, "Peter, First Epistle of," *ABD* 5:270.

[3] I am reminded of G. B. Caird's innovative approach to NT theology (*New Testament Theology* [ed. L. D. Hurst; Oxford: Clarendon, 1995]) in which he imagines a colloquium, convened by himself, consisting of at least twelve NT authors. Curiously, however, Peter, as a distinct witness, is not present. The most that can be said is that the anonymous author of 1 Peter appears as a proxy!

[4] *Saint Peter: The Underestimated Apostle* (trans. Thomas H. Trapp; Grand Rapids: Eerdmans, 2010).

the unanimous voice of the writers of the New Testament for pre-eminence is sufficient reason why he should demand our serious attention."[5]

## Constructing Petrine Theology

My readers are entitled to know how I intend to approach the task of synthesizing the theology of the apostle Peter. Accordingly, I set out the various methodological assumptions and decisions underlying this work.

## The Sources

A fundamental, methodological question immediately arises when one inquires into the theology of Peter. What are the relevant sources for such an undertaking? The Christian canon contains but two epistles attributed to Peter. Of these, the second is almost unanimously rejected as authentic by modern scholars, and a majority cast doubt on the genuineness of the first, leaving little but tradition.[6]

My approach accepts both letters as genuine. I also take seriously the tradition, supported by close textual study, which links all four Gospels to eyewitness testimony.[7] Accordingly, I see no reason to doubt the traditional view that the Gospel of Mark is based in large measure on the preaching of the apostle Peter at Rome.[8] Accordingly, Mark's

---

[5] *Peter: Prince of Apostles* (London: Hodder & Stoughton, 1927), p. xii.

[6] In *The Eerdmans Bible Dictionary* (Grand Rapids: Eerdmans, 1987), p. 818, Allen C. Myers renders a negative verdict on the whole undertaking:

> A "theology of Peter" cannot be reconstructed. The only materials that could be drawn on would be his speeches (Acts 2:14-40; 3:12-26; 4:8-12; 5:29-32; 10:34-43), which reflect the beliefs of the early Church for whom he spoke and the interests of the writer of Acts more than any distinctive ideas of Peter; possibly 1-2 Peter . . . and the gospel of Mark, which was associated with Peter at an early date but does not necessarily reflect his particular concerns.

[7] On this whole issue, see Robert H. Gundry, *The Old Is Better: New Testament Essays in Support of Traditional Interpretations* (WUNT 178; Tübingen: Mohr Siebeck, 2005). In defense of the reliability of the Gospels, see Craig L. Blomberg, "Gospels (Historical Reliability)," *DJG*, pp. 291-97; R. Riesner, "Archaelogy and Geography," *DJG*, pp. 33-46; Birger Gerhardson, *The Reliability of the Gospel Tradition* (foreword by Donald A. Hagner; Peabody, Mass.: Hendrickson, 2001) and Richard J. Bauckham, *Jesus and the Eyewitnesses: The Gospels as Eyewitness Testimony* (Grand Rapids: Eerdmans, 2006).

[8] Eusebius, a fourth-century historian of the early church, cites the following statement of Papias (first and second centuries A.D.), said to be from "the presbyter" (traditionally thought to be the apostle John, though some think it refers to an elder named John, who was in turn a disciple of the apostle John):

Gospel ought to be taken into account when seeking to formulate Peter's theology. On good historical grounds, I also accept the essential historicity and reliability of the book of Acts.[9] Inasmuch as Peter is the prominent figure and spokesperson in the first half of Acts, I include the sermons and speeches attributed to him as an adequate representation of his thought, even though they are now incorporated into the work of another author who has his own theological perspective and agenda.[10] For purposes of synthesizing Peter's theology, however, I will not incorporate material from the various apocryphal works attributed to Peter, since these lay outside the canonical boundary lines.[11] Chapters 15 and 16 will, however, briefly survey some of the fascinating, later traditions that emerge concerning Peter.

## Method of Presentation

A further methodological problem concerns the presentation of the material extracted from the sources. Should one's synthesis be set out in a strictly chronological order with regard to the actual sources in which information appears, or in terms of Peter's life, insofar as this can be reconstructed from the sources? If the former, one should be obliged to begin with Paul's letters, since there is a consensus that they are the earliest surviving Christian documents. The problem here concerns the

---

And the presbyter said this. "Mark having become the interpreter of Peter, wrote down accurately whatsoever he remembered. It was not, however, in exact order that he related the sayings or deeds of Christ. For he neither heard the Lord nor accompanied Him. But afterwards, as I said, he accompanied Peter, who accommodated his instructions to the necessities [of his hearers], but with no intention of giving a regular narrative of the Lord's sayings. Wherefore Mark made no mistake in thus writing some things as he remembered them. For of one thing he took especial care, not to omit anything he had heard, and not to put anything fictitious into the statements." This is what is related by Papias regarding Mark. (*Hist. eccl.* 3.39)

See Hengel's trenchant criticism of views denying Petrine theology behind Mark's Gospel (e.g., Udo Schnell) or detect an anti-Petrine tendency in Mark (e.g.,Terrence V. Smith) in *Saint Peter*, pp. 36-48.

[9]See Colin Hemer, *The Book of Acts in the Setting of Hellenistic History* (ed. Conrad H. Gempf; WUNT 49; Tübingen: Mohr, 1989).

[10]See F. F. Bruce, "Acts of the Apostles," *ISBE* 1:39-40, and J. B. Green, "Acts of the Apostles," *DLNTD*, pp. 10-12.

[11]For a full discussion of my methodology, see Larry R. Helyer, *The Witness of Jesus, Paul and John: An Exploration in Biblical Theology* (Downers Grove, Ill.: InterVarsity Press, 2008), pp. 26-44.

paucity of material. If the latter, one must necessarily begin with the Gospels since they purport to record events from Jesus' ministry (ca. A.D. 27-30). However, given the inherent problems, perhaps a chronological approach should be jettisoned for a thematic or topical scheme. Good arguments can be made for either.

I opt for a chronological approach in terms of Peter's life fully aware of the many problems and scholarly disagreements and quibbles such an option engenders.[12] Mark's Gospel, supplemented by the other Gospels, provide the primary materials for piecing together a general picture of what may be known: his home and profession, his call to be a disciple, his appointment as an apostle and, most importantly, his role as spokesperson of the Twelve at key moments during Jesus' ministry (chaps. 1 through 3). The book of Acts carries the canonical storyline forward and gives some indication of Peter's leadership in the early Jerusalem church and Judea (chap. 4). I pay special attention to Peter's sermons as recorded in Acts with leading themes and motifs highlighted that appear later in Peter's letters. To this are added the several references in Paul's letters that refer to Peter. These are examined in chapter 5 for any further contribution they may make to the task at hand.

The heart of the book focuses on Peter's two epistles, the primary content from which Peter's theological thought may tentatively be reconstructed. Chapters 6 through 10, devoted to 1 Peter, probe the theological substratum informing Peter's moral admonition and exhortation to believers in Anatolia (north central Turkey). Peter's contribution to the NT teaching on God the Father, the person and work of Christ and the role of the Holy Spirit come in for special attention, as does the practical problem that lies at the center of Peter's purpose in writing his first epistle: suffering for the name of Christ. Closely linked to this issue are Peter's reflections on the nature and purpose of the people of God. Along the way, several key theological ideas and themes are identified which recur in the teaching of Jesus, Paul and

---

[12]My approach is similar to that adopted by the participants in an ecumenical study titled *Peter in the New Testament* (ed. Raymond E. Brown, Karl P. Donfried and John Reumann; Minneapolis/New York: Augsburg/Paulist, 1973). My study, however, significantly differs in maintaining a high regard for the historical reliability of the Gospels and the book of Acts, as well as holding to the authenticity of both 1 and 2 Peter.

John, all with an eye to demonstrating the remarkable unity discovered in these four witnesses.

Chapters 11 through 14 focus on 2 Peter. Once again, I focus on the leading theological ideas and themes of this short pastoral letter. Sharp polemic against false teachers dominates, and trying to specify more narrowly their identity and the contours of their teaching presents considerable challenges. Closely linked to the foregoing, the eschatology of 2 Peter receives special attention since it is a major contribution of the epistle.

Chapters 15 through 17 survey the post-NT traditions and legends that gradually develop concerning Peter and his position in the Christian church. I briefly trace the veneration of Peter through the early centuries culminating in the Roman Catholic claim for the primacy of Peter and apostolic succession as essential for true catholicity. I conclude the book with a word of appreciation for the influence of Peter's life and thought and a brief summary of his theological contribution to NT theology.

***Central themes.*** The leading theological theme of 1 Peter already surfaces in the Gospel according to Mark and in the speeches of Peter as summarized in Acts. The overarching rubric that encapsulates Peter's theology is the meaning and significance of the cross which shapes Peter's first pastoral letter. The Christian life, according to Peter, is cruciform in nature. In his words, "To this you were called, because Christ suffered for you, leaving you an example, that you should follow in his steps" (1 Pet 2:21 TNIV). The echoes of Mark 8:34-38 are unmistakable. Admittedly, the Greek word for "cross" (*stauros*) occurs not even once in the two letters ascribed to Peter or in the speeches attributed to him in Acts. The Greek verb *stauroō* ("to crucify"), however, does occur eight times in the Gospel of Mark, and the concept is clearly present in all four sources. Furthermore, the special vocabulary of 1 Peter includes the word "to suffer" (*paschein*), occurring eleven times out of a total of forty occurrences in the NT. In four passages, the suffering in question is that of Christ on behalf of sinners and for sins (1 Pet 2:20, 23; 3:18; 4:1). Peter's burden is transparent: one cannot follow the Master without also treading the Via Dolorosa. An implied question confronts each reader: *Quo vadis* ("Where are you going")?

The overarching theological theme of 2 Peter is twofold: hope in the glory of God through Christ and certainty of God's judgment on evildoers. This glory reveals itself through participation in the divine nature and through experiencing the new heavens and new earth. For Peter, Christian hope is not just pie in the sky but a robust certainty, rooted in the prophetic promises and confirmed by the Lord Jesus Christ, molding and anchoring the believer in the seductions and storms of life. Second Peter is highly polemical in nature because false teachers are denying this central Christian doctrine: the imminent return of Jesus Christ in glory. False teachers are put on notice: their condemnation is not an idle threat.

## ACKNOWLEDGMENTS

I take this opportunity to thank once again my editor, Dr. Daniel Reid, academic and reference books editor of IVP. He has shepherded me through two previous books for IVP, and I am grateful he has persevered with me one more time. As always the editorial staff of IVP is superb, and I am indebted to them for their careful work. Special thanks go to the external reader of this manuscript whose input has considerably improved the book.

I also wish to acknowledge the important contribution of the graduate students who persevered with me in the Petrine Epistles course I taught at Taylor University during the fall of 2009. Their feedback and perceptive questions helped sharpen my own understanding—or called into question my misunderstanding—of Peter's letters.

As always, my wife has been a constant source of encouragement along the way. Sharing with her my findings and listening to her feedback has been a valuable and enjoyable part of writing this book.

Along the way, I have learned many things about Peter and his theology. But unresolved questions remain. Perhaps I can request an interview at Saint Peter's gate! In the meantime, I have to refocus on the Galilean fisherman's primary message: walking in the Master's steps—very big steps indeed.

# 1

## BACKGROUND OF
## SIMON PETER

◊

THE GOSPELS SERVE AS our primary source for sketching Peter's early years during which he becomes a disciple and then an apostle of Jesus the Messiah. This chapter considers some linguistic, historical-geographical and sociological clues imbedded in the Gospels that throw light on this remarkable man.

### HIS NAME

Peter was not the apostle's given name; Jesus gave it to him. Peter is a Greek name (*petros*) meaning "rock" or "stone" (Mk 3:16). His Aramaic name was *šim'ōn*, meaning something like "hearing" or "obedient."[1] But he also went by the good Greek name *Simōn* (occurring seventy-five times in the NT), though occasionally his name is transliterated into Greek as *Symeōn*, a spelling reflecting his Aramaic name (Acts 15:14; 2 Pet 2:1 [majority of Gk MSS]). The fact that he had both an Aramaic and a Greek name is significant; he was bilingual and lived in an environment that was heavily influenced by Hellenism. The disparaging view of the Jerusalem religious leaders that Jesus' disciples were "uneducated and ordinary men" (Acts 4:13) probably "means no more than that they were ignorant of the finer points of the rabbinical interpretation of the Jewish Torah."[2]

---

[1] *Šim'ōn* may be a diminutive of *šam'a'el*, meaning "God has heard."
[2] Ralph P. Martin, "Peter," *ISBE* 3:803. See also Jerome Murphy-O'Connor, "Fishers of Men: What We Know of the First Disciples from Their Profession," *BR* 25/3 (1999): 22-27, 48-49.

Simon or Simeon was a popular name shared by many Jews of the Second Temple period; several luminaries in Jewish history also bore it. From the Hebrew Scriptures, one recalls Simeon, second son of the patriarch Jacob and progenitor of the tribe bearing his name. In the early second century (ca. 180 B.C.), Ben Sira, a Jerusalem teacher, rhapsodizes on the virtues and ministrations of a certain high priest named Simon.[3] In the mid-second century B.C., a Simon Maccabeus achieved iconic status as a war hero during the national liberation movement against the Seleucids. The Jewish people bestowed on him the unprecedented honor of acclaiming him both ethnarch (ruler of a province or a people) and high priest (ca. 140 B.C.). He thus assumed national leadership in both the political and religious spheres. Not surprisingly, Jewish parents frequently chose to name their sons Simon. Ossuaries provide mute evidence that it was a well-worn name during Second Temple times.[4] Accordingly, at least nine different people, including Simon Peter, bear the name in the NT.[5]

Jesus apparently gave Simon the nickname "Peter" in keeping with a character trait appropriate to or desired for him. One recalls in Hebrew tradition the importance of name changes, especially when God is the one who bestows the new name. At critical moments in their life, Abram ("exalted father") becomes Abraham ("ancestor of a

---

Oscar Cullmann observes that "anyone brought up in Bethsaida would not only have understood Greek, but would also have been polished by intercourse with foreigners and have had some Greek culture" (*Peter: Disciple—Apostle—Martyr* [trans. Floyd V. Filson; Philadelphia: Westminster, 1953], p. 22). By contrast, Martin Hengel says, "We do not even know whether we can say for sure that Peter, who was once a Galilean fisherman, even knew how to write decently. The ability to read, already on the level of being able to know the Holy Scriptures, was more important and more widespread" (*Saint Peter: The Underestimated Apostle* [trans. Thomas F. Trapp; Grand Rapids: Eerdmans, 2010], p. 12 and n. 35).

[3]On the debated question of the precise identity of this Simon, see James C. VanderKam, *From Joshua to Caiaphas: High Priests After the Exile* (Minneapolis: Fortress, 2004), pp. 137-57.

[4]Of the 917 ossuaries possessed by the State of Israel, 231 are inscribed with names. Of these there are only 72 different names. Remarkably, 16 names comprise a full 75 percent of the entire collection. The most frequent female Jewish name is Salome (Shalom, Shlomzion), occurring 26 times, and the most frequent male name is, interestingly, Shim'on, also occurring 26 times. See L. Y. Rahmani, *A Catalogue of Jewish Ossuaries* (Jerusalem: Israel Antiquities Authority and the Israel Academy of Sciences and Humanities, 1994).

[5]See Nola J. Opperwall-Galluch, "Simon," *ISBE* 4:515-16. It may be noted that Shimon remains a relatively popular name among Israelis: witness a former prime minister and current president of Israel, Shimon Peres.

multitude," Gen 17:5) and Jacob ("he who grasps the heel" becomes Israel ("God strives," Gen 32:27-30; see also Is 62:2; 65:15).[6] A "Man of Rock" is someone who is solid and on whom you may depend.[7] Bedrock provides a solid foundation on which to build (Mt 7:24-25; Eph 2:20). Although Peter struggles at times, in the end, he lives up to the meaning of his new name bestowed by the Master.[8] For English speakers, perhaps we can best appreciate Simon's nickname by calling him "Rocky."[9]

The Aramaic equivalent of *petros* is *kēphās*, and the English cognate, "Cephas," occurs nine times in the NT as Peter's name (Jn 1:42; 1 Cor 1:12; 3:22; 9:5; 15:5; Gal 1:18; 2:9, 11, 14). The frequency with which his name appears in the NT (e.g., Peter, Simon, Simon Peter, Cephas) testifies to his significance in early Christianity. In the Synoptics his name occurs 75 times and in John, 35 times. Taking into account the entire NT, we find 181 occurrences, even more than that of Paul/Saul (177).[10]

## GALILEAN FISHERMAN

Here is what may be pieced together concerning Peter's background. Simon was a Galilean fisherman, and his home town was Bethsaida (Jn 1:44).

*Location of Bethsaida.* A problem of identification arises, however, and two candidates vie for recognition. The first location, today known as Et-Tell, was a city of some consequence in the Iron Age and was probably the capital of the small Aramean state called Geshur in the

---

[6]"But this fact is important if we desire to judge rightly the bearing of the fact that Jesus gave Peter this title. It corresponds to Jewish custom to choose as titles words which somehow point to the promise in a particular situation and lay an obligation on their bearer." Cullmann, *Peter*, p. 19.

[7]Hengel likes to use the appellations "the Man of Rock" or "Peter the Rock" in *Saint Peter*, pp. 16-22.

[8]"He was at least not always a model of rock-like firmness" (BDAG, p. 654).

[9]"To the best of our knowledge, the name 'Rock' was not an ordinary personal name in either Hebrew/Aramaic or in Greek. It would be more comparable to the American nickname 'Rocky' and therefore would have to be explained, e.g., the one who bears it has a rough or 'tough' character, etc. Compare the appellation *maqqāb(āy)*, 'hammer(like),' given to Judas Maccabeus." Raymond E. Brown, Karl P. Donfried and John Reuman, eds., *Peter in the New Testament* (Minneapolis/New York: Augsburg/Paulist, 1973), p. 90, n. 210.

[10]Hengel, *Saint Peter*, pp. 10-11.

OT (Josh 12:5; 13:11; 2 Sam 3:3, et al.). During the Hellenistic-Roman era, it was a Greek city serving as an administrative center for the district of Gaulanitis. In approximately A.D. 30, Herod Philip renamed it Julias in honor of Augustus's wife Julia/Livia, who died in A.D. 29.[11] Today, Et-Tell lies about 1.5 kilometers to the north of the shoreline, on the eastern bank of the Jordan River before it empties into the northeastern quadrant of the Sea of Galilee (called Kinneret in the OT [Num 34:11] and Sea of Galilee, Sea of Tiberius [Jn 6:1] and lake of Gennesaret [Lk 5:1] in the NT).[12]

The other candidate is a site called el-'Araj, a small village lying along the present-day shoreline and east of where the Jordan River empties into the Galilee. In NT times, however, the site lay on the *west* side of the Jordan because the river has changed its course over the centuries.

Can we decide between the two options? According to John's Gospel, Philip, in addition to Peter and Andrew, also came from "Bethsaida *in Galilee*" (Jn 12:21, italics added). Taking John strictly, in accord with precise geopolitical terminology, favors el-'Araj, because it, not Et-Tell, was located in Galilee, under the jurisdiction of Herod Antipas. But the course of the Jordan may have shifted since the first century so that in Peter's day, Et-Tell was in fact located in the district of Galilee. Or, it may be that John is content to locate Bethsaida regionally. Another objection to identifying Et-Tell as NT Bethsaida arises from Mark 8:22-23, in which Jesus leads a blind man who lived at Bethsaida outside the "village" (*kōmē*). One would have expected Mark to use the word city (*polis*) in keeping with Bethsaida's dignity as a district capital. But perhaps this expects more precision in the use of these two terms than is warranted. James Strange suggests that el-'Araj and a nearby site el-Misadiyeh are the remains of the fishing village of Bethsaida and Et Tell is the acropolis of Herod Philip's Hellenistic city of Julias.[13] This

---

[11]Reisner, "Archaeology and Geography," *DJG*, p. 39, points out that the NT uses only the Jewish name for the place. This should be taken into consideration in evaluating the age of the Gospel traditions. I follow the general consensus that Josephus was in error when he identified this Livia with Augustus's daughter.

[12]On the terminology used for the Sea of Galilee, see R. Steven Notley, "The Sea of Galilee: Development of an Early Christian Toponym," *JBL* 128 (2009): 183-88.

[13]"Bethsaida (Place)," *ABD* 1:692-93.

follows a suggestion offered by G. Schumacher in the 1880s.[14]

As early as 1838, Edward Robinson identified Et-Tell as NT Bethsaida. Modern excavations under the direction of Rami Arav support Robinson's view: "Probes and remote sensing (ground penetration radar) near the present-day shoreline at el-'Araj, the other contender as Bethsaida, have shown it to have been an *exclusively* Byzantine period settlement." Furthermore, an earthquake in A.D. 363 resulted in a massive flow of dirt and debris from some 9 kilometers north of Et Tell and a subsequent dislocation of the northern shore line some 2 kilometers to the south. Thus, in Jesus' day, Et-Tell was much closer to the Sea of Galilee than it is today.[15] Steven Notley, however, calls attention to "the inexplicable absence of first-century remains" at Et-Tell, and concludes that "for the time being, the location of ancient Bethsaida remains in question."[16]

At any rate, in the first century, the Jordan River was the border between the district of Galilee and the district of Gaulanitis (modern Golan). Bethsaida-Julias thus lay near a political border—just inside the jurisdiction of Herod Philip (Gaulanitis) and just to the east of the jurisdiction of Herod Antipas (Galilee). Almost certainly it possessed a customs office. Goods passing from one toparchy to another were subject to duty. "Toparchy" is a Greek term used to designate an administrative or tax district, perhaps equivalent to a county or state. This necessitated the presence of toll, tax and duty collectors along with military personnel to enforce the levies. Since Bethsaida-Julias was the capital of Gaulanitis, various administrative officials resided there, and, since Herod Philip's tetrarchy was inhabited by a large Gentile population, it reflected both Jewish and non-Jewish influence.[17] This means

---

[14]R. L. Alden, "Bethsaida," *ZPEB* 1:542-43, harmonizes the conflicting textual data by suggesting that "perhaps the fishing settlement first occupied the shore position [et-Araj], whereas the city that Herod Philip built [Et Tel] was located at a more advantageous site to the N. This identification would solve most of the questions presented in the gospel accounts as well as those of the ancient secular historians."

[15]Rami Arav, "Bethsaida (Et-Tell)," *NEAEHL* 5:1611-12 (italics added).

[16]Perhaps future excavations will resolve the question. Anson F. Rainey and R. Steven Notley, *The Sacred Bridge: Carta's Atlas of the Biblical World* (Carta: Jerusalem, 2006), p. 359.

[17]In area B at Et-Tell, excavation turned up sherds of limestone vessels. This is a significant diagnostic feature since, in the Second Temple period, limestone was considered unsusceptible to ritual impurity and thus "provides evidence of a Jewish presence." Arav, "Bethsaida (Et-Tell)," NEAEHL 5:1615.

that free association with Gentiles is a not inconsequential aspect of
Peter's background, especially when one remembers that he played the
leading role in opening the door for Gentile admittance to the nascent
church (Acts 10:1–11:18; 15:7-14).

*The fishing industry in Galilee.* The economy of Bethsaida, like that
of other towns and villages along the lake, depended heavily on the
fishing industry, as demonstrated by an abundance of fishing hooks,
lead weights, anchors, sail and net needles and other gear associated
with fishing uncovered in area A of Et-Tell, appropriately called the
"House of the Fisherman." In fact, fishing was an important aspect of
the socioeconomic fabric of first-century Palestine. Josephus, in his
nearly rhapsodic description of the region of Galilee and the Sea of
Gennesaret, mentions "a great number of ships" employed by the Jewish
rebels in their vain attempt to defeat the Romans (*J.W.* 3.10.1 §465; cf.
3.10.9 §531). In 1986, the remarkable discovery of an ancient boat dated
to the first century A.D. brought Josephus's reference to life. The so-
called "Jesus Boat" may have been one of those involved in the great
battle on the lake between the Jewish insurgents and the Romans in the
summer of A.D. 67.

Today, we can see the kind of sailing craft used for both fishing and
transportation in the time of Jesus. The "Jesus boat," 25.5 feet long, 7.5
feet wide and 4.1 feet high, carried a crew of five but could hold up to
fifteen passengers. Interestingly, the boat had a rear seat, nicely illustrating the vivid Markan account of a storm on the lake: "Jesus was in
the stern, sleeping on a cushion" (Mk 4:38 TNIV).[18] In such a vessel,
several of the apostles, before their call to preach the gospel, spent long
hours on the lake eking out a living. Recall Simon's response to Jesus'
command to let down his nets: "Master, we've worked hard all night
and haven't caught anything" (Lk 5:4-5 TNIV). In a similar boat, Jesus
and his disciples frequently crisscrossed the lake during his Galilean
ministry (Mk 4:35; 5:21; 6:32, 53; 8:10, 13).

The name Bethsaida means "House of the Fisherman," and the town
of Magdala Nunnaya (Magdala in the NT), on the northwestern shore

---

[18]For an account of the discovery and recovery of the vessel, see Shelley Wachsman, "The Galilee Boat 2,000 Year-Old Hull Recovered Intact," *BAR* 14/5 (1988): 18-33.

of the lake, means "Fish Tower," probably referring to a wooden structure in which fish were air-dried. Magdala was also called Taricheae, a Greek word meaning something like "Place of Salted Fish," evidence of a fish-processing facility just a few miles from Capernaum, which also appears to have been a center for salting fish. Processed fish from the Galilee was carted to Jerusalem and sold in its markets, as witnessed by the Fish Gate in postexilic Jerusalem (Neh 3:3).[19] Mendel Nun has discovered fifteen or sixteen ancient harbors located along the shoreline of the lake, all dating to the Second Temple period,[20] one of the most impressive of which served the village of Capernaum, almost certainly located at Tell Hum.[21] Not surprisingly, Nun also found one in proximity to Bethsaida.

Simon Peter and his brother Andrew appear as partners in a domestic fishing business with a man named Zebedee and his two sons, James and John (Lk 5:7, 9-10).[22] Simon owned one of the boats (Lk 5:3), perhaps one he inherited from his father. The family business, located in Capernaum, employed hired hands or day laborers (Mk 1:20; cf. Mt 20:1-16). These extra hands were necessary to assist in rowing, handling sails, managing and drying the large dragnets and sorting fish. Western readers should not superimpose a free market economy on the Gospel narratives. Such was not likely the case.[23] The Zebedee

---

[19]See Seane Freyne, *Galilee, Jesus and the Gospels: Literary and Historical Approaches to the Gospels* (Philadelphia: Fortress, 1988), p. 50, n. 44, and Murphy-O'Connor, "Fishers of Men," pp. 22-27, 48-49. For allusions to the fish-pickling industry at Taricheae, see Strabo, *Geogr.* 16.2.45.

[20]Mendel Nun, "Ports of Galilee," *BAR* 25/4 (1999): 8-31.

[21]Eusebius's *Onomasticon* locates Capernaum 2 miles from Chorazin, which fits Tell Hum, and the excavations there (the synagogue and "Peter's house") support that identification. See H. G. Andersen, "Capernaum," *ZPEB* 1:747. Reisner, "Archaeology and Geography," *DJG*, p. 39, says, "Excavations of recent years establish beyond any doubt that Capernaum is to be identified with the site of the ruins at Tel-Hum."

[22]The Greek word used for "partners" (Lk 5:7) is *metochois*, and in Luke 5:10, it is *koinōnoi*. For the latter there is an interesting parallel in the Amherst Papyrii: "Hermes the fisherman takes Cornelius as his partner" (*koinōnos*). See BAGD, pp. 439-40. Furthermore, this Cornelius is responsible as a partner for the sixth share of an annual rent assessed for fishing on a certain lake (MM 351).

[23]"Even fishers who may have owned their own boats were part of a state regulated, elite-profiting enterprise, and a complex web of economic relationships. These are symptoms of an 'embedded economy.' That is to say, economies in the ancient Mediterranean were not independent systems with 'free markets,' free trade, stock exchanges, monetization, and the like, as one finds in modern capitalist systems." K. C. Hanson, "The Galilean Fishing Economy and

fishing business was part of an imbedded domestic economy under the
oppressive control of elites, in this case, the Roman client government
of Herod Antipas and the aristocratic families who supported his
regime, probably the group called the Herodians (Mk 3:6; 12:13).
Herod's government arbitrarily exacted taxes in kind, that is, a percentage of the catch, and imposed rental fees or fishing licenses on the
Galilean fishermen.[24] Furthermore, local fishermen were required to
pay harbor usage fees.

The harbors discovered by Nun along the shores of the Sea of Galilee
were of such a nature as to make it unlikely individuals constructed or
maintained them since they required resources well beyond the capa-
bility of local fishermen.[25] In short, the government financed their in-
frastructure investment by levying usage fees. So in addition to tolls
and duties, Levi may have collected rental and license fees at his tax
booth in Capernaum (Mt 9:9). There were probably a number of toll
and tax collectors at Capernaum because it, like Bethsaida, was situated
next to a border separating two toparchies (Mk 2:15 mentions "many
tax collectors" at Levi's dinner party). Oppressive systems like this encourage hiding and lying about goods and assets as well as bitter, but
mostly ineffective, protests about excessive fees (*J.W.* 2.4).[26]

Fundamental to imbedded domestic economies is the extended
family that functions as the producing and consuming unit. Kinship is
a regular feature of guild or trade membership. Relatives and in-laws
work together as an extended family in the production of certain goods
and carefully preserve and protect required technologies. Whether we
should speak of these fishermen as middle-class entrepreneurs or Galilean peasants is a moot point.[27] Jonah (John), Simon and Andrew's

---

the Jesus Tradition," *BTB* 27 (1997): 99-111.

[24]Antipas exacted one third of the wheat raised in his domain and one half of all orchard pro-
duce (ibid., p. 111).

[25]Nun, "Ports of Galilee," p. 22, says, "The construction of the harbors required organizational
skill and economic planning. Breakwaters were built first, followed by piers and promenades,
repair shops for boats, administrative buildings, storehouses, tollhouses, watchtowers and
other facilities. Maintenance was, of course, necessary, and the breakwaters were continually
repaired and silt removed."

[26]Ibid.

[27]Murphy-O'Connor labels them a middle-class family; Hanson insists they are peasants. R.
Alan Culpepper says, "The evidence is insufficient to show that they were among the families

father (Mt 16:17; Jn 1:42; 21:15-17),[28] and Zebedee, father of James and John, were business partners and their sons shared in the partnership.

This leads to a conjecture. Simon was married (1 Cor 9:5), and his mother-in-law lived at Capernaum (Mk 1:30). Though neither woman is identified, I wonder if Simon was married to one of Zebedee's daughters. If so, his mother-in-law was none other than the mother of James and John, and she in turn may be the person named Salome, one of the women mentioned at the cross (cf. Mt 27:56 with Mk 15:40; 16:1; Jn 19:25). Perhaps Andrew married another Zebedee daughter. If so, the Zebedee-Jonah family fishing business was truly all in the family![29]

Not to be overlooked in all this is the fact that four, possibly seven, of the twelve apostles were part of an economic network linked to the Galilean fishing industry. Recall that Philip was also from Bethsaida (Jn 1:44) and Nathanael and Thomas participate in a postresurrection fishing venture with Simon Peter (Jn 21:1-3), quite different from fishing today with rod and reel—the skills required to operate a trammel net are not picked up on weekend outings! If Levi (Matthew) collected license and harbor usage fees at Capernaum, there are now at least five, possibly eight, of the twelve apostles who, before their call, owed all or part of their livelihood to the fishing industry on the Galilee. This is quite remarkable.

***Status of fishermen in Palestinian society.*** The status of Galilean fishermen within Jewish society is difficult to estimate. The NT provides no overt indication one way or the other. In Jewish culture generally, manual labor was not demeaned (*b. Ketub.* 59b; *b. Ned.* 49b) and

---

of the upper class, but neither did they share the desperate lot of hired servants and day laborers" (*John, the Son of Zebedee* [Columbia: University of South Carolina Press, 1994], p. 15).

[28]The textual evidence clearly favors the reading "John" at both John 1:42 and John 21:15-17. There is no obvious solution to the different patronymics recorded in Luke and John. Jonah and John are sufficiently different in Aramaic and Hebrew to preclude Jonah being a diminutive of John. It may be that early on there was confusion about the correct family name. If Jonah was the family name of Simon and Andrew, this is not without some irony. One recalls that their namesake, the prophet from Gath Hepher in Galilee, had a terrifying encounter with a great fish.

[29]Murphy-O'Connor, "Fishers of Men," p. 27, suggests a different reason for Simon and Andrew's move from Bethsaida to Capernaum: to avoid extra taxes levied on nonresidents of Galilee. Perhaps both reasons played a part.

fathers were enjoined to teach their sons a trade. But certain trades were despised because of ritual impurity infractions, for example, the tanning industry (Acts 9:43). Fishing would entail its share of ritual impurity issues, but there were means to rectify temporary ritual impurity, and there is no indication that fishing rendered one constantly unclean. In ancient Egypt, "The Satire on the Trades" informs us that the fish catcher "is more miserable than any (other) profession."[30] Closer in time (third to second century B.C.), the Roman Plautus mentions the low status of fishermen (*Rudens* 290-305). In the third century A.D., Athenaeus lumps fishmongers with moneylenders and considers them murderous, wealthy thieves (*Deipnosophistai* 6.226a, e; 6.228c; 7.309d). However, given the importance of fish for the economy and diet of Palestinian Jews, I think it is reasonable to assume that fishing was appreciated, but probably not highly regarded as an occupation.[31]

*Capernaum and Simon's house.* Jesus established Capernaum as the headquarters for his Galilean ministry (Mt 4:13; Lk 4:31). Mark's Gospel mentions a house belonging to Simon and Andrew (Mk 1:29). Based on the archaeological remains of first-century houses excavated just to the south of the synagogue at Capernaum, this house has probably been located. "Peter's house" is part of a larger complex of rooms or houses. That is to say, "several families lived together in a patriarchal fashion, sharing the same courtyard and the same exit."[32] According to Mark 1:29, after leaving the synagogue in Capernaum, Jesus, James and John "entered the house of Simon and Andrew." The Zebedee and John/Jonah families probably occupied rooms ("houses") surrounding the same central courtyard.[33] Peter and Andrew, born and raised in Bethsaida, lived in Capernaum during Jesus' ministry, the

---

[30]J. A. Wilson, *ANET*, pp. 433-34.

[31]Michael Grant observes that "these activities [fish pickling] were in considerable demand, not only from the inhabitants of the region, and the fish-shops of Jerusalem, but also from the Roman army of occupation, and the commerce of the Roman empire outside Palestine" in *Saint Peter: A Biography* (New York: Scribner, 1995), p. 56.

[32]Stanislao Loffreda, "Capernaum—Jesus' Own City," *Bible and Spade* 10/1 (1981): 5. Archaeologists designate such an area an *insula*.

[33]"The houses are characterized by large courts surrounded by small dwelling chambers. The life of an extended family centered around a communal court. In the courts were ovens, staircases for access to the roofs, and only one exit to the street." Vassilios Tzaferis, "Capernaum," *NEAEHL* 1:292.

town in which Zebedee and his sons plied their fishing trade. Jesus, not owning a house himself (Mt 8:20; Lk 9:58), was Simon and Andrew's guest during the Galilean ministry (Mk 1:36).[34] The degree of closeness and familiarity experienced by Jesus and his Galilean apostles is probably something that escapes most readers of the Gospels, especially North American readers who prize their privacy and space. It is also worth noting that, despite the extraordinary miracles Jesus performed at both Bethsaida and Capernaum, he denounces Chorazin, Bethsaida and Capernaum for their failure to repent (Mt 11:20-24; Lk 10:13-15).

*First-century fishing techniques and the Gospels.* The technique of fishing on the lake involved the seine net and the drag or trammel net. Both were made of linen. The former could be operated by one person standing along the shore or from a boat. The net was cast by hand and had weights attached, causing it to sink and entrap feeding fish (Mt 4:18). The drag or trammel net, by contrast, required a boat and several people to operate effectively. After the boat moved offshore into deep water, a large net with floats on the top edge and weights on the bottom was let out and allowed to sink forming a nearly vertical wall from the surface to the lake bottom. The boat was then rowed, parallel to the shore, with the net trailing behind and forming a long wall. The boat was then brought in to shore, and tow lines attached at both ends of the net were used to drag the net ashore with its catch. Depending on the size of the net, this would require several people on both towlines. A variation on this arranged the trammel net in a large barrel formation out in the deep water to encircle any feeding fish. A floating net would then be arranged around the outer edge of the barrel on the surface in order to capture fish that tried to jump over the top of the barrel net. This is known as the verranda method. In addition, one could sail into the middle of the barrel and employ a cast net. In this case, one must dive into the water and remove the fish from the mesh by hand. The description of a miraculous draft of fish in Luke 5:1-11 sounds like the verranda and cast net techniques. The final step was

---

[34]For floor plans of the house thought to be Peter's, see James F. Strange and Hershel Shanks, "Has the House Where Jesus Stayed in Capernaum Been Found?" *BAR* 8/6 (1982): 26-37.

labor intensive, requiring hand sorting to eliminate undesirable and inedible fish (Mt 13:47-50). There was a ready market for fish in the towns and villages of Galilee (Jn 6:9) in addition to the regions of Perea and Judea to the south.[35]

Angling, fishing by means of a line and hook, was not unknown and is mentioned once in the Gospel of Matthew. This is the episode involving the temple tax (Mt 17:24-27). At Jesus' request, Peter cast a hook into the lake and the first fish he caught had a coin in its mouth, a *stater* worth two didrachmas, thus providing the required payment for both Jesus and Peter. I will discuss the significance of this event later.

The foregoing affords a small opening through which we can peer into Peter's background. There are still many unanswered (and unanswerable) questions, but it at least provides some understanding of what it means to be a Galilean fisherman in the first century A.D.

For the most part, our portrait of Peter is dependent on episodes in the Gospels in which he is either mentioned or plays a leading role. Admittedly, reconstructing the life an individual on the basis of materials whose primary purpose is otherwise requires generous amounts of inference and not a little conjecture. In the nature of the case, it can hardly be otherwise. Still, in my opinion, the Gospels permit a reasonably reliable reconstruction and the attempt is well worth the effort.[36] In the next chapter, I will examine more closely the text of the Gospels for more clues about this man.

---

[35]Readers who have visited the Holy Land may even have enjoyed a delicious fish dinner consisting of fresh fish from the Sea of Galilee. A favorite is the so-called Saint Peter's fish, a species of tilapia called *musht* in Arabic because its dorsal fin resembles a comb. I highly recommend it!

[36]I am aware that some scholars who practice redaction and narrative criticism will be uncomfortable with my harmonistic approach to the Gospels. I appreciate the insights of both types of criticism but insist that a harmonistic approach, carefully employed, still has a place at the table and accords with basic methodology in historical studies generally. While it is true that my portrait of Peter is a reconstruction, so also are the various readings proposed by redaction and narrative critics. In other words, we need to acknowledge that none of our methodologies are hard sciences; they are subjective, and the results are often less than certain. This seems self-evident by the multiplicity of narrative readings of the Gospels. Evangelical biblical scholarship assumes that the Gospels are reliable historical accounts. Consequently, a reconstruction based on all four Gospels is not only a possible undertaking but also a desirable one—Tatian's harmony of the Gospels was not a misguided enterprise. In my view, no necessity or advantage requires the exegete to privilege one approach over the other.

## QUESTIONS FOR DISCUSSION

1. What value is there in trying to reconstruct the background of a leading figure in the early church?

2. What specifically does an examination of Peter's life as a Galilean fisherman contribute to understanding his later role as a respected leader in the Jesus movement?

3. Why did Jesus select a majority of his apostles from Galilee? Why didn't he select apostles from the religious center of Judaism in Jerusalem?

4. Why does Jesus give Simon a nickname? What relationship does this act have to the larger history of ancient Israel?

5. How does the conjecture about possible kinship ties with some of his apostles alter your understanding of Jesus' ministry and later early church history?

## FOR FURTHER READING

Brown, Raymond E., Karl P. Donfried and John Reuman, eds., *Peter in the New Testament*. Minneapolis/New York: Augsburg/Paulist, 1973. Pp. 7-20.

Cullmann, Oscar. *Peter: Disciple—Apostle—Martyr: A Historical and Theological Essay*. Translated by Floyd V. Filson. 2nd ed. Philadelphia: Westminster, 1962. Pp. 17-23.

Foakes-Jackson, F. J. *Peter: Prince of Apostles*. London: Hodder & Stoughton, 1927. Pp. 23-30.

Grant, Michael. *Saint Peter: A Biography*. New York: Scribner, 1995. Pp. 3-50.

Martin, Ralph P. "Peter." *ISBE* 3:802-3. Grand Rapids: Eerdmans, 1986.

Murphy-O'Connor, Jerome. "Fishers of Men: What We Know of the First Disciples from Their Profession." *BR* 25/3 (1999): 22-27, 48-49.

Nun, Mendal. "Ports of Galilee." *BAR* 25/4 (1999): 8-31.

Perkins, Pheme. *Peter: Apostle for the Whole Church*. Columbia: University of South Carolina Press, 1994. Pp. 18-26, 38-41.

Pixner, Bargil. *With Jesus Through Galilee According to the Fifth Gospel*. Rosh Pina: Corazin, 1992. Pp. 33-40.

# 2

## PETER IN THE GOSPELS

### PART ONE

#### Call to Confession

ALL FOUR GOSPELS INDICATE that Simon was among the first four individuals to become a disciple of Jesus (Jn 1:35-42; Mk 1:16-20; Mt 4:18-22; Lk 4:38).[1] His early acceptance of Jesus as Messiah was probably a factor in accounting for his preeminence among the Twelve.

### EARLY CONVERT

**Simon's summons to discipleship.** Jesus personally summoned Simon to be a disciple. His call occurs along the shore of the Sea of Galilee as he and his brother Andrew were casting their nets into the lake (Mk 1:16). Jesus calls them to "fish for people" (Mk 1:17). Shortly thereafter, Jesus calls another set of brothers, James and John, the sons of Zebedee, who were mending their nets (Mk 1:16-17). They not only leave their nets; they also leave their father and the hired hands in the boat (Mk 1:20; Mt 4:18-22). Luke's account of this call to discipleship is more fully developed and includes a miraculous catch of fish (Lk 5:1-11). This

---

[1]For helpful guidelines to interpret the Gospels, see Grant R. Osborne, *The Hermeneutical Spiral* (Downers Grove, Ill.: InterVarsity Press, 1991), pp. 153-72; Gordon D. Fee and Douglas Stuart, *How to Read the Bible for All Its Worth* (3rd ed.; Grand Rapids: Zondervan, 2003), pp. 127-48l; and Timothy Wiarda, *Interpreting Gospel Narratives: Scenes, People and Theology* (Nashville: B&H Academic, 2010). See also Wiarda's more technical *Peter in the Gospel Narratives: Pattern, Personality and Relationship* (WUNT 2.127; Tübingen: Mohr Siebeck, 2000). For a discussion of how narrative criticism operates and its limitations, see Mark Allan Powell, "Narrative Criticism," in *Hearing the New Testament: Strategies for Interpretation* (ed. Joel B. Green; Grand Rapids: Eerdmans, 1995), pp. 239-55.

episode depicts a dramatic change in Peter's understanding of who Jesus is, moving from respect ("Master") to reverence and awe ("Lord").[2] Simon first appears as an accommodating host who does Jesus a favor. Presumably, Simon listens to Jesus' teaching, along with the large crowd on the shoreline.[3] He then goes the extra mile and consents to Jesus' request to let down his nets again, even though he had labored all night with no results. The miraculous haul is presented with vivid detail ("filled both boats, so that they began to sink"). Luke's account thus provides a compelling reason for the four disciples' abrupt decision to walk away from their fishing business: Jesus confronts them with a display of divine power and authority. Simon's reaction, "Go away from me, Lord, for I am a sinful man!" (Lk 5:8) echoes that of the prophets Moses (Ex 3:5-6), Isaiah (Is 6:5) and Ezekiel (Ezek 1:28), each of whom experienced a theophany (manifestation of God in a visible form) in connection with their prophetic calls.[4]

John's Gospel further illuminates the disciples' abrupt commitment. There we learn that the Galilean summons to discipleship was not their first encounter with Jesus. Prior to this Simon was introduced to Jesus in the Jordan Valley in connection with John the Baptist's revival movement—a call for national repentance in preparation for the coming of Messiah. In fact, Jesus' first two converts appear to have been Andrew, Simon's brother, and an unnamed disciple, both of whom were disciples of John the Baptist. This unnamed disciple is commonly identified as "the one whom Jesus loved" (Jn 13:23; 19:25-27; 20:1-10; 21:1-14, 20-24), John the son of Zebedee.

After spending some time with Jesus, Andrew fetches his brother Simon and excitedly announces: "We have found the Messiah" (Jn

---

[2]Wiarda, *Interpreting Gospel Narratives*, pp. 14-20.

[3]Not far from Capernaum lies a little cove in which just such a scene could have occurred ("Bay of the Parables"). The acoustics have been tested and found quite adequate for a large crowd of several thousand. See Bargil Pixner, *With Jesus Through Galilee According to the Fifth Gospel* (Rosh Pina: Corazin, 1992), pp. 41-42.

[4]It is striking that the *Epistle of Barnabas*, a post-NT document generally dated to between A.D. 70 and 135, describes the apostles as people who "were sinful beyond all measure in order to demonstrate that 'he did not come to call the righteous, but sinners'" (*Barn.* 5:9). Michael Grant calls attention to a literary form called "divine commission" in the OT. Most of the features of a prophetic call find a parallel in the call and commission of Simon Peter in the NT. See Grant, *Saint Peter: A Biography* (New York: Scribner, 1995), pp. 106-7.

1:41). This episode implies that all three have previously responded to the Baptist's preaching (Jn 1:6-9). After emphatically denying his own messianic status (Jn 1:19-27), the Baptist explicitly identifies Jesus as "the Lamb of God who takes away the sin of the world" (Jn 1:29) and "the Son of God" (Jn 1:34) in the presence of Andrew and an unnamed disciple. Though they hardly grasp the full import of these titles, they believe Jesus to be the promised Messiah.[5]

Brimming with messianic fervor, Andrew brings Simon to Jesus. Looking at Simon, Jesus says, " 'You are Simon son of John. You are to be called Cephas' (which is translated Peter)" (Jn 1:42). This utterance, like a prophetic oracle, implies preternatural knowledge on the part of Jesus and should probably be interpreted in the same light as the ensuing interview with Nathanael (Jn 1:47-51). In his first meeting with Jesus, Peter's status and role in the Jesus movement are already foreshadowed. In short, Rocky is destined to be a leader among the apostles.[6] The ensuing call along the Sea of Galilee to be Jesus' disciple launches a career Simon could never have imagined.

***Observer of Jesus' first miracle at Cana.*** In the Gospel of John, Jesus next appears at a wedding in Cana of Galilee. In addition to Jesus and his family, his disciples are invited to the celebration (Jn 2:1-2). Kinship, friendship and business ties probably account for their being included.[7] In fact, Mary's sister may have been Salome, Zebedee's wife (see Mt 27:56; Mk 15:40; 16:1; Jn 19:25).[8] If this is the case, we arrive at the surprising conclusion that James and John, sons of Zebedee, were Jesus' first cousins.[9] Whether this is so or not, Jesus' first recorded miracle,

---

[5]See *Psalms of Solomon* 17:21-44; 18:5-9, perhaps emanating from Pharisaic circles. On this, see Larry R. Helyer, *Exploring Jewish Literature of the Second Temple Period* (Downers Grove, Ill.: InterVarsity Press, 2002), p. 389, and M. Lattke, "Psalms of Solomon," *DNTB*, p. 855. On Qumran messianism, see Craig A. Evans, "Messiahs," *EDSS* 1:537-42. Evans concludes, "it would appear that in most of the major points Qumran messianism is not much different from that of other pious, hopeful Jews" (1:539).

[6]"The name is probably proleptic, anticipating the time when Peter would take his place as a pillar apostle (Gal 2:9) and a foundation stone, which he and the other apostles were to be as original witnesses to the gospel (Eph 2:20; Rev 21:14)." Ralph P. Martin, "Peter," *ISBE* 3:803.

[7]G. R. Beasley-Murray assumes that disciples would be reckoned as Jesus' family (*John* [2nd ed.; WBC 36; Dallas: Word, 1999], p. 34).

[8]See the earlier discussion in chapter 1. See also Beasley-Murray, *John*, pp. 348-49, and Ben Witherington III, "Salome," *ABD* 5:906-7.

[9]A point argued by J. A. T. Robinson, *Priority of John* (London: SCM, 1985), pp. 118-22. By

changing water to wine, strengthens the disciples' conviction: he is indeed the Messiah (Jn 2:11).

*Jesus as Simon's house guest.* In John's Gospel, after the miracle at Cana, Jesus goes down to the village of Capernaum with his mother, his brothers and his disciples (Jn 2:12). According to Mark's Gospel, Jesus stays at Simon's house (Mk 1:21, 29; 2:1), a circumstance that makes sense if Salome, Zebedee's wife and Peter's mother-in-law, was also Mary's sister (Mt 27:56; Mk 15:40; Jn 19:25). Later, Mark informs us that Jesus' family, alarmed at his increasing notoriety and the shrill accusations leveled by the Jerusalem scribes, attempted to restrain him from continuing his ministry (Mk 3:21-22, 31-35). John's Gospel informs us that during his ministry even Jesus' brothers did not believe in him (Jn 7:5).[10]

During Jesus' residence in Simon's house, he heals Simon's mother-in-law of a fever—on a sabbath, no less (Mk 1:30). Remarkably, she immediately resumes her duties as hostess.[11] This healing, the first of five such healings of women recorded in Mark, further reinforces Simon's faith in Jesus as the promised Messiah. Very likely, many Jews already viewed a ministry of healing as a messianic signature. The discovery among the Qumran fragments of a messianic text called "Redemption and Resurrection" (4Q521) underscores this. This extraordinary text describes God's Messiah as one who liberates prisoners, gives sight to the blind, raises up those who are bowed down, heals the critically wounded, revives the dead, preaches good news to the afflicted and enriches the hungry (see Lk 7:18-23).[12] That evening, after

---

contrast, R. Alan Culpepper concludes "that while John the son of Zebedee's mother may have been named Salome, it is precarious to build other inferences on the basis of these lists" (*John, the Son of Zebedee* [Columbia: University of South Carolina Press, 1994], p. 9).

[10]Martin Hengel wryly observes that "[Jesus'] brothers . . . had an estranged relationship with their strange brother during Jesus' lifetime" (*Saint Peter: The Underestimated Apostle* [trans. Thomas H. Trapp; Grand Rapids: Eerdmans, 2010], p. 10).

[11]This may explain why the mother of James and John had the chutzpah to ask that her two sons be enthroned alongside Jesus (Mt 20:20-23). If Zebedee's wife, Salome, was Simon's mother-in-law, she was also the one whom Jesus healed. Thus Jesus not only had been a house guest but also had shown special favor to her. She may also have been his aunt. For these reasons, she may have presumed the right to request a place of special honor and privilege for her two sons, Jesus' first cousins. But even if my conjecture is unfounded, close association in the same village and faithful support of Jesus' ministry may have been motive enough for her overreaching request (Mt 27:55-56).

[12]For the text and brief commentary, see Michael Wise, Martin Abegg Jr. and Edward Cook,

sabbath, Jesus performs many other healings and exorcisms (Mk 1:32-34), boosting his already skyrocketing fame in Galilee (Mk 1:28, 37). Simon, like the crowds, can only wonder and exclaim: "We have never seen anything like this!" (Mk 2:12).

Significantly, it is Simon who heads up a search team to find Jesus when he momentarily withdraws from the hubbub for a time of quiet prayer and meditation in the early morning hours. Simon's exclamation, "Everyone is searching for you" (Mk 1:37), may suggest a certain impatience to get on with the messianic mission and perhaps already betrays a major misunderstanding about Jesus' mission as the promised Messiah of Israel.[13] This becomes evident later when Jesus rebukes Peter at Caesarea Philippi (Mk 8:32-33).

## LEADER AND SPOKESMAN IN THE JESUS MOVEMENT

Simon assumes the role as spokesman for the twelve apostles. He, along with James and John, constitute an inner circle of three within the larger group of twelve. But he is clearly the recognized leader even within this select group.

*Apostolic appointment.* Jesus' appointment of twelve apostles is a key moment freighted with symbolic meaning (Mk 3:13-19; Mt 10:1-4; Lk 6:12-16). There is wide agreement that the number twelve deliberately symbolizes a reconstitution of the ancient twelve tribes of Israel, a new Israel. Jesus views his movement as a new covenant community fulfilling the ancient prophecies of Jeremiah and Ezekiel (Jer 31:31-34; Ezek 34:25-31; 36:24-28; cf. Lk 22:20; 1 Cor 11:25).[14] His followers constitute the remnant of the true Israel (Is 10:20-23; Amos 9:9; Mic 5:3).

The triple tradition (material common to the Synoptic Gospels), supplemented by Acts (Mt 10:2-4; Mk 3:13-19; Lk 6:13-16; Acts 1:13),

---

*The Dead Sea Scrolls: A New Translation* (San Francisco: HarperSanFrancisco, 1996), pp. 420-21.

[13]Martin understands Simon as trying "to press on Him the role of a popular teacher" ("Peter," 3:803). See Joseph H. Hellerman, *Jesus and the People of God* (ed. Stanley E. Porter; New Testament Monographs 21; Sheffield: Sheffield Phoenix Press, 2007), pp. 90-122, for a helpful discussion of Jewish nationalism and Jesus' response to it.

[14]On this, see Scot McKnight, *A New Vision for Israel: The Teachings of Jesus in National Context* (Grand Rapids: Eerdmans, 1999), pp. 1-14, and Petrus J. Gräbe, *New Covenant, New Community* (Waynesboro, Ga.: Paternoster, 2006), pp. 51-57.

supplies a list of the apostles, and in all three, Simon is listed first; Matthew's Gospel explicitly designates Simon as "first" (*prōtos*). There can be little doubt that he is the recognized spokesman and acknowledged leader of the Twelve, as the Gospel narratives in which he is mentioned make clear (e.g., Mt 14:28; 15:15; 18:21; 26:35, 40; Mk 8:29; 9:5; 10:28; Jn 6:68).[15] The Master saw leadership potential in Rocky. To this group of twelve Jesus grants extraordinary power and authority, sending them out as missionaries, preaching the good news of the kingdom and performing healings and exorcisms (Mk 6:7-13).

*Member of the inner circle.* Mark's Gospel narrates three episodes in which only Peter, James and John are allowed to be present: the healing of Jairus's daughter (Mk 5:37), the transfiguration (Mk 9:2-13) and Jesus' agony in the Garden of Gethsemane (Mk 14:32-42).[16] Not without interest, in ancient Israel, King David's army also had three great warriors called "the Three" (2 Sam 23:8). In addition to the above episodes, when Jesus delivers his eschatological discourse on the Mount of Olives, Mark mentions only the three, plus Andrew (Mk 13:3-4). Andrew's presence is probably more a factor of his being Peter's brother and frequent companion than being part of an inner four. Apparently, Jesus deliberately groomed this inner group of three as leaders within the apostolate. This is confirmed by Paul's letter to the Galatians in which he describes James, Cephas and John as "acknowledged pillars" in the Jerusalem church (Gal 2:9). The James mentioned by Paul, however, is not James the son of Zebedee and brother of John, but Jesus' half-brother (Mk 6:3). James of Zebedee is listed third in the apostolic roster in Acts 1:13 but does not figure in any of the stories of the early Jerusalem church until mention of his martyrdom in Acts 12:2.

This special treatment may at first appear in tension with some of Jesus' teachings on discipleship. For example, he stresses that those who want to be first (*prōtos*) must be servant of all (Mt 20:27). Perhaps, however, the incongruity is more perceived than real. All

---

[15]"The numerous times the Galilean fisherman and disciple of Jesus is mentioned is without parallel in early Christianity," writes Hengel, *Saint Peter*, p. 29. See also his comments on pp. 34, 48, 75, 89 and 100.

[16]Matthew singles out the inner three at the transfiguration and Gethsemane (Mt 17:1; 26:37).

Jewish and Gentile communities of which we are aware in the first century relied on strong leaders. The difference between these and the Palestinian Jesus movement lay in the manner in which leaders exercised authority. The ethos in the Qumran community, with its decidedly top-down structure, rigid conformity and penal code, contrasts markedly with the Jesus movement.[17] Though not as strict and rigid, the Pharisees were highly authoritarian in terms of leadership. As we will see, differences in leadership style between the early Christians and other religious communities become apparent in Peter's first epistle (1 Pet 5:1-11).

*Peter walks on water.* Matthew narrates a unique and extraordinary episode involving Peter.[18] Following Mark, Matthew tells us that after the miraculous feeding of the five thousand (Mt 14:13-21), Jesus commands his disciples to get into the boat and cross over to the other (western) side of the lake. He dismisses the crowds and spends time alone in prayer on the hills overlooking the lake. The disciples, however, have great difficulty because they are trying to cross into a strong headwind. In the early morning hours, Jesus comes "walking toward them on the sea." Terrified, they cry out, "It is a ghost!" (Mt 14:26). Jesus replies, "Take heart, it is I; do not be afraid" (Mt 14:27).

At this point, Matthew inserts material unique to his Gospel (Mt 14:28-31). Peter requests Jesus' permission, which is granted, to join him on the water. Remarkably, we read, "So Peter got out of the boat, started walking on the water, and came toward Jesus" (Mt 14:29). As he does so, however, he becomes frightened by the powerful wind and

---

[17]On the organization of the Qumran community, see Geza Vermes, *An Introduction to the Complete Dead Sea Scrolls* (Minneapolis: Fortress, 1999), pp. 94-113, and Helyer, *Exploring Jewish Literature*, pp. 211-18, esp. pp. 221-24.

[18]G. D. Kilpatrick speaks of this episode as "standing quite unparalleled in whole or in part to the rest of the gospel material" in *The Origin of the Gospel According to St. Matthew* (Oxford: Clarendon, 1946), p. 40. Robert H. Gundry finds it "difficult to resist the conclusion that Matthew did not draw the material in vv 28-31 from tradition, but composed it as a haggadic midrash on discipleship" (*Matthew: A Commentary on His Literary and Theological Art* [Grand Rapids: Eerdmans, 1982], p. 300). W. D. Davies and Dale C. Allison Jr., however, are not so sure: "We find it all but impossible to come to any definite conclusion on the issue at hand. In view of the solid connexion with the feeding of the five thousand (which we think has an historical basis), it may be best to surmise some factual core" (*A Critical and Exegetical Commentary on the Gospel According to Saint Matthew* [ICC; 3 vols.; Edinburgh: T & T Clark, 1991], 2:499).

begins to sink. In desperation, he cries out, "Lord, save me!" Jesus grasps him by the hand and issues the climactic saying to which the episode builds: "You [sing.] of little faith, why did you [sing.] doubt?" (Mt 14:31). When they get into the boat, the wind immediately ceases. Adding an emphatic point to an already astonishing episode, the disciples worship Jesus saying, "Truly you are the Son of God" (Mt 14:33).

One can scarcely miss the pastoral intention of this episode. Peter functions as a typical disciple, the boat being the community of believers and the wind and waves depicting trials and tribulations assailing the church. The source of these assaults is probably satanic given the widespread imagery of the abyss as the domain of demonic forces (see Rev 13:1). When Peter leaves the safety of the church, turns his attention away from Jesus and focuses on the imminent danger, he begins to sink. Only as he cries out to Jesus is he saved from impending destruction. The application is clear: believers must keep focused on the Savior, who delivers them from peril.[19]

But how are we to understand Matthew's portrayal of Peter in this episode? Is this a negative depiction? Does he serve as a warning to disciples who lack faith? Does it portray Peter as an impulsive and vacillating man? Was he motivated merely by a desire for the sensational? Or is the portrayal rather more positive, showing genuine love and commitment, albeit exercised by a person who, in common with all disciples, experiences moments of weakness and failure?[20] I think the latter is more likely.[21] After all, Peter alone among the disciples requests Jesus to bid him walk on the water. Apparently, he initially suc-

---

[19]"The Jesus who multiplied the loaves and fish and who appeared to the disciples walking on the water and who saved Peter from sinking, this same Jesus is the Lord of the church who has brought salvation and who stands similarly prepared to save his people, even when they may doubt, from the evils that beset them. This Jesus who rules over nature and even the realm of evil is rightly worshiped as 'truly the Son of God.'" Donald A. Hagner, *Matthew 14–28* (WBC 33B; Dallas: Word, 1995), p. 425.

[20]"It is not so clear, however, whether Matthew intends us to see Peter in this incident as an example of valid faith which went wrong, or as from the beginning taking a foolhardy risk ether to impress the others or simply in a childish search for exhilaration. Peter's motivation for wishing to do as Jesus is doing is not explained." R. T. France, *The Gospel of Matthew* (Grand Rapids: Eerdmans, 2007), p. 567.

[21]Hagner, *Matthew*, p. 423, aptly observes that "Peter is here paradoxically a model both of faith and lack of faith."

ceeded.[22] Though addressed as "you of little faith," does he not at least have *a little* faith? No one else volunteers! Not to be overlooked is the fact that Jesus did indeed deliver Rocky. Believers may take comfort (especially in light of Peter's confession that soon follows), knowing that the church, built on Peter the Rock, will triumph over the "gates of Hades," a metaphorical expression for death (Mt 16:18).[23] Perhaps this episode came to mind when Peter later reminded believers that their inheritance is "kept in heaven for you, who are being *protected by the power of God through faith* for a salvation ready to be revealed in the last time" (1 Pet 1:4-5, italics added).

## PETER'S CONFESSION

Peter's confession at Caesarea Philippi serves as the hinge of Mark's Gospel (as well as in Matthew and Luke). In Matthew, however, it also becomes the occasion for an explicit recognition by the Master that Peter will lead the nascent church in the unspecified future (Mt 16:18-19). The importance of Peter's confession is underscored by its appearance in the triple tradition (Mk 9:27-30; Mt 16:13-20; Lk 9:18-21) with echoes in John's Gospel (Jn 1:40-42; 6:67-69).

At the midpoint of Jesus' ministry, amid rampant messianic speculation and increasing opposition, he withdraws from Galilee and spends time with his disciples in Herod Philip's territory near Caesarea Philippi, some twenty-five miles to the north of Capernaum (Mk 8:27; Mt 16:13). Jesus then takes his disciples aside and asks them, "Who do people say that the Son of Man is?" (Mt 16:13). After receiving various responses, including John the Baptist, Elijah, Jeremiah, or one of the prophets, Jesus then asks them the all-important question: "But who do you say that I am?" (Mk 8:29; Mt 16:15; Lk 9:20). All three Synoptic Gospels (cf. Jn 6:68-69) indicate that Peter speaks for the Twelve. His response strikes a keynote of each Evangelist: "You are the Christ" (Mk 1:1; Mt 1:1; Lk 3:21-38; Jn 20:31).

---

[22]The aorist tense of the two finite verbs in Matthew 14:29 should probably be taken as ingressive or inceptive (i.e., depicting the beginning of an action). See Daniel B. Wallace, *Greek Grammar Beyond the Basics* (Grand Rapids: Zondervan, 1996), p. 558.

[23]For the view that the "gates of Hades" refers to demonic powers, see J. Jeremias, "πύλη" *TDNT* 6:926-28.

"Christ" is here a title best rendered as "Messiah."[24] The term gathers up a long tradition concerning an expected Davidic descendant who restores the dynasty to its former glory and ushers in an unprecedented era of peace, righteousness and prosperity (2 Sam 7:14-17; Is 11; Jer 23:5-8; Ezek 34:23-31). In the ears of the first listeners, this term evoked nationalistic and political aspirations.[25] But is that all Peter intended? Mark's Gospel begins with a double affirmation: "The beginning of the good news of Jesus Christ, the Son of God" (Mk 1:1).[26] Viewed in light of his Gospel as a whole, the title "Son of God" transcends Jewish, messianic nationalism—it points to Jesus' divine nature. By not affirming the second title, are we to infer that Peter has not yet fully grasped this? So it would seem. It is not until an unnamed centurion makes the climactic confession at the foot of the cross ("Truly this man was God's Son," Mk 15:39) that we come full circle and reaffirm the opening confession of the Gospel (Mk 1:1).

The problem is that matters are somewhat different in Matthew's Gospel. He expands Peter's confession, adding the words, "the Son of the living God" (Mt 16:16). Luke's version has "the Messiah of God" (Lk 9:20), but this appears to be functionally equivalent to "Messiah." Should we then conclude that Matthew's "Son of the living God" is likewise synonymous with "Messiah"? This seems clearly to be the understanding of the high priest who later questions Jesus: "I put you under oath before the living God, tell us if you are the Messiah, the Son of God" (Mt 26:63; cf. Mk 14:61; Lk 22:69). In the OT, even the

---

[24]The NRSV and GNB have "the Messiah" in the text with "the Christ" in a footnote (Mk 8:29 and pars.). See also TEV, NAB and NEB. Most English versions, however, have "the Christ" in the text. A few provide a footnote with "Or the Messiah" (e.g., NASB, NIV). The Greek word *Christos*, in this context, is a title and should not be transliterated into English as "Christ" but as "Messiah" or "promised Savior" so that English readers can grasp the significance of this title.

[25]"In declaring Jesus as the Christ, Peter has supplied the proper title, but he has the wrong understanding . . . Jesus will don the servant's trowel rather than the warrior's sword; he will practice sacrifice above vengeance. He will not inflict suffering, but suffer himself as a 'ransom for many.' " James R. Edwards, *The Gospel According to Mark* (Grand Rapids: Eerdmans, 2002), p. 252.

[26]Many scholars think the title "Son of God" is secondary. See, e.g., Adela Yarbro Collins, *Mark: A Commentary* (ed. Harold W. Attridge; Hermeneia; Minneapolis: Fortress, 2007), p. 130. For the MS evidence, see Bruce M. Metzger, *A Textual Commentary on the Greek New Testament* (New York: United Bible Societies, 1971), p. 73.

Hebrew king could be styled as God's son (2 Sam 7:14; Ps 2:7; 89:26-27). Perhaps, then, Peter's confession in Matthew advances the thought no further than in Mark and Luke.

But there is good reason to suppose that it does. Usage of the title "Son of God" demonstrates that it is "one of the most exalted New Testament titles for Jesus, and at times it seems to have been yoked to 'Messiah' in order to correct any inadequacy in the understanding of messiahship and to introduce a divine element."[27] That this is the case in Matthew 16:16 seems evident by the fact that Jesus addresses him by his full name, "Simon Peter," praises him for his insight and attributes it to nothing less than a divine disclosure by the Father himself (Mt 16:16-17). To this should be added the manner in which Matthew treats the notion of Jesus as God's unique Son in his Gospel as a whole (Mt 1:20-23; 3:17; 4:1-11; 17:5).

Even though the Markan and Lukan narratives of Peter's confession at Caesarea do not include the title "Son of God," earlier episodes in both Gospels reveal that the apostles already recognize in Jesus certain attributes that God alone possesses (Mk 1:27; 2:7; 3:11; cf. Lk 4:41; Mk 4:41; cf. Lk 8:25). In short, they intuitively know that Jesus is in some sense divine. Matthew makes explicit what is implicit in Mark and Luke. But it is also important to note that Peter's confession of Jesus as the Son of God is at an elementary stage; he and the apostles still have a long way to go in their comprehension of this exalted person.[28] Only in the aftermath of the resurrection and the gift of the Holy Spirit at

---

[27]Raymond E. Brown, Karl P. Donfried and John Reuman, eds., *Peter in the New Testament* (Minneapolis/New York: Augsburg/Paulist, 1973), p. 86. "Matthew's interpretive expansion, ὁ υἱὸς τοῦ θεοῦ, 'the Son of God,' defines the Messiah as more than a human figure, as someone who is uniquely a manifestation of God, the very agent of God who somehow participates in God's being," writes Hagner, *Matthew*, p. 468. So also France, *Matthew*, pp. 618-19.

[28]Thus Peter's understanding of Christ at Caesarea Philippi is not yet at the level of the Evangelists who later composed the Gospels. A further problem arises in that Matthew's Gospel has all the apostles make this confession *prior* to Peter's confession (Mt 14:33). This seems to upstage Peter's confession at Caesarea Philippi. France, *Matthew*, p. 571, offers a plausible explanation: "Perhaps the difference is between the instinctive recognition of Jesus' more-than-human nature . . . in the context of an overwhelming miracle [Mt 14:33] . . . and the deliberate formulations at Caesarea Philippi of a christological confession which balances the supernatural ('Son of God') element of this exclamation with a functional identification of Jesus' role as Messiah."

Pentecost does a full-fledged high Christology suddenly emerge.[29] Thus when we turn to Peter's epistles, written about thirty years after Peter's confession, evidence of a greatly enlarged understanding of Jesus' divine Sonship now appears (e.g., 1 Pet 1:3, 19-21; 2:22; 3:18-19; 2 Pet 1:1, 11, 17; 2:1, 10; 3:18).

This brings us to some of the most bitterly disputed words in the NT. What precisely does it mean when Jesus says to Peter, "And I tell you, you are Peter, and on this rock I will build my church, and the gates of Hades will not prevail against it. I will give you the keys of the kingdom of heaven, and whatever you bind on earth will be bound in heaven, and whatever you loose on earth will be loosed in heaven" (Mt 16:18-19)?

The first question is this: Is Peter himself the rock, or is the rock the confession he makes? In the past, ecclesiastical affiliation virtually dictated one's response. Roman Catholics affirmed the former and Protestants the latter. This oversimplifies the situation, and today one finds a wider range of nuances. Still, these two options remain the primary contenders.

A face-value reading of the text equates Peter with the rock on which the church is to be built. Supporting this is the assumption of a pre-Matthean, Aramaic tradition lying beneath the Greek text of Matthew.[30] In Greek the play on words between "Peter" (*petros*, masc.) and "rock" (*petra*, fem.) requires a shift in gender. Such is not the case in Aramaic—it is the same word with the same gender in both instances (*Kephā'* and *kephā'*). Furthermore, one detects in the larger context of the passage a deliberate parallelism that further strengthens a face-value reading:

"You are the Messiah" (Mt 16:16)

"you are Peter" (Mt 16:18)

"you are a stumbling block" (Mt 16:23)

In each case, an individual, whether Jesus or Peter, is the subject of a

---

[29]See I. Howard Marshall, *The Origins of New Testament Christology* (Downers Grove, Ill.: InterVarsity Press, 1976), pp. 93-94, 119-23.

[30]Other indicators of an Aramaic tradition underlying this pericope are the expressions "Simon son of Jonah" (Simon bar Jonah), "gates of Hades," "flesh and blood" and "bind and loose." See Brown et al., *Peter in the New Testament*, pp. 90-91.

predication. Though possible, the interpretation that the rock is Peter's confession seems forced. Rather, Jesus designates Peter as the one who will exercise authority within the movement. The book of Acts amply documents Peter's leadership role in the early formative years of what later became Christianity.[31]

Such an interpretation is a far cry from the fully developed Roman Catholic teaching on the origin of the papacy. One is not logically or historically compelled to acknowledge the latter by affirming Peter (and the apostles) as the foundation of the church (Eph 2:20). Since my concern is with the NT itself and not its later interpretation in church history, I will not pursue it further.[32]

The second question concerns the meaning and nature of the authority bestowed on Peter. What does it mean for Peter to have the "keys of the kingdom of heaven" and thereby to "bind" and "loose" (Mt 16:19)? The idiom of "binding and loosing" appears in rabbinic Judaism. In the Mishnah (second-century A.D. codification of oral, rabbinic interpretation of biblical laws), for example, the expression refers to decisions rendered by rabbis, during the Tannaitic period (first two centuries A.D.), concerning actions or activities that were either prohibited (bound) or permitted (loosed). In context, these decisions were part of what is called *halakah*, that is, rules for the conduct of life. One also finds instances of this terminology in cases where individuals are banned from the synagogue or the ban is repealed.[33] The Qumran community likewise employed similar terminology and procedures for determining admittance to membership and disciplining errant members (1QH 5:36; 1QM 5:3; 1Q 22:3, 11; CD 13:10).

Peter's keys, then, likely refer to his authoritative role within the new covenant community. The idiom of binding and loosing with respect to judicial decisions regarding errant members also occurs in Matthew

---

[31]"Apparently Jesus actually meant that Peter is the rock upon which He would build His Church. Peter's vital role in the Early Church as shown in Acts substantiates this interpretation," according to B. Van Elderen, "Peter, Simon," *ZPEB* 4:734. Hengel, *Saint Peter*, p. 14, summarizes the situation as follows: "Peter functions as the ruling head of the circle of disciples and in the growing church."

[32]See also the ecumenical study by Brown et al., *Peter in the New Testament*, pp. 83-84.

[33]See further J. Neusner, "Rabbinic Literature: Mishnah and Tosefta," *DNTB*, pp. 893-97, and Hengel, *Saint Peter*, pp. 4-5.

18:18. Peter thus takes the lead in two broad areas: he announces the terms of admittance into the new covenant community and establishes the limits of acceptable behavior within that fellowship. Both kinds of authority were in fact exercised by Peter, as illustrated in the book of Acts (see, e.g., Acts 1:15-26; 2:14-41; 3:17-26; 4:8-12; 5:1-11, 29-32; 8:14-25; 10:34-48; 11:1-18).[34] It is also clear that this authority was not restricted to him; the picture that emerges from Acts is a collegial exercise of the "keys" by apostles and prophets (e.g., Stephen and Philip) within the Jesus movement.

***Jesus rebukes Peter.*** Most Bible readers are aware of Simon Peter's ups and downs. One moment he is the hero; the next he is the goat.[35] As seen in this episode (Mt 16:22-23), no sooner has he made a climactic confession of faith, been praised for having received divine revelation and elevated to the role of leader in the church than he is on the receiving end of a stinging rebuke by the Master.

In response to Jesus' direct prediction of his approaching death at the hands of the religious authorities, Peter takes him aside and rebukes him: "God forbid it, Lord! This must never happen to you" (Mt 16:22). Jesus discerns in Peter's effort another assault by the Dark Lord. Satan did not withdraw and cede the field after his initial failure to deter Jesus from his redemptive mission (Mt 4:1-11); he bided his time, waiting for another occasion, "an opportune time" (Lk 4:13). Peter unwittingly provides that opportune time. I previously commented on the fact that Peter almost certainly harbors nationalistic hopes for the Jesus movement. Although Jesus has spoken openly about his impending death, Peter cannot fathom how that fits into the politics of the messianic kingdom.[36]

Christians in the United States of America can sympathize with Peter; sometimes, we too fall prey to equating nationalism and political

---

[34]As Davies and Allison put it, "Peter is the authoritative teacher without peer," *Saint Matthew*, p. 639.

[35]Wiarda, *Interpreting Gospel Narratives*, p. 180, notes six episodes in the Gospel of Matthew in which "Peter says or does something with good intentions, but then immediately encounters corrections or failure."

[36]"Jesus must now begin to teach the *true* meaning of Peter's confession. For this, Peter and the disciples are quite unprepared" (Edwards, *Mark*, p. 252, italics in original). "The idea of a suffering Messiah was foreign to him [Peter], and that is why he was said to have been so harshly reprimanded for this 'Satanic' mistake" (Grant, *Saint Peter*, p. 66).

preferences with Jesus' kingdom. Like Peter, we are guilty of "setting your mind not on divine things but on human things" (Mt 16:23). Jesus' rebuke of Peter is personal but not unique; that is to say, as the leader and spokesperson for the Twelve, he is rightly chastised. But make no mistake about it, he is not alone in his sentiments; the others also cherish the same confused view as Peter, and his rebuke is theirs as well. Peter will finally get it right. His letters reflect his mature views. In his first letter, he now clearly grasps the necessity of Jesus' sufferings before his glory: "the Spirit of Christ within them [the prophets] indicated when it testified in advance to the sufferings destined for Christ and the subsequent glory" (1 Pet 1:11). Not even a whiff of Jewish, nationalistic messianism may be detected in Peter's epistles.

Peter's confession, linked with Jesus' announcement of his impending death, his rebuke of Peter and the requirements for discipleship stand at the midpoint of Jesus' ministry in the Synoptic Gospels (Mt 16:13-27; Mk 8:27-38; Lk 9:18-27).[37] The die is now cast, and Jesus "set[s] his face to go to Jerusalem" (Lk 9:51). Our next chapter retraces Peter's journey to Jerusalem and the climactic events of Passion Week.

## QUESTIONS FOR DISCUSSION

1.  Compare Peter's summons to be a disciple with accounts of prophetic calls in the OT. What similarities and differences do you detect?

2.  How does combining all four Gospel accounts of Peter's summons throw light on this important episode? What changes when each Gospel is read without reference to the others?

3.  Why do you think Jesus selected Peter as the future leader of the Jesus movement?

4.  Do you agree with the view that Jesus' choice of twelve apostles

---

[37]The Gospel of John is organized according to an entirely different scheme: a book of signs (Jn 1:19–12:50) followed by a book of glory (Jn 13:1–20:31). This is not contradictory but complementary to that of the Synoptics. All of the foregoing Synoptic themes reappear in John, though in differing contexts and with different formulations (see, e.g., Jn 6:68-69; 2:19-22; 12:23-33; 8:12–10:42; 13:6-9). Luke also has a different and more overarching organizational scheme for this two-volume work, involving distinct eras or periods of salvation history. Within this larger structure, however, Peter's confession is still a decisive moment in the time of Jesus' ministry. The same can be said of Matthew's Gospel.

is significant and symbolizes a new Israel? If not, what is your explanation?

5. Why do you think Jesus provided Peter, James and John unique experiences and information not granted the other apostles? Is this a sound method in training leaders?

6. Do you agree that in the episode of walking on water (Mt 14:28-33), Matthew portrays Peter as a paradigm for all believers?

7. Why is Peter's confession at Caesarea Philippi a turning point in the Synoptic Gospels?

8. What is your interpretation of Jesus' declaration: "You are Peter, and on this rock I will build my church, and the gates of Hades will not prevail against it" (Mt 16:18)?

9. Do you agree with my claim that Christians sometimes confuse the kingdom of God with their own political views? Can we gain insight from church history in this regard?

## FOR FURTHER READING

Brown, Raymond E., Karl P. Donfried and John Reumann, eds. *Peter in the New Testament*. Minneapolis: Augsburg, 1973. Pp. 57-69, 75-101, 109-19.

Cullmann, Oscar. *Peter: Disciple—Apostle—Martyr*. Philadelphia: Westminster, 1953. Pp. 17-32.

Edwards, James R. *The Gospel According to Mark*. Grand Rapids: Eerdmans, 2002.

Foakes-Jackson, F. J. *Peter: Prince of Apostles*. London: Hodder & Stoughton, 1927. Pp. 45-62.

France, R. T. *The Gospel of Mark: A Commentary on the Greek Text*. Grand Rapids: Eerdmans, 2002.

———. *The Gospel of Matthew*. NICNT. Grand Rapids: Eerdmans, 2007.

Grant, Michael. *Saint Peter: A Biography*. New York: Scribner, 1995. Pp. 53-85.

Hengel, Martin. *Saint Peter: The Underestimated Apostle*. Translated by Thomas F. Trapp. Grand Rapids: Eerdmans, 2010. Pp. 1-48.

Hurtado, L. W. "Gospel (Genre)." *DJG*. Downers Grove, Ill.: InterVarsity Press, 1992. Pp. 276-82.

Martin, Ralph P. "Peter." *ISBE*. Grand Rapids: Eerdmans, 1986. 3:802-7.

Osborne, Grant R. *The Hermeneutical Spiral*. Downers Grove, Ill.: Inter-
    Varsity Press, 1991. Pp. 149-73.
Perkins, Pheme. *Peter*: *Apostle for the Whole Church*. Columbia: University of
    South Carolina Press, 1994. Pp. 52-62, 66-74, 84.
Perrin, Nicholas. "Gospels." *DTIB*. Grand Rapids: Baker, 2005. Pp. 264-68.
Van Elderen, B. "Peter, Simon." *ZPEB*. 5 vols. Grand Rapids: Zondervan,
    1977. 4:733-39.

# 3

## PETER IN THE GOSPELS

### PART TWO

#### *Transfiguration to Resurrection*

THE TRANSFIGURATION PREPARES for the climactic moment of Jesus' ministry. Descending from the mount, he sets his face for a final visit to Jerusalem and the inevitable confrontation with the religious leaders (Mk 9:30-32; Mt 17:22-23; Lk 9:51). Peter will be swept up and nearly overwhelmed by the ensuing events. Remarkably, he emerges from his time of "sifting" (Lk 22:31) as the recognized leader of a movement now proclaiming an astonishing message, truly good news, centering on the saving deeds of Jesus of Nazareth (Acts 2:22-36).

### WITNESS TO THE TRANSFIGURATION

All three Synoptic Gospels record Jesus' transfiguration (Mk 9:2-8; Mt 17:1-8; Lk 9:28-36). For a moment, the inner three, Peter, James and John, glimpse Jesus' divine nature. Some scholars reckon this as a postresurrection appearance story read back into Jesus' ministry.[1] In my view, we are dealing with a historical event that took place as narrated on the slopes or summit of Mount Hermon.[2] The impact of this un-

---

[1]See, e.g., Rudolf Bultmann, *History of the Synoptic Tradition* (New York: Harper, 1968), pp. 259-61. Raymond E. Brown, Karl P. Donfried and John Reuman, eds., *Peter in the New Testament* (Minneapolis/New York: Augsburg/Paulist, 1973) do not even discuss it, implying their rejection of its historicity. For a defense of its historicity, see W. L. Liefeld, "Transfiguration," *DJG*, pp. 834-41.

[2]The traditional site of the transfiguration is Mount Tabor, on whose summit rest two churches, Roman Catholic and Greek Orthodox, commemorating the event. According to

veiling of Jesus' divinity was overwhelming. Mark says, "they were terrified" (Mk 9:6); Matthew expands this and says "they fell to the
ground and were overcome by fear" (Mt 17:6).

Once again, Peter is the spokesman. In response to this divine
manifestation (cf. Ex 24; Dan 7:9-14) and the sudden appearance of
Moses and Elijah (Lk 9:31), Peter blurts out a suggestion: "Rabbi, it
is good for us to be here; let us make three dwellings, one for you, one
for Moses, and one for Elijah" (Mk 9:5). Mark, followed by Luke,
indicates that Peter was so frightened he did not know what to say
(Mk 9:6; Lk 9:33). Peter's reference to dwellings recalls the Feast of
Tabernacles (Heb *sukkôt*) in which observant Jews build temporary
huts and live in them for a week in order to commemorate the wilderness wanderings and God's faithful provision both then and now
(Lev 23:23-25, 39-43; Deut 16:13-15). Perhaps the transfiguration
occurred just prior to the festival, suggesting to Peter an appropriate
response.[3] Perhaps Peter wanted to prolong this intense, highly privileged, spiritual experience. Whatever his intention, Jesus does not
criticize or correct him. Matthew, in line with his pastoral concerns,
fittingly adds that Jesus touched the three apostles and said, "Get up
and do not be afraid" (Mt 17:7).

The experience left an indelible impression. In his second epistle,

---

Jerome Murphy-O'Connor, "Eusebius (d. 340) hesitates between Tabor and Mount Hermon,
while the Pilgrim of Bordeaux (333) places it on the Mount of Olives. The Mount of Olives
has little to commend it being fully in view of Jerusalem and only rising to about 2700ft. In
348 Cyril of Jerusalem decided on Tabor, and the support of Epiphanius and Jerome established the tradition firmly" (*The Holy Land: An Oxford Archaeological Guide From Earliest Times
to 1700* [5th ed.; Oxford: University Press, 2008], p. 413). Another possible candidate is Jebel
Jermuk, the highest elevation in Upper Galilee at 4,000 feet. There were several Jewish centers and towns in the vicinity that could explain the presence of scribes shortly after Jesus'
transfiguration (Mk 9:14). However, the immediate context of the transfiguration, Peter's
confession near Caesarea Philippi (Mk 8:27), the reference to a "high mountain" (Mk 9:2) and
the presence of a Roman camp on the summit of Mount Tabor during Jesus' day favor nearby
Mount Hermon, rising to over 9,000 feet in elevation. See discussion by M. H. Scharlemann,
"Transfiguration," *ISBE* 4:888-89.

[3]In Matthew 17:22 Jesus addresses Jewish pilgrims who "were gathering in Galilee." Most com-
mentators assume this was in preparation for a Passover. But if John 7:1–10:39 fits between
Matthew 17:22 and Matthew 19:1, the Feast of Tabernacles may be the chronological setting
for the transfiguration. B. D. Chilton's view that Jesus' last visit to Jerusalem was during the
Feast of Tabernacles ("Festivals and Holy Days: Jewish," *DNTB*, p. 375) has little support. See
M. O. Wise, "Feasts," *DJG*, pp. 234-41.

Peter recalls this moment "on the holy mountain" (2 Pet 1:18) in which Jesus revealed his divine nature. The transfiguration anticipates the ultimate vindication and glorious coming of the Lord Jesus Christ at the end of the age (2 Pet 1:16-21) and so powerfully validates Peter's prior confession: "You are the Messiah, the Son of the living God" (Mt 16:16). No wonder the apostle insists "the prophetic message [is] . . . fully confirmed" (2 Pet 1:19).

## PETER AND THE TEMPLE TAX

Matthew alone inserts a curious episode concerning the temple tax (Mt 17:24-27).[4] This tax, though voluntary, was expected of all Jewish males above twenty years of age, whether living in Palestine or the Diaspora, and was levied in the Jewish month of Adar, corresponding to March in our calendar (Neh 10:32-33; *J.W.* 6.281; *m. Šeqal.* 1:3-4). Matthew thus narrates an episode occurring about a month before the Passover (cf. Mt 17:22). The temple tax was intended to maintain the ritual and sacrificial needs of the Jerusalem temple. Collectors of

---

[4]This episode is often viewed as unhistorical. Some see it as a parable, but the literary indicators of that genre are lacking. After admitting that "Jesus' words about the fish and the coin read like a mater-of-fact instruction which Peter is expected to carry out to the letter," R. T. France goes on to say, "there is no account of the proposed miracle actually taking place" (*The Gospel of Matthew* [Grand Rapids: Eerdmans, 2007], p. 667). He concludes that "Jesus' words should not be taken at their literal face-value but read in the context of popular belief as an ironical comment on their lack of resources. Whether Jesus and the Twelve did in fact pay the tax, and, if so, how the money was raised, are questions which Matthew tantalizingly leaves open" (ibid., p. 671). But since a face-value reading of the text implies that Peter did "carry out to the letter" Jesus' instructions, one must provide more convincing evidence than an argument from silence. Despite objections that it reads like a fable, which it does not, the account is not improbable. See C. Brown, "Tax," *NIDNTT* 3:752-54. The fish in question may have been a large, bottom-feeding carp like the barbell. Carp are known to ingest a wide range of junk, and coins are just the kind of thing one might expect. In this regard, popular stories of valuable objects being found in the mouth of fish reflect what may occur in reality. Robert H. Mounce counters moral objections to the story and highlights a fundamental issue in the interpretation of Scripture:

> The "miracle" is held to be contrary to the moral principle that God does not do for us what we can do for ourselves. It is also thought to violate Jesus' own decision not to use miraculous power for his own benefit. Although we may acknowledge the distinctiveness of this miracle, the recommended solutions are inadequate. To declare that a historical narrative is folklore has far-reaching implications for the reliability of the text. To suggest that the whole event is no more than an example of Jesus' sense of humor makes a farce of serious exegesis. Better to assume that Peter did exactly what Jesus told him to do and in fact found a four-drachma coin in the mouth of the first fish he caught. (*Matthew* [Peabody, Mass.: Hendrickson, 1991], p. 172.)

the half-shekel tax (equivalent of a day's wage and levied on an annual basis) inquire of Peter whether his teacher pays the tax, a detail assuming Peter's role as a leader within the group.[5] Peter affirms that he does and goes inside the house to inform Jesus about the levy. Jesus asks Simon, "From whom do kings of the earth take toll and tribute? From their children or from others?" Peter's answer, based on his experience in the Galilean fishing industry, is straightforward: "From others."

Jesus' response is carefully nuanced. On the one hand, he implies that Peter and the rest of the disciples, because they are members of the kingdom of heaven ("children"), are not obligated to pay the temple tax. As becomes clear in the Gospel accounts, especially John's Gospel, the Jesus movement transcends the ancient traditions and institutions of Judaism, including that magnificent edifice that embodies and symbolizes the central affirmations of the ancestral faith. Jesus' answer thus constitutes an indirect indictment of the current religious authorities in Jerusalem, inasmuch as they fail to acknowledge his message about the kingdom. On the other hand, Jesus decides that his Jewish followers should, for now, pay the tax and avoid unnecessary conflict with the powers that be. The principle of avoiding unnecessary resistance to the gospel message becomes a primary missionary strategy among the early Christians. The apostle Paul, in particular, insists on this point in several of his letters (1 Cor 9), and Peter clearly echoes it in his first epistle as well (1 Pet 2:13-17; 3:16-17).

## PETER AND THE RICH YOUNG RULER

In the context of Jesus' approaching ascent to Jerusalem for the Passover,[6] a man of some means comes up and asks him, "Good Teacher, what must I do to inherit eternal life?" (Mk 10:17). Luke says he was a ruler (Lk 18:18), and Matthew adds that he was young (Mt 19:22). Jesus challenges him to sell his possessions, give the money to the poor and become a disciple. The man reluctantly declines the invitation and leaves (Mk 10:21-22). Jesus observes, "How hard it will be for those

---

[5]B. Van Elderen, "Peter, Simon," *ZPEB* 4:734.

[6]The distance from Jericho to Jerusalem is only about 15 miles, but in the process one must ascend nearly 4,000 feet to the summit of the Mount of Olives overlooking Jerusalem to the west.

who have wealth to enter the kingdom of God" (Mk 10:23), a statement running counter to the view that material abundance was a sign of divine blessing and approval on one's life.[7] The disciples are stunned and ask, "Then who can be saved?" (Mk 10:26), to which Jesus replies, "For mortals it is impossible, but not for God; for God all things are possible" (Mk 10:27).

At this point, Peter enters the narrative (Mk 10:28; Mt 19:27; Lk 18:28). Obviously, wealth is not an obstacle since he has already made considerable financial sacrifice to follow Jesus. But does Peter still feel threatened by the high demands Jesus makes for securing eternal life? Is he anxious about whether he qualifies? Or does his remark convey "perhaps a touch of smugness"?[8] It is hard to be sure. What Jesus does is assure him and his fellow disciples that their sacrifices are worth it; indeed, they will be matched by rewards beyond compare (Mk 10:28-30). Included in the list of future blessings, however, is the unexpected addition of "persecutions" (Mk 10:30). As we will see, the paradox that joy and blessing can co-exist with suffering is a major theme in Peter's first letter (1 Pet 1:6, 8; 2:9; 4:13; 5:10).

## PETER AND PASSION WEEK

All four Gospels focus on the last week of Jesus' ministry on earth, the final visit to Jerusalem for the Passover. In keeping with Greco-Roman biography, the Gospels put great emphasis on the events surrounding the death of the leading character. They break new ground, however, in that the passion of Jesus is much more than the tragic death of a noteworthy person; it proclaims the bedrock events, the death, burial and resurrection of Christ (cf. 1 Cor 15:1-8), that constitute the good news of salvation.[9]

*Curse on a fig tree.* On the day after Jesus' entry into Jerusalem, which was fraught with messianic overtones (cf. Zech 9:9-10), Peter witnessed Jesus' curse on a fig tree (Mk 11:12-14) followed, the next day, by his observation and report of its dramatic fulfillment: the tree

---

[7]See Peter H. Davids, "Rich and Poor," *DJG*, pp. 701-10.
[8]France, *Mark*, p. 407.
[9]On this point, see further L. W. Hurtado, "Gospel (Genre)," *DJG*, pp. 276-82.

was "withered away to its roots" (Mk 11:20-24). At first glance, Jesus' curse seems out of character. Why would he curse a fig tree especially when, as Mark tells us, "it was not the season for figs" (Mk 11:13)?[10] Furthermore, Mark seems to imply in the sequel that the key issue is one of faith, in which disciples should boldly request the seemingly impossible (moving mountains into the sea) because God will grant "whatever you ask for in prayer" (Mk 11:24).

Two factors help us make sense of this episode. First, Mark uses a technique called intercalation or the "sandwich story."[11] The cursing of the fig tree (Mk 11:12-14; cf. Mt 21:18-19) and its fulfillment (Mk 11:20-21) frame Jesus' visit to the temple and his driving out the money changers and the sellers of sacrificial animals in the temple precincts (Mk 11:15-19). Most likely, then, the episode of the fig tree bears some direct relationship to what happened on the Temple Mount. Second, the episode conforms to the long-established prophetic tradition of the symbolic action or acted parable whereby a message is conveyed by performing an action that dramatically visualizes the content. Classic examples include Jeremiah's linen belt (Jer 13 NIV), earthenware jug (Jer 19) and yoke of straps and bars (Jer 27).[12] In similar fashion, the fig tree probably functions as a symbol (cf. Deut 8:8; 1 Kings 4:25; Jer 8:13; 24; Hos 9:10; Mic 4:4). By cursing the fig tree, Jesus dramatically foretells the fate befalling the Second Commonwealth and its crown jewel, the Second Temple. In fact, the prophet Micah's lament over the Judean temple state in the eighth century B.C. almost serves as a template for Jesus' curse: "there is no first-ripe fig for which I hunger. The faithful have disappeared from the land, and there is no one left who is upright" (Mic 7:1-2). Furthermore, Luke includes in his Gospel a parable about a fig tree that implies what Jesus' curse in Mark vividly portrays ("cut it down," Lk 13:6-9).

---

[10]Winter figs typically ripen in May and June, although baby fig buds may appear as early as February (W. E. Shewell-Cooper, "Fig Tree," *ZPEB* 2:534); Passover occurs variously in the months of March and April. H. W. Hoehner argues that Jesus died on Friday, Nisan 14, which corresponds to April 3, A.D. 33 in our calendar ("Chronology," *DJG*, pp. 119-22).

[11]See Timothy Wiarda, *Interpreting Gospel Narratives: Scenes, People and Theology* (Nashville: B & H Academic, 2010), pp. 191-92, and Craig A. Evans, *Mark 8:27–16:20* (WBC 34B; Nashville: Thomas Nelson, 2001), pp. 151-52.

[12]See further Larry R. Helyer, *Yesterday, Today and Forever: The Continuing Relevance of the Old Testament* (2nd ed.; Salem, Wis.: Sheffield, 2004), pp. 274-77.

Peter and the early Jerusalem church, following the teaching of Jesus, come to understand that they are the remnant of Israel and give their allegiance to the great descendant of David who is the "righteous Branch" (Jer 23:5-6; 33:15), the "shoot . . . from the stump of Jesse" (Is 11:1), the one who "shall branch out in his place, and . . . build the temple of the LORD" (Zech 6:12). As we will see in 1 Peter, Peter holds that believers in Jesus now constitute "a spiritual house" and "holy priesthood" (1 Pet 2:5). For Peter, the Jerusalem temple, a place that was supposed to be "a house of prayer for all nations" but had been deformed into "a den of robbers" (Mk 11:17 citing Is 56:7 and Jer 7:11) has now been superseded by a new community of faith in which believing prayer accomplishes great things (Mk 11:23-25; cf. 1 Pet 1:17; 4:7; 5:7). Jesus' curse on the fig tree and the subsequent Olivet Discourse, to which we next turn, were transformational in the apostle Peter's understanding of God's new people (see 1 Pet 2:9-10).

***Instruction on the Mount of Olives.*** Probably on Wednesday of Passion Week, Peter, in company with Andrew, James and John, receive private instruction concerning the consummation of the kingdom of God. This teaching is generally designated as the Olivet Discourse, and its occurrence in the triple tradition signals its importance (Mk 13; Mt 24; Lk 21).

On his way back to his host's home in Bethany, Jesus pauses on the summit of Olivet. He sits down and gazes westward across the Kidron to view the splendid panorama. Before him lay Jerusalem the Golden, crowned with one of the wonders of the ancient world, the Second Temple. Its glistening, polished marble walls and columns with gilded gold adornment was truly a visual delight.[13] The rabbis extolled its virtues: "He who has not seen the temple of Herod, has never seen a beautiful building" (*b. Sukkah* 51b).

The four apostles, however, are subdued and stunned. Moments before, as they were making their way out of the temple complex, an

---

[13]That Josephus (*J.W.* 5.201-24) and the rabbis were not embellishing the facts when they mention gold-plated building stones is now confirmed by Benjamin Mazar's excavations along the southern wall of the Temple Mount. For a discussion and picture of such a stone, see "Gold-Plated Building Stone Found Near Temple Mount," *BAR* 35/1 (January-February 2009): 14.

unnamed disciple calls Jesus' attention to the splendor of the buildings. Jesus' reply is unexpected: "Do you see these great buildings? Not one stone will be left here upon another; all will be thrown down" (Mk 13:2). Now the four privately inquire, "Tell us, when will this be, and what will be the sign that all these things are about to be accomplished?" (Mk 13:4). Jesus responds with his famous discourse outlining the course of this age and his triumphant return in glory.[14]

Though differing on specifics, scholars generally agree on the following salient points: Jerusalem is doomed, the Second Temple will be destroyed, and the messianic community will experience violent persecution. A majority of evangelical scholars also hold that the discourse forecasts the eschatological consummation: cosmic upheaval and distress, the unexpected but glorious return of the Son of Man and a gathering of the elect. Not surprisingly, Peter, in both his letters, discusses this core affirmation of Christianity: Jesus Christ will return in glory (1 Pet 1:5, 7, 11, 13; 4:5, 7, 13, 17; 5:4, 10; 2 Pet 1:16, 19; 2:9; 3:1-13), a truth enshrined in the Apostles' Creed, "From thence he shall come to judge the quick and the dead." Not without interest is the likely source of this creed in the ancient Roman church.

*Peter in the upper room.* Reflecting Peter's leadership role among the Twelve, Jesus assigns Peter and John the task of preparing a place in the city to observe the Passover meal (Lk 22:8-13).[15] This detail is im-

---

[14]I am aware that in some circles there is strong disagreement about the eschatological referent of this discourse. Some, like N. T. Wright (*Jesus and the Victory of God*, vol. 2 of *Christian Origins and the Question of God* [Minneapolis: Fortress, 1996], pp. 339-68), think that only the destruction of Jerusalem and the temple in A.D. 70 is in view. In my opinion, this is quite mistaken. The destruction of Jerusalem does lie in the foreground, but the climax of the discourse is clearly the parousia. In response to Wright, see France, *Mark*, pp. 500-503, and Thomas Schreiner, *New Testament Theology* (Grand Rapids: Baker, 2008), pp. 803-13. The literature on this topic is voluminous. See T. J. Geddert, "Apocalyptic Teaching," *DJG*, pp. 20-26, for a helpful overview.

[15]This is a matter of longstanding debate. Was the Last Supper a Passover Seder or not? The condensed Gospel accounts place the meal in the context of Passover, and a few features seem to reflect the traditional Seder. However, there are some significant omissions. We leave this an open question. What seems reasonably established are Passover allusions and motifs in the meal Jesus celebrated with his apostles. For a helpful discussion of the issues involved in the nature and timing of the Last Supper, see Joseph A. Fitzmyer, *The Gospel According to Luke X-XXIV* (AB 28A; Garden City, N.Y.: Doubleday, 1985), pp. 1378-84, and R. H. Stein, "Last Supper," *DJG*, pp. 444-50.

portant for understanding Jesus' later arrest.[16] Peter and John do not know the place where the supper is to be held until after they meet an anonymous man carrying a water jar just inside the city. They are instructed to follow this person to the home of the unnamed host for the supper and there make preparations (Lk 22:9-13). None of the other apostles knows the location until they arrive later with Jesus. This secrecy allows Jesus to spend time with his apostles, instructing and preparing them for what is to follow without fear of arrest or interruption. Luke tells us that Judas had already begun "to look for an opportunity to betray him to them when no crowd was present" (Lk 22:6). What Judas does know, however, is the location where they would all sleep that night, namely, the Garden of Gethsemane (Jn 18:2). After Judas leaves the upper room (Jn 13:21-30), he goes to the authorities and tells them where they can arrest Jesus when only his disciples are present.

John's Gospel significantly augments the Synoptic accounts of the events leading up to the arrest. Especially meaningful for generations of Christians is the so-called Upper Room Discourse of John 13–17. Two episodes in this section feature the apostle Peter. The first is the famous foot-washing incident.

In a deeply moving, symbolic action, Jesus assumes the role of a servant and begins washing the feet of each apostle. But when it is Peter's turn, Peter demurs: "Lord, are you going to wash my feet?" (Jn 13:6).[17] On being informed that he will understand what it means later (Jn 13:7), he adamantly refuses: "You will never wash my feet" (Jn 13:8).[18] Once again, Peter's distorted concept of the Messiah interferes with his understanding of Jesus' mission. For Peter, it is demeaning for Jesus the Messiah to assume the role of a servant; after all, he is the king of Israel! If there is to be any foot washing, let the apostles wash those of the Master, not vice versa.

Jesus' gentle but firm response puts in sharp relief the symbolic

---

[16]It also anticipates the future prominence of Peter and John in the nascent church. See Brown et al., *Peter*, p. 113.

[17]The word order of the Greek conveys the total disconnect Peter experienced. See further G. R. Beasley-Murray, *John* (WBC 36; 2nd ed.; Dallas: Word, 1999), p. 233.

[18]Peter's emphatic refusal is indicated in Greek by the use of the double negative, *ou mē*. Hence the NRSV, and most English translations, render this by using the temporal adverb "never."

meaning of the gesture and its theological significance. Jesus' action speaks of two realities: identification with him and imitation of him. To be the recipient of undeserved grace and mercy is the essence of being a member of the new covenant community. Accordingly, humility is the hallmark of membership and the pattern for mutual relations among family members. "For I have set you an example, that you also should do as I have done to you" (Jn 13:15). Self-giving love authenticates those who belong to Jesus: "By this everyone will know that you are my disciples, if you have love for one another" (Jn 13:35). Peter did eventually get the point, as a thoughtful reading of his first letter eloquently testifies. In the letter, the voice of one who experienced self-giving love in action appeals to the reader to replicate the pattern (1 Pet 3:8; 4:8-10; 5:1-6).

A second moment of high drama involving Peter occurs in the upper room. After the shocking disclosure that one of them would betray Jesus, Simon Peter signaled to "the one whom Jesus loved" and who "was reclining next to him" (Jn 13:23) to ask Jesus who the betrayer was.[19] One may be fairly certain what would have happened had Jesus plainly told Peter who it was (see Jn 18:10). Judas' sudden departure did not arouse suspicion because he was the treasurer and some thought Jesus instructed him either to buy provisions for the feast or make a donation to the poor (Jn 13:29-30).

Another unsettling disclosure follows. Jesus informs the apostles that he is leaving them. Simon Peter speaks for all the apostles: "Where are you going?" (Jn 13:36). When told he cannot follow Jesus now but will do so later, Peter inquires: "Lord, why can I not follow you now? I will lay down my life for you" (Jn 13:37). Then the bombshell: "Will you lay down your life for me? Very truly, I tell you, before the cock crows, you will have denied me three times" (Jn 13:38). All four Gospels narrate Peter's denial. Luke, however, adds unique material by in-

---

[19]Contrary to Leonardo da Vinci's masterpiece, the apostles did not sit at a table; the participants reclined in a U-shape around a low table lying in the center. Each person reclined on his left side and ate with his right hand. This posture, modeled after Roman custom, signified the new status of Israelites as freedmen and no longer slaves. I follow the traditional view that the disciple whom Jesus loved was John the apostle. For alternative views and a defense of the traditional understanding, see M. J. Wilkins, "Disciples," *DJG*, pp. 179-80.

forming us that Satan requested permission to test Peter's faithfulness, recalling the book of Job (Job 1:6-12; 2:1-7). Jesus prays that Peter's faith will not fail and then, knowing full well he will momentarily stumble, predicts Peter's full restoration to leadership (Lk 22:31-34). The Synoptics all narrate Peter's vociferous denial that he would ever deny knowing the Lord (Mk 14:29; Mt 26:33; Lk 22:33). In just a few short hours, Peter's emphatic resolve crumbled.

***Peter in the Garden of Gethsemane.*** During the last week of Jesus' earthly ministry, he daily taught the people and engaged in discourse and debate with the religious leaders. Things were clearly heading for a showdown. During the days leading up to the Passover sacrifice and meal, Jesus stayed with the family of Mary, Martha and Lazarus in the village of Bethany. Bethany is on the eastern slopes of Olivet, out of view from Jerusalem to the west. The religious leaders determined to arrest Jesus and put him to death. However, they had a problem: Jesus was very popular among the thousands of Galilean pilgrims who now flooded the city. Rather than risk a riot by publicly arresting Jesus, they tried to arrest him secretly. Since Jewish tradition specified that Passover night be spent within the environs of greater Jerusalem, and Bethany was beyond these limits, Jesus selects another place to sleep that night.[20] The Garden of Gethsemane, just across the Kidron Valley, at the foot of Mount Olivet, had a dense olive grove and cave, providing a safe house within proximity to the Temple Mount. According to the Gospel of John, "Jesus often met there with his disciples" (Jn 18:2). After leaving the upper room, Judas reveals the location of this hideout to the authorities. He not only leads them to the spot but also identifies Jesus for them in the darkness of night by his infamous kiss (Mk 14:44-46).

Peter's role in the ensuing events is less than stellar (Mk 14:32-50). Soon after Jesus arrives at the garden with his disciples, he requests the presence of the inner three and withdraws with them for prayer. In

---

[20]Stein, "Last Supper," *DJG*, p. 446. Jesus may also have been concerned about putting Mary, Martha and Lazarus at risk by his staying with them. The name Gethsemane is derived from two Hebrew words, *gat* ("press") and *šĕmānîm* ("oil"), hence the meaning "place of the olive press."

deep, inner turmoil, Jesus then withdraws from the three and requests that they watch with him in prayer (Mk 14:33-34). For their part, exhausted and unaware of imminent danger, they fall asleep. In Mark's Gospel, when Jesus returns and finds them asleep, he singles out Peter and reproves him: "Simon, are you asleep? Could you not keep awake one hour? Keep awake and pray that you may not come into the time of trial; the spirit indeed is willing, but the flesh is weak" (Mk 14:37-38). Jesus withdraws once again for prayer. This sequence happens two more times (Mk 14:40-42), anticipating Peter's impending threefold denial. In keeping with Mark's less than exemplary depiction of the disciples, he informs his readers: "their eyes were heavy; and they did not know what to say to him" (Mk 14:40). I think we hear an echo of Peter's failure to stay awake in his admonition to Christians in Asia Minor: "Therefore prepare your minds for action; discipline yourselves. . . . Be serious and discipline yourselves for the sake of your prayers. . . . Discipline yourselves, keep alert" (1 Pet 1:13; 4:7; 5:8).

Once Peter realizes what is happening, he springs into action. Wielding a sword—there were only two swords among the entire group and, not surprisingly, he has one of them (Lk 22:38)—Peter lops off the right ear of one of the high priest's servants, a man named Malchus (Jn 18:10). But instead of a melee breaking out, the Master squelches all resistance by a stern rebuke ("No more of this!" [Lk 22:51; cf. Mt 26:52]). According to John's Gospel, the rebuke was directed at Peter: "Put your sword back into its sheath. Am I not to drink the cup that the Father has given me?" (Jn 18:11). In keeping with what we have already seen, Peter has no idea what that cup entails. A suffering Messiah is not on his radar. Then, remarkably, Jesus proceeds to heal the ear of Malchus (Lk 22:51). Once the apostles realize Jesus is not going to resist, they escape into the night.

This episode becomes paradigmatic (serving as a model) for Peter's later understanding of how Christians should react to betrayal, persecution and opposition. What a different approach permeates Peter's parenesis (exhortation) in his letter to believers under fire than the one he himself displayed in the Garden of Gethsemane (1 Pet 2:21-23; 3:13-17; 4:1, 12-19).

***Peter in the courtyard of the high priest.*** Peter and an unnamed disciple, whom I take to be John, double back and follow Jesus and his captors from afar to the home of the high priest (Mk 14:54; Jn 18:15-16). Throughout the early morning hours, however, as the reality of what is happening sinks in, Peter experiences a meltdown while sitting around a fire with the servants of the high priest. He vehemently denies even knowing Jesus. Luke poignantly portrays what happens after the third, decisive denial: "The Lord turned and looked at Peter. Then Peter remembered the word of the Lord, how he had said to him, 'Before the cock crows today, you will deny me three times.' And he went out and wept bitterly" (Lk 22:61-62).[21]

Peter's denial can never be taken back. It happened, and he had to live with the painful memory. But rather than letting his failure cripple him spiritually and emotionally, he used it as a means of building up the flock of God (cf. Paul in 1 Tim 1:12-16). He becomes a living illustration of forgiveness and a second chance. He possesses a degree of compassion and understanding for wavering believers that others, sometimes rather self-righteously, are incapable of showing. We hear a tenderness in Peter's first epistle that springs out of a bitterly disappointing failure in his own life (1 Pet 5:1-11). Jesus' prayer for Peter was wonderfully answered: "I have prayed for you that your own faith may not fail; and you, when once you have turned back, strengthen your brothers" (Lk 22:32). These words prepare Peter for the missionary role he performs in volume two of Dr. Luke's account of Christian beginnings.[22] Believers in Rome and "the exiles of the Dispersion" (1 Pet 1:1) were greatly encouraged and comforted by the story of the big fisherman's failure and subsequent forgiveness.

***Jesus appears to Simon on the first day of the week.*** We do not know where Peter went after his denial (Lk 22:62). He is not mentioned as being present at the cross, in contrast to "the beloved disciple" (Jn 19:26-27). Though perhaps he was among the "great number of people" who followed Jesus to the cross, more likely, he stayed away, especially

---

[21]Brown's comment here is apt: "The human interest touch is typical of Lucan style, and probably reflects Lucan redaction" (*Peter*, p. 112, n. 249).

[22]For a brief rehearsal of how this plays out in Acts, see Fitzmyer, *Luke*, pp. 1422-23.

in light of his overwhelming sense of failure at having denied the Lord.[23] All four Gospels tell us that the women who discovered the empty tomb on the first day of the week and heard the angelic announcement about Jesus' resurrection ran and informed "the eleven and . . . all the rest" (Mk 16:1-8 [the shorter ending of Mark]; Mt 28:8; Lk 24:9; Jn 20:2). Peter was among this group and, in company with "the other disciple" (Jn 20:3), ran to the tomb to see for himself (Lk 24:12; Jn 20:3-10). It may be that the home of John Mark's mother served as a meeting place for the apostles. This may also have been the residence having a guest room, an upper room, in which the Last Supper was observed and served as a regular meeting place (Acts 1:6, 13-14).[24]

More important, however, is the early tradition that Jesus appeared to Peter and that this appearance was the first to an apostle (1 Cor 15:5). The gospel tradition is also quite clear that Jesus first appeared to women disciples, Mary Magdalene being the first believer to see the risen Lord (Mk 16:9 [the longer ending of Mark]; Mt 28:8; Jn 20:14-18). It has often been observed how remarkable this fact is given the generally low credibility accorded women as witnesses in Second Temple Judaism.[25] This datum argues for the historicity of the resurrection accounts in that one would hardly suppose the disciples invented the story.[26] The fact that the Lord appeared to Peter before any of the rest of the apostles seems to have a twofold significance: it makes clear that Peter was truly forgiven for his denial ("But go, tell his disciples *and Peter*" [Mk 16:7]; "The Lord has risen indeed, and *he has appeared to Simon!*" [Lk 24:34, italics added]), and it anticipates his

---

[23]"That weekend must have been a period of remorse, soul-searching, and introspection for Peter; he bitterly regretted his cowardice that night, and it is not surprising that he had a significant place in the post-resurrection appearances of Jesus" (Van Elderen, "Peter, Simon," 4:736).

[24]Archaeological excavations have shown that the area now called Mount Zion was an affluent neighborhood during Second Temple times (Nahman Avigad, *Discovering Jerusalem* [Jerusalem: Shikmona and Israel Exploration Society, 1980], pp. 64-204). This is reflected in the model of first-century A.D. Jerusalem now located near the Shrine of the Book in modern West Jerusalem. The model shows palatial homes having enclosed rooms on top of flat roofs. These "upper rooms" probably illustrate the meeting place of the disciples.

[25]The first-century Jewish historian Josephus says, "From women let no evidence be accepted, because of the levity and temerity of their sex" (*Ant.* 4.8.15 [219]).

[26]See, e.g., N. T. Wright, "Resurrection Narratives," *DTIB*, p. 675.

future role as leader of the Jesus movement in which he will "feed my sheep" (Jn 21:15-19).

A mystery surrounds Jesus' appearance to Peter; we have no narrative account of the circumstances. According to Luke's Gospel, on the first day of the week, Jesus joins two disciples, one named Cleopas (Lk 24:18), on the road to Emmaus and spends a considerable part of the afternoon with them (Lk 24:29). After recognizing Jesus, they hasten back to Jerusalem to inform the disciples. On their arrival, however, the disciples who remained in Jerusalem confirm this report with their own joyous announcement: "The Lord has risen indeed, and he has appeared to Simon!" (Lk 24:34). But if Jesus was at Emmaus, how could he have appeared to Simon? Surely, the anonymous disciple was not Simon, or Luke would have said so. Raymond Brown conjectures that this is a "stray item of kerygmatic proclamation that Luke has fitted awkwardly into his condensed Gospel sequence."[27] But given that several morning hours were available for such an encounter, I hardly see how this counts as a problem. Jesus' appearance to Simon was probably not long after his appearance to Mary Magdalene in the garden (Jn 20:11-18). In Jerusalem, the sun rises before 6:00 a.m. in the month of Nisan, and the women set out for the tomb before sunrise (Jn 20:1; Mk 16:2).[28] The distance from the upper room to the holy sepulchre is only about half a mile.[29] If we allow time for them to walk to the site and then return (hurriedly) to the disciples with their news and have Peter and John run to the tomb and then return, this could all have transpired before 8:00 a.m. This would allow for a period of several hours before Jesus appears at Emmaus (Lk 24:29). Since Jesus is now in his glorified state, distance is no longer a problem!

---

[27] *Peter*, p. 126. John Nolland says that "Luke rather cleverly makes use of a narrative setting in which resumé reporting is the appropriate form" (*Luke 18:35—24:53* [WBC 35C; Dallas: Word, 1993], p. 1206).

[28] In 2009, the State of Israel began daylight saving time on March 27, and Easter sunrise occurred at 6:14 a.m.

[29] I assume the traditional view, supported by modern archaeological and historical investigation, that the upper room was located on what is today called Mount Zion. It may well be that the traditional site, though Crusader in its present form, is located on or near the actual site. See M. Broshi, "Excavations in the House of Caiaphas, Mount Zion," in *Jerusalem Revealed* (ed. Yigael Yadin; New Haven and London: Yale University Press and the Israel Exploration Society, 1976), pp. 57-60.

## Jesus' Appearance and Commission to Simon

The final Gospel episode about Simon occurs back in Galilee, along the lake where his initial call took place (Jn 21). In this respect, his story comes full circle. But as it turns out, this is the beginning of a new phase—in his life as well as that of the Jesus movement.

So, what happened on that momentous occasion? Seven disciples (Peter, Thomas, Nathanael, James, John and two unnamed disciples) are together at the Sea of Tiberias (Jn 21:1). Most likely they are at Capernaum, where Peter and the sons of Zebedee lived. Perhaps Andrew is one of the unnamed disciples (Jn 1:40-41, 44; 6:8; 12:22). Peter suggests they all go fishing.

What should we make of this? Many preachers and commentators chastise Peter and the others for slipping back into their old ways and forgetting their commission to preach the gospel. But this goes beyond what can fairly be inferred. Mark and Matthew make it clear that soon after his resurrection, Jesus instructed the apostles to meet him in Galilee (Mk 16:7; Mt 28:7, 10). After completing the Festival of Unleavened Bread in Jerusalem, they return to Galilee in anticipation of meeting up with Jesus. This, according to Matthew, is precisely what happened (Mt 28:16, 17). It seems reasonable to assume that before the entire group assembled, there was some down time. What is more natural for these men than going back out on the lake and doing what they have done since their youth? Furthermore, there may have been some pressing financial needs in their families that a good catch could alleviate. As it turns out, they haul in a windfall, assisting them in the transition to full-time ministry.[30]

At first, however, the fish are not biting. In fact, the entire night nets nothing. As morning light dawns, Jesus suddenly appears along the beach and calls out to the weary fishermen: "Children, you have no fish, have you?" To their dejected report, Jesus orders them to let down their nets on the right side of the boat. When they do so, their nets suddenly ensnare a huge school of fish, including 153 large ones to be exact (Jn 21:11).[31] Memories are activated; the story has come full circle (cf. Lk

---

[30]See further, in support of my interpretation, Beasley-Murray, *John*, p. 399.

[31]To canvass the supposed significance of this number requires more time and space than it deserves. Suffice it to say, the precision points to the eyewitness quality of the report. The text

5:1-11); the "disciple whom Jesus loved" told Peter, "It is the Lord!" (Jn 21:7).[32] Peter, who had been working naked, put on his loincloth and swam to shore. The others row the boat in, dragging the net behind. When they all get ashore, Jesus has a fish breakfast, cooked over coals, already prepared for them. Jesus "took the bread and gave it to them, and did the same with the fish" (Jn 21:13). Once again, memories are jogged and the disciples remember the miraculous feeding of the multitudes with five loaves and two fishes (Jn 6:1-14). If there were any lingering doubts about how they will manage in the future, this incident vividly reinforces Jesus' earlier assurance: "Do not worry about your life, what you will eat or what you will drink, or about your body, what you will wear . . . your heavenly Father knows that you have need of all these things. But strive first for the kingdom of God and his righteousness, and all these things will be given to you as well" (Mt 6:25, 32-33).

What next follows is the climactic moment of the episode. Jesus asks Peter, three times, if he loves him.[33] The thrice-repeated question is not incidental; it is intentional, gently but painfully reminding Peter of his threefold denial. This time Peter does not swear or take an oath; his only recourse is to appeal to Jesus' extraordinary understanding of the human heart: "Lord, you know everything; you know that I love you" (Jn 21:17; cf. 1:48; 2:24-25). Each time Peter reaffirms his love for Jesus, Jesus counters by commissioning him: "Feed my lambs" (Jn 21:15), "Tend my sheep" (Jn 21:16), and "Feed my sheep" (Jn 21:17).[34] The imagery of shepherd and sheep points to Peter's primary role as pastor of the emerging church.

---

implies that there were also smaller fish in the catch. It should also be noted that *musht* (Saint Peter's fish) typically feed in large schools. See Mendel Nun, "Ports of Galilee," *BAR* 25/4 (1999): 8-31.

[32]This detail points to John of Zebedee as the disciple whom Jesus loved. He was present the first time Jesus performed a miracle involving a huge catch of fish (Lk 5:1-11). Ben Witherington's conjecture that the beloved disciple was Lazarus is improbable (*Letters and Homilies for Hellenized Christians*, vol. 1: *A Socio-Rhetorical Commentary on Titus, 1-2 Timothy and 1-3 John* [Downers Grove, Ill.: IVP Academic, 2006], pp. 232-61). Lazarus lived in Judea, far removed from the life of fishing on the Galilee.

[33]Sermons drawing a distinction between the two Greek words *phileo* and *agapaō* probably read too much into this because they are used synonymously in this passage. See Beasley-Murray, *John*, p. 394.

[34]Nor should one find any significant difference between *boskō* ("feed") and *poimainō* ("tend"). They are essentially synonymous in this context.

This is a deeply moving moment for Peter. He is forgiven and reinstated as leader. The Master has full confidence in him, and the ensuing history of the early church confirms that confidence was not misplaced. It is no accident that Peter's first epistle employs the same metaphor to remind the elders in the house churches of Asia Minor of their primary responsibility: "I exhort the elders among you to tend the flock of God that is in your charge" (1 Pet 5:1b-2a).

There is another aspect of being a shepherd. In the words of Jesus, "the good shepherd lays down his life for the sheep" (Jn 10:11). The last recorded conversation in John's Gospel is somber but inspiring: Peter will eventually follow Jesus in death by crucifixion (Jn 21:18-19). This fulfills Peter's earlier, vehement claim: "Lord . . . I will lay down my life for you" (Jn 13:37; cf. Lk 23:33). Jesus' revelation powerfully shapes Peter's consciousness. He knows in advance that he will imitate his Lord through death on a cross. "I know that my death will come soon, as indeed our Lord Jesus Christ has made clear to me. And I will make every effort so that after my departure you may be able at any time to recall these things" (2 Pet 1:14-15). Though he lacked the courage the first time he faced this prospect, he will not fail a second time. In the upper room, Peter had asked Jesus, "Lord, where are you going?" To this question, Jesus replied, "Where I am going, you cannot follow me now; *but you will follow afterward*" (Jn 13:36, italics added).[35] No wonder the shadow of the cross falls across Peter's theology.

Peter then inquires about the destiny of the beloved disciple. Jesus' response is terse and enigmatic: "If it is my will that he remain until I come, what is that to you? Follow me!" (Jn 21:21-22). An editorial comment implies that a misunderstanding of this saying was already widespread: Jesus did not affirm that the beloved disciple would live until Jesus' glorious return. The point of the saying is that the time of a disciple's death lies entirely in Jesus' hands and prying into such matters should not be a concern. What matters is being a faithful witness and resting in the Lord of life and death. Peter got the point: "Let those suffering in accordance with God's will entrust themselves to a faithful

---

[35]As Brown notes, this is "most probably an invitation to martyrdom" (*Peter*, p. 145).

Creator, while continuing to do good" (1 Pet 4:19).

This concludes my sketch of Peter's life as reconstructed from the Gospels. The next phase of Peter's life witnesses an extraordinary growth and expansion of the Jesus movement. In fact, under Peter's pastoral oversight, it begins to transform into a universal faith called Christianity.

## QUESTIONS FOR DISCUSSION

1.  Outline the key moments in Peter's life as pieced together from the four Gospels. Is there a discernible pattern in this synthesis?
2.  Sketch a personality profile of Peter based on the information gleaned from the Gospels. What made Peter a good leader?
3.  Why was the transfiguration of Jesus so important for Peter's understanding of Jesus, and how is that new understanding reflected in his epistles?
4.  Do you think there are unhistorical episodes narrated in the Gospels (such as the temple tax and the curse on the fig tree)?
5.  What is pastorally significant in the fact that Peter's failures are clearly evident in the Gospels?
6.  Do you find the links and parallels made in this chapter between the life of Peter as reconstructed from the Gospels and various passages cited in 1 and 2 Peter convincing? Are there others that should be added?
7.  How does the Upper Room Discourse throw light on Peter's first epistle?

## FOR FURTHER READING

Brown, Raymond E., Karl P. Donfried and John Reumann, eds. *Peter in the New Testament*. Minneapolis/New York: Augsburg/Paulist, 1973. Pp. 57-147.

Bruce, F. F. *Peter, Stephen, James and John: Studies in Non-Pauline Christianity*. Grand Rapids: Eerdmans, 1979.

Cullmann, Oscar. *Peter: Disciple—Apostle—Martyr. A Historical and Theological Essay*. 2nd ed. Philadelphia: Westminster, 1962.

Foakes-Jackson, F. J. *Peter: Prince of Apostles*. London: Hodder & Stoughton, 1927. Pp. 63-73.

Grant, Michael. *Saint Peter: A Biography*. New York: Scribner, 1995.

Hengel, Martin. *Saint Peter: The Underestimated Apostle*. Grand Rapids: Eerdmans, 2010.

Martin, Ralph P. "Peter." *ISBE*. Grand Rapids: Eerdmans, 1986. 3:802-7.

Perkins, Pheme. *Peter: Apostle for the Whole Church*. Columbia: University of South Carolina Press, 1994. Pp. 62-108.

Van Elderen, B. "Peter, Simon." *ZPEB*. Grand Rapids: Zondervan, 1977. 4:733-39.

Wiarda, Timothy. *Peter in the Gospels: Pattern, Personality and Relationship*. WUNT 2.127. Tübingen: Mohr & Seibeck, 2000.

———. *Interpreting Gospel Narratives: Scenes, People and Theology*. Nashville: B&H Academic, 2010.

# 4

---

# PETER AND
# THE EARLY CHURCH

◇

*The Book of Acts*

OUR PRIMARY SOURCES for understanding the role of Peter in the
earliest years of the church are the book of Acts and a few snippets from
Paul's letters. Several problems surface in seeking to reconstruct Peter's
life during this amazing period of approximately A.D. 30-65. These will
be addressed as they arise. I attribute the authorship of Acts to Luke,
Paul's travel companion.[1] The following chapter summarizes episodes
in Acts in which Peter figures prominently.

## APOSTLE AND LEADER OF THE JERUSALEM CHURCH

According to Acts, during a forty-day postresurrection period, Jesus
appeared frequently to his disciples, confirming their faith and in-
structing them further concerning the kingdom of God (Acts 1:3).
Jesus ordered them to wait in Jerusalem for the gift of the Holy Spirit
(Acts 1:4; cf. Jn 14:16-17, 26; 15:26; 16:7-15). Soon after Jesus' ascension
(Acts 1:9-11), Peter begins to use the keys of the kingdom of heaven
(Mt 16:19).

---

[1]On the authorship, background, genre and reliability of Acts, see F. F. Bruce, "Acts of the
Apostles," *ISBE* 1:43-44; Colin J. Hemer, *The Book of Acts in the Setting of Hellenistic History*
(WUNT 49; ed. Conrad H. Gempf; Tübingen: Mohr, 1989); Ben Witherington III, ed., *History, Literature and Society in the Book of Acts* (Cambridge: Cambridge University Press, 1996);
idem, *The Acts of the Apostles: A Socio-Rhetorical Commentary* (Grand Rapids: Eerdmans, 1998),
pp. 1-65; J. B. Green, "Acts of the Apostles," *DLNTD*, pp. 7-12; Bruce W. Winter et al., eds.,
*BAFCS* (6 vols.; Grand Rapids: Eerdmans, 1993-1997).

*Election of Matthias.* The first thing Luke narrates about the fledgling community is a decision made at Peter's initiative.[2] Peter, who is listed first in the apostolic roster (Acts 1:13), introduces his counsel with this statement: "the scripture had to be fulfilled" (Acts 1:16). Judas's defection is not mere happenstance; it is foreordained and foreseen in Scripture (Pss 69:25; 109:8). Peter then informs the group of about 120 believers that it is necessary to fill the vacancy of Judas.[3] As noted earlier, the number twelve is significant in that it represents the ancient covenant tradition of the twelve tribes of Israel. The Jesus movement, in line with the teachings of the Master himself, views itself as the true Israel. Peter now reads the Scriptures christologically, that is, he perceives that they point toward and foreshadow Jesus as the fulfillment of Israel's prophetic hope. This too was learned from the Master (cf. Lk 24:27, 44-49).

Peter stipulates the requirements for a replacement: participation in the movement from the days of John the Baptist and personal witness to the resurrection of Jesus (Acts 1:21-22). The community selects two qualified candidates and, after prayer, allows the drawing of lots to determine election to office (cf. Lev 16:8; Josh 18:6; 19:51). Matthias fills the spot vacated by Judas's defection. The episode shows that the community recognizes Jesus' conferral of leadership on Peter, and he now assumes that responsibility.

*Pentecost: Peter announces the terms for admission to the kingdom.* Pentecost may be dubbed "the birthday of the church," marking the

---

[2]David J. Williams calls attention to the fact that Luke's method of writing history is very similar to that of the Roman historian Livy, for whom history must perforce be a record of people and their deeds. "[Luke] tells his story by means of paradigmatic people and events. The events of this chapter illustrate the opposition that the church soon encountered from the Jewish authorities, and the man on whom the spotlight is focused is Peter" (*Acts* [NIBC; Peabody, Mass.: Hendrickson, 1995], p. 63).

[3]The Qumran community required that for every ten members there be a priest (1QS 6:3-4). There is another tradition: "And how many residents must there be in a town so that it may be suitable for a sanhedrin? One hundred and twenty" (*m. Sanh.* 1.6; Jacob Neusner, *Mishnah: A New Translation* [New Haven: Yale University Press, 1988]). Bock, however, cautions against making the connection with Acts 1:15; Darrell L. Bock, *Acts* (BECNT; Grand Rapids: Baker, 2007), pp. 80-81. Beverly Gaventa likewise questions the parallel and suggests that it "serves primarily to indicate that the community's strength already extends well beyond the small circle of the apostles and the women who had traveled with Jesus" (*The Acts of the Apostles* [ANTC; Nashville: Abingdon, 2003], p. 69).

first of three major doors Peter unlocks with his keys of the kingdom. In reality, each door is essentially the same door, the "narrow door" (Lk 13:24) "that leads to life" (Mt 7:14), open for "everyone who calls on the name of the Lord" (Acts 2:21). The distinction involves the audience invited to enter. The first invitation is offered to Peter's fellow Jews in Jerusalem (Acts 2:14) and extended to include "the entire house of Israel" (Acts 2:36), a temporal priority also recognized by the apostle Paul (cf. Rom 1:16; 2:9). As we will see shortly, the second and third keys unlock doors for quite different and unexpected audiences. The coming of the promised Holy Spirit on Pentecost ignites a veritable evangelism explosion. When Peter the preacher begins his sermon, there are 120 Spirit-filled believers. By the time he finishes and gives an invitation, 3,000 people respond. The Jesus movement shifts into high gear. Several features of this account require comment.

1. Peter is depicted as "standing with the eleven" (Acts 1:14) when he delivers his Pentecost sermon. Whereas Peter is the acknowledged spokesperson for the Jesus movement, his witness is a shared one. Collectively, the apostles witness to the resurrection of Jesus and thereby function as the leaders of the movement. Collegial rather than hierarchical best describes the pattern of leadership displayed in Acts. The collegial nature of early church leadership manifests itself some thirty years later when Peter appeals "as an elder myself" to the elders in Anatolia (1 Pet 5:1).

2. Peter's message resonates with the motif of promise-fulfillment. His initial text is appropriately taken from Joel's prophecy about the outpouring of the Spirit "in the last days" (Joel 2:28-32). The implications are staggering: the last days have begun! The distinguishing sign of that era—an outpouring of the Holy Spirit on both genders and spanning all age groups—is now in effect. As we will see in our study of the Petrine Epistles, the assumption that redemptive history is now in its last stage clearly manifests itself (1 Pet 1:10-13; 2:12; 4:5, 13; 5:1, 4, 6, 10; 2 Pet 1:19; 3:1-15).

3. This display of the Holy Spirit's power and presence is based on Jesus' atoning death and resurrection. Peter briefly summarizes the ministry of Jesus, marked by "deeds of power, wonders and signs" (Acts

2:22) and quickly moves to the heart of the matter. He demonstrates to his Jewish listeners that Jesus' crucifixion is not just another instance of falling afoul of the occupation forces; in reality it is the key moment of a divinely ordained and prophesied plan. God raised Jesus of Nazareth from the dead and thereby demonstrates that "this Jesus whom you crucified" is "exalted at the right hand of God" and declared "both Lord and Messiah" (Acts 2:33, 36).

Peter's bold assertion is buttressed by two key proof texts, both from the book of Psalms (Pss 16:8-11; 110:1).[4] According to Peter, when Psalm 16:8-11 speaks about the "Holy One," whom God "will not abandon . . . to Hades or let . . . experience corruption" (Acts 2:27), this refers to Jesus of Nazareth and his resurrection (Acts 2:31). Perhaps Peter dramatically pointed toward the tomb of David, a prominent landmark in the city (Neh 3:16; *Ant.* 7.15.3 §392-394; 13.8.4 §249; 16.7.1 §179-183), when he said, "I may say to you confidently of our ancestor David that he both died, and was buried, and his tomb is with us to this day." And just as confidently, Peter asserts, "this Jesus God raised up, and of that all of us are witnesses" (Acts 2:32). This emphasis on Peter and the apostles as witnesses also characterizes Peter's letters (1 Pet 5:1; 2 Pet 1:16).

Following the lead of the Master (Mt 22:41-46; cf. Mk 12:35-37; Lk 20:41-44), Peter now understands the "my Lord" of Psalm 110:1 to be none other than the Lord Jesus who is exalted to the right hand of the Lord God of Israel. The identification in both psalm texts of "your faithful one" and "my Lord" as Jesus the Messiah and the linkage with deliverance from death and exaltation to God's right hand provides Peter with a compelling argument to his Jewish audience. Such a christological reading of the OT, especially the Psalms and Prophets, reappears in Peter's letters (1 Pet 2:3-4, 6-10; 2:22-25; 3:12-15; 2 Pet 3:8-13).

4. The hearers come under conviction and raise an agonized question:

---

[4]Peter's use of the OT is similar to a technique called *pesher.* The Hebrew word *pesher* refers to a mode of interpreting Scripture "in which a verse of Scripture is interpreted with reference to the interpreter's own time and situation, which is usually seen as the last days" (Arthur G. Patzia and Anthony J. Petrotta, *Pocket Dictionary of Biblical Studies* [Downers Grove, Ill.: InterVarsity Press, 2002], p. 92). See Larry R. Helyer, *Exploring Jewish Literature of the Second Temple Period* (Downers Grove, Ill.: InterVarsity Press, 2002), pp. 227-45.

"Brothers, what should we do?" (Acts 2:37). Peter takes out his keys and issues a pronouncement concerning admission to the new messianic community: repent and be baptized. This at first sight strikes a note similar to the one John the Baptist sounded at the beginning of his ministry (Lk 3:7). However, a significantly new meaning attaches to the act of baptism; it is now performed "in the name of Jesus Christ" (Acts 2:38). Whereas John's baptism was preparatory, baptism in the name of Jesus Christ is initiatory; it represents admission to the kingdom of God. On the basis of Jesus' death and resurrection both forgiveness of sins and the gift of the Holy Spirit are predicated. The unifying factor of the new Israel is no longer adherence to Torah and temple but faith in Jesus Christ the Lord who fulfills and transcends the intent of both. This is the key admitting one to the kingdom: embrace the message concerning Jesus' saving deeds and identify with him in baptism (Acts 2:41).

The hallmark of those who sincerely accept Jesus is a continuance in "the apostles' teaching and fellowship . . . the breaking of bread and the prayers" (Acts 2:42).[5] The transforming power of the Jesus movement results in a growing number of converts to this new sect of Judaism, known simply as "the Way" (Acts 9:2). "And day by day the Lord added to their number those who were being saved" (Acts 2:47). Adherence to apostolic teaching is a keynote of 2 Peter (2 Pet 2:1, 12-21; 2:15, 21; 3:1-2, 15-18).

*Peter and the Samaritan Pentecost.* Peter's second use of his keys to unlock the door leading to life involves an unlikely people group, the Samaritans. As the Gospels make clear and Josephus confirms, Jews and Samaritans were bitter enemies. Although Samaritans shared a belief in the authoritative Pentateuch (the Samaritan version, however, differs from the Hebrew version in several significant ways) and some religious customs, Jews despised Samaritans as religious hybrids and

---

[5]Opinions vary on whether "breaking of bread" refers to common meals or the Lord's Supper. Ernst Haenchen thinks it refers to "the Christians' communal meal" (*The Acts of the Apostles: A Commentary* [trans. B. Noble and G. Shinn; Oxford: Blackwell, 1987], p. 191). John B. Polhill (*Acts* [NAC 26; Nashville: Holman, 1992], p. 119) and Joseph A. Fitzmyer (*The Acts of the Apostles* [AB 31; New York: Doubleday, 1998], pp. 270-71) argue that it is the Lord's Supper. Bock says "it is unclear" (*Acts*, p. 150).

prohibited their entry into the sacred precincts of the Jerusalem temple. But Samaritans identified Mount Gerizim as the sacred mount where Abraham nearly sacrificed Isaac, a view exacerbating the hostility already existing between the two groups (*Ant.* 11.8.2 §306-312; 13.10.2 §275-281; 18.2.2 §29-30; cf. Jn 4:20-21).[6] When the religious leaders of Jerusalem sought to vilify Jesus, they hurled this insult: "Are we not right in saying that you are a Samaritan?" (Jn 8:48). Much blood was spilled during ethnic-religious conflict between Jews and Samaritans preceding the birthday of the church.[7]

After Stephen's martyrdom and a period of intense persecution spearheaded by none other than Saul of Tarsus, "Philip went down to the city of Samaria and proclaimed the Messiah to them" (Acts 8:5). This Spirit-directed mission reaps a harvest of souls (cf. Jn 4:35-38).[8] Luke pens his endorsement of the enterprise with one of his signature phrases: "So there was great joy in that city" (Acts 8:8; cf. Acts 13:52; 16:34; Lk 1:14, 44, 58; 10:17, 21; 24:52).

News of this unexpected response reaches Jerusalem. Significantly, the apostles dispatch Peter and John (Gal 2:9, "acknowledged pillars") to assess the situation in Samaria (Acts 8:14).[9] Realizing that the Sa-

---

[6]Archaeological excavations on Mount Gerizim confirm that the Samaritans built a temple on its summit in the middle of the fifth century B.C. during the governorship of Sanballat the Horonite, an enemy of Nehemiah (see Neh 2:10, 19; 4:1-3, 7-9; 13:28). An even larger temple was built over that one at the beginning of the second century B.C., and it was this temple that John Hyrcanus destroyed (ca. 114-111 B.C.). The 21st of Chislev, said to be the date of the destruction of the Samaritan temple, became a Jewish holiday on which it was forbidden to mourn. This reflects the intense antagonism Jews felt toward the Samaritans. See Itzhak Magen, "Gerizim, Mount," *NEAEHL* 1:484-92, and idem, "Gerizim, Mount," *NEAEHL* 5:1742-48.

[7]For more background on the Samaritans, see J. L. Kelso, "Samaritans," *ZPEB* 5:244-47, and H. G. M. Williamson and C. A. Evans, "Samaritans," *DNTB*, pp. 1052-61.

[8]The mission to the Samaritans spearheaded by Philip the deacon was not, however, an unprecedented initiative; Jesus proclaimed his messianic status there during his earthly ministry (Jn 4:25-26, 42). Jesus even made a Samaritan a role model of piety in his famous parable of the Good Samaritan (Lk 10:29-37), much to the indignation of his Jewish audience and probably also his own disciples (Lk 9:51-55). On one occasion, Jesus healed ten lepers in an area between Galilee and Samaria. What is significant is that only one of the ten returned to thank Jesus, and Luke especially emphasizes the ethnicity of this grateful man: "And he was a Samaritan" (Lk 17:11-16).

[9]Witherington (*Acts*, p. 289) comments: "Confirmation of true conversion would be needed by the mother church . . . the same sort of infallible confirmation that Peter later remarks on a proof that God also accepts Gentiles among his people (cf. 11:15-17)."

maritan believers have not yet received the Holy Spirit, they lay hands on them (Acts 8:17). Immediately, the Samaritans receive the Spirit, evidenced by observable effects, perhaps speaking in tongues and other sign miracles, authenticating the Samaritans' conversion experience. In effect, it constitutes a Samaritan Pentecost. "The Way" breaches a major religious-ethnic barrier, and Peter himself validates the breakout. But an even greater barrier looms ahead, and its breaching will not be so easy or without lingering reservations and repercussions.

## THE CONVERSION OF CORNELIUS

No ethnic-religious divide in the Roman Empire during the first century A.D. was more pronounced and fraught with tension than that between Jew and Gentile.[10] For the first decade or so, the apostles never entertained the notion that Jesus intended to incorporate Gentiles into a new Israel. That some Gentiles might be saved was not in question, but that they would be accorded equal status with believing Jews was quite beyond their expectations. That is why the episode of Cornelius's conversion is so pivotal, a veritable sea change.[11] Highlighting its importance, Luke recounts the story not once but three times in his second volume (Acts 10; 11:1-18; 15:1-29). And the apostle Peter occupies center stage, wielding his kingdom keys for the third and decisive time, and in so doing, completely altering the course of the Christian church history.

Luke's first narration of the "Cornelius Affair" is a carefully crafted account, designed to demonstrate divine initiative and approval. The story is introduced by an intriguing lead-in: "Meanwhile he [Peter] stayed in Joppa for some time with a certain Simon, a tanner" (Acts 9:43).[12] The profession of tanner rendered one ritually unclean because it involved daily contact with animal hides. Being a former fisherman

---

[10]I think Tessa Rajak understates the situation when she speaks of "rare occasions of tension" between Jews and Greeks ("The Location of Cultures in Second Temple Palestine," in *The Book of Acts in Its Palestinian Setting* [ed. Richard J. Bauckham; *BAFCS*, ed. Bruce W. Winter et al.; Grand Rapids: Eerdmans, 1995], 4:1-14).

[11]"What began as a Jewish movement struggling for acceptance within Judaism has now expanded to become a movement to reach all people" (Bock, *Acts*, p. 383).

[12]Readers may be surprised by another Simon in the book of Acts. But as noted in chapter 1, Simon is one of the most frequently occurring names in Jewish inscriptional evidence during Second Temple times.

in Galilee, Peter had never observed all the Pharisaic ritual requirements either—that would have been extremely difficult given his occupation; but we do learn, perhaps surprisingly, that Peter observed the
dietary restrictions expected of all Jews (Acts 10:14; cf. Lev 11).
Whereas Pharisees avoided contact with tanners to prevent ritual de-
filement, Peter is obviously not constrained by such scruples. One
wonders if this brief notice is Dr. Luke's way of showing how Peter is
being prepared to bridge a major ethnic-religious fault line.

The central figure in this dramatic story is a Roman centurion
named Cornelius. Luke even specifies his unit as "the Italian Cohort,"
a not inconsequential detail given Luke's purpose to show the spread of
the gospel to the very capital of the empire.[13] Even more important, "he
was a devout man who feared God with all his household; he gave alms
generously to the people and prayed constantly to God" (Acts 10:2). As
we learn in the book of Acts, "God-fearers," Gentiles who acknowledged the God of Israel and observed many of the commandments of
Torah—short of undergoing circumcision and converting to Judaism—
are among the most responsive people groups in the empire to the
preaching of the gospel. Here is a man whose heart has been divinely
prepared to accept the Jewish Messiah. Two providentially prepared
men are about to have a divine appointment.[14]

Luke juxtaposes two visionary experiences. An angel of God first
appears to Cornelius at three in the afternoon, the time for the *Tamid*
or perpetual burnt offering in the Jerusalem temple (cf. Acts 3:1). He is
assured that his prayers have been heard and is commanded to send for
"Simon who is called Peter" (Acts 10:5) and given his address. The next
day at about noon, Peter is praying on the rooftop of his Joppa residence. Falling into a trance and seeing a large sheet let down from
heaven with all manner of unclean beasts, Peter is bidden by a heavenly
voice to eat. He protests, "I have never eaten anything that is profane or
unclean" (Acts 10:14). This happens three times, reminding us of Pe-

---

[13]This cohort of auxiliary archers is known to have served in Syria from 69 B.C. into the second
century A.D. (Fitzmyer, *Acts*, 449).

[14]One of the strengths of Gaventa's commentary is her insistence that, in Acts, we "see God at
work from the beginning until well past the end" (*Acts*, p. 26).

ter's three denials and the Lord's threefold question, "Simon, son of John, do you love me?" (Jn 21:15-17).

While Peter is trying to make sense of this strange vision, Cornelius's Gentile servants appear at the gate and inquire about Simon Peter's presence. Still trying to sort out the meaning of the vision and wondering what these strangers want, Peter receives direct guidance from the Holy Spirit: "Now get up, go down, and go with them without hesitation; for I have sent them" (Acts 10:20). Peter does so and moves further across Jewish boundary lines by inviting them to stay the night before returning to Caesarea (cf. Acts 10:28). The next day they set out for Caesarea, the provincial capital of Judea and the Roman imperial headquarters. Interestingly, some believers from Joppa accompany Peter as well. It will be extremely important for Peter to have Jewish Christian eyewitnesses to what is about to unfold.

What happens next is truly amazing. Cornelius gathers his relatives and close friends (Acts 10:24) to attend to what Peter says. As Peter peers into the faces of these Gentiles eager to be instructed, the vision on the rooftop and the emissaries from Cornelius now make sense: a new era for the people of God has begun (Acts 11:28).[15] Peter inquires into the nature of the request for his presence, and Cornelius briefly recaps his visionary experience. He concludes with these words: "So now all of us are here in the presence of God to listen to all that the Lord has commanded you to say" (Acts 10:33). Peter does not even have an opportunity to extend an invitation: the Holy Spirit falls on the listeners and a Gentile Pentecost occurs. Perhaps the most telling line in Luke's account is the following: "The circumcised believers who had come with Peter were astounded that the gift of the Holy Spirit had been poured out even on the Gentiles" (Acts 10:45). Peter, discerning the Holy Spirit's leading, seizes the moment and asks rhetorically: "Can anyone withhold the water for baptizing these people who have received the Holy Spirit just as we have?" (Acts 10:47). Hearing no objection, he orders "them to be baptized in the name of Jesus Christ" (Acts 10:48). Gentiles, without first converting to Judaism, receive the

---

[15]"God's Spirit first uses the symbolism of clean and unclean food to teach Peter a proper understanding of Gentiles in the divine plan of salvation" (Fitzmyer, *Acts*, p. 454).

promised gift of the Holy Spirit. A massive wall had just been breached. But would the breach stand or would Jewish Christians rush in to plug the gap and maintain the status quo?

Luke stays with this story because it sparks a heated controversy in the Jerusalem church (Acts 11:1-18). Only the acknowledged authority invested in Peter and the extraordinary events surrounding the episode save the day for Gentile freedom.[16] Peter's actions immediately come under fire by Jewish Christians, the "circumcised believers" (Acts 11:2-3). In response, Peter explains "step by step" the events that led to Cornelius's conversion and baptism (Acts 11:4). Especially interesting are the added details. For example, now we learn that the Spirit told Peter "not to make a distinction between them and us" (Acts 11:12) while he was still pondering what to do on the rooftop. In addition, we learn that *six* brothers accompanied Peter and entered Cornelius's home with him (Acts 11:12).[17] Finally, Peter informs us that he remembered that Jesus had said: "John baptized with water, but you will be baptized with the Holy Spirit" (Acts 11:16). This then sets up his self-evident conclusion: "If then God gave them the same gift that he gave us when we believed in the Lord Jesus Christ, who was I that I could hinder God?" (Acts 11:17).

The response of the Jerusalem church speaks volumes about the difficulty for Jewish believers to embrace unreservedly this unexpected turn of events: "When they heard this, they were silenced. And they praised God, saying, 'Then God has given *even to the Gentiles* the repentance that leads to life'" (Acts 11:18, italics added). However, as the rest of Acts and Paul's letters to the Galatians, Romans and Philippians make clear, the response was far from unanimous and some viewed the "Cornelius Affair" as an exception to the rule, a divinely permitted aberration, not the norm for Gentile admittance to the church. The mission of the apostle Paul to the Gentiles reignites this controversy and draws Peter into the fray once again.

---

[16]"It was in other words no 'freelance' who began the mission to the Gentiles, but the legitimate, apostolic Church" (Haenchen, *Acts*, p. 360).

[17]This doubles or triples the required minimum number of witnesses in capital cases (Deut 17:6; 19:15; Num 35:30; Mt 18:16; 1 Tim 5:19: Heb 10:28).

## Jerusalem Council

Peter's last appearance in the book of Acts is in connection with one of the most significant councils of Christian church history, the council of Jerusalem (Acts 15).[18] After Peter's mysterious departure "to another place" (Acts 12:17), Luke shifts to an account of the second leading figure in his volume 2. The apostle Paul, the man who spearheaded the Gentile mission and led the charge in taking the gospel "to the ends of the earth" (Acts 1:8), now comes on center stage.

Paul and Barnabas's so-called first missionary journey acutely raises the issue of the terms of Gentile admission to the church because their standard operating procedure was immediate admittance for all Gentiles who professed faith in Jesus Christ. According to Luke, controversy broke out after Paul and Barnabas returned to Antioch and reported the results of their initial foray among the Gentiles. "Certain individuals came down from Judea" and insisted that "unless [Gentiles] are circumcised, according to the custom of Moses, [they] cannot be saved" (Acts 15:1). This ultimatum directly contradicts the earlier verdict concerning Cornelius and generates "no small dissension and debate with them" (Acts 15:2).

Luke's account of the Jerusalem Council summarizes seven distinct phases leading to a landmark decision:

- The Antioch church appoints a delegation, including Paul and Barnabas, the point men in the Gentile mission, to discuss the contested issue with the apostles and elders in Jerusalem (Acts 15:2).

- En route, Paul and Barnabas report on their successful Gentile mission to the churches in Phoenicia and Samaria, bringing "great joy to all the believers" (Acts 15:3). Apparently, there were no dissenting voices among those who heard the report.

- After arriving in Jerusalem and being welcomed by the church, they report what God accomplished through them. Their report elicits strong criticism from the believers who still identified themselves as

---

[18]Fitzmyer reminds us that this meeting "is never counted as one of the councils in the history of Christianity." Nonetheless, he points out that it is "the episode in the early church that eventually leads to the convening of official councils of later date" (*Acts*, p. 543).

Pharisees: "It is necessary for them to be circumcised and ordered to keep the law of Moses" (Acts 15:5).

• The dispute requires a full hearing presided over by the apostles and elders. Initially, there appears to be open discussion by various members of the church, some pro and some con.

• Significantly, the apostle Peter is the first major witness to testify. He rehearses the extraordinary events surrounding Cornelius's conversion, stressing that God selected him to be the one through whom the Gentiles "would hear the message of the good news and become believers" (Acts 15:7).[19] He then observes that God granted his Holy Spirit to these Gentiles quite apart from any commitment to the law of Moses, thus showing that there was now no distinction between Jew and Gentile in terms of being part of the new people of God (Acts 15:8). He concludes by rebuking Jewish believers for imposing a yoke on Gentile believers and by insisting that salvation comes to both Jew and Gentile through the grace of the Lord Jesus alone (Acts 15:10). Peter's view thus dovetails with that of Paul and Barnabas.

• The second witnesses were Barnabas and Paul. Their testimony highlights the signs and wonders accomplished among the Gentiles during their missionary trip. The correlation of these signs and wonders with the prophecy of Joel (Joel 2:30) could hardly escape the listeners, especially in light of Peter's citation of this very text when he first used his keys of the kingdom on the day of Pentecost (Acts 2:16-21). More importantly, however, their recital "served to answer any objection that the Cornelius episode was an isolated example and not intended as normative."[20]

• The final witness is the half-brother of Jesus and now recognized leader of the Jerusalem church, James the Just. His speech is quite remarkable and requires comment.

He begins his testimony by reaffirming the pivotal role of Peter in

---

[19]Gaventa draws attention to the "unrelenting focus on God's activity" in this narrative (*Acts*, p. 215).

[20]R. H. Mounce, "Apostolic Council," *ISBE* 1:201.

opening the door of the kingdom to Gentiles. This is crucial: James respects the stature of the apostle Peter and does not for a moment undercut his reputation.[21] James reinforces Peter's testimony by linking it to Scripture: "This agrees with the words of the prophets" (Acts 15:15). Though James refers to the prophets (plural), he cites one passage in particular as a proof text, Amos 9:11-12. According to James, Amos's prophecy about rebuilding the "dwelling of David" is now being fulfilled in the church. What is especially relevant and decisive for the present controversy is the prophetic word that "all other peoples may seek the Lord—even all the Gentiles over whom my name has been called" (Acts 15:17).

James concludes with an authoritative ruling: "I have reached the decision" (Acts 15:19). No mention is made of a vote or a call for consensus; James pronounces a verdict and plans are immediately made to implement his ruling. As to substance, James announces a compromise, not with respect to admission requirements but rather in the matter of fostering harmonious relations between Jews and Gentiles. Gentiles will not be required to observe the essential boundary markers that distinguish Jews from Gentiles, but they are urged to avoid certain behaviors that would inhibit amiable social intercourse with Jewish Christians.[22]

However one interprets the list, the primary boundary markers of circumcision, dietary restrictions and sabbath observance are not imposed on Gentile believers. In effect, this amounts to a major victory for the law-free gospel preached by Paul and endorsed by Peter. Whether Paul and Peter were completely satisfied with this ruling is debated; Luke depicts Paul as passing along this ruling to the church in Antioch and later to his primarily Gentile churches in Galatia (Acts 16:4), whereas one of Paul's letters to the Corinthians evidences a more liberal approach (1 Cor 8–10).

---

[21]"The crucial point in the entire argument was Peter's experience at Caesarea. It is to this that James redirected the thinking of the Council" (ibid., 1:202).

[22]The precise meaning of the list of prohibited behaviors is disputed. For further discussion, see Richard J. Bauckham, "James and the Jerusalem Church," in *The Book of Acts in Its Palestinian Setting* (*BAFCS* 4; Grand Rapids: Eerdmans, 1995), pp. 458-62; Fitzmyer, *Acts*, pp. 556-58; Bock, *Acts*, pp. 505-7.

The consequences of this ruling can hardly be overstated. In the book of Acts, "the legitimation of the mission to the Gentiles is Peter's last work."[23] Not forcing Gentiles to become Jews before they can be part of the new covenant community prepares the way for the emergence of a truly universal faith. The apostle Peter could scarcely have envisioned the scope of his actions when he used his keys to open the door of the kingdom for the Gentile Cornelius. Today, Saint Peter's Basilica in Rome tangibly testifies to the remarkable transformation of the original Jesus movement into a universal faith.

## PETER THE MIRACLE WORKER

In addition to using his keys of the kingdom, the apostle Peter performs a number of high-profile miracles, on the same order of magnitude as those of his Master. Luke singles out one in particular that brings the movement under scrutiny by the religious authorities in Jerusalem (Acts 3:1-10). Peter and John attend a 3:00 p.m. service, the second of two daily sacrifices accompanied by set prayers (Ex 29:39; Lev 6:20; Num 28:4; Josephus, *Ant.* 14.65).[24] At the Beautiful Gate, Peter encounters a man born lame more than forty years of age (Acts 4:22). This man begged daily on the steps leading up to the gate. Sadly, the lame man's physical handicap prohibited him from entering (Lev 21:17-20; 2 Sam 5:8). Ironically, he is about to enter the kingdom of God, thanks to Peter. In short, the man is instantly healed by the power of "Jesus Christ of Nazareth" (Acts 3:6) and, in all likelihood, joins the Jesus movement.

This miracle is similar to two others in the NT: Jesus healed an invalid of thirty-eight years in a generally similar manner at the Pool of Bethzatha (Bethesda) just north of the Temple Mount (Jn 5:1-9), and Paul was instrumental in healing a man in Lystra who had never walked (Acts 14:8-10). The fact that these two leading apostles perform mir-

---

[23]Martin Hengel, *Acts and the History of the Earliest Christianity* (London: SCM, 1979), p. 125.

[24]The morning and evening sacrifice is called the *Tamid* (i.e., the "regular"; so Jacob Milgrom in JPS) or "continuous" (most English translations) sacrifice. It is noteworthy that the earliest believers in Jerusalem continued to worship in the temple and from all outward appearances were indistinguishable from their fellow Jews.

acles so closely resembling that of the Master is not a coincidence.[25] Luke surely intends readers to understand that the Lord Jesus continues to work through the Spirit-filled apostles to build his church and that Paul is no less an apostle than is Peter, the acknowledged leader of the earliest church.[26]

This miraculous healing, occurring in such a public location, quickly attracts a crowd, and Peter seizes the opportunity. Standing in Solomon's Portico, he proclaims the good news about Jesus. Here is the substance of his message as summarized by Luke:

- God's servant, Jesus, accomplished the miraculous healing.

- The people of Jerusalem and their rulers are liable for the death of Jesus, the holy and righteous One, the Author of life.

- God vindicated and raised Jesus from the dead, and his power is now very much present to heal and to save.

- Israel's tragic mistake was foretold by the prophets.

- Repentance and faith are required to obtain forgiveness and experience the messianic era.

- Jesus is the prophet foretold by Moses: listen to him!

- Failure to believe Jesus will result in being cut off from Israel; now is the predicted time of blessing.

When we turn to 1 and 2 Peter, several of these themes reappear. Although Peter does not use the titles "the holy One," "the righteous One" or the "Author of life" in his letters, he does refer to these essential attributes of Jesus. Thus Jesus is the one "without defect or blemish" (1 Pet 1:19), who "committed no sin and no deceit was found in his mouth" (1 Pet 2:22). Furthermore, "the righteousness of our God and Savior Jesus Christ" (2 Pet 1:1) was supremely displayed when he

[25]Polhill notes: "Of the many miracles recounted in Acts, none has more formal resemblance to the miracles of Jesus in the Gospels than this one. There is one major difference—Jesus healed by His own authority; Peter healed by the 'name' of Jesus, which was indeed by Jesus' authority at work through the agency of the apostle" (*Acts*, p. 124).
[26]See Gary M. Burge, Lynn H. Cohick and Gene L. Green, *The New Testament in Antiquity* (Grand Rapids: Zondervan, 2009), p. 232, for a convenient chart displaying the intended Lukan parallels between Peter and Paul in Acts.

"suffered for sins once for all, the righteous for the unrighteous" (1 Pet 3:18) so that believers "might live for righteousness" (1 Pet 2:24). That Jesus Christ is the author of life is demonstrated in that he makes a new birth possible through his word (1 Pet 1:3, 23; 2:2), enables believers to become "participants of the divine nature" (2 Pet 1:4) and ensures their "entry into the eternal kingdom" (2 Pet 1:11). Punctuating both letters is the recurring motif that God has vindicated and exalted Messiah Jesus to his right hand (1 Pet 1:7, 11, 21; 2:6-7; 3:22; 4:5, 11, 13; 5:1, 4, 6, 10; 2 Pet 1:11, 16-18; 3:10, 18).

Peter's two epistles also strike the keynote of fulfillment: Jesus' saving activity unfolded in accordance with the prophetic Scriptures and so will his judging activity when he returns. Noteworthy also is the portrayal of Jesus as the Servant of the Lord, especially in 1 Peter. One hears the echoes of Isaiah's Suffering Servant in both Peter's sermons (Acts 2:23-24, 32-33; 3:13, 18; 4:27-30) and 1 Peter (1 Pet 1:11; 2:22-24; 3:18; 4:13). Both letters warn against rejecting Christ's offer of salvation. Second Peter especially warns against turning away from the true message. And both letters accent what Peter here urges of his fellow Jerusalemites: Listen to him! In short, they resonate with Luke's synopsis of Peter's preaching some thirty years earlier.

Peter's message, emphasizing Jesus' bodily resurrection and laying culpability for his death at the feet of the religious leaders, predictably enough leads to the arrest of Peter and John (Acts 4:3). The next day, when summoned before the high priests, Peter, "filled with the Holy Spirit," uses the occasion to fearlessly proclaim the gospel (Acts 4:8-12).

Note especially the scriptural appeal to Psalm 118:22, the passage about the rejected cornerstone, an important proof text figuring prominently in the argument of 1 Peter (1 Pet 2:7). Luke also draws attention to the impact of Peter's bold witness on the high priests: "they were amazed and recognized them as companions of Jesus" (Acts 4:13). This is a far cry from Peter's prior performance, when he cursed and swore an oath: "I do not know this man you are talking about" (Mk 14:71). When ordered to cease speaking and teaching about Jesus of Nazareth, he stands firm: "we cannot keep from speaking about what we have seen and heard" (Acts 4:20). Echoes of this episode may be detected in

1 Peter 3:14-16: "Do not fear what they fear, and do not be intimidated, but in your hearts sanctify Christ as Lord. Always be ready to make your defense to anyone who demands from you an accounting for the hope that is in you; yet do it with gentleness and reverence."

Several more Lukan episodes emphasize Peter's power as a miracle worker. The story about Ananias and Sapphira is not a healing miracle, but rather a demonstration of divine judgment (Acts 5:1-11). Recalling the story of Achan (Josh 7), Peter confronts the duplicity and hypocrisy of this couple, resulting in sudden death for both. This stunning intervention served as a salutary warning to the entire community of faith to take seriously the moral and ethical requirements of the gospel.[27] Perhaps echoes of this episode reverberate when Peter rails against the hypocrisy of the false teachers in 2 Peter 2:19-20.

Likewise, the story of Simon Magus (Acts 8:9-24) severely censures the mercenary attitude of a professed follower of the Way: "May your silver perish with you, because you thought you could obtain God's gift with money" (Acts 8:21). In 2 Peter 2:3, the false teachers are lambasted for their greed. There may be an even closer connection between Acts 8 and 2 Peter if early church fathers like Justin Martyr, Irenaeus, Hippolytus and Epiphanius are correct that Simon Magus was the taproot of Gnosticism and if some form of Gnosticism lies behind the false teaching in 2 Peter.[28]

Luke mentions that the apostles performed "many signs and wonders ... among the people" (Acts 5:12). This remarkable feature of those early years was in accord with the prophecy of Joel mentioned earlier as a key text for Peter's Pentecost sermon: "I will show portents in the heavens and on the earth" (Joel 2:30; Acts 2:15). Luke proceeds to give a dramatic example, showcasing the apostle Peter: "They even carried out the sick into the streets, and laid them on cots and mats, in order that

---

[27]The role of Peter as disciplinarian recalls the Qumran community with their overseers charged with disciplining erring members. There are, however, significant differences between the Jesus movement and Qumran, such as the rigid legalism and ritual purity emphasis of the latter that is not present in the former. See further Helyer, *Exploring Jewish Literature*, pp. 221-24.

[28]See A. F. Walls, "Simon Magus," *NBD*, pp. 1104-5, and B. F. Harris. "Simon Magus," *ZPEB* 5:442-44.

Peter's shadow might fall on some of them as he came by" (Acts 5:15). According to the Gospel of Mark, during Jesus' ministry, "they laid the sick in the marketplaces, and begged him that they might touch even the fringe of his cloak; and all who touched it were healed" (Mk 6:56). The Master's words were coming true: "Very truly, I tell you, the one who believes in me will also do the works that I do and, in fact, will do greater works than these, because I am going to the Father" (Jn 14:12).[29]

Luke narrates two more miracle stories involving Peter. The setting for both is on the Plain of Sharon (Acts 9:35) at Lydda (modern Lod) and Joppa (modern Jaffa). Peter is pictured as going "here and there among all the believers" (Acts 9:32), probably engaging in itinerate evangelism and pastoral oversight. The first miracle involves a paralyzed man who had been bedridden for eight years. The healing is instantaneous and complete; its effect on the vicinity is profound: "And all the residents of Lydda and Sharon saw him and turned to the Lord" (Acts 9:35).

The second miracle is more expansively narrated and noteworthy for its attention to details. A woman of Joppa named Tabitha (Dorcas) passed away while Peter was ministering in nearby Lydda (Acts 9:36-37). The believers held her in high esteem and deeply mourned her death. Peter was urgently summoned back to Joppa (Acts 9:38). Are we to assume they expected Peter to bring her back to life just as Jesus had restored Lazarus after four days in a tomb (Jn 11:17)?[30] In any case, when Peter arrived, he was taken to an upper room where her body lay. Like his Master had done in his presence about a decade earlier (Mk 5:38-43), Peter dismissed the mourners, knelt down at her bed and directly addressed the deceased: "Tabitha, get up" (Acts 9:40; cf. Mk 5:41). She opened her eyes, sat up and, taking Peter's hand, got up (Acts 9:40). Peter summoned the mourners back to the room and presented

---

[29]As Luke informs us, the apostle Paul was by no means lacking this charism either: "God did extraordinary miracles through Paul, so that when the handkerchiefs or aprons that had touched his skin were brought to the sick, their diseases left them, and the evil spirits came out of them" (Acts 19:11-12). Peter and Paul are mirror images of each other in Acts. Fitting that they should end their ministries together in the city to which Luke's narrative inexorably leads.

[30]This account also resembles miracles in the ministries of Elijah (1 Kings 17:17-24) and Elisha (2 Kings 4:18-37).

to them the now quite alive Dorcas. As at Lydda, this stunning miracle resulted in many coming to faith in Jesus (Acts 9:42).

In addition to the miracle-working power granted Peter by the Holy Spirit, Luke narrates two episodes of divine intervention and rescue. Alarmed by the attention gained by this new Jewish movement and its obvious attraction for many, the religious authorities cracked down "and put [the apostles] in the public prison" (Acts 5:18). That night "an angel of the Lord opened the prison doors, brought them out" (Acts 5:19). Ordered by the angel to return to their preaching posts in the temple porticoes, the apostles are preaching by daybreak. Meanwhile the high priests summon a council meeting and order that the apostles be conveyed from prison to their chambers. Imagine their surprise to learn that the prison doors were securely locked but the apostles were gone! Their surprise turns to perplexity when news arrives that the apostles are "standing in the temple and teaching the people" (Acts 5:25)! The temple captain rounds them up and brings them before the council. The high priest bitterly reproaches them for ignoring his prior warning and for continuing to lay blame on him and his colleagues for Jesus' death (Acts 5:28). Once again, Peter is spokesperson for the apostles. His reply is a courageous but courteous refusal to comply: "We must obey God rather than any human authority" (Acts 5:29).

The religious leaders are so incensed they intend to execute all the apostles, but a Pharisee named Gamaliel, probably the teacher of Saul of Tarsus (Acts 22:3), cautions the high priests against capital punishment and counsels patience. Conforming to Pharisaic belief in divine providence, Gamaliel argues that if "this undertaking is of human origin, it will fail; but if it is of God, you will not be able to overthrow them—in that case you may even be found fighting against God!" (Acts 5:38-39). Gamaliel's advice prevails. The council orders the apostles flogged, severely warns them to stop their evangelistic preaching and lets them go. But Luke laconically notes, "every day in the temple and at home they did not cease to teach and proclaim Jesus as the Messiah" (Acts 5:42).

The second miraculous escape occurred sometime after Emperor Claudius appointed Herod Agrippa I king of Judea in A.D. 41. James,

John's brother, became Herod's first victim; he was put to the sword. According to Luke, this "pleased the Jews," so Herod "proceeded to arrest Peter also" (Acts 12:3). Though not named in Luke's account, the context indicates that Peter was incarcerated in the fortress and barracks called Antonia, named after Mark Antony. This massive four-tower complex was located at the northwest corner of the Temple Mount.[31] Not wanting a repeat performance of Peter's earlier escape, Herod assigns four squads to guard Peter and binds him with two chains. Even Houdini would not have been able to escape! Luke places this episode during the Festival of Unleavened Bread, the same time of year Jesus had been executed some ten years earlier.

Once again, during the night, an angel of the Lord is dispatched to the rescue. The two soldiers next to Peter fall into a deep sleep, as do the two outside the cell door. The angel gently awakens Peter and tells him to get up. As he does so, the chains fall off his wrists. The angel instructs Peter to follow him, and the two of them proceed to walk out of the cell. They pass two more detachments of guards, presumably fast asleep, and then come to "the iron gate leading into the city," which opens "of its own accord" (Acts 12:10). After going down a lane, the angelic visitor suddenly vanishes. Peter, realizing this was not a dream, "went to the house of Mary, the mother of John whose other name was Mark, where many had gathered and were praying" (Acts 12:12).[32] The maid Rhoda's excited announcement about Peter's presence outside the courtyard door illustrates Luke's fondness for understated humor (Acts 12:13-15).[33] After being admitted to the house, Peter relates the details of his miraculous deliverance (Acts 12:17).

What follows next is one of the most mysterious lines in the book of

---

[31]For a description of the Antonia fortress with photos and reconstructions, see Ehud Netzer, "A New Reconstruction of Paul's Prison," *BAR* 35/1 (January/February 2009): 44-51, 71. It should be noted that both Peter and Paul spent time in this formidable fortress (Acts 21:31-40; 22:24; 23:10, 16, 23, 32).

[32]See Jerome Murphy-O'Connor for the identification of the Cenacle (upper room) as the probable location for this home ("The Cenacle—Setting for Acts 2:44-45," in *The Book of Acts in Its Palestinian Setting* [ed. Richard J. Bauckham; *BAFCS*, ed. Bruce W. Winter et al.; Grand Rapids: Eerdmans, 1995], 4:303-21).

[33]Gaventa comments that "developments at Mary's house smack of slapstick humor" (*Acts*, p. 185).

Acts: "Then he left and went to another place" (Acts 12:17). Where was this? What did he do there?[34] We hear of Peter only one more time in the book of Acts, at the Jerusalem Council in A.D. 49, as previously discussed. After that, he drops off the radar in the book of Acts. Is there any other credible source that can throw light on the period after the council and before his martyrdom in about A.D. 64, or must we be content with this black hole?

Here is where Paul's letters come into play. Several references to Peter occur in the Pauline collection, and from these we may glean at least a few more details about Peter's life and ministry. That is our next stop.

## QUESTIONS FOR DISCUSSION

1. How does Luke's portrayal of Peter in the first section of Acts correspond to Jesus' appointment of Peter as the leader of the movement?

2. How does Peter's role in Acts demonstrate his use of the keys of the kingdom?

3. What relationship is there between Peter's sermons in Acts and the content of Peter's letters?

4. Why is it essential for Peter and John to validate the reception of the gospel by the Samaritans?

5. Why is the conversion of Cornelius so important for church history?

6. How important is Peter's testimony at the Jerusalem Council?

7. Explore the possible interpretations of "another place" (Acts 12:17).

## FOR FURTHER READING

Bock, Darrell L. *Acts*. BECNT. Grand Rapids: Baker, 2007.

Brown, Raymond E., Karl Donfried and John Reumann, eds. *Peter in the New Testament*. Minneapolis: Augsburg, 1973.

---

[34]Eusebius (*Hist. eccl.* 2.14.5) has Peter go to Rome during the reign of Claudius (A.D. 41-54). See Oscar Cullmann, *Peter: Disciple—Apostle—Martyr* (trans. Floyd V. Filson; Philadelphia: Westminster, 1953), pp. 37-55, and Martin Hengel, *Saint Peter: The Underestimated Apostle* (trans. Thomas F. Trapp; Grand Rapids: Eerdmans, 2010), pp. 48-49, 79, for various options, and Fitzmyer, *Acts*, p. 490, for bibliography.

Conzelmann, Hans. *Acts of the Apostles*. Edited by Eldon Jay Epp. Translated by James Limburg, A. Thomas Kraabel and Donald H. Juel. Hermeneia. Philadelphia: Fortress, 1987.

Cullmann, Oscar. *Peter: Disciple—Apostle—Martyr*. Translated by Floyd V. Filson. Philadelphia: Westminster, 1953.

Fitzmyer, Joseph A. *The Acts of the Apostles*. AB 31. New York: Doubleday, 1997.

Foakes-Jackson, F. J. *Peter: Prince of Apostles*. London: Hodder & Stoughton, 1927.

Gaventa, Beverly Roberts. *The Acts of the Apostles*. ANTC. Nashville: Abingdon, 2003.

Grant, Michael. *Saint Peter: A Biography*. New York: Scribner, 1994. Pp. 103-21.

Haenchen, Ernst. *The Acts of the Apostles: A Commentary*. Translated by R. McL. Wilson. Philadelphia: Westminster, 1971.

Hengel, Martin. *Saint Peter: The Underestimated Apostle*. Grand Rapids: Eerdmans, 2006. Pp. 48-57.

Marshall, I. H. *The Acts of the Apostles: An Introduction and Commentary*. TNTC 5. Grand Rapids: Eerdmans, 1980.

Polhill, John B. *Acts*. NAC 26. Nashville: Holman, 1992.

Rainey, Anson F., and R. Steven Notely, eds. *The Sacred Bridge: Carta's Atlas of the Biblical World*. Jerusalem: Carta, 2006. Pp. 370-73.

Witherington, Ben, III. *The Acts of the Apostles: A Socio-Rhetorical Commentary*. Grand Rapids: Eerdmans, 1998.

# 5

## PETER IN PAUL'S LETTERS

THE PAULINE LETTERS ARE our other source for reconstructing Peter's role in the early church. Though brief, they carry considerable weight because they are among the earliest surviving Christian writings we possess, close in time to Peter's missionary activity.

### GALATIANS: PETER THE PILLAR

By far the most important reference to Peter in Paul's letters occurs in Galatians. Here we learn of a confrontation between these two apostolic leaders in which Paul rebukes Peter for a failure to be consistent with the gospel message.

Paul's purpose in writing Galatians is to prevent a defection from the law-free gospel he preaches. Undermining Paul's house churches in Galatia are Jewish Christian missionaries, the "circumcision faction" (Gal 2:12), who endeavor to bring Gentile Christians under the yoke of the Torah. These Judaizers ("to live like a Jew") apparently arrive after Paul departs and discredit Paul's apostleship and gospel. They insist that the traditional Jewish badges or boundary markers must be observed for salvation and that Paul is a renegade rather than a recognized apostle. Apparently, according to the Judaizers,[1] although Paul is dependent on the Jerusalem apostles for his gospel, he deliberately distorts it in order to facilitate Gentile admission to enter the church, es-

---

[1] I say "apparently" because nowhere in the text do we read the Judaizers' arguments; rather, these must be inferred from a close reading of Paul's rhetoric. This is an instance of mirror reading, an inexact but necessary technique in reading letters.

pecially in regard to circumcision, an issue of no little significance for Gentile males.[2]

Paul's response is white-hot with righteous indignation. After his salutation, he immediately launches into a counterattack on his Judaizing opponents—Galatians is the only Pauline letter in which he skips his typical thanksgiving and prayer opening. In the first two chapters, Paul sets out to accomplish two things: defend his independent, apostolic status and commission to preach to the Gentiles and defend his version of the gospel message: Christ alone, grace alone, faith alone. It is within this highly polemical context that Paul brings the apostle Peter into the conversation.

In order to defend his independent status as a genuine apostle, Paul rehearses the events surrounding his conversion and call to apostleship (Gal 1:13–2:14). In this section, we learn that God revealed his Son to Paul and commissioned him to preach the gospel to the Gentiles (Gal 1:15-16), correlating with Luke's narrative of Paul's Damascus Road experience (Acts 9:3-6, 15-19). Paul emphatically insists, "I did not confer with any human being, nor did I go up to Jerusalem to those who were already apostles before me" (Gal 1:16-17), almost certainly refuting the Judaizers' accusation that he was originally dependent on the Jerusalem apostles for his gospel. On the contrary, says Paul, it was not until three years later that he even met with one of the Twelve, who, as it turns out, was none other than Cephas (Gal 1:18). This fifteen-day visit, however, occurred after Paul had already been engaged in extensive evangelism in Damascus, according to Luke's account in Acts (Acts 9:19-25). Paul's point is plain: Cephas did not impart to him or modify in any way his gospel (Gal 2:6).[3]

The next event Paul narrates involving Peter occurs fourteen years later.[4] The implications of Paul's mission to the Gentiles are causing ripples back in the mother church. According to Paul, he, Barnabas and Titus go up to Jerusalem in response to a revelation (Gal 2:1-2). If

---

[2]It will come as no surprise to learn that more Gentile women converted to Judaism than men.
[3]The NAB renders the last part of Galatains 2:6: "those of repute made me add nothing."
[4]Debate continues on whether Paul means fourteen years after his conversion or fourteen years after he visited with Cephas. For our purposes, it makes little difference.

we identify the revelation with the prophecy of Agabus concerning an impending famine (Acts 11:27-30), then Galatians 2 is an account of the so-called famine visit. Alternatively, if Galatians 2 is equated with the visit to the Jerusalem Council (Acts 15), the precise nature of the revelation is unstated and uncertain.[5] In either event, Paul meets with Peter once again in Jerusalem. According to Paul, he had a private meeting with the "acknowledged leaders" (Gal 2:2), of whom Peter (Gal 2:7), also called Cephas (Gal 2:9), was a member. Paul wanted "to make sure that I was not running, or had not run, in vain" (Gal 2:2). Particularly relevant to the Galatian crisis is Paul's reference to Titus, who accompanied him to Jerusalem. According to Paul, "even Titus, who was with me, was not compelled to be circumcised, though he was a Greek" (Gal 2:3). In this context, Paul then makes two highly significant statements: the acknowledged leaders of Jerusalem "contributed nothing to me," and James, Cephas and John fully endorsed Paul's mission to the Gentiles, symbolized by their extending the right hand of fellowship to him (Gal 2:9). In short, the Jerusalem apostles are in full accord with Paul's gospel and mission to the Gentiles. In Galatians, however, Paul must contend with missionaries "who are confusing [the believers] and want to pervert the gospel of Christ" (Gal 1:7) and who are almost certainly appealing to Cephas in support of their agenda.[6] As the book of Acts indicates, this is without foundation. Paul is unsparing in his censure: it is "a different gospel—which is really no gospel at all" (Gal 1:6-7 NIV), with the result that the perpetrators are "accursed" (Gal 1:8-9) and, like Hagar and her child (Gen 21:9-10), should be driven out of the Galatian house churches (Gal 4:30).

The third episode involving Paul and Cephas in Galatians is both surprising and disappointing (Gal 2:11-14). In no uncertain terms, Paul

---

[5]For a concise discussion on the problem of correlating Paul's visits to Jerusalem in Galatians and Acts, see G. W. Hansen, "Galatians, Letter to the," *DPL*, pp. 326-29. In defense of the view equating the famine visit (Acts 11:27-30) with Galatians 2:1-10, see R. H. Mounce, "Apostolic Council," *ISBE* 1:198-203, and Richard N. Longenecker, *Galatians* (WBC 41; Dallas: Word, 1990), pp. lxxiii-lxxxviii.

[6]Raymond E. Brown, Karl P. Donfried and John Reuman, eds., *Peter in the New Testament* (Minneapolis/New York: Augsburg/Paulist, 1973), p. 25.

rebukes this "acknowledged pillar" (Gal 2:9) and indicts him because "he stood self-condemned" (Gal 2:11) on account of a glaring instance of inconsistency with regard to "the truth of the gospel." Specifically, Cephas participated in table fellowship with Gentile Christians until "certain people came from James," after which "he drew back and kept himself separate for fear of the circumcision faction" (Gal 2:12). Paul calls this hypocrisy; he intuitively understands where such actions lead: either the church will have a two-tiered membership with Gentile Christians occupying the lower tier, or there will be two distinct churches distinguished by ethnicity. For Paul, this would be a travesty because "there is no longer Jew or Greek, there is no longer slave or free, there is no longer male and female; for all of you are in Christ Jesus. And if you belong to Christ, then you are Abraham's offspring, heirs according to the promise" (Gal 3:28-29).

The nuances of Paul's diction require further discussion. What are we to make of Paul's reference to "the acknowledged leaders" (Gal 2:2), "those who were supposed to be acknowledged leaders (what they actually were makes no difference to me; God shows no partiality)" (Gal 2:6). Do we detect a scent of sarcasm? What does "supposed" imply? In short, how does Paul view Peter in his angry letter to the Galatians?

This is more difficult to decide than it might seem. One important piece of evidence concerns the purpose of Paul's private meeting with the acknowledged leaders: "in order to make sure that I was not running, or had not run, in vain" (Gal 2:2). Does this mean that Paul recognized his subordinate relationship to the Jerusalem apostles and was fearful lest he had strayed from the true gospel message? In my opinion, viewed from the larger context of the entire letter to the Galatians, and particularly 1 and 2 Corinthians, this is unlikely. Alternatively, one might suggest that Paul was concerned lest the Jerusalem church withdraw its earlier acquiescence to Paul's law-free gospel and impose circumcision for Gentile admittance to the church. Of course, this is all hypothetical because, as it turned out, the Jerusalem leaders endorsed Paul's law-free Gentile mission and extended the right hand of fellowship to Paul and Barnabas.

It is hard to be certain, but there appears to be some ambivalence in

Paul's attitude toward Cephas. Human nature being what it is, Paul may have harbored some envy of this "acknowledged pillar"—Paul displays all the characteristics of an alpha male. Furthermore, Paul's confrontation with Peter at Antioch (Gal 2:11-14) likely generated animosity between these two apostolic leaders with lingering consequences.[7] Adding to the difficulty is the problem of capturing just the right nuance for the key Greek expression *hoi dokountes*. For example, note the difference in nuance between "reputed" (ASV), "seemed to be" (ESV), "acknowledged" (NRSV) and "esteemed" (TNIV). The first two renderings allow for a degree of reservation, whereas the last two imply full recognition and respect. So which is it? Of the five occurrences of the word *dokeō* ("think, believe, appear") in Galatians (Gal 2:2, 6 [twice], 9; 6:3), the last passage has a decidedly negative connotation ("For if those who are nothing think [*dokei*] they are something, they deceive themselves"). Do the other occurrences in Galatians likewise bear a negative or "at least relativizing" overtone?[8] Perhaps, but we should also note that Paul takes seriously the reputation these leaders possess and makes a concerted effort to meet with them in order to gain their tacit approval for his mission.[9] I think Richard Longenecker strikes just the right balance:

> Paul . . . recognizes in his use of the expression the legitimate role of the Jerusalem apostles in the church, yet without compromising his claim that his gospel stems from God and Christ apart from any human authority. Contrary to many who deny irony in Paul's usage, it seems hard to ignore at least a certain "dismissive" tone in Gal 2.[10]

What might have happened had the Jerusalem leaders reimposed the traditional badges of Jewish identity on Gentile believers as a precon-

---

[7]See Martin Hengel for a discussion of the far-reaching consequences of this confrontation (*Saint Peter: The Underestimated Apostle* [trans. Thomas F. Trapp; Grand Rapids: Eerdmans, 2010], pp. 57-79).

[8]According to Gerd Schunack, "this designation for the Jerusalemites appears to have an accent that is for Paul, who is struggling for the unity of the Church in the freedom of faith, if not negative, at least relativizing." "*dokeō*," *EDNT* 1:341.

[9]As favored by D. Müller, "*dokeō*," *NIDNTT* 3:822: "This is not necessarily an ironic point here against the other apostles, for this expression is often found of a recognized authority in extra-biblical literature."

[10]*Galatians*, p. 48.

dition for full membership in the new community of faith? I doubt very much Paul would have backed down and submitted (see Gal 2:5).

Finally, how should we evaluate Peter's actions in the affair at Antioch? His vacillation is not unprecedented, as we have seen in our overview of his life in the Gospels. But by this time in his career we are disappointed by his inconsistency.[11] However, we are probably expecting too much. As Peter later reminds his readers, we must "grow into salvation" (1 Pet 2:2), "make every effort" (2 Pet 1:5) and "strive to be found by him at peace" (2 Pet 3:14). Paul forthrightly admits to the Philippians that he had not yet "reached the goal" (Phil 3:12). In short, neither apostle was without sin; that remains for the day of resurrection (1 Cor 15:42-57; Rom 8:23; Phil 3:21). Consequently, we must frankly acknowledge that Peter behaved inappropriately and Paul was harsh in correcting him. What saves the day is Peter's willingness to accept rebuke and move on without bitterness or recrimination. Peter's second letter contains a touching reference to "our beloved brother Paul" (2 Pet 3:15).[12] Here is a trait that Christ saw in Peter from the beginning, a trait that enabled him to become the leader he was. Christian church history is littered with too many leaders unwilling to acknowledge errors and repent of misdeeds.

## 1 CORINTHIANS: PETER ON A PEDESTAL

Sometimes leaders are placed in awkward situations by well-meaning admirers. Apparently that happened to Peter at Corinth. Four times in 1 Corinthians Paul refers to Peter, using his Aramaic nickname Cephas (1 Cor 1:12; 3:22; 9:5; 15:5), raising further, tantalizing questions about this man and his role in the earliest churches.

I take up the last reference first because we discussed it earlier in connection with the Gospel portrait of Peter. Paul is the earliest Christian writer to assert that the risen Christ first appeared to Peter (1

---

[11]I remind the reader that we hear only Paul's side of this episode and not Peter's. In Hengel's view the account is both "one-sided and overstated" (*Saint Peter*, p. 59).

[12]Herein lies a marked difference between those who reject the Petrine authorship of 1 and 2 Peter (e.g., Hengel and Brown) and those who receive them as genuine. The former ignore these letters as irrelevant to the above discussion.

Cor 15:5).[13] This testimony is supported by the Lukan account of postresurrection events (Lk 24:34). Paul's statement occurs in a passage having the earmarks of a confessional formulation probably going back to the earliest believers in Jerusalem.[14] Perhaps Peter himself conveyed this profound experience to Paul during their fifteen-day visit in Jerusalem, three years after Paul's conversion (Gal 1:18). What is striking is the fact that Peter's primacy among the Twelve is matched by (should we also say confirmed by?) the temporal priority of Jesus' resurrection appearance to him. Peter cast a long shadow in the early years of the Jesus movement, a shadow that only lengthened with time. As 1 Corinthians shows, however, being a pillar in the church has a downside.

The first reference to Cephas occurs as Paul replies to a report delivered by "Chloe's people," describing a situation in which the Corinthian house churches are wracked by factionalism and quarreling (1 Cor 1:11). Once again adopting mirror reading, I infer that the believers are divided on the basis of loyalty to a single, esteemed leader. In this case, there appears to have been four factions championing, respectively, Paul, Apollos, Cephas and Christ. That Paul was one of the leaders put on a pedestal is understandable given his role in establishing the church on this second missionary journey (Acts 18:1-18).

Surprisingly, we also have an Apollos faction, about whom we know little other than what Luke briefly narrates about him in Acts (Acts 18:24–19:1) and the few references in 1 Corinthians (1 Cor 1:12; 3:4-6, 22; 4:6; 16:12). According to Luke, this Alexandrian Jew came to Ephesus and proclaimed Jesus "with burning enthusiasm" (Acts

---

[13]Once again, this statement is qualified by the intended comparison: it was the first appearance to any of the apostles. The Gospel testimony is quite clear that the first witnesses were women.

[14]I briefly mention here theories concerning the significance of the two groupings of witnesses in 1 Corinthians 1:5-8. (see Brown, *Peter*, pp. 32-36). Some scholars suggest that the first group, Cephas, the Twelve and the more than five hundred, are those who followed Jesus during his earthly ministry. The second group, such as James and Paul, are those who experienced a postresurrection appearance. Other scholars view the first group as "church founding" appearances and the second as "mission inaugurating." More extreme are those scholars who think we have two rival groups that Luke has combined, creating a superficial sense of harmony. In my opinion, the first suggestion has some merit, but it must be admitted that all three are speculative and read more into the list than is warranted. There is no good reason to reject a chronological ordering, especially since Paul later uses the same temporal particles to sketch a chronological sequence of bodily resurrections (1 Cor 15:23-28).

18:25). After he had caught the attention of Priscilla and Aquila, they "explained the Way of God to him more accurately" (Acts 18:26). Soon afterwards, the Ephesian church introduced him to the churches of Achaia, of which Corinth was a leading center, and "he powerfully refuted the Jews in public, showing by the scriptures that the Messiah is Jesus" (Acts 18:28). Apparently he made a big impression on the Corinthian believers, so much so that a faction formed touting him as their apostle.

This brief snapshot into the inner dynamics of church life at Corinth reflects a distinctive Greek ethos. Factionalism and great emphasis on oratorical skill characterized Greek politics and culture. Apollos conforms to the preconceived notions of many Corinthians concerning the desired qualifications for preeminence. As becomes clear in 1 and 2 Corinthians, Paul does not always measure up in the eyes of some Corinthian believers. We thus learn of a faction who identify with and praise the virtues of Apollos, while being critical and dismissive of Paul (1 Cor 2:1-5; 3:1-9; 4:1-21; 9:1-23; 2 Cor 1:12-14, 17-19; 10:1–13:10).[15] Apollos himself may have been quite innocent in this development; we do not have enough evidence to be sure, one way or the other. However, Paul's remarks in 1 Corinthians give the impression that no deep-seated animosity existed between these two figures ("our brother Apollos," 1 Cor 16:12).

Then we have the Cephas party. It is of more than passing interest that Paul uses Peter's Aramaic name, Cephas, not his Greek name. Perhaps this relates to one of the reasons why a faction gravitated to the leader of the Twelve. Cephas identifies Peter with the earliest, and thus, perhaps, in the minds of the Corinthians, the most authentic version of the faith, having its roots in Jerusalem.[16] After all, this man was among the first disciples, spent three years of itinerant ministry with the Master, was groomed to be the apostolic leader, was "a witness of the sufferings

---

[15]In my view, both letters give evidence of Corinthian believers who are critical of Paul. In this I agree with Gordon Fee against some other commentators who largely dissociate the opponents in the two letters.

[16]Hengel conjectures that "those associated with Peter later considered him to be the actual 'founder' of the mission to the Gentiles on the basis of the narrative about Cornelius" (*Saint Peter*, p. 57).

of Christ" (1 Pet 5:1) and, as we noted, was the first of the apostles to see Jesus alive after his crucifixion. This is an impressive résumé. Should we then suppose that this faction was predominately Jewish Christian? That would make sense, but a partiality for what was deemed original might equally appeal to Greek Christians. At any rate, the presence of a "Cephas party" at Corinth carries intriguing implications.

The "Christ party" probably exhibits one-upmanship by some who sought to seize the high ground in the quarrels that swirled about the house churches. Perhaps it is this group that considered itself as "spiritual people" (1 Cor 3:1). If so, Paul quickly disabuses them of this conceit (1 Cor 3:1)!

The question is: Does the presence of a "Cephas party" prove that Peter visited Corinth? This goes beyond what can be demonstrated, but a desire to be linked to the acknowledged leader of the Twelve is a plausible explanation for the existence of such a faction.[17] There is, however, another piece of information in 1 Corinthians that suggests Peter did in fact visit Corinth.

In 1 Corinthians 9, Paul defends his nonuse of certain apostolic privileges and, in the course of his argument, asks rhetorically: "Do we not have the right to be accompanied by a believing wife, as do the other apostles and the brothers of the Lord and Cephas?" (1 Cor 9:5). At the least, this passage supports the NT evidence (Gal 2:7-8, 11; Acts 12:17 [?]; 1 Pet 1:1; 5:13) and later traditions that Peter engaged in itinerant missionary work in the Diaspora. But it also implies that Peter visited Corinth because Paul's passing reference to Peter seems to require that the Corinthians knew from firsthand experience rather than mere hearsay that Peter's wife accompanied him.

How does Paul handle this tendency to place human leaders on a pedestal, form fierce loyalties around them and, consequently, foster rivalry and quarrels? He forthrightly chastises such behavior as "human wisdom," the "wisdom of this age," and not "God's wisdom" (1 Cor 2). He further characterizes conduct like "jealousy and quarreling" as a

---

[17]It is worth noting that both Philo (*Hypoth.* 6.1) and Josephus (*C. Ap.* 1.1-8) make much of the antiquity of Moses and the Law in arguing for the superiority of Judaism over against paganism.

clear indication of spiritual immaturity and "behaving according to human inclinations" (1 Cor 3:1-3). He then provides a theological perspective for Christian ministry and evangelism, stressing a division of labor, equality of workers, unity of purpose and accountability to the Lord. Essential to the entire effort is the necessity of building on the foundation of Jesus Christ (1 Cor 3:5-15). In sum, "we [the apostles] are God's servants, working together; you [the Corinthians] are God's field, God's building" (1 Cor 3:9).

It is within this context that Paul mentions Cephas again (1 Cor 3:22). As he wraps up his contrast between mere human wisdom and God's wisdom, Paul admonishes his readers not to "boast about human leaders" (1 Cor 3:21). It is too limiting to orient one's life around the personality, teachings and example of one human leader. The Christian life requires a much wider frame of reference. In Paul's expansive prose, "all things are yours." Among the "all things" are apostles and preachers like Paul, Apollos and Cephas. Each has a place; each should be valued; none should be enshrined on a pedestal.

The order of names may be significant. We are probably justified in thinking that a majority of Corinthians held Paul in high regard since he was their founding missionary. Consequently, the Pauline party was probably the largest (cf. 2 Cor 2:6). "For though you might have ten thousand guardians in Christ, you do not have many fathers. Indeed, in Christ Jesus I became your father through the gospel" (1 Cor 4:15). The fact that Apollos comes next and is referred to specifically several more times in Paul's letter (1 Cor 3:5-6; 4:6; 16:12) suggests that the most serious rival faction championed this silver-tongued preacher of the gospel. The Cephas faction was perhaps the smallest. Still, his reputation and ties to the historical Jesus gave him credentials the other two lacked. And if we add to this the evidence from 2 Corinthians, which strongly suggests that the interlopers whom Paul castigates had ties to the Jerusalem church and identify themselves with the apostle Peter, we now have the ingredients for bitter rivalry and divisions.[18]

So, how would Peter have responded to Paul's letter to the Corin-

---

[18]I agree with Fee and Hengel that one must read 2 Corinthians in light of 1 Corinthians.

thians? Based on Peter's first letter, to which we next turn, I think he would have endorsed Paul's sentiments. Peter did not want to be placed on a pedestal; he knew all too well the precarious nature of such a position ("Keep alert. Like a roaring lion your adversary prowls around, looking for someone to devour," 1 Pet 5:8). His final exhortation, directed to the elders of the house churches in Anatolia, captures his pastoral perspective, one quite in harmony with that of Paul: "Do not lord it over those in your charge, but be examples to the flock . . . all of you must clothe yourselves with humility in your dealings with one another" (1 Pet 5:3, 5; cf. Eph 4:2; Phil 2:3; Col 3:12; Tit 3:2).

Finally, I return to 1 Corinthians 15:3-11 for one further observation. Paul concludes this section with a note of gratitude: "Whether then it was I or they, so we proclaim and so you have come to believe" (1 Cor 15:11). Cephas must be included in the "they" since 1 Corinthians 15:11 "makes it clear that the Corinthians had also heard the kerygma from other apostolic preachers—a message that the Corinthians had received in faith (15:1) at the time of their conversion. Besides Paul, the most likely example of such an apostolic preacher is Cephas."[19] This further strengthens our opinion that the apostle Peter at least preached at Corinth and likely spent some time there ministering to the house churches.

## CONCLUSION: PETER IN PAUL'S LETTERS

The above discussion allows us make some assumptions about the "missing" period in Peter's career. The church traditions concerning Peter have him ministering in Syria, Greece, Anatolia and Rome.[20] These traditions are not manufactured out of thin air. Paul's letters give evidence that Peter was indeed in Antioch of Syria and almost certainly

---

[19]Brown, *Peter*, p. 36.

[20]Eusebius (*Hist. eccl.* 2.14.6) and Jerome (*Vir. ill.* 1) place Peter at Rome as early as the reign of Claudius (ca. A.D. 42). According to Hengel, "the Western communities knew the apostle himself or learned about him from messengers. These messengers had been sent forth by him and thus were influenced by him either directly or indirectly, and indeed not only in Syria, Antioch, and Rome but also in important communities located in between, in the capital cities of provinces such as Ephesus and Corinth" (*Saint Peter*, p. 49). See also his quotation of Hans von Campenhausen, *Kirchliches Amt und geistliche Vollmacht in den ersten drei Jahrhunderten* (BHT 14; Tübingen, Mohr, 1953), p. 21, to the same effect (ibid., n. 166).

visited Corinth. As I will argue in 1 Peter, there is good reason to believe that Peter addresses the believers in Anatolia because he is in some sense their apostle. It may be that many of these people were members of Roman house churches before being forcibly relocated to the eastern fringes of the empire.[21] This correlates with the tradition that the apostle Peter actively served the church in Rome for some years. In short, it is likely that Peter evangelized among Jews and Greeks in the western Diaspora, including Rome, over a period of at least sixteen or seventeen years and possibly more.

But this raises a problem. Does not Paul's letter to the Galatians state that Peter and Paul had an agreement about their respective spheres of ministry? Peter would go "to the circumcised" and Paul would "go to the Gentiles" (Gal 2:9). In all likelihood, this understanding, formulated in the aftermath of the Jerusalem Council, proved unworkable in light of the ethnic diversity and interconnectedness of Diaspora communities.[22] Peter and Paul accepted the facts on the ground and quietly dropped their prior arrangement.

Another problem surfaces. Why doesn't Paul mention Peter in his letter to Rome in A.D. 56/57? If Peter were there, surely Paul would have made reference to such an important figure. Those who deny that Peter was ever at Rome lay great weight on this striking absence.[23] Martin Hengel stresses that the incident at Antioch caused great injury to both apostles and was to some extent never completely healed. He thus attributes the silence to residual hard feelings left over from the Antioch confrontation.[24] Oscar Cullmann, by contrast, suggests

---

[21]This point, leaning on the work of Karen Jobes, will be argued in the next chapter. In spite of the fact that Hengel rejects Petrine authorship of 1 Peter, he nonetheless argues that "the pseudepigraphic apostolic author carried authority in these regions" (*Saint Peter*, p. 49).

[22]"The distinction that was agreed upon at the Apostolic Council in Jerusalem between the mission to the Jews and the mission to the Gentiles turned out later to be unrealistic since it could not be maintained consistently in practice outside the motherland, especially since the 'Gentiles' were originally closely tied to the synagogue as 'God-fearers' and were more or less congruent with Judaism. For this reason Paul also started at each new site at the synagogue, since he could speak to the Godfearers there, who were considered legally still to be uncircumcised Gentiles" (ibid., pp. 55-56).

[23]For a historical overview of scholarship on this issue, see Cullmann, *Peter*, pp. 71-80.

[24]"*The deep divide that was signified by the dramatic, public, drawn-out dispute between Peter and Paul is something we cannot portray deeply enough*" (Hengel, *Saint Peter*, p. 63, italics in original. See his entire discussion, pp. 57-65).

that this unexpected silence has a rather straightforward explanation: Peter was away from the capital on a mission trip at the time of writing.[25] However we account for this omission, to pit an argument from silence against the widespread tradition linking Peter and Rome seems ill-advised.

This brief foray into Paul's letters provides sufficient evidence to confirm the early traditions of a Petrine mission throughout portions of the western Diaspora. There are no convincing historical arguments refuting Peter's activity beyond Caesarea Maritima in Palestine. Neither does the tradition linking Peter to Rome appear to be an after-the-fact creation. There is, however, evidence that tension existed between Paul and Peter. As we will see in 2 Peter, however, Christian charity appears to have healed the deep wounds inflicted by this incident.

## QUESTIONS FOR DISCUSSION

1. Why are Paul's letters important in reconstructing the career of the apostle Peter?
2. Assess Paul's view of Peter as reflected in Galatians.
3. How significant was the incident at Antioch, and what effect did it have?
4. What can we learn about Peter's missionary work in the Diaspora from Galatians and 1 Corinthians?

## FOR FURTHER STUDY

Brown, Raymond E., Karl P. Donfried and John Reumann. *Peter in the New Testament*. Minneapolis/New York: Augsburg/Paulist, 1973. Pp. 23-38.

Cullmann, Oscar. *Peter: Disciple—Apostle—Martyr*. Translated by Floyd V. Filson. Philadelphia: Westminster, 1963. Pp. 33-55.

Fee, Gordon. *The First Epistle to the Corinthians*. NICNT 24. Grand Rapids: Eerdmans, 1987.

Grant, Michael. *Saint Peter: A Biography*. New York: Scribner, 1994. Pp. 122-31. Marked by considerable skepticism concerning the reliability of Acts.

---

[25]"Otherwise he [Peter] could not possibly have been omitted from the list of the persons addressed in this letter" (Cullmann, *Peter*, p. 79). See also J. Wenham, "Did Peter Go to Rome in A.D. 42?" *TynBul* 23 (1972): 94-102.

Hansen, G. W. "Galatians, Letter to the." *DPL*. Downers Grove, Ill.: Inter-
    Varsity Press, 1993. Pp. 323-34.

Hengel, Martin. *Saint Peter: The Underestimated Apostle*. Translated by
    Thomas H. Trapp. Grand Rapids: Eerdmans, 2006. Pp. 48-99.

Longenecker, Richard N. *Galatians*. WBC 41. Dallas: Word, 1990.

Michaels, J. R. "Peter." *DPL*. Downers Grove, Ill.: InterVarsity Press, 1993.
    Pp. 701-3.

Perkins, Pheme. *Peter: Apostle for the Whole Church*. Columbia: University of
    South Carolina Press, 1994. Pp. 109-30. Flawed by undue historical skep-
    ticism.

Stein, R. H. "Jerusalem." *DPL*. Downers Grove, Ill.: InterVarsity Press, 1993.
    Pp. 463-74.

# 6

◇

# 1 PETER

◇

*Encyclical to Exiles*

*Probably no document in the NT is so theological as 1 Peter,*
*if "theological" is taken in the strict sense of teaching about God.*

RALPH P. MARTIN

*1 Peter is about God and the ramifications*
*of orienting life wholly around him.*

JOEL B. GREEN

PETER'S COMMISSION TO "feed my sheep" is nowhere more concretely
demonstrated than in the letter called 1 Peter. This encyclical, addressed to house churches in five Roman provinces of Asia Minor
(modern Turkey), is a heartfelt exhortation to persevere in the midst of
trials and persecution. Indeed, there are indications in the letter that
the present situation is likely to worsen. In light of this, Peter the apostle
and pastor urges his readers to remember their "living hope," their "inheritance . . . in heaven" and "the grace Jesus Christ will bring you
when he is revealed" (1 Pet 1:3-4, 13), "the true grace of God" in which
they must "stand fast" (1 Pet 5:12). The shadow of a cross falls across
the pages of this letter, and the suffering of Jesus on behalf of his people

serves as a paradigm for discipleship: "you should follow in his steps" (1
Pet 2:21). My task in the next four chapters is to study the theological
substructure underlying Peter's pastoral exhortation.[1]

## CRITICAL ISSUES

Before extracting some features of Peter's theology from this occasional letter (i.e., written for a particular purpose), I briefly touch on
several issues arising from historical-critical and rhetorical-social research. Not least among these is the matter of authorship. Is this letter
genuine? Did Peter write it, or should it be attributed to some other
early Christian figure, whether known or unknown? Or should we
speak instead of a Petrine school perpetuating the tradition and
teachings of the revered apostle? To whom was it written, what was
the situation and circumstances of the addressees, and why was it
written? Or, is this document a pastoral letter at all? Does it serve a
quite different literary function? Is 1 Peter a composite work, and if so
can we identify its sources? These are the leading questions that require investigation if we are to understand more fully the meaning and
significance of this writing.

## GENRE AND INTEGRITY

I quickly dispense with one rhetorical critical question: Is 1 Peter a
genuine letter or has an original baptismal homily been adapted to a
letter format? The latter view, in vogue during the first half of the
twentieth century, has largely been abandoned by critical scholarship
today. As J. H. Elliott notes, "the consistency and coherence of its language, style, themes, arrangement, and line of argumentation indicate
that 1 Peter from the outset was conceived, composed, and dispatched
as an integral, genuine letter. This conclusion represents the majority
position of recent research on 1 Peter."[2]

---

[1]Even if, according to some scholars, this is a rather daunting task. "The First Letter of Peter is
a puzzling text. . . . It nevertheless appears to have a clear message. . . . Scholars do not agree,
however, on what that message actually is, and what is the *theology* or *ideology* behind the text."
Lauri Thurén, *Argument and Theology in 1 Peter: The Origins of Christian Paraenesis* (JSNTSup
114; Sheffield: Sheffield Academic Press, 1995), p. 14, italics in original.
[2]J. H. Elliott, *1 Peter: A New Translation with Introduction and Commentary* (AB 37B; New York:

## AUTHORSHIP AND DATE OF COMPOSITION

Not so quickly resolved are the issues of authorship and date. Here are some factors arising from a close inspection of the document itself and external evidence bearing on the question.

1. The prescript to the book identifies the implied author as "Peter, an apostle of Jesus Christ" (1 Pet 1:1). In 1 Peter 5:1 the author describes himself both as "an elder" and "a witness of the sufferings of Christ." The latter self-description, at face value, suggests an eyewitness, although it may refer to one who bears witness to the life, death and resurrection of Jesus.[3] The postscript implies that our author is writing from "Babylon" (1 Pet 5:13), acknowledged by most interpreters as a code word for Rome. Early church tradition locates Peter in Rome near the end of his life, and in Rome he and the apostle Paul suffered martyrdom.[4] The author mentions the presence of "my son Mark" (1 Pet 5:13), probably a figurative expression of affection for

---

Doubleday, 2000), p. 11. For a survey of scholarship on this question see his entire discussion and bibliographic sources in pp. 7-12. "In comparison with other ancient letters, 1 Peter absolutely can be considered to count as one." Reinhard Feldman, *The First Letter of Peter: A Commentary on the Greek Text* (trans. Peter H. Davids; Waco, Tex.: Baylor University Press, 2008), p. 29.

[3]See BDAG, p. 618. Selwyn holds that "the writer . . . claims to have been an eyewitness of Christ's passion" (E. G. Selwyn, *The First Epistle of Saint Peter* [London: Macmillan, 1947], p. 228), but Elliott argues that the meaning of *martys* [witness] is "one who bears witness *to* something" (*1 Peter*, p. 819) rather than one who is an "eye-witness *of* something," involving "personal presence, interpretation, and engagement for what has been witnessed" (J. Beutler, "*martys*," *EDNT* 2:394). The syntactical and contextual arguments against taking *martys* as an eyewitness are that one definite article governs both nouns *sympresbyteros* and *martys* and the noun *sympresbyteros* requires that those addressed share that attribute with the author. Furthermore, the further descriptor, "as well as one who shares in the glory to be revealed" implies that at least two of the three self-descriptions are shared by author and addressees. Michaels avers that *martys* in this context "is virtually equivalent to *symmartys*, 'fellow witness'" (J. Ramsey Michaels, *1 Peter* [WBC 47; Waco, Tex.: Word, 1988], p. 280). See also H. Strathmann, "*martys*," *TDNT* 4:494-95; Peter H. Davids, *The First Epistle of Peter* (NICNT; Grand Rapids: Eerdmans, 1990), pp. 176-77; Karen H. Jobes, *1 Peter* (BECNT; Grand Rapids: Baker, 2005), p. 301. For a discussion of the Granville Sharp rule, see Daniel B. Wallace, *Greek Grammar Beyond the Basics* (Grand Rapids: Zondervan, 1996), pp. 270-90.

[4]In chapter 7, I sketch the traditions about Peter's residence, preaching, martyrdom and burial in Rome. C. H. Hunzinger's argument from silence that no instance has come to light of "Babylon" used as a code word for Rome earlier than A.D. 70 ("Babylon als Deckname für Rom und die Datierung des 1. Petrusbriefes," in *Gottes Wort und Gottes Land* [ed. H. Graf Reventlow; Göttingen: Vandenhoeck & Ruprecht, 1965], p. 71, cited in Reinhard Feldmeier, *The First Letter of Peter* [trans. Peter H. Davids; Waco, Tex.: Baylor University Press, 2008], p. 33) has been refuted by C. P. Thiede, *Simon Peter: From Galilee to Rome* (Exeter: Paternoster, 1986).

John Mark, a cousin of Barnabas, known from Acts and Paul's letters and author of the Gospel bearing his name (Acts 13:13; 15:37-39; Col 4:10; 2 Tim 4:11; Philem 24). Church tradition places Mark in Rome with Peter near the end of the latter's life and says that Mark wrote his Gospel based on Peter's preaching (Eusebius, *Hist. eccl.* 2.15). Finally, the author gratefully acknowledges the assistance of Silvanus (Silas) either in composing or in delivering the letter.[5] He was Paul's frequent companion and fellow worker (Acts [fourteen times]; 2 Cor 1:19; 1 Thess 1:1; 2 Thess 1:1). Two members of the Pauline circle are thus present with the implied author in Rome, nicely dovetailing with the church traditions about Peter.

2. There are features of the letter that comport with the apostle Peter as the real author. For example, at least four passages seem to evoke key moments in Peter's life during Jesus' ministry: Peter's being tested by Satan (1 Pet 1:7 and Lk 22:31); Peter's restoration and recommissioning (1 Pet 5:10 and Mk 16:7) the metaphor of shepherd and sheep to describe Jesus' ministry and the ministry entrusted to Peter and church elders (1 Pet 2:25; 5:2 and Mk 14:27; Jn 21:15-17); and humility as a hallmark of Christian service as demonstrated in Jesus' washing of the apostles' feet in the upper room (1 Pet 5:5-6 and Jn 13:4-16).[6] Ralph Martin calls attention to "impressive correspondences between Peter's language in Acts and in this Epistle."[7] In addition, Robert Gundry detects fifteen allusions to *verba Christi* ("words of Christ") in the letter drawn from Gospel contexts

---

[5] A number of commentators hold that the preposition *dia* points to Silvanus's active role in composition. BDAG is more circumspect and says "perhaps" this is the usage in 1 Peter 5:14, citing a possible parallel in Eusebius, *Hist. eccl.* 4.23.11 (p. 180). Michaels, however, holds that "more likely it indicates that Silvanus was the bearer of the letter" (*1 Peter*, p. 306).

[6] I am indebted to Selwyn (*Peter*, p. 28) for these allusions. Especially noteworthy is the Greek verb used in 1 Peter 5:5 for "clothe yourselves", depicting the act of tying a garment around one's body, like a slave would a towel, in order to wash feet. The image of Jesus in the upper room comes immediately to mind (Jn 13:4; not, however, the same Greek verb as in 1 Peter 5:5, which is *diazōnnumi*). See further Ceslas Spicq, "*enkomboomai*," *TLNT* 1:404.

[7] Ralph P. Martin, *New Testament Foundations* (2 vols.; Grand Rapids: Eerdmans, 1978), 1:330-31. These are (1) the description of God as one "who shows no partiality" (Acts 10:34; cf. 1 Pet 1:17); (2) depiction of Christ as "the stone that was rejected" (Acts 4:11; cf. 1 Peter 2:7) based on Psalm 118:22; (3) emphasis on "the name of the Lord" (Acts 3:5, 16; 4:10, 12; 5:41; 10:43; cf. 1 Pet 4:14, 16); and (4) stress laid on the fulfillment of OT messianic prophecies (Acts 3:18, 14; cf. 1 Pet 1:10-12).

in which Peter is present.[8] Furthermore, the implied author does not trade on his status as an apostle but prefers to identify himself as a fellow elder and shepherd of the flock. A similar restraint characterizes the apostle John's writings (2 Jn 1:1; 3 Jn 1:1; Rev 1:4, 9). It should also be noted that a couple of ironies in the letter work well if Peter is the real author and thus corroborate the foregoing evidence.[9]

3. Attestation for Peter as the real author is widespread among the early church fathers and unchallenged until the rise of the historical-critical method in the eighteenth century.[10] This is no guarantee that the Fathers were right, and it must be admitted that much has been learned about the background and composition of the NT in the modern era. Still, such an early and persistent tradition should not be dismissed without convincing evidence.

4. However, a majority of critical scholars believe that the preponderance of evidence points to someone other than the apostle Peter. In short, here are the leading arguments.

4.1. Linguistically, 1 Peter exhibits a high level of Greek proficiency. Is it likely that a Galilean fisherman could achieve this level of control?[11] Two things need to be said. First, while the Greek of 1 Peter is good, it is hardly the best in the NT; Hebrews and Acts take top billing in that regard. More importantly, Karen Jobes argues that the Greek of 1 Peter betrays an author whose native language is Semitic.[12] Second, it is always

---

[8] " 'Verba Christi' in 1 Peter: Their Implications Concerning the Authorship of 1 Peter and the Authenticity of the Gospel Tradition," *NTS* 13 (1966-1967): 336-50. Werner Kümmel comments that such an attempt "does not come off" and cites the work of E. Best, "I Peter and the Gospel Tradition," *NTS* 16 (1969-1970): 95-113. One should, however, carefully read Gundry's response to Best ("Further Verba on Verba Christi in First Peter," *Bib* 55 [1974]: 211-32).

[9] E.g., in 1 Peter 2:6, Christ is the stone, whereas Jesus designated Peter as "the Rock" in Matthew 16:18. Peter is the stumbling block in Matthew 16:23, whereas in 1 Peter, it is Jesus (1 Pet 2:8).

[10] "The earliest undoubted attribution of the Epistle to St. Peter is by Irenaeus" (Selwyn, *Peter*, p. 37; cf. Irenaeus, *Haer.* 4.9.2.; 16.5; 5.7.2). See also the important passage (*locus classicus* according to Selwyn) in Eusebius, *Hist. eccl.* 3.3. Probably the earliest quotation (ca. A.D. 96) occurs in *1 Clement* 30:2 (1 Pet 5:5) and *1 Clement* 49:5 (1 Pet 4:8). Polycarp (ca. A.D. 135) also quotes from it several times in his letter to the Philippians. See *The Apostolic Fathers* [ed. Michael W. Holmes; trans. J. B. Lightfoot and J. R. Harmer; 2nd ed.; Grand Rapids: Baker, 1992], pp. 207-21).

[11] Werner Kümmel says it is "inconceivable" (*Introduction to the New Testament* [trans. Howard Clark Kee; rev. ed.; Nashville: Abingdon, 1975], p. 423).

[12] "Excursus: The Syntax of 1 Peter: How Good Is the Greek?" in *1 Peter*, pp. 325-33. According to Nigel Turner, "there are some strong Semitic features." He concludes "that 1 Peter wears a

surprising how confident modern scholars can be about what is or is not possible in terms of linguistic achievement. Not a few examples of individuals having little or no formal training becoming literary virtuosos may be adduced.[13] Why couldn't this have happened in the ancient world?

There is an important parallel that is highly relevant to this discussion. Flavius Josephus, a Galilean Jew and near contemporary of the apostle Peter, participated in and survived the great Jewish war against Rome in A.D. 66-73. After retiring to Rome under the protection and patronage of the Roman emperor, he penned a gripping account of this epic war. This work, in Greek, is a fine example of Greek prose. We learn, however, that he wrote a first edition in his native tongue (Hebrew/Aramaic). He later translated this into Greek, the only edition that has survived from antiquity. Of great interest is Josephus's comment on this latter project: "It . . . [is] a difficult thing to translate our history into a foreign, and to us unaccustomed, language" (*Ant.* pref. §7). He then goes on to sing the praises of one Epaphroditus, a patron and encourager of Josephus's work (§§8-9). Did Epaphroditus also lend stylistic and compositional assistance or provide someone who could? Since Josephus does not explicitly say, we cannot be certain. What Josephus does say is that he worked very hard on the project.

Why couldn't Peter, also working very hard, accomplish something comparable? A number of NT scholars have suggested that Silvanus, or someone unnamed,[14] assisted Peter as an amanuensis (scribe or secretary). This is only a conjecture, but one that is plausible and may account for the high level of Greek in 1 Peter. The fact that Peter grew up in a bilingual region and, by the time he wrote this letter, had spent twenty to thirty years preaching and teaching in Greek should be factored into the equation. To be sure, oral and writing skills are not

---

veneer of good stylistic revision upon a basic draft of the same kind of Greek that is found elsewhere in the NT. It is tempting to ascribe the veneer to an amanuensis, not necessarily Silvanus" (*A Grammar of New Testament Greek* [Edinburgh: T&T Clark, 1976], pp. 124, 130).

[13]Feldmeier (*First Peter*, p. 47, n. 39) lists Lucian of Samosata and Josef Teodar Nalecz Korzeniowksy as an ancient and a modern example, repectively. He also cites Neugebauer's trenchant comments in this regard: "Arguments such as these base themselves on deceptive academic images and often result from a lack of contact with so-called simple people" (F. Neugebauer, "Zur Deutung und Dedeutung des 1. Petrusbriefes," *NTS* 26 [1980]: 72).

[14]Michaels's view (*1 Peter*, p. lxii).

always on a par, but to dismiss the possibility that Peter was incapable of composing the Greek of 1 Peter, especially if he had assistance from someone who was highly literate, displays a modern, academic bias.

4.2. Theological considerations are often appealed to as evidence against Petrine authorship. The argument goes like this: several passages demonstrate similarity to Pauline phrasing and thought. This is especially the case in epistles designated as deutero-Pauline, that is, supposedly written not by Paul but by a Paulinist (Ephesians, Colossians and the Pastorals). In this regard, F. W. Beare made much of the similarities between Ephesians and 1 Peter, even positing that the latter drew on the former. Since these supposed deutero-Pauline epistles postdate Paul's death, and the tradition is uniform that Paul and Peter died at about the same time, the presence of "Paulinisms" in 1 Peter is said to point toward pseudonymity.

In response, several things should be mentioned. First, similarity to Pauline expressions is neither surprising nor determinative in ruling out Petrine authorship. After all, both Peter and Paul share a common apostolic tradition and significant interaction in Jerusalem, Syrian Antioch and Rome. Paul himself expresses his indebtedness to the apostolic traditions in his letters pointing to a shared Christian tradition among all the apostles (1 Cor 15:3). First Peter contains a relatively high percentage of material having a liturgical and confessional character.[15] Consequently, we should be surprised if there were no common features shared by Paul and Peter. But the differences between 1 Peter and the Pauline letters are not negligible; the thought of 1 Peter charts its own independent course.[16] Finally, the case for deutero-Pauline epistles is not nearly as secure as its adherents maintain, a key plank in their argument that 1 Peter is literarily and theologically indebted to them.[17]

---

[15]"More recent study has remarked that the common matter relates mainly to liturgical interest . . . and that the closeness of the parallels may best be accounted for by the access of both writers to a common fund of liturgical and catechetical material" (Martin, *Foundations*, 2:332).

[16]J. H. Elliott argues persuasively for a distinctive Petrine formulation of Christianity having its own independent existence ("The Rehabilitation of an Exegetical Step-Child: 1 Peter in Recent Research," *JBL* 95 [1976]: 243-54), though he does not support direct Petrine authorship (*1 Peter*, 124-30).

[17]See, e.g., P. T. O'Brien, "Colossians," *DPL*, pp. 150-52; C. E. Arnold, "Ephesians," *DPL*, pp. 240-43; E. E. Ellis, "Pastoral Letters," *DPL*, pp. 659-61.

4.3. Many scholars detect in the letter evidence of a post-Petrine life setting. For example, the kind of persecution implied in the letter is said to be more likely in the time of Domitian (A.D. 81-96) or even Trajan (A.D. 111/112). If this is so, it clearly places the letter well after Peter's death. In addition, the organization of the church is thought to reflect a situation more in keeping with the end of the first century and beginning of the second than with the mid-first century. Furthermore, many think the problem of how Christianity took root in the northern provinces of Asia Minor requires a dating of the letter after the lifetime of Peter. Historical evidence connecting an apostle or a group of Christian evangelists with a mission to those regions does not exist. Consequently, most critical scholars assume a gradual spread from the southern areas of Asia Minor where Paul initially founded house churches. In their view, for Christians to achieve a critical mass and come to the attention of the governing authorities requires a date sometime in the 80s or 90s, at the earliest. In fact, the first documentation we possess of Christians in Bithynia and Pontus (i.e., excluding 1 Peter) is Pliny the Elder's letter to Trajan (ca. 111-118).

This argument is even less secure than the previous one. In fact, the life setting implied in 1 Peter does not require any formal state persecution, nor is there even unambiguous evidence of mob-incited acts of violence. Rather, slander, ostracism and abuse appear to be the primary manifestations of the hostility. Dating the letter to the time of Trajan, as championed by Beare, is now increasingly abandoned. As for an emerging Catholicism in terms of church organization, this reads far too much into the text and does not carry conviction. The pattern of leadership implied in the letter easily fits into the decades of the 50s and 60s. In short, there is no need to posit a dating later than the 60s.[18] As I will mention shortly, there is another life setting that fits the implied circumstances of the letter quite well and allows for a date as early as the 50s.

4.4. Finally, the notion of epistolary pseudonymity as an accepted

---

[18]"If the Epistle of 1 Peter was published with Peter's personal authorization and as representing his own apostolic teaching, a date in the earlier part of the seventh decade is required. This seems very probable" (Martin, *Foundations*, 2:334).

literary feature in the early church is suspect. That several letters were explicitly excluded from the canon by the early fathers because they were pseudonymous should be a red flag (Eusebius, *Hist. eccl.* 6.12.3; Tertullian, *Bapt.* 17; Cyril of Jerusalem, *Cat.* 4.36). I think it unlikely that any of the NT letters are pseudonymous.[19] In short, I think the external and internal evidence taken together still favors Petrine authorship.[20]

## RECIPIENTS AND PLACE OF COMPOSITION

Most of the early fathers identify the original recipients of this letter as Jewish Christians. The majority view today is that most of the readers were Gentile Christians. The reason for this reversal arises from the text itself. There are several statements made by the implied author that are hard to square with a Jewish Christian audience. For example, would Peter exhort Jewish believers "not [to] be conformed to the desires that you formerly had in ignorance" (1 Pet 1:14)? Would he say to them, "You know that you were ransomed from the futile ways inherited from your ancestors" (1 Pet 1:18), and, even more telling, "You have already spent enough time in doing what the Gentiles like to do, living in licentiousness, passions, drunkenness, revels, carousing, and lawless idolatry" (1 Pet 4:3)? The latter reference to idolatry appears especially incompatible with an assumed Jewish Christian readership.

However, Jobes queries whether we may so easily assume that all Diaspora Jews eschewed "what the Gentiles like to do." For example, Paul's scathing critique of Jewish morality and behavior in Romans 2 builds to this indictment: "The name of God is blasphemed among the Gentiles because of you" (Rom 2:24). According to Paul, Jews "are doing the very same things" as Gentiles (Rom 2:1, 3, 9, 21-23). Nor should we forget Jesus' stinging indictment of Pharisaic leaders in the heartland of Judaism (Mt 23). Furthermore, Josephus's account of the Jewish war depicts some Jews exhibiting a shocking degree of inhu-

---

[19]See further D. A. Carson, "Pseudonymity and Pseudepigraphy," *DNTB*, pp. 857-63.

[20]"If ever there was a weak case for pseudonymity, surely it is in respect to this letter." I. Howard Marshall, *1 Peter* (IVPNTC 17; Downers Grove, Ill.: InterVarsity Press, 1991), p. 21. Marshall's concise treatment of the authorship question is highly recommended (pp. 21-24).

manity and depravity. Another contemporary of Josephus, Philo of Alexandria, had a nephew, Tiberius Alexander, who assimilated into the Greco-Roman society of Alexandria, Egypt, a course of action adopted by other Jews as well.[21] All of this should give us pause before we conclude that the readers of 1 Peter could not be Jewish in ethnicity.

That brings us to the designation applied to the recipients. They are called "the exiles of the Dispersion" (1 Pet 1:1), a description that, at face value, sounds very Jewish and recalls the existential situation of a majority of Jews during the first century A.D. who lived outside the Holy Land in the Diaspora. Since the recipients are clearly Christians (1 Pet 4:16), this implies that they are Jewish converts. In this regard, one finds a close parallel in James, where the addressees are called "the twelve tribes in the Dispersion" (Jas 1:1). By common consent, the addressees in James are Jewish Christians. It would seem, then, that we should follow suit in 1 Peter. But as already indicated, most modern interpreters regard the recipients of 1 Peter as primarily Gentiles because of the internal evidence already discussed. They understand the phrase "exiles of the Dispersion" as a metaphorical expression applied to the believers in Asia Minor as members of the new Israel, the church of Jesus Christ.

Here is where Jobes's thesis is helpful. She does not deny a metaphorical use of terms at home in Judaism and applied to Christians, but she argues that one must take seriously the literal description of these people as "aliens" (*paroikous*) and "exiles" (*parepidēmous*) (1 Pet 2:11). Linked to this is the intriguing question of how Christianity took root in the hinterland provinces of Pontus, Bithynia and Cappadocia. We know that Paul planted house churches in southern Galatia and Asia and that he was prevented by the Holy Spirit from entering Bithynia (Acts 16:7). So who brought the gospel to the other three provinces? One suggestion, found among the early fathers, is that Jewish pilgrims from these regions embraced the gospel on the day of Pentecost and brought their newfound faith with them. This may be, but there is no corroborating evidence. Another suggestion is

---

[21]See R. M. Wilson, "Philo Judaeus," *ISBE* 3:847.

that Peter himself was responsible for evangelizing the area during the approximately eight-year hiatus in the book of Acts during which he is not mentioned (see Acts 12:17; 15:7-11).[22] This would account for his writing an apostolic letter to these believers. Once again, this is possible, but there is no explicit documentary evidence for such a Petrine mission.

But 1 Peter is also addressed to believers in Asia and Galatia, provinces in which, according to Acts, Paul was the founding missionary. This raises a question: Would these two formidable apostles have labored in the same general area? What are we to make of Paul's statement in Galatians 2:7, which, at face value, seems to be a formal agreement demarcating ministry zones? As argued in the previous chapter, this agreement was probably not a perpetually binding arrangement. Acts depicts Peter's initial work in opening the door to Gentiles (Acts 10) and portrays Paul initiating church plants by first visiting local synagogues or Jewish places of prayer (Acts 13:5, 14; 14:1; 16:13; 17:1, 10; 18:4, 19; 19:8). In short, the documentary evidence does not *exclude* the possibility that Peter evangelized in all five Roman provinces. Still, the area represented is huge; something like the entire state of Montana in extent.

Jobes has a neat solution. She hypothesizes that the addressees were former residents of Rome, relocated by imperial mandate as part of a "policy of urbanization through colonization" to the fringes of the empire.[23] More specifically, she places this colonization during the reign of Claudius (A.D. 41-54), known for his focus on precisely the five provinces mentioned in 1 Peter and for his edict of expulsion of Jews from Rome in A.D. 49 (Acts 18:2). If this background for the recipients of 1 Peter is assumed, they were in fact "aliens and exiles" living in a new and somewhat threatening situation. Peter takes it on himself to write a letter to these displaced persons because he had previously ministered to them as apostle and pastor in Rome. This theory, of course, accepts the tradition that Peter lived in Rome well before his martyrdom and that he functioned there as an apostle. Furthermore, this allows for an

---

[22]As argued by J. Wenham, "Did Peter Go to Rome in AD 42?" *TynBul* 23 (1972): 94-102.
[23]Jobes, *1 Peter*, p. 28. See pp. 28-41 for the complete discussion.

even earlier date of composition, perhaps even in the mid to late 50s. An objection to this view is that Paul wrote a letter to the Romans (ca. A.D. 57) and does not even mention Peter, even though he greets a number of Roman believers by name. Of course, Peter may not have been in Rome at that particular time because he was elsewhere on a mission trip.[24] After all, Paul implies that Peter was active in evangelizing during this very period in 1 Corinthians 9:5: "Do we not have the right to be accompanied by a believing wife, as do the other apostles and the brothers of the Lord and Cephas?" Also, is it likely there would have been a "Cephas faction" at Corinth if Cephas had not personally been there at some time (see 1 Cor 1:12)? In short, a credible, but by no means certain, case can be argued that Peter writes to former residents of Rome who have been relocated by the imperial government to the hinterlands for purposes of colonization.[25] Peter thus addressees them in a twofold sense: they are living away from their former home in Rome and, at the same time, living away from their ultimate home, their heavenly home. In short, both a literal and metaphorical meaning aptly applies.[26] This thesis has much to commend it and, while it cannot be proven, "it explains a number of issues."[27]

## PETER'S PURPOSE AS AN ENTRÉE INTO HIS THEOLOGY

Peter's purpose is to encourage his readers to remain steadfast in their faith, hope and love ("the true grace of God"). To this end, he earnestly exhorts the readers to live lives full of courage and commitment, respect and submission, gentleness and compassion. Peter's parenesis (ethical exhortation and admonition) is paradoxical in a twofold sense. On the one hand, Christians should live their lives with "an indescribable and glorious joy" coupled with a sober seriousness (cf. 1 Pet

---

[24]Wenham, "Did Peter Go?" pp. 94-102.

[25]Leonhard Goppelt makes the interesting observation that "through the greeting in 5:13 our letter becomes the first explicit Christian writing known to us that builds the arch of church contact from Rome to Asia Minor that in the second century would become the basis for the Catholic Church" (Der erste Petrusbriefe [KEK 12; Göttingen: Vandenhoeck & Ruprecht, 1978], p. 353, cited by Feldmeier, First Peter, p. 42, n. 61).

[26]Feldmeier accepts the view that "Babylon" in 1 Peter 5:13 is both a cryptogram for Rome and a metaphor for the dispersion (First Peter, p. 41).

[27]Jobes, 1 Peter, p. 39.

1:6-8, 4:13 with 1 Pet 4:7; 5:8). On the other, they should respect the cultural institutions of which they are a part (1 Pet 2:13-17) but resist that which is inimical to their true status as members of God's household (1 Pet 1:14; 2:1, 11-12; 4:3, 15). These two primary exhortations summon the readers to live as resident aliens, both in their new provinces and, more importantly, in the world as opposed to their true, heavenly home. They are also charged to bear up under intense trials and persecution as Christians and resist impulses to retaliate and take revenge for wrongs. Underlying his exhortations are fundamental theological convictions.

In what follows, I seek to identify and explain what these are and why they are still important for modern Christians. I am mindful of the limits and difficulties of this endeavor, since we are dealing with a relatively short, occasional letter. Still, in this piece of missionary correspondence, one is brought into the narrative world of a mind and heart deeply touched by his personal encounter with Messiah Jesus. This encounter is an ongoing, developing relationship. Peter believes that Jesus is alive and well and works through him to "feed the flock of God." The same Holy Spirit, the "Spirit of Christ," who spoke to the OT prophets speaks to him and is available to his readers. An extraordinary thing has happened to this man: He has been transformed by the living Christ. He assumes that every believer is on a similar journey. The road, however, is not easy; indeed, perils constantly threaten each pilgrim's progress. Nonetheless, because of Peter's great confidence in the God and Father of Jesus Christ and the living hope secured by Jesus Christ through the Holy Spirit, there is every reason to persist and be joyful. In short, what Peter believes dictates his behavior. And what he believes deserves careful reflection.[28]

## PETER'S UNDERSTANDING OF GOD

Paternal imagery shapes Peter's parenesis in 1 Peter 1:3–2:3. Peter places high theological importance on the fact that God is the heavenly Father (1 Pet 1:2-3, 17). No need to speculate on the source of this

---

[28]"1 Peter is more extensively used as a text for preaching than any other biblical document" (Feldmeier, *First Peter*, p. 43).

teaching; Peter learned it at the feet of the Master: "Our Father in heaven" (Mt 6:9; cf. Mk 14:36). Though the fatherhood of God is mentioned in the OT, Jesus takes it to an unprecedented level.[29] Peter, like the other apostles, assumes this new intimacy as foundational for all believers in Christ. Praise (1 Pet 1:3) and petition (1 Pet 1:17) are directed to the heavenly Father.

More specifically, Peter indicates that the Father is the primary agent who determines who his children are: he chooses those who belong to him; he causes them to experience spiritual rebirth; and he judges and evaluates their deeds. Each of these requires further treatment.

*The God who elects.* A longstanding puzzle and controversy involves the relationship between God's sovereignty and human freedom as it relates to salvation. This issue did not first arise as a post-Reformation debate between the followers of John Calvin and Jacob Arminius. Already in Second Temple Judaism, one overhears this theological question being vigorously debated. Sadducees championed human freedom as the determining factor; each person was free to choose for or against God. The Essenes represented a diametrically opposed alternative; God decided each person's destiny before he or she was even born. The Pharisees represented a delicate balance in the middle; God determines all things, but human freedom is part of the equation.[30] In short, Pharisees affirmed an antinomy (a seeming contraction between two reasonable concepts). It is precisely this balancing act, acknowledging both factors simultaneously, that surfaces in the thought of the apostle Paul (see Rom 8–10). Let us see if we can detect what the apostle Peter says on this vexed question.

In his salutation, Peter addresses his readers as "exiles of the Dispersion . . . who have been chosen and destined by God the Father" (1 Pet 1:1-2). The NRSV rendering "destined" translates two Greek words,

---

[29]See Larry R. Helyer, *The Witness of Jesus, Paul and John* (Downers Grove, Ill.: InterVarsity Press, 2008), pp. 153-56, 158-59, 174-75.

[30]This position is nicely encapsulated in the following aphorism attributed to R. Akiva (A.D. 50-135): "All is foreseen, but freedom of choice is given" (*'Abot* 3:17). This view is already reflected in the speech placed in Gamaliel the Elder's mouth by Luke in the book of Acts (Acts 5:38-39). See Jonathan Klawans, "The Dead Sea Scrolls, the Essenes and the Study of Religious Belief: Determinism and Freedom of Choice," in *Rediscovering the Dead Sea Scrolls* (ed. Maxine Grossman; Grand Rapids: Eerdmans, 2010), pp. 264-83.

*kata prognōsin*, literally, "according to, in conformity with or on the basis of, foreknowledge." The precise meaning of the preposition *kata* is rather important here, as is the intended nuance of the noun *prognōsis*. As to the former, M. J. Harris says that, in this passage, "the notion of conformity is totally displaced, with *kata* denoting the basis. Thus, election is based on the foreknowledge of God the Father."[31] As to the latter, when used of God, as it is here, "the idea of election is always present" (cf. Rom 8:29; 11:2) and "this election is based on God's decree and obligates the chosen person to a responsibility that is manifested above all in obedience."[32] Thus the intended meaning in this passage refers to more than mere prescience; included is a creative willing, an overarching determination. Just like Christ, who "was destined before the foundation of the world" (1 Pet 1:20) to be the Passover Lamb, so believers are destined "to be obedient to Jesus Christ" (1 Pet 1:2). Does this mean then that Peter leaves no place for human freedom? Has it been overridden by God the Father's sovereign decree? Immediately following 1 Peter 1:20, Peter goes on to say, "Through him [Christ] you have come to trust in God . . . so that your faith and hope are set on God. Now that you have purified your souls by your obedience to the truth . . . " (1 Pet 1:21-22).[33] Neither God the Father nor Christ exercises trust on behalf of believers; this is an indispensable, saving act that must be performed by the individual. So, like Paul, Peter apparently has no difficulty setting side by side two seemingly opposed notions. We do well, like the Pharisees before us, to let stand these two great theological truths, being careful not to exclude or obscure one or the other.[34]

***The God who begets.*** The human process of birth serves admirably as a metaphor for becoming a member of God's covenant family. In John's

---

[31]"Appendix," *NIDNTT* 3:1201.

[32]A. Sand, *"prognōsis,"* *EDNT* 3:153-54.

[33]I. Howard Marshall explains the foreknowledge of God as "a way of saying that he took the initiative in bringing the church into being." *New Testament Theology: Many Witnesses, One Gospel* (Downers Grove, Ill.: InterVarsity Press, 2004), p. 644.

[34]P. Jacobs and H. Krienke insist that "any interpretation in terms of an impersonal constraint (such as destiny, fate or doom), or of an autonomy which removes itself from the normal course of world events, would contradict the NT use of these words" ("Foreknowledge," *NIDNTT*, 1:693).

Gospel, Jesus challenges Nicodemus the Pharisee with this imperative: "You must be born from above" (Jn 3:7). In fact, in Johannine theology, this is a favorite metaphor to describe entrance into the community of faith in Jesus (Jn 1:13; 3:3, 7-8; 1 Jn 2:29; 3:9; 4:7; 5:1, 4, 18). The apostle Paul rarely uses this idiom (see Tit 3:5)—he prefers to speak of a new creation, a coming to life.[35] Peter, like John, affirms that God "has given us a new birth" (1 Pet 1:3).

If the election of believers is grounded in God's foreknowledge, according to Peter, their spiritual rebirth is based on God's great mercy. In the OT, mercy is sometimes found in a context in which a father expresses his deep, emotional attachment for his son (Jer 31:20). Often the context implies notions of loyalty, devotion and faithfulness on God's part that persist in spite of human rebellion and faithlessness (Jer 3:11-25). Especially noteworthy are the OT contexts reflecting a covenantal relationship between God and his people (Ex 20:6; Deut 5:10). The NT carries this over and deepens it; indeed, 1 Peter 2:9-10 taps into this rich fund of covenantal language and reapplies it to the Christians of Anatolia: "You are a chosen race, a royal priesthood, a holy nation, God's own people."

How can this be? Peter has at hand a key OT text from the prophet Hosea that explains this wondrous transformation. They are now the people of God because they have received God's mercy (Hos 2:23). One may say that, in the NT, God demonstrates his mercy by extending his love to human beings even though they are in a most miserable state (Rom 5:6-11). Peter's pastoral letter opens with this doxology: "By his great mercy he has given us a new birth into a living hope" (1 Pet 1:3). The creative agency through which God accomplishes this supernatural rebirth is expressly identified as "the living and enduring word of God" (1 Pet 1:23), further specified as "the good news that was announced to you" (1 Pet 1:25). The connection between the creative word of God in Genesis 1 and the word of God conveyed through the

---

[35]In fact, as Kelly points out, Peter's statement finds a close parallel, though with different imagery, in Ephesians 2:4-5: "But God, who is rich in mercy, out of the great love with which he loved us . . . made us alive together with Christ." See J. N. D. Kelly, *A Commentary on the Epistles of Peter and of Jude* (HNTC; New York: Harper, 1969), p. 47.

preaching of the gospel is quite remarkable. God alone is the source of all life, whether physical or spiritual. This theological conviction closes the door on any recourse to therapeutic techniques or self-help schemes, to say nothing of magical formulas and mantras. It is, in fact, "a sheer miracle."[36] Peter, in harmony with the witness of the entire NT, affirms that "a person is inwardly transformed through a believing acceptance of the word of God."[37]

*The God who judges.* Peter insists that all must stand before God the Father "who judges all people impartially according to their deeds" (1 Pet 1:17; 4:6). Believers dare not "rely on their privileged status as his children" because the Father's "decisions will be determined solely by the quality of each [person's] actions."[38] Consequently, this obligates believers to "live in reverent fear during the time of [their] exile" (1 Pet 1:17). Such a lifestyle results in ultimate vindication and causes Gentiles who malign Christians to "glorify God when he comes to judge" (1 Pet 2:12). Furthermore, unbelievers "have to give an accounting to him who stands ready to judge the living and the dead" (1 Pet 4:5).[39] Peter's assumption that there is accountability after death counters a widely held pagan view. In short, "death does not invalidate either the promises or the warnings of the gospel of Jesus Christ."[40] Peter does not elaborate on the nature of punishment for unbelievers; it is enough to say that "the face of the Lord is against those who do evil" (1 Pet 3:12; cf. Ps 34:16).[41] Peter exhorts believers who are suffering because of their faith in Christ (1 Pet 4:16) to remain steadfast knowing that the heavenly judge is also their heavenly Father. When he comes, he will exalt them

---

[36]Leon Morris, *New Testament Theology* (Grand Rapids: Zondervan, 1986), p. 317.

[37]F. Porsch, *"anagennaō," EDNT* 1:76.

[38]Kelly, *Epistles of Peter*, p. 71. Beare nicely captures Peter's point: "Our knowledge of Him as Father must not dispel our dread of Him as our Judge" (F. W. Beare, *The First Epistle of Peter* [3rd. ed., rev.; Oxford: Blackwell, 1970], p. 100).

[39]The expression "the living and the dead" is a merism (i.e., a figure of speech whereby two opposites are conjoined in order to express a universal). Thus all people without exception must stand before God the Judge.

[40]Jobes, *1 Peter*, pp. 270-71.

[41]Almost certainly Peter accepted the reality of punishment in Gehenna, as reflected in various texts emanating from the period of Second Temple Judaism (*1 En.* 10:13; 18:11-16 et al., *Jub.* 9:15; 1QH 3.29-36; *2 Bar.* 37:1) and, even more decisively, from the teaching of Jesus (Mt 5:20, 22; 10:28; 18:9; 23:15, 33; Mk 9:43, 45, 47; Lk 12:5; cf. 2 Pet 2:1-10, 12, 17).

(1 Pet 5:6) and reward their faithfulness with an everlasting inheritance and a participation in the glory of God (1 Pet 1:4; 4:13; 5:1, 10), symbolized by a crown of glory (1 Pet 5:4). Though Peter does not describe the nature of this glory, there are indications in the OT and the teaching of Jesus that it manifests itself in radiant light (Mt 22:30; 2 Pet 1:19).

A difficult text dealing with judgment occurs in 1 Peter 4:6: "For this is the reason the gospel was proclaimed even to the dead, so that, though they had been judged in the flesh as everyone is judged, they might live in the spirit as God does." Precisely who are "the dead" and how and when are they judged? Some interpreters understand this passage as speaking of a postmortem opportunity to hear and respond to the gospel.[42] Though in some respects attractive, this reads a lot into a little, with questionable NT support (Eph 4:9; Rom 10:7) and scant support in later Christian tradition.[43] A majority of interpreters opt for the view that the dead are deceased Christians who responded to the gospel during their lifetime.[44] Presumably, the judgment "in the flesh" was physical death (see Rom 5:12-21). Since this passage is perhaps related to the even more difficult text in 1 Peter 3:18-22, sometimes called the *descensus ad inferos* ("descent into hell"), I postpone further discussion until later.

Finally, Peter reminds his Christian readers that "the time has come for judgment to begin with the household of God" (1 Pet 4:17). Peter's reminder probably alludes to the OT prophet Ezekiel. In Ezekiel 9 God orders an angel to place a mark on the forehead of all those who mourn over the sad spiritual state of the city of Jerusalem. Six destroying angels are then dispatched with orders to kill all who are not repentant: "And begin at my sanctuary" (Ezek 9:6). This is the key phrase that Peter lifts out and applies to the situation facing his readers. Though not precisely reflecting the historical context of Ezekiel,[45]

---

[42]See, e.g., Jerry L Walls, *Heaven: The Logic of Eternal Joy* (Oxford: Oxford University Press, 2007).

[43]First attested in Clement of Alexandria (ca. A.D. 150-215).

[44]As carefully argued by Thomas R. Schreiner, *1, 2 Peter, Jude* (NAC 37; Nashville: Broadman & Holman, 2003), pp. 205-10.

[45]Jobes argues that Peter always utilizes OT quotations in light of their historical context. Because Ezekiel 9 does not neatly relate to Peter's meaning in 1 Peter 4:17, she denies that it is the text to which Peter alludes. Rather, she selects snippets from Zephaniah and Malachi. In my

Peter draws attention to a uniform feature of redemptive history: God's people are the first to be judged. It is not without interest that in Matthew 25, Jesus gives three parables illustrating some aspect of eschatological judgment. In each case, the ten maidens, the talents and the sheep and goats, believers are first judged and rewarded before unbelievers face their judgment and punishment. We should also note that Peter's argument reflects one of Hillel's seven exegetical principles, namely, *qal wahomer* (i.e., an inference from the lesser, *qal*, to the greater, *homer*).[46] Since judgment first begins with God's people, how much more certain it is that unbelievers will also stand before the "one who judges all people."

*The God who rules.* From the above considerations, Peter clearly understands God as the sovereign God who directs salvation history toward its appointed goal. Everything is unfolding according to his purpose and plan (1 Pet 1:5, 10-12, 20-21; 2:8-10; 3:18-22; 4:12, 17; 5:4, 10). The similarity to the thought in Ephesians 1, which I take to be genuinely Pauline, has often been noted. Several times the apostle Peter mentions "the will of God" (1 Pet 2:15; 3:17; 4:2, 19) in connection with the readers' sufferings. I discuss this in more detail later but for now draw attention to the fact that Peter specifically locates suffering within God's will. The pastoral application of this theological conviction is significant: the implied readers should not view themselves as victims of whim and fate; in spite of their outward circumstances, they are being "protected by the power of God through faith for a salvation ready to be revealed" (1 Pet 1:5). And the power of God is not inadequate for the task: he has already raised Christ from the dead and given him glory (1 Pet 1:21). Believers are destined to share in Christ's resurrection and glory. Accordingly, they must set their faith

---

view, Ezekiel 9:6 is more likely the text to which Peter is indebted. In line with Second Temple Judaism generally, NT writers sometimes employ the OT more creatively and allusively than is often admitted. See Helyer, *Exploring Jewish Literature*, pp. 238-47. Schreiner holds that the language of 1 Peter 4:17 is taken from Ezekiel 9:6 but the theology is closer to Malachi 3:1-4 because the former concerns judgment for rebellious sinners and the latter refers to refining believers for acceptable worship (*1, 2 Peter, Jude*, p. 227).

[46]Hillel. a contemporary of Jesus and Paul, was one of the most influential rabbis of the era. His formulation of exegetical principles exercised a long-lasting influence in rabbinic Judaism (i.e., the Judaism that dominated after A.D. 70 up until modern times).

and hope on God to accomplish their appointed destiny (1 Pet 1:21) because he will not fail to "exalt [them] in due time" (1 Pet 5:6). Peter reminds his readers that "the word of the Lord endures forever" (1 Pet 1:25; cf. Is 40:6-8). He is "the living God," and his power is forever and ever (1 Pet 5:11).

*The God who creates.* Thoroughly in keeping with his Hebraic heritage, Peter affirms belief in God as Creator. This affirmation occurs in a passage exhorting believers, in the midst of suffering, to "entrust themselves to a faithful Creator" (1 Pet 4:19). In so doing, believers imitate their heavenly Father. As the great Creator, he made all things good (see Gen 1:10, 12, 18, 21, 25, 31); they, for their part, continue "to do good" (1 Pet 4:19). And this is hardly an onerous or unreasonable task because "[they] have tasted that the Lord is good" (1 Pet 2:3).

*The God of glory.* It is assumed without argument that God alone is the proper object of worship and devotion. Not surprisingly, Peter includes "lawless idolatry" in a short vice list (1 Pet 4:3). He also sketches a picture of the church as a dynamic "spiritual house," that is, a temple composed of a "holy priesthood" who "offer spiritual sacrifices acceptable to God through Jesus Christ" (1 Pet 2:5). As priests, Christians have the high calling to "proclaim the mighty acts of him who called [them] out of darkness into his marvelous light" (1 Pet 2:9). The holiness of God serves as a basic paradigm for behavior: "as he who called you is holy, be holy yourselves in all your conduct; for it is written, 'You shall be holy, for I am holy'" (1 Pet 1:15-16 quoting Lev 11:44-45; 19:2; 20:7). For the Christian, all of life is lived "in God's sight" (1 Pet 3:4), and thus "in reverent fear" (1 Pet 1:17). The highest calling of each believer is to "glorify God" (1 Pet 2:12).

*The God who reveals himself as a complex unity.* An important theological question arises in connection with the nature of God. The salutation immediately confronts us with language that sounds trinitarian. Peter places side by side God the Father, the Spirit and Jesus Christ (1 Pet 1:2). Are we to assume that he already grasps the doctrine of the Trinity, even if not couched in the precise trinitarian phrasing of Nicea and Chalcedon? Only the most hidebound traditionalist would hazard as much. We are better advised to acknowledge development in

Christian doctrine and not read later formulations into the NT. Having said that, however, I still think it is important to emphasize that Peter's diction represents a significant advance beyond his Judaic heritage. His thought, along with that of Paul, John and Hebrews, represents "one giant leap for mankind."[47] Peter's thought contains the rudiments of later trinitarian faith, though lacking its precise formulations.[48] What it does provide is a functional understanding of these three persons who sit comfortably alongside each other. Each has a distinctive role in redemptive history, although a certain priority is accorded God the Father.[49] No more can be confidently stated, but no less should be. Monotheism is not abandoned; it is modified.[50] Our next chapter investigates how Jesus fits into this modified monotheism.

## Questions For Discussion

1. What is your assessment of the arguments for and against Petrine authorship of 1 Peter?
2. How important is the question of genuineness?
3. Discuss whether 1 Peter fits the genre of letter.

---

[47]I borrow Neil Armstrong's famous words after he stepped off the ladder of the Apollo lunar module and placed his left boot on the surface of the moon, the first human being to do so.

[48]Green strikes a nice balance in this regard:

> Though it would be a mistake to suggest that, writing in the first century, Peter embraced the Trinitarian formulations to be generated in subsequent centuries, we can nevertheless see both how Peter anticipates those formulations and how Peter's theology is hospitable to a reading that takes its point of departure from the ecumenical creeds. That is, far from obscuring our understanding of 1 Peter, the classical theological tradition helps us to identify the relations of Father, Christ, and Spirit, which otherwise might have escaped our attention. (*1 Peter*, p. 207)

Ladd stated it this way: "Peter's concept of God contains the raw materials of trinitarian theology, but his expression is altogether practical rather than theoretical." See George Eldon Ladd, *A Theology of the New Testament* (ed. Donald A. Hagner; rev. ed.; Grand Rapids: Eerdmans, 1993), p. 644.

[49]I concede that Pauline and Johannine Christology is "higher" than that of 1 Peter. But one should not make more of this than is warranted given the circumstantial nature of the evidence. If we had a larger Petrine corpus, perhaps we would be in a better position to draw a firmer conclusion in this regard.

[50]See further L. W. Hurtado, *Lord Jesus Christ: Devotion to Jesus in Earliest Christianity* (Grand Rapids: Eerdmans, 2003); idem, *How on Earth Did Jesus Become a God? Historical Questions About Earliest Devotion to Jesus* (Grand Rapids: Eerdmans, 2005); and N. T. Wright, *Christian Origins and the Question of God*, vol, 3: *The Resurrection of the Son of God* (Minneapolis: Fortress, 2003).

4. Discuss the relationship of the implied author to the implied recipients of this letter.

5. What is the purpose of this letter, and what rhetorical strategy does the author adopt to achieve his aim?

6. How would you summarize the author's understanding of God as reflected in this pastoral letter?

7. Is the theology of 1 Peter trinitarian?

## For Further Study

### Commentaries

Achtemeier, Paul J. *1 Peter: A Commentary on First Peter*. Edited by Eldon J. Epp. Hermeneia. Minneapolis: Fortress, 1996.

Davids, Peter H. *The First Epistle of Peter*. NICNT. Grand Rapids: Eerdmans, 1990.

Elliott, J. H. *1 Peter: A New Translation with Introduction and Commentary*. AB 37B. New York: Doubleday, 2000.

Feldmeier, Reinhard. *The First Letter of Peter*. Translated by Peter H. Davids. Waco: Baylor University Press, 2008.

Green, Joel B. *1 Peter*. The Two Horizons New Testament Commentary. Grand Rapids: Eerdmans, 2007.

Grudem, Wayne A. *The First Epistle of Peter: An Introduction and Commentary*. TNTC 17. Grand Rapids: Eerdmans, 1988.

Jobes, Karen H. *1 Peter*. BECNT. Grand Rapids: Baker, 2005.

Kelly, J. N. D. *A Commentary on the Epistles of Peter and of Jude*. HNTC. New York: Harper, 1969.

Marshall, I. Howard. *1 Peter*. IVPNTC 17. Downers Grove, Ill.: InterVarsity Press, 1991.

Michaels, J. Ramsey. *1 Peter*. WBC 47. Waco: Word, 1988.

Selwyn, E. G. *The First Epistle of Saint Peter*. London: Macmillan, 1947.

Schreiner, Thomas R. *1, 2 Peter, Jude*. NAC 37. Nashville: Broadman & Holman, 2003.

### Biblical Theologies and Special Studies

Goppelt, Leonhard. *Theology of the New Testament*. Vol. 2: *The Variety and Unity of the Apostolic Witness to Christ*. Edited by Jürgen Roloff. Grand Rapids: Eerdmans, 1982.

Marshall, I. Howard. *New Testament Theology: Many Witnesses, One Gospel.* Downers Grove, Ill.: InterVarsity Press, 2004. Pp. 642-59.

Martin, Ralph P. *New Testament Foundations.* 2 vols. Grand Rapids: Eerdmans, 1978. 2:329-45.

Morris, Leon. *New Testament Theology.* Grand Rapids: Zondervan, 1986. Pp. 316-17.

Schreiner, Thomas R. *New Testament Theology: Magnifying God in Christ.* Grand Rapids: Baker, 2008. Pp. 154-56.

# 7

---

# PETER'S CHRISTOLOGY

LIKE THAT OF THE OTHER apostolic witnesses, Peter's portrait of
Christ is polychromatic; his canvas displays a diverse palette applied
with bold brushstrokes. Nonetheless, his perspective is sharply focused,
centering around the dominant feature of the epistle, namely, its emphasis on undeserved suffering. Just as the letter is intended for those
who are "reviled for the name of Christ" (1 Pet 4:14) and suffering because they bear this name (1 Pet 4:16), so also it showcases the sufferings of Christ; indeed, the shadow of the cross shapes its christological reflections. In Mark's Gospel, disciples are challenged to "take
up their cross and follow me" (Mk 8:34). In Peter's letter, believers are
exhorted, "since therefore Christ suffered in the flesh, *arm yourselves*
also with the same intention" (1 Pet 4:1, italics added). The paradoxical
nature of this militaristic exhortation recalls the apostle John's exquisite
use of paradox and irony in both his Gospel and the Apocalypse.[1]

Three great christological affirmations punctuate 1 Peter (1 Pet
1:18-21; 2:21-25; 3:18-22). Though each has its own distinctive content,
each focuses on the death of Christ on behalf of sinners. Here is the
primary quarry from which Peter's Christology may be mined. Before
looking at each in some detail, I draw attention to the conceptual similarities found in Pauline passages widely regarded as creedal or hymnic
(e.g., Phil 2:5-11; Col 1:15-20; 1 Tim 3:16). In other words, this ma-

---

[1]See further Larry R. Helyer, *The Witness of Jesus, Paul and John* (Downers Grove, Ill.: InterVarsity Press, 2008), pp. 326-32. Albrecht Oepke, "*hoplizō*," *TDNT* 5:295, says, "There is thus an
intentional element of paradox in the expression."

terial was, in all likelihood, already part of the catechetical and liturgical life of the church. The importance of this observation can scarcely be overemphasized: these confessions put us in touch with the earliest and formative stages of "the apostles' teaching" (Acts 2:42). The case for a very early high Christology is compelling.[2]

## JESUS CHRIST AS LAMB OF GOD

Peter's salutation already forces the reader to come to grips with the person and work of Jesus Christ. Believers have been chosen and destined for a specific purpose: "to be obedient to Jesus Christ and to be sprinkled with his blood" (1 Pet 1:2). There can be little doubt that Peter is recalling the narrative of Israel's covenant-making ceremony with Yahweh at Mount Sinai.[3] An essential part of the solemn ceremony involved a vow of obedience and a symbolic sprinkling with blood:

> Moses took half of the blood and put it in basins, and half of the blood he dashed against the altar. Then he took the book of the covenant, and read it in the hearing of the people; and they said, "All that the Lord has spoken we will do, and we will be obedient." Moses took the blood and dashed it on the people, and said, "See the blood of the covenant that the Lord has made with you in accordance with all these words." (Ex 24:6-8)

In the passage in Exodus, blood represents life taken by death. The Israelite cult (public worship practices) involved the offering of animal sacrifices as cleansing and restorative actions. The animals served as substitutes for guilty sinners. The malign effects of sin are covered by such ritual actions. The Lord accepts these rituals, when accompanied by sincere confession and repentance, as a means of maintaining fellowship with a sinful people.[4] The apostles, following the teaching of

---

[2]See, e.g., C. F. D. Moule, *The Origin of Christology* (Cambridge: Cambridge University Press, 1977), pp. 35-46 and esp. L. W. Hurtado, *Lord Jesus Christ: Devotion to Jesus in Earliest Christianity* (Grand Rapids: Eerdmans, 2003).

[3]On the meaning and importance of the Sinai covenant, see Larry R. Helyer, *Yesterday, Today and Forever: The Continuing Relevance of the Old Testament* (2nd ed.; Salem, Wis.: Sheffield, 2004), pp. 138-48.

[4]For more background on the meaning of sacrifice in the OT, see ibid., pp. 126-29.

the Master, now understand those ancient rituals as foreshadows and types of Christ's atoning death—in the words of the writer to the Hebrews, "sketches of the heavenly things" (Heb 9:23).

Thus Peter's use of this imagery indicates both continuity and discontinuity with the grand narrative of Israel. Christ continues the story of Israel in that he now offers, by his blood (i.e., death), a sacrifice that cleanses and restores guilty sinners. Believers who accept this sacrifice on their behalf take a vow of obedience and commit to their new Lord. Peter presupposes that Christians are brought into a new covenant relationship with Christ as Lord and thus have been "spiritually" sprinkled with Christ's blood.[5] As 1 Peter 3:18 makes clear, however, the death of Christ is discontinuous with Israel's sacrificial cult in that Christ offers himself as a sacrifice "once for all." The implication is clear: in terms of salvation history, Christ's death both culminates and terminates ancient Israel's sacrificial system.

Another way of stating this is to recognize that the death of Christ on behalf of his people constitutes a decisive, new moment in salvation history. It is a new exodus in which the people of God are once again rescued from bondage, only this time from bondage worse than the political, social and economic bondage of ancient Israel. The new Israel is delivered from sin, a force that enthralls and enslaves.

Another allusion to the exodus and its associated festival of Passover occurs in 1 Peter 1:19. In a section appealing to his readers to realize how incredibly blessed they are to be redeemed from their former way of life (1 Pet 1:18), Peter reminds them of the great cost involved in their redemption. It was "not with perishable things like silver and gold, but with the precious blood of Christ, like that of a lamb without defect or blemish." This alludes to the cultic requirements for the Passover lamb (Ex 12:5; cf. Lev 23:12) and the fulfillment of the Nazarite vows (Num 6:14). A lamb without blemish or spot was demanded. Peter understands these texts typologically, that is, as types of Christ; transposing ritual purity into the key of moral and ethical purity, he

---

[5]"The sprinkling with the blood of Christ is, so to speak, *the new covenant.*" Reinhard Feldmeier, *The First Letter of Peter* (trans. Peter H. Davids; Waco, Tex.: Baylor University Press, 2008), pp. 58-59, italics in original.

views Christ as fulfilling and transcending the OT requirements.[6] In his role as the Suffering Servant, Jesus "committed no sin, and no deceit was found in his mouth" (1 Pet 2:22 quoting Is 53:9). As pointed out earlier in our brief survey of Peter's life, one may also hear echoes of John the Baptist's testimony: "Here is the lamb of God who takes away the sin of the world!" (Jn 1:29), a testimony Andrew surely conveyed to his brother Peter (Jn 1:41). Later, at the Last Supper, Peter himself witnessed this sacred drama: Jesus took "a loaf of bread, and after blessing it he broke it, gave it to them, and said, 'Take; this is my body.' Then he took a cup, and after giving thanks he gave it to them, and all of them drank from it. He said to them, 'This is my blood of the covenant, which is poured out for many'" (Mt 26:26-28). The confession of Jesus as the sinless Lamb of God who takes away the sin of the world lies at the core of apostolic doctrine and runs like a scarlet thread through NT literature.

## JESUS CHRIST AS THE SUFFERING SERVANT

Peter also projects a portrait of Jesus through the lens of the Suffering Servant of Isaiah 52:13–53:12. This unique OT passage, depicting a righteous individual who suffers and dies on behalf of "us all" and the "many," provides both background and foreground for Peter's exhortation.[7] Obviously, Peter has pondered deeply the profound connection between the Suffering Servant of Isaiah and Jesus of Nazareth.[8] We may say, with a high degree of probability, that Peter did not discover

---

[6]"The mention of a lamb moves us into the imagery of sacrifice. Christ's death was both a ransom and a sacrifice, and everything that was foreshadowed in the sacrifices of old is fully brought to pass in Christ." Leon Morris, *New Testament Theology* (Grand Rapids: Zondervan, 1986), p. 318.

[7]According to J. H. Elliott, there are "at least eight citations of the OT (LXX) and from ten to twelve allusions." *1 Peter: A New Translation with Introduction and Commentary* (AB 37B; New York: Doubleday, 2000), p. 12. Of these, 1 Peter 2:25 is a citation of Isaiah 53:6 with an introductory formula (*gar*). The following are allusions: 1 Peter 2:22 (Is 53:9); 1 Peter 2:23 (Is 53:6, 12); 1 Peter 2:24d (Is 53:5); 1 Peter 2:25a (Is 53:6). Possible allusions include 1 Peter 1:19 (Is 53:7); 1 Peter 1:21 (Is 52:13); 1 Peter 3:18b (Is 53:11 LXX). In addition, Elliott lists Isaiah 52–53 as an incipient allusion ("OT reference dependent on an exegetical tradition for its recognition") lying behind 1 Peter 1:19 (pp. 13-14).

[8]"Without once identifying Jesus Christ as 'servant,' its Servant of God Christology, elaborated through use of the servant song in Is 53, is one of the most developed and moving expressions of this Christology in the early Church" (ibid., p. 151).

this linkage on his own. He, along with his fellow apostles, learned to read the OT at the feet of the Master. Jesus believed he was the Suffering Servant of Isaiah 53 and, consequently, so did his followers (see Acts 8:30-35).[9]

Peter's second christological passage (1 Pet 2:21-25) occurs in part two of his letter, signaled by the direct address, "beloved" (1 Pet 2:11; cf. 1 Pet 4:12), in which the focus falls on "the honorable behavior of this household of God in the larger society."[10] The institution of slavery and the patriarchal family placed certain demands and expectations on the various members of the Greco-Roman household. In this section, Peter adapts well-known Hellenistic household codes, outlining expected behavior, by reframing these cultural expectations in a Christian context. As a "chosen race, a royal priesthood, a holy nation, God's own people" (1 Pet 2:9), believers both respect and transcend the traditional expectations. Here is a new morality, unity and love far exceeding that of which paganism was capable. The motive force behind this new ethic is the death of Christ on behalf of his people.

In 1 Peter 2:18-20, Peter addresses a major social division and distinction within the empire (cf. Gal 3:17-29). In the capital city of Rome, estimates of slavery run as high as 400,000 out of a population of about 1,200,000. This was potentially the most volatile social issue early Christians faced. Slavery as a state institution drove the economy of the empire, and no literary evidence from the Roman era exists condemning slavery as morally wrong. What is the response of Christianity to this unjust and oppressive system? Even Christian sources, like 1 Peter, contain no direct condemnation. Rather than confront it directly, the apostle Peter, in agreement with apostolic protocol, lays out a Christian response. He urges deference not defiance, respect not revolution.

But why should Christian slaves acquiesce in this institutional evil? Peter prefaces his remarks with this general admonition: "For the Lord's sake accept the authority of *every human institution*, whether of

---

[9]At the same time, I think Karen H. Jobes is correct that "we are . . . indebted to the apostle Peter alone for his distinctive Christological use of the Suffering Servant passage to interpret the significance of the suffering and death of Jesus" (*1 Peter* [BECNT; Grand Rapids: Baker, 2005], p. 193).

[10]Elliott, *1 Peter*, p. 456.

the emperor as supreme, or of governors. . . . As servants of God, live as free people, yet do not use your freedom as a pretext for evil" (1 Pet 2:13-16, italics added). Notice how this recasts the way in which slavery is viewed from a Christian perspective: slaves discover true freedom in Christ, and paradoxically, Christian freed men and women find true freedom in being slaves of Christ. Furthermore, the NRSV rendering "accept the authority of" is better than "submit." As Joel Green suggests, *hypotassō* more likely conveys the meaning of "finding and occupying responsibly one's place in society, and not passive or unreflective subjection."[11]

The theological underpinning for Peter's counsel about slavery rests on the example of Christ's unjust suffering (1 Pet 2:21-25): Christ suffered as the uniquely sinless one. Here Peter directly quotes Isaiah 53:9 about the Suffering Servant: "He committed no sin, and no deceit was found in his mouth." And how did he, the "cornerstone, chosen and precious" (1 Pet 2:6), react to this unjust suffering? Alluding to Isaiah 53:7, Peter describes Jesus' response: "When he was abused, he did not return abuse; when he suffered, he did not threaten; but he entrusted himself to the one who judges justly" (1 Pet 2:23). In Peter's words, Christ left you "an example, so that you should follow in his steps" (1 Pet 2:21). It may also be that in the back of Peter's mind is a dominical saying: "Servants are not greater than their master. If they persecuted me, they will persecute you" (Jn 15:20; Mt 10:24-25). Be that as it may, the pattern for Christian slaves is clear: neither violent resistance nor a sullen, passive resistance is a Christian option. "Ironically, the suffering of Christ has become central to the Christology of the apostle who most strongly objected to Jesus' predictions of his death (Mt 16:21-23; Mk 8:31-33)."[12]

This may disappoint some modern Christian readers who tend to be impatient with social injustice, and rightly so. How can Peter be claimed as an inspired teacher of spiritual truth when he—and the apostle Paul for that matter (1 Cor 7:21-24; Col 3:22–4:1)—seem to lack moral courage? Instead of finding fault with the pragmatic approach employed

---

[11]Joel B. Green, *1 Peter* (Grand Rapids: Eerdmans, 2007), p. 79.
[12]Jobes, *1 Peter*, p. 192.

by the early Christian missionaries, one must first understand their situation and circumstances. Though aware of the injustice and oppressive nature of this dehumanizing institution ("if . . . you endure pain while suffering unjustly . . . if you endure [beating] when you do right and suffer for it" [1 Pet 2:19-20]), the apostles apparently reckoned that direct resistance would provoke massive retaliation and threaten the movement with destruction. Violent resistance was not an option for early Christianity. The short-term solution for Christian slaves lay in a profound recognition of their true freedom ("live as free people," 1 Pet 2:16) and a powerful witness to a transformed life. Doing the right thing and acceptance of the authority of masters, even "those who are harsh" (1 Pet 2:18), demonstrates something quite unheard of and accomplishes God's will by silencing "the ignorance of the foolish" (1 Pet 2:15).

The long-term answer to institutional slavery lay in a leavening process whereby the gospel message permeates society. Tragically, the abolition of slavery has been a very long, tortuous process, with some American Christians defending and even participating in slavery until after the American Civil War—and many are oblivious to its continued existence in many parts of the world today.[13] We have at our disposal today international human rights groups and declarations, resources, agencies and political clout whereby slavery can be aggressively combated. Desperately needed are people like a William Wilberforce who will doggedly persist in the eradication of human rights violations, sexual slave trafficking, and the like. For multitudes of contemporary Christians who find themselves enslaved, abandoned and beyond the reach of those concerned, the pattern of Christ's undeserved suffering remains a valid response and beckons them to trust in the one who judges justly (1 Pet 2:23).

Before leaving this passage, I draw attention to the explicit teaching on vicarious, substitutionary atonement. Once again drawing on the phrasing and imagery of the Suffering Servant, Peter affirms that

---

[13]For a brief survey of slavery and the Christian tradition, see Irving Hexham, "Slavery," *NDT*, pp. 643-45. J. A. Harrill, "Slavery," *DNTB*, pp. 1124-27, and S. S. Bartchy, "Slave, Slavery," *DLNTD*, pp. 1098-1102, also provide helpful, though somewhat differing, surveys of slavery as practiced in NT times in the Roman Empire.

Christ "himself bore our sins" (Is 53:4a, 12) and that it was precisely "by his wounds you have been healed" (Is 53:5d).[14] Peter's addition to the quotation from Isaiah 53:4, "in his body on the cross, so that, free from sins, we might live for righteousness" (1 Pet 2:24), more narrowly specifies where and how Jesus "bore our sins" and what it accomplished: His death on a Roman cross liberates believers from the reign of sin and inaugurates a new reign of righteousness (cf. Rom 6:5-14). Thus Jesus' death is not merely an instance of Roman injustice, even though Peter's readers were then experiencing a form of Roman injustice; nor is it primarily a pattern for Christian discipleship, though it entails that. Rather, the death of Christ is supremely a substitutionary sacrifice that makes possible a right relationship with God and with one's fellow human beings.[15] In short, the cross unlocks the meaning of righteousness. Among the various ways of proclaiming the death of Christ in the NT, the notion that Christ died in our place and as our substitute is a fundamental Christian truth that fundamentally alters one's view of reality.[16]

---

[14]Those who insist that physical healing is an entitlement based on Christ's sacrificial death appeal to this verse. But interpreted carefully in its context, it hardly guarantees that faith in Christ inevitably results in physical healing in this life. Jobes has correctly caught the meaning of the quotation from Isaiah 53:5: "The fatal, physical wounds of the Suffering Servant . . . heal fatal, spiritual wounds" (*1 Peter*, p. 198). Green notes that "were we to adopt a view of disease at home in the world of 1 Peter, we would recognize that the two images—from death to life, and healing—speak to the same reality: cleansing for holiness. This is because, both in antiquity and in much of the non-Western world today, healing refers to human recovery, to the restoration of health in all its respects, and, then, to patterns of health in which we are fully alive" (*1 Peter*, p. 90).

[15]I think Donald Guthrie captures the significance of Peter's prose: "The example of Christ is not regarded as an interpretation of his death, i.e. that people should see how he suffered and died and should regard this as a pattern for themselves. It is the reverse. Christ in his suffering becomes an example because he has first become a substitute. The linking of the ideas, moreover, shows that for Peter as for Paul, Christian ethics were firmly rooted in Christian doctrine" (*New Testament Theology* [Downers Grove, Ill.: InterVarsity Press, 1981], p. 474). See also I. Howard Marshall, *1 Peter* (IVPNTC 17; Downers Grove, Ill.: InterVarsity Press, 1991), pp. 91-95.

[16]Green speaks of a "sanctifying atonement" rather than a substitutionary atonement in which penal satisfaction is rendered. Indeed, he even says that "atonement is not something that happens outside a person but it his or her proceeding through death into life, a cleansing from sin that opens up new life" (*1 Peter*, p. 89). His Wesleyan perspective strikes a quite different note from that of the Calvinists Peter H. Davids, *The First Epistle of Peter* (NICNT; Grand Rapids: Eerdmans, 1990), p. 113; Wayne Grudem, *The First Epistle of Peter: An Introduction and Commentary* (Leicester: Inter-Varsity Press, 1988), pp. 131-34; and Thomas R. Schreiner, *1, 2 Peter, Jude* (NAC 37; Nashville: Broadman & Holman, 2003), pp. 145-47. Another Wesleyan,

The third christological passage (1 Pet 3:18-22) constitutes one of the most perplexing and debated passages in the book. Because of this, I devote a separate and following chapter to this challenging text. Before doing so, however, I draw attention to two more christological descriptions and a christological title in 1 Peter that deserve careful consideration.

## JESUS CHRIST THE CORNERSTONE

In 1 Peter 2:4-8, Peter both encourages and exhorts his readers by employing the striking metaphor of a great temple. Changing from a parental metaphor (1 Pet 2:2), Peter now likens believers to "living stones" who are steadily being incorporated into a growing "spiritual house" (1 Pet 2:5). I will return to this notion later, but for now, my focus lies on Peter's further elaboration of the temple's central feature, namely, "a living stone, though rejected by mortals yet chosen and precious in God's sight" (1 Pet 2:4). For Peter, the living stone is clearly Jesus Christ (1 Pet 2:5), who is the cornerstone (1 Pet 2:6). He supports this identification with three OT quotations (Is 28:16; Ps 117:22 [LXX]; Is 8:14), although he "creatively transposes them in light of the new reality inaugurated by Christ's resurrection."[17]

The metaphor of the stone is not a Petrine innovation. In fact, Second Temple Judaism already draws upon this OT motif in order to express its messianic expectations. The earliest instance comes from the LXX translation of Isaiah 28:16: "and he who believes *in him* [*ep' autō*] shall not be ashamed." The addition of the third person, masculine pronoun (not present in MT) "suggests a personal understanding."[18] *Targum Jonathan* on Isaiah 28:16 reads, "Behold, I will appoint in Zion a king, a strong king, powerful and terrible, whom I will uphold and

---

Ben Witherington III, says, "It cannot be stressed enough that Peter envisions the sacrifice of Christ as both substitutionary and penal in character" (*The Indelible Image.* vol. 1: *The Individual Witnesses* [Downers Grove, Ill.: InterVarsity Press, 2009], p. 345). See Henri A. G. Blocher, "Atonement," *DTIB*, pp. 72-76, for an insightful essay on the meaning of atonement.

[17]Jobes, *1 Peter*, p. 142. For a full discussion, see G. K. Beale and D. A. Carson, eds., *Commentary on the New Testament Use of the Old Testament* (Grand Rapids: Baker, 2007), pp. 1023-30, and Elliott, *1 Peter*, pp. 423-34.

[18]J. Jeremias, "*lithos*," *TDNT* 4:272.

strengthen."[19] Many other examples from rabbinic literature may be cited.[20] It is likely that the Jewish historian Flavius Josephus, a contemporary of the apostle Peter, alludes to the widespread view that the stone of Isaiah 28:16 was none other than the Messiah (*Ant.* 10.210). The Dead Sea Scrolls provide no instance in which the epithet is applied to the Messiah, but the Qumran Community, probably following the interpretation of its revered Teacher of Righteousness, did view itself as the stone mentioned in Psalm 118 (1QS VIII 7).[21]

The most likely source for Peter's understanding of the passages about the stone in the OT, however, is Jesus. In the triple tradition (Mk 12:10-12; Mt 21:42-46; Lk 20:17-19), Jesus applies the imagery in Psalm 118:22-23, Isaiah 8:14-15 and Isaiah 28:16 to himself. Peter thus learns it from the Master and appeals to it with great effect in his defense before the Jewish religious leaders in Jerusalem (Acts 4:8-12). And Peter is not alone in this regard. The apostle Paul directly quotes the passages from Isaiah in Romans 9:33 and alludes to Isaiah 28:16 in Ephesians 2:20, in both cases, with the same understanding as the apostle Peter that the stone is Christ. Evidently, there was a shared tradition in apostolic circles whereby the passages about the stone in the OT were linked with Jesus.

So what does it mean to call Jesus the cornerstone? The Greek word *akrogōniaion* most likely denotes "the foundation stone at its farthest (foremost) corner with which a building is begun—it firmly fixes its site and determines its direction."[22] Some argue that the word refers to the capstone of an arch or "the final stone in a building, probably set over a gate."[23] Others suggest that both meanings apply. But it is hard to imagine how one might stumble over a capstone.[24] To be sure, one might envision the arch collapsing and the capstone crashing down on

---

[19]For background on the Targums, see Craig A. Evans, *Noncanoncial Writings and New Testament Interpretation* (Peabody, Mass.: Hendrickson, 1992), pp. 97-113.

[20]Jeremias, "*lithos*," 4:272. To be sure, many of these citations are much later than the NT. Nonetheless, the tradition behind them probably goes back to the first Christian century.

[21]See Craig A. Evans, "Messiahs," *EDSS* 1:537-42.

[22]H. Krämer, "*gōnia*," *EDNT* 1:268.

[23]Joachim Jeremias, "*gōnia*," *TDNT* 1:791.

[24]As Carson observes, "it is difficult to imagine how a capstone could do that" (i.e., cause someone to stumble) (*New Testament Use*, p. 1028).

someone, but that is not the imagery Peter explicitly employs. To call Jesus the cornerstone means that he determines the orientation and direction of the church, the new covenant community. He is the completely indispensable "living stone" (1 Pet 2:4) without which the "living stones" (1 Pet 2:5) may not properly function. As Jesus told Peter, "on this rock I will build *my* church" (Mt 16:18, italics added). Catholics and Protestants may differ in their interpretation of what precisely "this rock" means, but they share a deep conviction that the church belongs to and is Christ living in his people (see Eph 5:30, 32).

But the cornerstone is also a stumbling stone, as foretold by Isaiah (Is 8:14-15). Those who reject Christ as the all-important cornerstone consign themselves to judgment, here depicted as stumbling or falling. In Isaiah's day both the civil and religious leaders of Judah and Jerusalem failed to trust in the Lord as a sanctuary and, in so rejecting him, stumbled and fell, failing to find true security. As a consequence, they experienced national judgment and devastation at the hands of Assyria. In Peter's day, the same essential error was being repeated: disobeying the word (1 Pet 2:8) about Christ the Lord, the living stone and cornerstone, is tantamount to stumbling and falling, that is, exclusion from the "spiritual house" composed of living stones. Indeed, in the imagery of Daniel 2:34-35, 44-45, they will be crushed by the stone not cut out by human hands.

The pastoral relevance of this citation of "stone passages" is apparent. "Even if Peter's readers find themselves alienated from their society and suffering a loss of status, Peter assures them that they have become part of a much grander and everlasting community."[25] The living one creates living ones who in turn participate in a life-giving ministry. And these living ones, living in troublous times (like their OT counterparts) "will not be put to shame" (1 Pet 2:6; cf. Ps 34:5).

But can the Anatolian believers be sure that Jesus is the cornerstone of God's spiritual building, that is, the only means of salvation? This is an acute question for the Anatolian believers be they Jewish or Gentile. The reality was that a majority of both Jews and Gentiles rejected the

---

[25]Jobes, *1 Peter*, p. 149.

gospel message. Why is this the case? Peter's citation of these passages provides "a convincing explanation as to why so few shared their belief that Jesus was the fulfillment of prophecy about the Messiah."[26] Each passage points to a critical moment in the history of Israel in which the nation (and, of course, its individual citizens) had to decide whether to trust in the Lord God of Israel or turn to other so-called gods, trusting in their own devices. In each case, an inspired spokesperson prophesies that most would fail to trust in the foundation stone laid in Zion, a tested stone, the chief cornerstone, a stone over which many stumble (Is 28:16; Ps 118:22; Is 8:14-15). Peter's readers should not be surprised or alarmed that, in their own day, the same results were unfolding; indeed, it is "destined" (1 Pet 2:8). Rather, they must remain committed to this enduring truth: "Christ is the only way of salvation; to reject him is to land oneself in ruin and destruction."[27]

Ironically, Peter himself is once called a "stumbling block" (*skandalon*) by the Master (Mt 16:23). On that occasion, Peter protests against Jesus' stunning announcement that "he must go to Jerusalem and undergo great suffering at the hands of the elders and chief priests and scribes, and be killed" (Mt 16:21). Peter now understands and wants his listeners to understand too. The death of the Messiah was necessary; it was destined (1 Pet 1:11). The fact is, however, that the suffering and death of Jesus on a Roman cross constitutes an inevitable scandal. In the words of the apostle Paul, "Christ crucified [is] a stumbling block to Jews and foolishness to Gentiles" (1 Cor 1:23). But, says Peter, for those who believe, he is "chosen and precious in God's sight" (1 Pet 2:4). Finally, it is not without pastoral relevance that the "the living stone" and the living stones" share in a Via Dolorosa experience. In Paul's words, "If we have died with him, we will also live with him; if we endure, we will also reign with him" (2 Tim 2:11).

## JESUS CHRIST AS SHEPHERD AND GUARDIAN

Another descriptive title for Christ in Peter's first epistle also has roots deep in the OT and in the ministry of Jesus. At the end of the second

---

[26]Marshall, *1 Peter*, p. 70.
[27]Ibid., p. 73.

christological passage, Peter portrays Christ as "the shepherd and guardian of your souls" (1 Pet 2:25). Then, as he concludes his epistle, Peter returns to this idea by describing Christ as "the chief shepherd" (1 Pet 5:4) under whom pastors serve their house churches, "the flock of God" (1 Pet 5:2).

"Shepherd" is a common ancient Near Eastern royal title and appears in Hebrew traditions going back to Israel's premonarchic days. It is a fitting description for the type of ruler the people of God should elevate to this important post (Num 27:17). To an agrarian and pastoral people, the metaphor of the shepherd conveys positive connotations; in fact, it is frequently applied to the God of Israel (Gen 48:15, 49:24; Ps 28:9; 80:1; Is 40:11; Jer 31:10; Ezek 34:16). Foreign rulers could also be described as shepherds (Nah 3:18), and the Lord even acknowledges the pagan king Cyrus as "my shepherd" because Cyrus accomplishes the Lord's will, even if unknowingly (Is 44:28). Kings of Israel were expected to rule over their people like shepherds (2 Sam 7:7). A shepherd lives with his sheep, leads and cares for them in spite of adverse circumstances and even lays his life on the line in defense of them against predators. The matchless cadences of Psalm 23 readily come to mind. One recalls the meteoric rise to fame of the Judean shepherd boy who courageously confronted lions and bears and the giant Goliath. Eventually, all the tribes of Israel come to David and reaffirm the Lord's special commission to him: "It is you who shall be shepherd of my people Israel, you who shall be ruler over Israel" (2 Sam 5:2). Later, the Lord, through the prophet Nathan, reminds David of his sacred charge "to shepherd my people Israel" (2 Sam 7:7). In his day, Ezekiel laments the unworthy shepherds of Israel who were interested only in their own gain and glory (Ezek 34:1-6). For this they stand accountable and condemned (Ezek 34:7-10). Zechariah likewise excoriates worthless shepherds (Zech 10:2; 11:16-17). But in contrast to these hirelings, Ezekiel foresees a day in which the Lord himself will gather his scattered sheep Israel and personally lead and judge them (Ezek 34:11-22). He will also raise up a true and faithful shepherd, "my servant David" (Ezek 34:23), apparently referring to a Davidic descendant, the Messiah. This dovetails with Micah's prophecy, which proclaims that from Bethlehem comes a ruler who "shall stand and feed his flock in the strength of the Lord" (Mic 5:4). This repository of shepherd imagery contributes to an emerging messianic hope in Israel. During Second Temple times, the expectation of a messianic shepherd-king, who would faithfully lead Israel in the coming days, continues to find expression. In a stirring passage describing the future Messiah, the anonymous author of *Psalms of Solomon* writes, "Then who will succeed against him, mighty in his actions and strong in the fear of God? Faithfully and righteously shepherding the Lord's flock, he will not let any of them stumble in their pasture" (*Pss. Sol.* 17:39-40).[28]

Building on this tradition, Jesus brings this theme to its fulfillment. Dramatically, after celebrating the Last Supper with his disciples, Jesus identifies himself with the shepherd spoken of by Zechariah the prophet: "Awake, O sword, against my shepherd, against the man who is my associate, says the Lord of hosts. Strike the shepherd, that the sheep may be scattered" (Zech 13:7; Mk 14:27 par. Mt 26:31). Shortly thereafter, the eleven disciples, stunned and scared by Jesus' arrest in the Garden of Gethsemane, desert him and flee (Mk 14:43-50; Mt 26:47-56). Both Mark and Matthew record an earlier moment in Jesus' ministry when he feels great compassion for the large crowds that follow him, "because they were like sheep without a shepherd" (Mk 6:34; Mt 9:36). Matthew, in keeping with his purpose of portraying Jesus as the rightful heir to David's throne, narrates an episode in which Herod the Great inquires of the chief priests and scribes where the Messiah was to be born. Employing his characteristic formula of fulfillment from prophecy, Matthew has the authorities cite in full Micah 5:2 about the future ruler who is to shepherd Israel.

The Gospel of John shares Peter's shepherd Christology in which Jesus is portrayed as the good shepherd who "lays down his life for the sheep" (Jn 10:11, 15, 17-18). In stark contrast, the religious leaders are depicted as thieves and faithless, hired hands reminiscent of Ezekiel 34:1-10 (Jn 10:11-13). Furthermore, the entire Gospel of John is structured around the motif of the Passover Lamb. At the outset of the

---

[28]Translation by R. B. Wright, *OTP* 2:668.

Gospel, John the Baptist draws attention to Jesus "the Lamb of God who takes away the sin of the world!" (Jn 1:29; cf. Jn 1:36) and, at the cross, the Evangelist informs the reader that none of Jesus' bones were broken, in keeping with the ritual requirements for the Passover Lamb (Jn 19:36). And then, as already discussed in connection with the life of Peter, John's Gospel concludes with Jesus' threefold commission to Peter: "Feed my lambs . . . tend my sheep . . . feed my sheep" (Jn 21:15-17). The analogy of shepherd and sheep left a deep impression on the heart and mind of Peter.

The context of Peter's first appropriation of this imagery is within the household code section of the letter (1 Pet 2:13–3:12).[29] Peter reinforces his admonition to slaves by incorporating his second christological confession. He concludes with a poignant and comforting reminder: "For you were going astray like sheep, but now you have returned to the shepherd and guardian of your souls" (1 Pet 2:25). The terms "shepherd" and "guardian" appropriately depict the care, affection, oversight and leadership exercised by Christ on behalf of his "sheep." "Guardian" is literally "overseer" (*episkopos*). Leon Morris observes that this word later designates the church office of bishop, but "it is probably a little too early for us to understand it in this sense."[30]

The second reference to the shepherd metaphor occurs near the end of Peter's letter, where he exhorts fellow elders to carry out their responsibilities diligently, willingly, eagerly and worthily, as befitting "examples to the flock" (1 Pet 5:3). Especially deplorable for elders is serving "for sordid gain," a phrase recalling Ezekiel's denunciation of unworthy shepherds in his day. Then he mentions the ultimate motive for faithfully performing their duties: "And when the chief shepherd appears, you will win the crown of glory that never fades away" (1 Pet 5:4). Of particular concern to Peter is the danger of elders or overseers lording it over members in the flock (1 Pet 5:3). He thus reminds them of their accountability to "the chief shepherd," the only one who is truly

---

[29]For background on household codes, see P. H. Towner, "Household Codes," *DLNTD*, pp. 513-20.

[30]Morris, *New Testament Theology*, p. 317. See also J. Rhode, *"episkopos," EDNT* 1:35-36, for references to the usage of the term in Greek society and especially in Qumran where its Hebrew equivalent is used for leaders in that community.

Lord. One also thinks here of Paul's extended warning about the quality of one's work being tested when Christ returns (1 Cor 3:10-15). There the danger was that if one's work amounted to wood, hay or straw, it would be burned and the worker would suffer loss on the day of judgment. Peter prefers to admonish by urging the elders to serve with their eyes on the prize, the crown of glory, bestowed on those who pattern their lives after Christ. It is not without interest that Peter begins this section by mentioning "the sufferings of Christ" (1 Pet 5:1). As we have seen, this motif lies just below or on the surface of Peter's parenesis throughout the letter. Christian ministry must always be exercised in the shadow of the Cross.

## JESUS THE CHRIST

In addition to descriptive titles, Peter also employs the title "Christ" in reference to Jesus. Many modern readers assume that "Christ" is part of Jesus' personal name when in fact it is a title carrying a rich history and tradition. *Christos* in Greek translates *mashiaḥ* in Hebrew, meaning "one who is anointed with oil." In the OT, priests, kings and sometimes prophets were anointed with oil on their installation. Anointing with oil conveys a sacramental meaning, namely, a setting apart and consecration to a particular task and calling. The action symbolizes a special enabling by the Spirit of God to perform the task entrusted.

The messianic idea in Israel springs from the notion of kingship. Samuel anointed the first two kings of Israel, Saul and David. In both instances the Spirit of God came on them and enabled them to lead Israel at critical moments in the national history. Tragically, Saul disobeyed and the Spirit of God departed from him. Consequently, he lost his life, kingdom and dynasty. But to David, "the man after God's heart," the Lord promised never to take away his Spirit; indeed, the Lord promised that David's throne and kingdom would never cease (2 Sam 7:16). This Davidic promise and covenant is picked up by the prophets Amos (Amos 9:15), Isaiah (Is 7; 9; 11; 32), Jeremiah (Jer 31) and Ezekiel (Ezek 34) and provided hope during hard times in the history of Israel. The hope of a great Davidic king who would someday—in the great "Day of the Lord"—reign in righteousness and peace sustained the people of Israel throughout the dark night of exile and beyond.[31]

This expectation of a future Davidic king who restores and reigns over Israel becomes a fixed feature of Second Temple Judaism (see *Pss. Sol.* 18-19). Accordingly, the NT places considerable emphasis on this theme and identifies Jesus of Nazareth as the fulfillment of this expectation. The title "Christ" is thus appended to Jesus' name in a titular sense: Jesus the Messiah. In time, the OT background of this title fades and Gentile Christians, who make up the majority of believers, view it simply as part of his name. One finds in the NT various ways of expressing Jesus' messianic status such as "the Christ," "Jesus Christ," "Christ Jesus," "Christ the Lord," "the Lord's Christ" or the full title "the Lord Jesus Christ." However, the Jewish Christian authors of the NT never lose sight of its OT roots and connotations. In fact, there are a number of passages where *christos* would better be translated as "Messiah," and 1 Peter is a good case in point (see also Mt 1:16; 2:4; 16:16, 20; 26:23; Rom 9:5 et al.).

Here is a breakdown of Peter's use of this title:

**Table 7.1.**

| Compound title | Substantive + title | Substantive + compound title | Absolute use of title | Preposition + title |
|---|---|---|---|---|
| Jesus Christ<br>Lord Jesus Christ<br>(1 Pet 1:1, 2, 3, 7, 13; 2:5; 3:21; 4:11) | Spirit of Christ<br>Sufferings of Christ (2 times)<br>Blood of Christ (2 times)<br>Name of Christ (1 Pet 1:11, 19; 4:13, 14) | Resurrection of Jesus Christ (1 Pet 3:21) | Christ (1 Pet 2:21; 3:15, 18; 4:1) | In Christ (2 times)<br>(1 Pet 3:16; 5:10, 14) |

Several observations are pertinent.

- Peter shows a preference for a compound title bringing together the essential truths about Jesus' identity. Jesus of Nazareth is the promised messiah ("Christ") of Israel's prophetic hope, to be sure, but he is much more than that. By appending the title "Lord," Peter transcends a strictly nationalistic conception of the Messiah, since we are now talking about a person who is identified as none other than the sovereign Lord of all creation and history. The majestic

---

[31]See further Helyer, *Yesterday, Today and Forever*, pp. 175-78, 182-86, 302-4.

strains of Isaiah 40–50 ring in our ears as we contemplate this compound title, "the Lord Jesus Christ." In this connection, it is worth noting that the imperial cult of Rome made pretentious claims about Caesar being "Lord" (*kyrios*). In reality, how hollow this sounds in comparison with the claims for Jesus the Messiah. With the apostle Paul, Peter affirms that "Jesus is Lord" (cf. Rom 10:9).

- Peter's use of a substantive plus the title "Christ" is especially noteworthy because of its pastoral relevance. The two references each to the "blood of Christ" and the "sufferings of Christ" draw attention to the burden of Peter's parenesis. The Anatolian believers are urged to withstand the pressures exerted against them by their pagan neighbors, and critical for this resolve is the recognition that Christ's destined but undeserved suffering on their behalf provides both a spiritual power and pattern for their own undeserved sufferings. In this regard, they should count themselves blessed if they are persecuted for "bearing" the name of Christ. Peter's one reference to "the resurrection of Jesus Christ" draws attention to the hope that sustains believers whose future may well involve more than ostracism and verbal abuse; indeed, it may be that a veritable "fiery ordeal" looms on the horizon. Peter's one reference to "the spirit of Christ" draws attention to the actual involvement of Christ in redemptive history. The OT prophets were guided in their reception and communication of divinely revealed truth by none other than the same person who would play such a central role in the salvation about which they spoke.

- One should also note the two occurrences of the "in Christ" formula, so familiar from Paul's letters, especially the prison letters (Ephesians, Philippians and Colossians). The notion of corporate solidarity of all believers in Christ is part of a shared conviction among the apostles. Paul emphasizes it most, but he is not alone in this understanding.

- Finally, Peter four times uses "Christ" absolutely. These instances reflect the messianic hope of Second Temple Judaism and are better translated into English as "Messiah." Three of the four occurrences connect Messiah with his vicarious sufferings (1 Pet 2:21; 3:18; 4:1) in which he fulfills the mission of the Suffering Servant of Isaiah. The one exception occurs in a passage in which believers are urged to give a reason for the hope that is in them (1 Pet 3:15). They are to confess that "the Messiah" is also Lord. Here we are brought to that most fundamental affirmation about Jesus that differentiates believer from nonbeliever: "Jesus is Lord" (cf. Rom 10:9; 1 Cor 12:3; Phil 2:11). This is also the great divide that separates Judaism from Christianity.

In short, Peter's relatively short pastoral letter surprises us with its dense christological substructure. But even more surprising is the famous christological passage in 1 Peter 3:18-22 to which we now turn. All our exegetical and hermeneutical skills will be truly tested in this text.

## Questions for Discussion

1. How does 1 Peter demonstrate that its theology is circumstantial in nature?

2. What relevance does the portrayal of Jesus as sacrificial lamb have to the life setting of this letter?

3. What are the probable sources of Peter's christological affirmations in this letter, and what significance should be attached to our findings?

4. What is your reaction to the way Peter handles the issue of slavery in this letter?

5. Discuss whether Peter believes in Jesus' death as vicarious and substitutionary.

6. What is the theological and practical significance of Peter's portrayal of Jesus as the cornerstone?

7. How does the description of Jesus as shepherd relate to the Gospel of John, and what does that imply?

8. What insights emerge when one studies the titles of Christ in 1 Peter?

## For Further Study

For commentaries, see the bibliography following the preceding chapter.

### Special Studies and Biblical Theologies

Guthrie, Donald. *New Testament Theology*. Downers Grove, Ill.: InterVarsity Press, 1981.

Hurtado, L. W. *Lord Jesus Christ: Devotion to Jesus in Earliest Christianity*. Grand Rapids: Eerdmans, 2003.

Ladd, George Eldon. *A Theology of the New Testament*. Edited and revised by Donald A. Hagner. Grand Rapids: Eerdmans, 1993. Pp. 640-48.

Marshall, I. Howard. *New Testament Theology: Many Witnesses, One Gospel*. Downers Grove, Ill.: InterVarsity Press, 2004. Pp. 648-59.

Matera, Frank J. *New Testament Theology: Exploring Diversity and Unity*. Louisville: Westminster, 2007. Pp. 379-83.

Morris, Leon. *New Testament Theology*. Grand Rapids: Zondervan, 1986. Pp. 316-21.

Moule, C. F. D. *The Origin of Christology*. Cambridge: Cambridge University Press, 1977.

Schreiner, Thomas R. *New Testament Theology: Magnifying God in Christ*. Grand Rapids: Baker, 2008. Pp. 403-6.

Thielman, Frank. *Theology of the New Testament: A Canonical and Synthetic Approach*. Grand Rapids: Zondervan, 2005. Pp. 569-84.

Witherington, Ben, III. *The Indelible Image: The Theological and Ethical Thought World of the New Testament*. Vol. 1: *The Individual Witnesses*. Downers Grove, Ill.: InterVarsity Press, 2009. Pp. 330-47.

# 8

---

# CHRIST AND THE SPIRITS,
# CHRIST AND THE HOLY SPIRIT

◊

EMPLOYING LANGUAGE, IMAGERY and narrative movement recalling the Suffering Servant of Isaiah 52–53 and combining with it the triumphant "lord" of Psalm 110:1, who is invited to sit at the right hand of the "Lord," 1 Peter 3:18-22 vividly depicts Christ's redemptive work, beginning at the cross and culminating with his exaltation at the right hand of God. In this regard, Philippians 2:5-11 offers a striking parallel. When the essential actions of the Pauline and Petrine passages are enumerated, the outline of what later becomes the Apostles' Creed emerges. There is a scholarly consensus that an early Christian creedal formulation lies behind 1 Peter 3:18-22.

## INTERPRETATION OF 1 PETER 3:18-22

Beyond this, the scholarly consensus evaporates and the unsuspecting reader enters a labyrinth of exegetical and theological options.[1] Perhaps it would be most helpful at this point to list the crucial exegetical questions. These may be narrowed down to the following:[2]

---

[1]"This complex passage has long challenged scholars and poses a host of questions concerning the syntax and structure of these verses, their sources and conceptual background, their coherence and meanings, their relations to 4:1-6, their rhetorical function, and their relation to the concept of Christ's 'descent into hell,' despite the fact that neither 'descent' nor 'hell is mentioned here" (J. H. Elliott, *1 Peter: A New Translation with Introduction and Commentary* [AB 37B; New York: Doubleday, 2000], p. 638). W. J. Dalton calls this "a notoriously difficult text" (*Christ's Proclamation to the Spirits: A Study of 1 Peter 3:18–4:6* [Rome: Pontifical Biblical Institute, 1965], p. 6).

[2]Although it is theoretically possible that the various permutations could total as many as 180

- Where did Christ go after having been made alive "in the Spirit (or spirit)"?

- When did Christ go there?

- Who are "the spirits in prison"?

- What was the nature of the proclamation to them?

In the welter of exegetical options, three leading interpretations have emerged.

1. Christ preached (in the spiritual realm or by the Holy Spirit) through Noah to the pre-flood generation. This preaching resulted in only eight souls being saved; the others were condemned.

2. Christ preached in the spiritual realm to the souls of deceased humans. Three distinct options may be entertained in this regard.

- The souls in question were only those who perished during the great flood of Noah.

- The souls consisted of all those who died before the incarnation of Christ.

- All souls without exception have a postmortem opportunity to respond to the gospel.

In the first two options, the preaching occurred during the interval between Christ's crucifixion and his resurrection. Some hold to the possibility of postmortem conversion; others that this preaching was a proclamation of impending judgment. Often coupled with the second interpretation is the notion that subsequently Christ transferred righteous believers from Hades to the third heaven (paradise) when he ascended to the right hand of God (the so-called harrowing of hell).

3. Christ proclaimed his victory over the rebellious spirits (fallen angels and/or their demonic offspring) who were imprisoned as a consequence of their sin (Gen 6).[3] This preaching, which was not an invi-

---

(Millard Erickson, "Is There Opportunity for Salvation After Death?" *BSac* 152 (1995): 131-44), in actuality, there are not quite this many options available! Gerhard Friedrich, "*kēryssō*," *TDNT* 3:707, lists five exegetical questions, including Who is the preacher? and What is meant by *phylakē* ("prison")? These are, however, subsumed in the four questions listed above, for which I am indebted to Karen H. Jobes, *1 Peter* (BECNT; Grand Rapids: Baker, 2005), p. 237.
[3] J. Ramsey Michaels argues that the "spirits in prison" are not strictly speaking the fallen angels

tation to be saved, announced their certain, final judgment and took place during his ascension.

A detailed commentary on this passage would unnecessarily lengthen the discussion, so I simply indicate my preference for the third interpretation and offer the following arguments in support and objections to the alternative positions.[4]

Exegetes must account for the two dative phrases *sarki* ("in the flesh," NRSV) and *pneumati* ("in the spirit," NRSV). Many interpreters insist that these datives must be parallel to one another in usage since they occur in the same sentence. If this is correct, one has two basic options:

1.  They are local datives juxtaposing two spheres of existence (i.e., the visible, physical realm over against the invisible, spiritual realm).

2.  They are instrumental datives of agency (i.e., *by* human beings and *by* the Holy Spirit). On this understanding, *pneumati* refers not to Christ's spirit but to the Holy Spirit.

Neither option is without problems. As to the first, it is a bit difficult to understand how Christ could be put to death in his body, the realm of the physical, while also being made alive in the spiritual realm. Doesn't this imply that his spirit also died on the cross? While it is conceivable Christ suffered spiritual death ("My God, my God, why have you forsaken me?" [Mk 15:34]) and thus had to be reborn spiritually, this seems farfetched and at odds with the NT insistence that Christ was the sinless one (see 1 Pet 1:19; 2:22; 2 Cor 5:21; Heb 4:15; 1 Jn 3:5). Consequently, one must either tweak the meaning of these key nouns or not insist on the parallelism of the two datives.

But perhaps even more decisively, is a local meaning in harmony

---

of Genesis 6 but their demonic offspring: "The 'spirits in refuge' are neither the souls of those who died in the flood nor precisely the angels whose sin brought the flood on the earth, but rather the 'evil spirits' who came from the angels—probably identified in Peter's mind with the 'evil' or 'unclean' spirits of the Gospel tradition. If the authors of *1 Enoch* saw the 'evil spirits' of their day as offspring of the angelic 'watchers,' there is no reason why Peter may not have viewed the 'unclean spirits' of his own Christian tradition in a similar light" (*1 Peter* [WBC 47; Waco, Tex.: Word, 1988], p. 208).

[4]For a detailed exegetical and theological defense of this view, see Thomas R. Schreiner, *1, 2 Peter, Jude* (NAC 37; Nashville: Broadman & Holman, 2003), pp. 179-98.

with the larger context of the passage? In other words, is this passage really about what Christ supposedly did in the spiritual realm of the dead after his death on the cross? Doesn't the accent fall rather on his triumphant resurrection by the power of the Holy Spirit and his exaltation to the right hand of God (1 Pet 3:21-22)?

The second option requires that the first dative, like the second, signify agency, in which case it refers to human beings who put Christ to death on the cross. The problem here is that equating the phrase "by flesh" with "by human beings" is forced and found nowhere else in the NT.

The way out of the impasse is to recognize that the two datives are not parallel in usage. The first dative, *sarki*, is a local dative ("in the sphere of the flesh"), but the second dative, *pneumati*, is probably a dative of agency, meaning "by the Holy Spirit."[5] Here is the 1984 version of the NIV's rendering of 1 Peter 3:18d-19: "He was put to death *in the body* but made alive *by the Spirit*, through whom also he went and preached to the spirits in prison" (italics added). This seems to me an improvement on the NRSV.

Peter's description of Christ's saving work, in addition to its clear indebtedness to the OT, displays striking parallels to the pseudepigraphal work *1 Enoch* 6-22. The latter is a pre-Christian account of the antediluvian patriarch Enoch, who was commissioned to go and proclaim to the "Watchers" (the angels who sinned [Gen 6]) God's irreversible sentence of final judgment. Although the passage in 1 Peter does not mention Enoch,[6] there are several salient points of similarity

---

[5]"It is often objected that the Holy Spirit cannot be in view because the two datives of v 18 (*sarki*, *pneumati*) would then have a different syntactical force (sphere, means). But if 1 Pet 3:18 is a hymnic or liturgical fragment, this can be no objection because of 'poetic license.' Poetry is replete with examples of grammatical and lexical license, not the least of which is the use of the same morpho-syntactic categories, in parallel lines, with different senses (note e.g., the dat. expressions in 1 Tim 3:16)." Daniel B. Wallace, *Greek Grammar Beyond the Basics* (Grand Rapids: Zondervan, 1996), p. 343, n. 76.

[6]A few scholars have offered an ingenious emendation at 1 Peter 3:19 whereby the proper name Enoch is inserted into the phrase so that it reads: "in which also Enoch." According to them, the proper name Enoch fell out of the text. But as Metzger points out, this "breaks the continuity of the argument by introducing an abrupt and unexpected change of subject from that of ver. 18." Bruce M. Metzger, *A Textual Commentary on the Greek New Testament* (New York: United Bible Societies, 1971), p. 693.

to *1 Enoch*,[7] not least of which is the importance of Noah and the flood
story in *1 Enoch* and in 1 Peter 3:20-21 (see also 2 Pet 2:5). Evidence
exists demonstrating a widespread knowledge of various flood stories
in Anatolia, well before and during the Christian era.[8] The point is that
even Gentile believers would possess some background by which to
make sense of Peter's exposition. All things considered, I think it
probable that Peter has drawn on the Enoch tradition in order to emphasize the victory of Christ over the "angels, authorities, and powers"
(1 Pet 3:22).

Reading the text in terms of a descent into hell (*descendus ad inferos*),
as enshrined in the Apostles' Creed, encounters considerable difficulty.
Not least is the observation that the notion of a descent is not unam-
biguously stated in this passage.[9] In only one other place in the NT does
the verb *poreuomai* ("go, journey, conduct one's life") perhaps mean "de-
scend," and that is in Acts 1:25: "Judas turned aside to go to his own
place." But even this reference is debatable. However, the verb is used
figuratively of Jesus' going to his Father in heaven (Jn 14:12, 28; 16:28).
In my opinion, the context of our passage in 1 Peter 3 implies not a descent to hell but an ascent to the right hand of the Father (1 Pet 3:22). In
this regard, it lines up with other NT creedal or confessional statements
(Eph 1:20-21; 2:6; 4:9-10; Phil 2:9-10) and with a widespread tradition
in Second Temple Judaism of heavenly journeys, as exemplified in
*1 Enoch* in particular. The early church fathers who advocate the view of
descent are trying to answer two questions: What about the righteous
who never heard the gospel before the advent of Christ? What was
Christ doing during the interval between his death and resurrection?
Their solution, however, invites more problems than it solves.[10]

---

[7]For a thorough listing and analysis of these similarities, see Elliott, *1 Peter*, 697-705. In Elliott's view, "This heavenly journey of Enoch and his announcement to the sinful angelic
spirits constitutes the closest analogy for the action of Christ as described here in 1 Peter and
in all likelihood provided the conceptual model for the Petrine author" (p. 654).

[8]See Jobes, *1 Peter*, pp. 251-52, for the evidence.

[9]Friedrich Hauck and Siegfried Schulz, "*poreuomai*," *TDNT* 6:577, admit that "the proper term
here is *katabainō*." Nonetheless, they argue that "a general examination of this difficult passage
justifies our referring it to the descent of Christ."

[10]For a sampling of the various opinions among the Fathers, see *James, 1-2 Peter, 1-3 John, Jude*
(ACCS 11; ed. Gerald Bray; Downers Grove, Ill.: InterVarsity Press, 2000), pp. 106-14.

The view that Christ preached through Noah to the pre-flood generation has notable advocates (Augustine[11] and Calvin among them) but in the end fails to account adequately for the context.[12] At face value, the text states that Christ personally made proclamation rather than through a proxy.[13] Furthermore, the flow of 1 Peter 3:18-22 seems to follow a chronological sequence of redemptive acts moving from crucifixion to exaltation. A digression describing what Christ did in the days of Noah interrupts this progression. Better to say that the digression identifies who the spirits in prison are and why they are there rather than narrating what Christ did (through Noah) before the flood. This view also has difficulty explaining why Peter singles out only Noah's generation for this proclamation. To reply that they serve as an example of the wickedest of sinners and thus witness to God's patience, grace and mercy in extending salvation to all seems arbitrary. As it stands, the text does not clearly state that the time of Christ's preaching to the spirits was the days of Noah.

The view that Christ preached the gospel to all the dead during the interval between the crucifixion and resurrection, thus offering them a postmortem opportunity to receive the gospel, appeals to a basic sense

---

[11]Though Augustine seems to have changed his mind later. See n. 14 below.

[12]Wayne Grudem, *The First Epistle of Peter* (TNTC; Grand Rapids: Eerdmans, 1988) and John Feinberg, "1 Peter 3:18-20, Ancient Mythology and the Intermediate State," *WTJ* 48 (1986): 303-36, are contemporary, evangelical scholars who defend this position.

[13]Grudem's concession, "Although it might appear on an initial reading that 'spirits in prison' must refer to those who were incarcerated at the time the preaching took place, this is not necessarily the case," is revealing (*First Epistle of Peter*, p. 209). In my opinion, his effort to demonstrate otherwise fails and is predicated on his refusal to accept *1 Enoch* as an important background source for Peter's thought in this passage. See especially his questionable argumentation in pp. 205-6, 211-12, 216-17, 220-23. His conclusion on p. 223, "A vast preponderance of biblical and extra-biblical literature seems to require the conclusion that they were not sinful angels but human beings who sinned while Noah was building the ark" is an example of overstatement. On the contrary, see Jobes's arguments and evidence for the importance of *1 Enoch* for understanding this passage (*1 Peter*, pp. 242-51) and the impressive evidence marshaled by Elliott, *1 Peter*, pp. 697-710. Notice how much more balanced is Elliott's conclusion: "While the foregoing conclusions regarding the terms of 1 Peter are inferences based on their close similarity to concepts and themes of Israelite and Christian tradition, their likelihood is strengthened by their consistency with both the content and structure of the Petrine text as a whole (vv. 19-22), has no exact parallel in either Israelite or contemporary Christian sources, and represents an original contribution of the Petrine author" (p. 706).

of fairness.[14] However, does this open the door too wide in terms of the biblical message as a whole?[15] While I think we need to reconsider carefully "the wideness of God's mercy," this particular option seems to run against the grain of several undisputed passages (e.g., Lk 16:26; Heb 9:26-28; Mt 15:10-13).

***Christological affirmations of 1 Peter 3:18-22.*** After the exegetical dust settles, what theological truths emerge? Peter creatively melds OT and Second Temple Jewish traditions with Christian tradition in order to make a pastoral point: believers in Jesus must prepare heart and mind to endure, if God so wills, undeserved suffering (1 Pet 3:17). Their role model is none other than the righteous, innocent sufferer par excellence, Jesus Christ. In holding forth the pattern of Christ's life, a christological narrative unfolds in which the central saving acts of redemption are outlined:

- Christ died for our sins (1 Pet 3:18)

- (Christ was buried) (1 Pet 3:18d; not stated explicitly but implied)

- Christ was raised from the dead (1 Pet 3:18e, 21d)

- Christ proclaimed his victory over rebellious spirits (1 Pet 3:19a-20a)

- Christ ascended to heaven (1 Pet 3:22b)

- Christ was exalted to the right hand of God (1 Pet 3:22a)

---

[14]Augustine's comment on this passage strikes a chord with which many Christians resonate:

The question which you put to me about the spirits in hell is one which disturbs me profoundly. . . . What troubles me most is why only those who were imprisoned in the days of Noah should deserve this benefit. Think of all the others who have died since Noah's time and whom Jesus could have found in hell. The meaning must be that the ark of Noah is a picture of the church, and so those who were imprisoned in his days represent the entire human race. In hell Christ rebuked the wicked and consoled the good, so that some believed to their salvation and others disbelieved to their damnation." (*Letters* 164 cited in ACCS 11, p. 109)

Joel B. Green, *1 Peter* (Grand Rapids: Eerdmans, 2007), pp. 122, 133-34, holds to a postmortem opportunity to hear the gospel, as does Clark H. Pinnock, *A Wideness in God's Mercy: The Finality of Jesus Christ in a World of Religions* (Grand Rapids: Zondervan, 1992).

[15]Two important hermeneutical principles are the analogy of faith and the analogy of Scripture. This means that a particular text must be interpreted in agreement with the overall theological meaning of Scripture and that obscure passages are interpreted in light of clear ones, not vice versa. See further Henry M. Knapp, "Protestant Biblical Interpretation," *DTIB*, pp. 634-35. To be sure, one can abuse these principles and suppress difficult texts with one's received tradition.

- Christ was installed as Lord over all spiritual beings and forces (1 Pet 3:22c)

Peter's christological confession is not unique but shares common ground with confessional and creedal statements found in other portions of the NT, especially Paul's letters. This observation is not appreciated as much as it should be in modern NT studies where diversity tends to drown out unity.

1 Corinthians 15:1-5
- Christ died for our sins (1 Cor 15:3)
- He was buried (1 Cor 15:4)
- He was raised on the third day (1 Cor 15:4)
- He appeared to many (1 Cor 15:5-8)

Romans 8:34
- Christ Jesus died
- He was raised
- He is at the right hand of God
- He intercedes for us

Philippians 2:5-11
- Christ Jesus takes on human flesh (incarnation; Phil 2:6-7)
- He is crucified (Phil 2:8)
- He is exalted above every name (Phil 2:9-10)
- Jesus Christ receives homage from all created beings as Lord of all (Phil 2:9-10)

Colossians 2:13-20; 2:9-15; 3:1-4
- He rescues, transfers, redeems and reconciles his people (Col 2:13-14, 20)
- He is buried (Col 2:12)
- He is the firstborn from the dead (i.e., raised from the dead; Col 1:18; 2:12)
- He triumphs over the rulers and authorities (Col 2:15)
- He is exalted over all creation and seated at the right hand of God (Col 1:15, 18, 20; 2:10; 3:1)

Ephesians 1:20-22
- God raises Christ from the dead (Eph 1:20)
- God exalts him to his right hand (Eph 1:20)
- All creatures and creation made subject to Christ (Eph 1:21-22)

1 Timothy 3:16
- He is revealed in flesh (incarnation)
- He is vindicated in spirit (resurrection or proclamation to spirits in prison?)
- He is "taken up in glory" (ascension and exaltation)

Hebrews 1:1-3
- He makes purification for sins (Heb 1:3)
- He sits down at the right hand of God (Heb 1:3)
- He receives homage from the angels (Heb 1:4, 5-13)

Revelation 5:9-13
- The Lamb is slaughtered and ransoms people for God (Rev 5:9, 12)
- The Lamb is seated at the right hand of God (Rev 5:13)
- The Lamb receives worship and praise from all creatures and creation (Rev 5:9, 11, 13)

## PASTORAL APPLICATION

Peter's third christological passage, like the first two, functions pastorally: he is exhorting and encouraging his Christian readers to remain steadfast in their commitment to Christ in the face of severe persecution.[16] A practical rather than a theoretical function emerges from the implied narrative theology.

---

[16]Frank J. Matera nicely captures this point: "The Christology of 1 Peter is a Christology of suffering. . . . By focusing on the sufferings of Christ, 1 Peter shows the intimate relationship between Christology and the Christian life: the *past* suffering of Christ is the *present* condition of believers, while the *present* glory of Christ is the *future* glory of those who follow in the steps of the suffering Christ. While the Christology of 1 Peter may not be the most developed of the New Testament, it is among the most pastorally sensitive" (*New Testament Christology* [Louisville: Westminster John Knox, 1999], p. 184, italics in original).

1. Jesus Christ suffered and died as the innocent, righteous Lord. Paradoxically, his unjust death (from a human perspective) resulted in justice for all. Christians must be prepared to imitate their Lord by living righteously and, if need be, by suffering and dying for that very reason. There is no indication that martyrdom is efficacious in atoning for their own sins, much less the sins of others. Only the truly righteous one suffers vicariously. In harmony with apostolic teaching, Peter reminds his readers that Christ's suffering as the righteous one "on behalf of" (Gk *hyper*) the unrighteous was "once for all" (Gk *hapax*). He does, however, indicate that once a believer has died (lit., "suffered"), sin no longer exerts its malign influence (1 Pet 4:1).

2. Not to be overlooked in this section is the additional confession of Christ's exaltation at the right hand of God, thus advancing the christological formulation found in 1 Peter 2:21-25. The implication is clear: believers set their hope on personal, ultimate vindication, exaltation and glorification alongside the one who sits on the right hand. His destiny is theirs. This hope sustains them in the midst of their suffering.

3. The digression about Noah and baptism dovetails with Peter's pastoral concern as seen in the following points:

- Just as Noah and his family were a persecuted minority, so also are Peter's readers (1 Pet 3:12-14; 4:4, 12-13)

- Though not explicitly mentioned by Peter, his readers are aware of the tradition that Noah was a preacher of righteousness (2 Pet 2:5; cf. Heb 11:7).[17] For this he was reviled and rejected by his contemporaries. So too, Peter's readers are called to live righteous lives and "always be ready to make your defense to anyone who demands of you an accounting for the hope that is in you; yet do it with gentleness and reverence. Keep your conscience clear, so that, when you

---

[17]A point not explicitly made in Genesis 6–8. However, "the Dead Sea Scrolls illustrate almost every aspect of this postbiblical fascination with Noah and the Flood narrative" (John Reeves, "Noah," *EDSS* 2:613). Here is just one of many instances illustrating P. Enns's contention that "the NT's use of the OT is a phenomenon that cannot be treated in isolation from the hermeneutical milieu of Second Temple biblical interpretation" ("Biblical Interpretation, Jewish," *DNTB*, p. 165). See also Larry R. Helyer, "The Necessity, Problems and Promise of Second Temple Judaism for Discussions of New Testament Eschatology," *JETS* 47/4 (December 2004): 597-615.

are maligned, those who abuse you for your good conduct in Christ may be put to shame" (1 Pet 3:15-16).

- In Noah's day judgment was imminent; likewise, Peter reminds his readers that God's final judgment on the world is imminent (1 Pet 4:5, 7; cf. 2 Pet 3:10).

- In Noah's day, God waited patiently before executing judgment on that generation; likewise, in 2 Peter, the apostle emphasizes God's continuing patience before final judgment on the world begins (see 2 Pet 3:9-10).

- Of great importance, Peter draws attention to the fact that only eight people were saved through the ark from the great flood. Accordingly, believers should not despair because of their isolation and small numbers. They, too, shall certainly be saved (1 Pet 3:21) and share in the exaltation and triumph of Christ (1 Pet 3:22; 4:14; 5:10).

## THE HOLY SPIRIT: AGENT OF REVELATION AND REDEMPTION

Four verses refer to the work of the Spirit, dealing with revelation and redemption (1 Pet 1:2, 11-12; 4:14). In spite of this relative paucity, Peter makes some important affirmations about the Spirit, affirmations reflecting a common source in apostolic teaching.

1. Peter draws attention to the sanctifying work of the Spirit (1 Pet 1:2). The NRSV rendering "by the Spirit" rightly captures the sense of the Greek phrase *en pneumati* since the dative case is best taken as an instrumental dative connoting agency and "Spirit" is best capitalized, since it probably refers to the Holy Spirit, not the human spirit.[18] A quick perusal of Paul's letters immediately turns up several texts in which the Holy Spirit plays a key role in progressively producing holiness and Christ-like virtues in believers (Rom 1:4; 7:6; 8:2, 4-6, 9-16; 15:16; 1 Cor 6:19; 2 Cor 3:17-18; Gal 5:16-22; Eph 4:30; 5:18; 1 Thess 5:23). One of the Holy Spirit's prime responsibilities is to conform believers into the image of Christ (Col 3:10; cf. Rom 8:29). Leon Morris notes that "the Spirit's work of sanctifying, setting people apart and making them fit for the service of God is an integral part of the Christian salvation."[19]

---

[18]So also Jobes, *1 Peter*, pp. 70-71, and many others.
[19]*New Testament Theology* (Grand Rapids: Zondervan, 1986), p. 319.

2. The second reference to the Spirit occurs in 1 Peter 1:11 in the phrase "Spirit of Christ." An exegetical question requires vetting. Does this expression refer to the preincarnate Christ who was working in the hearts and minds of the OT prophets, or does it speak of the Holy Spirit, who takes a back seat and draws attention to Christ?[20] The latter is probably the intention. Paul also employs the expressions "Holy Spirit" and "Spirit of Christ" almost interchangeably (Rom 8:9; cf. 2 Cor 3:17-18; Gal 4:6; Phil 1:19). The point Peter is making seems to be this: the Holy Spirit was active in guiding the OT prophets. The Spirit revealed truth about the Messiah and messianic age to the OT prophets.

3. The self-same Spirit also worked mightily in the life and ministry of Christ and now works in his church, most notably in the preaching of the gospel "by the Holy Spirit sent from heaven" (1 Pet 1:12). "Peter thereby shows a continuity of the presence of the Spirit with the prophets and with the Christians, who receive the gospel of God's mercy centered in the suffering and glorification of Jesus Christ."[21] What is especially noteworthy is Peter's comment that the Spirit of Christ revealed to the OT prophets that they were serving subsequent generations (1 Pet 1:12); that is, their prophecies pointed toward the end times. It is precisely this notion of eschatological fulfillment that Peter proclaims in his sermon at Pentecost (Acts 2:16-21).

4. The fourth reference to the Holy Spirit occurs in a passage dealing with suffering (1 Pet 4:14). Peter reassures the Anatolian believers that if they suffer for the name of Christ, a special blessing rests on them. This special blessing is described as "the Spirit of God . . . resting" on them. Two things should be noted. First, this word of encouragement recalls Jesus' teaching in which a special blessedness attaches to those who undergo persecution on his account (Mt 5:11; 10:22). Jesus promised his persecuted disciples that their "reward is great in heaven" (Mt 5:12). Here Peter speaks not of an eschatological blessing but of a present blessedness. Already believers are experiencing a reward for steadfastly adhering to Jesus Christ. This is but one example of many in

---

[20]Cf. the Johannine saying, "He will glorify me, because he will take what is mine and declare it to you" (Jn 16:14).

[21]Jobes, *1 Peter*, p. 101.

this letter of the "already but not yet" tension that characterizes apostolic teaching, rooted in the teaching of Jesus himself. Second, the word *resting* is the same Greek verb used in the LXX of Isaiah 11:2 (*anapauomai*). In that passage, describing the future messianic king, the spirit of the Lord is said to "rest on him." The Spirit endows the king with special abilities to rule with righteousness and faithfulness. Peter's point appears to be that believers who withstand persecution for the sake of Christ share a special charism with him; namely, the "resting" of the Holy Spirit on them resulting in a life also characterized by righteousness and faithfulness. In short, there is a bond, a fellowship of suffering, that joins the messianic community together, a bond that is strengthened not broken by persecution. Similar echoes from Paul readily come to mind (2 Cor 1:3-7; 4:10-11; Phil 3:10-11).

## CONCLUSION

Peter's portrayal of God the Father, the Lord Jesus Christ and the Holy Spirit is akin to a beautifully constructed mosaic that conveys a powerful sense of harmony, truth and beauty. The God who emerges from the pages of this pastoral letter is a supremely loving, merciful, just, righteous, powerful and wise heavenly Father. He foreknows both redeemer and redeemed. His plans and purpose for both are unshakable. Through his Son Jesus Christ and the work of the Holy Spirit, salvation is revealed to and reserved for the redeemed. A mainstay for the saints is this recurring motif: the Savior, the Suffering Servant, suffered on their behalf; they must be prepared to "follow in his steps." After suffering comes glory: a pattern that works itself out in the lives of both Savior and saints. Paradoxically, in the midst of severe persecution, they already experience inexpressible joy in fellowship with the triune God who sustains them. In 1 Peter theology leads to doxology.

## QUESTIONS FOR DISCUSSION
1. What are the leading interpretations of this passage, and which one do you think best explains the text?
2. How decisive should the Apostles' Creed and the early church fathers be in determining the meaning of this passage?

3. Evaluate the postmortem view. Does it cohere with Scripture and Christian tradition?
4. Do you think Peter has drawn on the Enoch tradition in this passage? Why or why not?
5. What are the implications of the common christological confessions found in the NT?
6. What is the relevance of the Noah story to Peter's parenesis?
7. What contribution does 1 Peter make to the NT teaching on the Holy Spirit?

## FOR FURTHER STUDY

In addition to the commentaries and theologies listed in the bibliography of the preceding two chapters, here are some germane specialized studies:

Bandstra, A. J. "'Making Proclamation to the Spirits in Prison.' Another Look at 1 Peter 3:19." *CTJ* 38 (2003): 120-21.

Collins, John J., and Daniel C. Harlow, eds. *EDEJ*. Grand Rapids: Erdmans, 2010. Among the relevant articles are the following: "Ascent to Heaven," "Enoch, Ethiopic Apocalypse of (1 Enoch)," "Noah" and "Suffering Servant."

Dalton, W. J. *Christ's Proclamation to the Spirits: A Study of 1 Peter 3:18–4:6.* 2nd ed. AnBib 23. Rome: Pontifical Biblical Institute, 1989.

Erickson, Millard. "Is There Opportunity for Salvation after Death?" *BSac* 152 (1995): 131-44.

Feinberg, John S. "1 Peter 3:18-20, Ancient Mythology and the Intermediate State." *WTJ* 48 (1986): 303-36.

France, R. T. "Exegesis in Practice: Two Examples." In *New Testament Interpretation: Essays on Principles and Methods.* Grand Rapids: Eerdmans, 1977.

Hiebert, D. E. "The Suffering and Triumphant Christ: An Exposition of 1 Peter 3:18-22." *BSac* 139 (1982): 146-58.

Johnson, S. E. "The Preaching to the Dead." *JBL* (1960): 48-51.

Reicke, Bo. *The Disobedient Spirits and Christian Baptism: A Study of I Petr. III.19 and Its Context.* ASNU 13. Copenhagen: 1946.

Skilton, J. H. "A Glance at Some Old Problems in First Peter." *WTJ* 58 (1996): 1-9.

# 9

---

# SUFFERING FOR JESUS

◇

*There are a number of emphases in the contemporary church*
*that continue to distort its life. One, has to do with the erroneous*
*idea that the Christian life is basically a fair-weather experience.*

CHARLES RINGMA

*Modern Western believers may revolt at the thought—but unless*
*we find our identity as God's people in the midst of suffering and*
*persecution, we will sadly discover that we have no identity.*

NIK RIPKEN

*To follow Christ is to embrace suffering and the Cross.*
*And, at times, to say with Jesus, "My God, my God,*
*why did you abandon me?"*

CHUCK COLSON

THE NEXT TWO CHAPTERS deal with two intertwining themes in
Peter's first epistle. The first is undeserved suffering for the sake of
Christ. The second concerns the corporate identity of people who so
suffer, "the family of believers" (1 Pet 2:17). The pastoral necessity of
addressing these two themes is apparent: people who are marginalized,

ostracized and brutalized because of their new religious convictions need guidance on how to respond to persecution. They also need to recover a sense of self-esteem. Peter's letter does both and gives his readers reasons to rejoice in their present sufferings. In short, 1 Peter redirects the readers' attention away from the privations and unpleasantness of their present situation and focuses instead on what is happening from a larger, theological perspective.

## PRAISING GOD FOR BEARING THE NAME OF CHRISTIAN

The name *christianos* (lit., "a partisan or follower of Christ") was apparently first attached to believers in Jesus as a term of reproach by outsiders in the Syrian city of Antioch (Acts 11:26; cf. Acts 26:28) and is used only by Peter in the epistolary literature of the NT (1 Pet 4:16). As noted earlier, the persecution presupposed in 1 Peter appears to be more in the nature of slander, ridicule and ostracism rather than physical violence.[1] However, the language of 1 Peter 4:12, "fiery ordeal," might imply that violence was now an imminent threat or even being experienced. Some scholars note that at 1 Peter 4:12 the tone of the letter changes dramatically and suggest that Peter is referring to the Neronian persecution of A.D. 64. This was indeed a horrific massacre that involved Christians being burned alive (Tacitus, *Ann.* 15.44.17-20). Perhaps Peter received news of this outbreak as he was dictating his letter and added 1 Peter 4:12 to 1 Peter 5:14 "as a postscript hastily written."[2] Most interpreters prefer a metaphorical interpretation, though conceding that 1 Peter 4:12 may signal a ratcheting up of intensity of persecution.

Peter's pastoral letter invites theological reflection on several aspects of persecution. I set this out in the form of four primary affirmations.

***Suffering for the name of Christ is destined.*** The suffering of the

---

[1]This is not to trivialize the nature of verbal abuse, as Luke Timothy Johnson so eloquently reminds: "scorn and contempt are slow-working acids that corrode individual and communal identity. Social alienation is not a trivial form of suffering. Persecution may bring death, but with meaning. Societal scorn can threaten meaning itself, which is a more subtle form of death." See *The Writings of the New Testament: An Interpretation* (Philadelphia: Fortress, 1986), p. 435.

[2]Glenn W. Barker, William L. Lane and J. Ramsey Michaels, *The New Testament Speaks* (New York: Harper & Row, 1969), p. 342. Michaels was the primary writer on 1 Peter.

Anatolian Christians was not unique; it should be seen as part of a much larger story of suffering, a story having its roots in the OT. Just as God called Abraham and his descendents to be resident aliens in a foreign land, the land of Canaan, a land that would ultimately be their inheritance (Gen 12:1-3, 7), so God has now caused these "exiles of the Dispersion" to be reborn having "an inheritance that is imperishable, kept in heaven" (1 Pet 1:3-4, 17). Abraham and Sarah experienced a number of trials that greatly tested their faith, but through them all God proved himself faithful.[3] The Anatolian believers likewise "have had to suffer various trials" (1 Pet 1:6). Like Abraham who "rejoiced that he would see [Christ's] day" (Jn 8:56), so the Anatolian Christians, though they have not seen Christ, nonetheless "love him . . . [and] believe in him and rejoice with indescribable and glorious joy" (1 Pet 1:8). Christian wives found themselves in a particularly difficult situation when married to unbelievers. Peter reminds them that "the holy women who hoped in God . . . [accepted] the authority of their husbands" (1 Pet 3:5). Indeed, Sarah "obeyed Abraham and called him lord. You have become her daughters as long as you do what is good and never let fears alarm you" (1 Pet 3:6). Just as the descendents of Jacob were rescued from "the iron-smelter, out of Egypt, to become a people of his very own possession" (Deut 4:20), so these believers were being "tested by fire" (1 Pet 1:7) and are reminded that they are "protected by the power of God through faith for a salvation ready to be revealed in the last time" (1 Pet 1:5).

A key theological idea that permeates 1 Peter is the predestined sufferings of Christ on behalf of his people (1 Pet 1:20). Peter emphasizes that the same prophets "who prophesied of the grace that was to be yours" (1 Pet 1:10) also prophesied about the "sufferings destined for Christ" (1 Pet 1:11). A distinctive pattern of redemptive history emerges: suffering precedes glory. Christ's sufferings prefigure a corporate expe-

---

[3]The rabbis spoke of "the ten trials of Abraham." For a more detailed discussion of this feature in the patriarchal narratives see Larry R. Helyer, *Yesterday, Today and Forever: The Continuing Relevance of the Old Testament* (2nd ed.; Salem, Wis.; Sheffield, 2004), pp. 91-109; idem, "Abraham's Eight Crises: The Bumpy Road to Fulfilling God's Promise of an Heir," in *Abraham and Family: New Insights into the Patriarchal Narratives* (ed. Herschel Shanks; Washington D.C.: Biblical Archaeology Society, 2000), pp. 41-52.

rience for those who bear his name. Accordingly, Christians must prepare their hearts and minds (1 Pet 1:13) to "follow in his steps" (1 Pet 2:21) and arm themselves with the intention to suffer in the flesh, if it is God's will (1 Pet 3:17), and show solidarity with their Savior and Lord (1 Pet 4:1). Peter exhorts his readers: "Beloved, do not be surprised at the fiery ordeal that is taking place among you to test you, as though something strange were happening to you. But rejoice insofar as you are sharing Christ's sufferings" (1 Pet 4:12-13). And their suffering as part of Messiah's people is not exceptional or isolated: "your brothers and sisters in all the world are undergoing the same kinds of suffering" (1 Pet 5:9).

This theological understanding of suffering is not peculiar to Peter. In fact, we may confidently say that it harmonizes perfectly with our major witnesses, Jesus, Paul and John. In addition, given our conviction that the Gospel of Mark is indebted to the preaching of Peter in Rome, it is not without interest that one hears precisely this same motif in its pages. "As Mark was read in the Christian meetings there were notes peculiarly appropriate to the Roman situation. Jesus spoke openly of the persecution that could be expected in the Christian life."[4] Immediately following Jesus' baptism, he is depicted in the wilderness, undergoing an ordeal, a trial at the hands of Satan, and he finds himself surrounded "with the wild beasts" (Mk 1:13).[5] One already hears echoes of persecution, rejection and opposition that intensify as the narrative moves to its inevitable crisis at the cross (Mk 2:6-8; 3:1-6, 30; 4:17; 8:34-38; 10:39; 11:27-28; 12:12; 13:9-13; 14:1-2, 10, 30-31). Especially telling in this regard is Jesus' response to Peter's personal testimony: "Look, we have left everything and followed you" (Mk 10:28). Jesus assures Peter that such commitment is not without its reward, not least being eternal life in the age to come. But tucked into a list of present blessings is this ominous note: "with persecutions" (Mk 10:30).

In what many count as Paul's earliest letter, and for that matter,

---

[4]Lane, *New Testament Speaks*, p. 256. Lane was the primary writer on the section covering the Gospel of Mark.

[5]As Lane observes, this enigmatic saying corresponds with the experience of persecuted Christians in A.D. 64 who found themselves in the arena at Rome confronted by wild beasts (ibid.).

perhaps the earliest surviving Christian document we possess, 1 Thessalonians, Paul reminds his readers that "in spite of persecution you received the word with joy inspired by the Holy Spirit" (1 Thess 1:6). He further reminds them that before coming to Thessalonica, he and his missionary team had endured "great opposition" (1 Thess 2:2). The present suffering of the Thessalonians, stemming largely "from [their] own compatriots" (1 Thess 2:14), followed the same pattern as the churches of Judea. Paul's anxiety over his new converts "that no one would be shaken by these persecutions" (1 Thess 3:3) compelled him to dispatch Timothy back to Thessalonica to strengthen and encourage them (1 Thess 3:2, 5). Striking precisely the same note as Peter in his first letter to the Anatolians, Paul reminds the Thessalonians, "Indeed, you yourselves know that this is what *we were destined for*" (1 Thess 3:3, italics added). That things continued to be difficult in Thessalonica is attested in 2 Thessalonians, in which Paul commends them "for [their] steadfastness and faith during all [their] persecutions and . . . afflictions" (2 Thess 1:4). One could give a long string of references from Paul's letters highlighting the ever-present reality of persecution for the name of Christ (e.g., 2 Cor 1:3-11; 4:8-12; 6:4-10; 11:23-29; 12:10; Rom 8:18-25, 35-36; 12:14-21). One text in particular, however, seems to capture precisely the point Peter makes in his first letter. In Colossians 1:24, Paul says, "I am now rejoicing in my sufferings for your sake, and in my flesh I am completing *what is lacking in Christ's afflictions* for the sake of his body, that is, the church" (italics added). The italicized words are "not a denigration of Christ's death, but a reflection of the apocalyptic belief that God's people must suffer before the culmination of history" (1 Cor 4:9; Rev 6:9-11).[6]

The witness of John chimes in with that of Paul. The Johannine Christ both warns and exhorts his disciples: "In the world you face persecution. But take courage; I have conquered the world!" (Jn 16:33). Already the prologue of John's Gospel establishes a fundamental opposition that governs salvation history: "The light shines in the darkness, and the darkness did not overcome it. . . . He was in the world, and the

---

[6]Jennifer K. Berenson, *The New Oxford Annotated Bible* (ed. Michael D. Coogan; 3rd ed.; Oxford: Oxford University Press, 2001), p. 336 (NT).

world came into being through him; yet the world did not know him. He came to what was his own, and his own people did not accept him" (Jn 1:5, 10-11). Opposition of the darkness to the true light is persistent and systemic. No wonder then that "the world [hates believers] because they do not belong to the world, just as [Jesus does] not belong to the world" (Jn 17:14). This thought recurs in 1 John, where the readers are reminded: "Do not be astonished, brothers and sisters, that the world hates you" (1 Jn 3:13). The Johannine corpus concludes with the definitive word on persecution.[7] The inaugural vision of the Apocalypse introduces the keynote: "I, John, your brother who share with you in Jesus the persecution and the kingdom and the patient endurance" (Rev 1:9). The fellowship of Jesus is a fellowship of the cross. Following the initial vision of the risen, triumphant Christ, John hears these words of encouragement and hope: "Do not be afraid; I am the first and the last, and the living one. I was dead, and see, I am alive forever and ever; and I have the keys of Death and of Hades" (Rev 1:17-18). This word of exhortation is certainly needed as the drama of redemptive history reaches its climactic struggle against the powers of darkness. The saints must understand clearly what is coming: "Let anyone who has an ear listen: If you are to be taken captive, into captivity you go: if you kill with the sword, with the sword you must be killed. Here is a call for the endurance and faith of the saints" (Rev 13:9-10).

The verdict is clear: the people of God must realize that salvation history, by its very nature, entails an inevitable consequence, opposition and persecution by the powers of darkness and those unwittingly or willingly swept along in their wake. This is not something strange but something unavoidable, even predestined. So what lies behind Peter's pastoral parenesis is an awareness of a larger story, the story of redemption as sketched out in the OT and now being fulfilled "in the last days" (Acts 2:17). The movement from suffering to vindication and exaltation works only if one brings the NT gospel into the story. Without the rubric of promise and fulfillment, the OT ends with a whimper of

---

[7]"The authors of 1 Peter and Revelation are intensely interested in understanding and interacting with the problem of suffering in their communities." William J. Webb, "Suffering," *DLNTD*, p. 1135.

unfulfilled hopes. Second Temple Judaism is painfully aware of this lack of fulfillment. One overhears this poignant recognition in the words of the two disciples on the way to Emmaus who lament: "But we had hoped that he was the one to redeem Israel" (Lk 24:21). More despondent still are the words of an anonymous, apocalyptic Jew writing in the aftermath of the destruction of Jerusalem: "If the world has indeed been created for us, why do we not possess our world as an inheritance? How long will this be so?" (*2 Esd.* 6:59). In striking contrast, listen to Peter on the day of Pentecost: "Therefore let the entire house of Israel know with certainty that God has made him both Lord and Messiah, this Jesus whom you crucified" (Acts 2:36). He follows that up with another sermon in Solomon's Portico in which he boldly proclaims:

> God fulfilled what he had foretold through all the prophets, that his Messiah would suffer. Repent therefore, and turn to God so that your sins may be wiped out, so that times of refreshing may come from the presence of the Lord, and that he may send the Messiah appointed for you, that is, Jesus, who must remain in heaven until the time of universal restoration that God announced long ago through his holy prophets. (Acts 3:18-21)

That same confidence rings out in this letter: "in your hearts sanctify Christ as Lord" (1 Pet 3:15).

An important qualification must be appended before we leave this topic, a qualification that somewhat ameliorates the situation. Whereas corporate suffering for the name of Jesus Christ is inevitable, the same is not true for individual believers. That is, some, perhaps many, believers will not travel down this road. They do not suffer reproach and persecution for their faith, as did the Anatolian believers.

This observation arises from three passing phrases easily overlooked in Peter's letter. The first occurs in 1 Peter 1:6: "even if now for a little while you have had to suffer various trials." The Greek phrase *oligon arti ei deon [estin]* (lit., "for a little [while] now if it must be") should be understood as referring to potential, not necessary, suffering. This is matched later in the letter by another phrase qualifying undeserved suffering for one's faith: "if suffering should be God's will" (1 Pet 3:17). The Greek is *ei theloi to thelēma tou theou* (lit., "if wills the will of God").

This phrase, involving the optative mood of the verb "to will"—a mood which is rare in the NT and views the action as possible—once again shows that Peter does not envision persecution as a necessary condition of Christian faith but a potential one.[8] The same point is made in 1 Peter 3:14, where Peter says, "But even if you do suffer for doing what is right." The mood of the verb "suffer" is also in the optative mood, indicating a possibility rather than a certainty or probability.

Here we peer into the mystery of God's providence. Why do some Christians undergo intense persecution for their faith and others do not? Peter himself confronts this question after his reconciliation and recommissioning along the shore of the Sea of Galilee. When Jesus enigmatically implies that Peter will follow him in crucifixion (Jn 21:18-19), Peter inquires about the destiny of the beloved disciple (probably the apostle John): "Lord, what about him?" (Jn 21:21). Jesus answers, "If it is my will that he remain until I come, what is that to you?" (Jn 21:22). Like his Master ("not what I want, but what you want," Mk 14:36), Peter embraced God's will for his life and accordingly did not attempt to answer his Anatolian brothers and sisters' unspoken question: "Why me and not him or her?" Instead, like his Master, Peter urges that each must carry his or her own cross (Mk 8:34; cf. 1 Pet 2:21; 4:1). Whether that cross includes persecution must be left in the hands of the one who summons us to follow in his steps wherever they lead.

## SUFFERING FOR THE NAME OF CHRIST IS NOT A NECESSARY CONSEQUENCE OF POSTCONVERSION SIN

Peter's primary explanation for Christian suffering at the hands of unbelievers is thus grounded in the inherent nature of redemptive history. Does he, however, also entertain notions of merited suffering because of human sinfulness? Is there a kind of "Christian karma"

---

[8]On this point see J. H. Elliott, *1 Peter: A New Translation with Introduction and Commentary* (AB 37B; New York: Doubleday, 2000), pp. 339-40, 634-35. For the grammar of the optative mood see Daniel B. Wallace, *Greek Grammar Beyond the Basics* (Grand Rapids: Zondervan, 1996), pp. 480-84. Wallace even goes so far as to say, "*Prima facie*, the readership of this letter has not yet suffered for righteousness, and the possibility of such happening soon seems remote" (p. 484). In my opinion, the letter clearly indicates that suffering was indeed a present reality for the Anatolian believers.

that must inevitably work itself out in the lives of sinning believers? Is it possible that suffering for the name of Jesus is a divine response to failed discipleship?

One must carefully nuance the answer. As baldly stated above, this idea is not found in Peter's epistle or in any of the other NT witnesses. One thinks of the episode of the man born blind in John's Gospel. The disciples ask Jesus: "Rabbi, who sinned, this man or his parents, that he was born blind?" (Jn 9:2). Jesus' answer is unambiguous: "Neither this man nor his parents sinned; he was born blind so that God's works might be revealed in him" (Jn 9:3). Similarly, Jesus rejected the easy assumption of most Second Temple period Jews that painful experiences were the direct result of divine judgment:

> "Do you think that because these Galileans suffered in this way [a massacre by the Roman governor Pilate] they were worse sinners than all other Galileans? No, I tell you; but unless you repent, you will all perish as they did. Or those eighteen who were killed when the tower of Siloam fell on them—do you think that they were worse offenders than all the others living in Jerusalem? No, I tell, you; but unless you repent, you will all perish just as they did." (Lk 13:2-5)

The confidence with which many moved backward from baneful result to sinful cause finds no place in NT thought (cf. *Wis* 8:19-20; *Gen Rab.* 63:[39c] on Gen 25:22).

However, several NT passages may be cited in which sinful behavior and subsequent suffering is explicitly linked. In this case, the suffering is an expression of divine discipline. Paul does not mince words with the Corinthians concerning their abuses of the Lord's Supper: "For this reason [partaking of the cup of the Lord in an unworthy manner] many of you are weak and ill, and some have died" (1 Cor 11:30). He also enjoins that the person guilty of incest be expelled from the fellowship "for the destruction of the flesh" (1 Cor 5:5). In the first instance, the form of suffering was physical illness, leading, in some cases, to death. In the second, the nature of "the destruction of the flesh" is not spelled out. Possibly, suffering as the result of persecution was involved, but more likely this too was in the form of physical illness.

The apostle Peter's ministry, as recorded in the book of Acts, throws light on our discussion. The episode of Ananias and Sapphira (Acts 5:1-11) seems very similar to the two instances of church discipline mentioned above from the Pauline corpus. We can only conjecture at the cause of this couple's death, though a stroke seems plausible. In addition, in Acts 8:14-24, Peter encounters a certain man named Simon who, out of selfish motives, wished to obtain the ability to heal in Jesus' name. Peter confronts this Simon (called "Great" by the Samaritans) and urges immediate repentance. The larger context of the earlier chapters in Acts implies that if he would not, something comparable to what happened to Ananias and Sapphira would befall him.

But can we detect such disciplinary suffering as the result of disobedience in 1 Peter? There is only one text that could be so construed. After warning his Christian readers not to suffer "as a murderer, a thief, a criminal, or even as a mischief maker," Peter announces, "For the time has come for judgment to begin with the household of God" (1 Pet 4:15, 17). A close reading of the context, however, indicates that Peter's point moves in a different direction.[9] Alluding to an episode from the prophet Ezekiel, in which six destroying angels were commissioned to slay wicked Jerusalemites (Ezek 8–9), Peter fastens on a particular command issued to the angels: "begin at my sanctuary" (Ezek 9:6; cf. Zech 13:9; Mal 3:1-3). In Ezekiel's day, retribution began at the temple of God, the place where God's holiness and glory should have been honored and extolled. Tragically, the elders trashed this notion with degrading and disgusting behavior. There were, however, some in Jerusalem who "[sighed and groaned] over all the abominations that [were being] committed in it" (Ezek 9:4). These were the faithful who were marked with a special sign on their foreheads and, like Jeremiah, were maligned and abused for their faithfulness (cf. Jer 11:18-20; 15:10-21; 17:14-18; 18:18-23).

In Peter's day, suffering by the people of God—whom he likens to a temple of God (1 Pet 2:4-5)—likewise precedes eschatological retri-

---

[9]See further Paul J. Achtemeier, *1 Peter: A Commentary on First Peter* (ed. Eldon J. Epp; Hermeneia; Minneapolis: Fortress, 1996), pp. 315-19, and D. A. Carson, *Commentary on the New Testament Use of the Old Testament* (ed. G. K. Beale and D. A. Carson; Grand Rapids: Baker, 2007), pp. 1041-42.

bution poured out on the unbelieving and wicked, when Christ's glory is revealed (1 Pet 4:13) and God judges the living and the dead (1 Pet 4:5). Furthermore, believers are now marked out by bearing the name of Christ and thus being a Christian (1 Pet 4:14, 16). Indeed, it would appear that deeply embedded in redemptive history is a recurring pattern: God first judges his people, then the wicked. A quick perusal of the Hebrew prophets bears this out (see Amos 3:2; Mal 3:1-5), and Jesus' teaching reinforces it (see Mt 25:31-46). In short, Peter is not warning his readers that their particular sins will find them out; rather, sinners will find them out.[10] Consequently, Christians must be prepared to withstand abuse and "entrust themselves to a faithful Creator, while continuing to do good" (1 Pet 4:19). He adds a further warning by quoting Proverbs 11:31: "If it is hard for the righteous to be saved, what will become of the ungodly and the sinners?" The point is clear: "Christians facing situations where denial of their faith could appear to alleviate their suffering . . . will in fact only guarantee that their eventual end will involve suffering far worse than any they must now endure."[11]

*Suffering for one's faith plays a role in sanctification.* Stated positively, Peter emphasizes that suffering for the name of Christ refines and strengthens one's faith (1 Pet 1:6-7). He effectively employs a metallurgical metaphor in which faith, like gold, "is tested by fire." He explains that "[suffering] various trials" demonstrates "the genuineness of . . . faith" and results in "praise and glory and honor when Jesus Christ is revealed." Christians should also bear in mind that, although pagans may now malign them as evildoers, there will be a day of vindication. In fact, pagans will see believers' "honorable deeds and glorify God when he comes to judge" (1 Pet 2:12).[12] It is thus mandatory for believers to do right in order to "silence the ignorance of the foolish" (1 Pet 2:15).

---

[10]Contrary to Leonhard Goppelt, *Theology of the New Testament*, vol. 2: *The Variety and Unity of the Apostolic Witness to Christ* (ed. Jürgen Roloff; Grand Rapids: Eerdmans, 1982), p. 175.

[11]Achtemeier, *1 Peter*, p. 316.

[12]I agree with Achtemeier that this passage probably does not imply the conversion of pagans but "points rather to the time of the final judgment" (*1 Peter*, p. 178). So also J. Ramsey Michaels, *1 Peter* (WBC 47; Waco, Tex.: Word, 1988), p. 118, and Karen H. Jobes, *1 Peter* (BECNT; Grand Rapids: Baker, 2005), p. 172.

Peter can also see great value in suffering because it carries with it God's stamp of approval. This theologically grounded explanation is given to slaves who are exhorted to endure pain and suffering even when doing what is right (1 Pet 2:20). But on what basis does Peter infer that undeserved suffering garners God's approval? He says, "For to this you have been called, because Christ also suffered for you" (1 Pet 2:21). Immediately thereafter, he launches into the second of three great christological passages prefaced by "you should follow in his steps" (1 Pet 2:21). Once again, Peter's argument appears to be predicated on a certain destiny that must unfold.

Perhaps another story lies thinly veiled beneath the surface of Peter's parenesis. Might not the story of Joseph the Hebrew slave in Potiphar's house (Gen 39) also inform Peter's word to slaves? To be sure, no explicit clues point in that direction, but general similarities and appropriateness are intriguing. Young Joseph finds himself in slavery in a foreign land; so do these Christian slaves being addressed by Peter. Rather than resist, Joseph submits to his master and applies himself diligently to his assigned tasks with the result that he finds favor and is appointed overseer of Potiphar's house. Without promising the same outcome, Peter nonetheless exhorts Christian slaves "to accept the authority of your masters with all deference, not only those who are kind and gentle but also those who are harsh" (1 Pet 2:18). Peter also urges slaves to be "aware of God" when they "endure pain while suffering unjustly" (1 Pet 2:19). Joseph wards off seduction by a similar awareness: "How then could I do this great wickedness, and sin against God?" (Gen 39:9). Peter assures slaves that when they do suffer unjustly, they "have God's approval" (1 Pet 2:20), reminiscent of a refrain in the story of Joseph: "But the LORD was with Joseph and showed him steadfast love; he gave him favor in the sight of the chief jailer" (Gen 39:21). What is especially interesting are Joseph's words at the grand conclusion of his personal ordeal: "Even though you intended to do harm to me, God intended it for good, in order to preserve a numerous people, as he is doing today" (Gen 50:20). No wonder Peter introduces his letter by reminding his readers that their destiny is "an inheritance that is imperishable, undefiled, and unfading" (1 Pet 1:4). He concludes it with a reminder that God "has called you to his eternal glory in Christ" (1 Pet 5:10). There will always be mystery concerning suffering on behalf of Christ, but there must be no uncertainty or doubt about its reality: "To this we have been called."

Complementary to the notion of predestined sufferings is a comforting truth, namely, suffering for the sake of Christ demonstrates one's membership in the fellowship of the cross. This creates a strong bond of solidarity among believers, a necessary attribute in order to survive a hostile, economic and social environment. As Joel Green observes:

> Suffering may be the consequence of society's attempts to clothe followers of Christ in humiliation and shame, but Peter turns this interpretation on its head. To the contrary, suffering is a sign of the genuineness of one's faith, an affirmation of one's identity before God, and a concrete measure of the value in which the believing community is held by God.[13]

Peter's address to slaves in the household code section of his letter (1 Pet 2:18–3:7) is followed by admonitions to the entire community of believers (1 Pet 3:8-17), signaled by the phrase "all of you" (1 Pet 3:8). His comments about suffering made to the slaves are essentially restated. All believers undergoing undeserved suffering in the form of persecution are reminded that they are thus blessed (1 Pet 3:14). Instead of fear and intimidation, believers must exhibit unflinching loyalty to Christ as Lord and witness to the reason for their robust hope, an attitude in short supply in the depressing world of Greco-Roman society generally (1 Pet 3:13-15; cf. Eph 2:12).[14] This must be done with a clear conscience, that is, Christian conduct must be irreproachable. If they do so, believers turn the tables on their detractors who seek to dishonor and shame them.

There is one disputed text which, taken at face value, seems to affirm

---

[13]Joel B. Green, *1 Peter* (Grand Rapids: Eerdmans, 2007), p. 226.

[14]As Cranfield reminds us, "The world of ancient Greek and Roman civilization was a world of fascinating beauty. It could boast of splendid courage, high intellectual power, and superb loveliness of poetry and art; but in spite of all the grandeur and charm, it was a world without hope." C. E. B. Cranfield, *The First Epistle of Peter* (London: SCM Press, 1950), p. 22.

that innocent suffering on the part of believers leads to a cessation of sin. "Since therefore Christ suffered in the flesh, arm yourselves also with the same intention (for whoever has suffered in the flesh has finished with sin)" (1 Pet 4:1). Did Peter mean that such suffering enables a believer to achieve a sinless state? If so, this flies in the face of the general tenor of the NT (see Mt 7:11) and specific passages from both Paul and John (Phil 3:12; 1 Jn 1:8–2:2).[15] Consequently, we should probe more deeply Peter's syntax and diction. The conjunction "for" (Gk *hoti*), beginning the disputed clause (placed in parentheses in the NRSV), can have two basic meanings: (1) "that" and (2) "because or for." In the former, *hoti* functions epexegetically, that is, it further specifies the content of the "same intention" of Christ. In the second meaning, *hoti* provides the reason for what follows. J. H. Elliott claims that "content and context favor the second alternative (so the majority of commentators)."[16] But Karen Jobes, likewise appealing "to the flow of Peter's argument," decides that "it is more likely epexegetical" and gives a list of respected scholars supporting that view.[17] This is a close call, but I opt for the causal interpretation. The imperative "arm yourselves" is rooted in the indicative of "Christ suffered in the flesh" and thus serves as the reason why "whoever has suffered in the flesh has finished with sin."

But we still have two significant problems of interpretation. In the first place, who is the "whoever"? Does this refer to a believer or is it still referring to Christ? A majority of commentators conclude that it refers to a believer, especially since the immediately succeeding verse (1 Pet 4:2, "so as to live for the rest of *your* earthly life" [italics added]) clearly has believers in mind.[18] Furthermore, as Elliott points out, several difficulties disallow any reference to Christ: "Christ has already been declared 'righteous' (3:18) and free from sin (2:22-23) and therefore

---

[15]One might appeal to several passages in 1 John that could be construed as teaching precisely the same as 1 Peter 4:1 (see 1 Jn 3:6, 8-9; 5:4, 18)

[16]Elliott, *1 Peter*, p. 714.

[17]Jobes, *1 Peter*, p. 263. Achtemeier, *1 Peter*, p. 278, is one of these.

[18]The discussion of Jobes, *1 Peter*, pp. 262-66, is helpful in sorting out the issues. Michaels takes this clause as referring to Christ and views it as a parenthesis inserted to remind his readers what Christ's intention was (*1 Peter*, p. 228).

cannot be said to have 'ceased from sin.' Moreover, if Christ has termi-
nated the sins of others there would be no point in urging the abandonment of sinning, as is done in vv. 2-4."[19]

One must still decide precisely what "has finished with sin" means.
Here is a very literal rendering: "the one having suffered in flesh has
ceased of sin." Given that Peter does not appear to use the word for sin
(*hamartia*) to refer "to a power that controls human beings [as Paul
does], but to acts that go counter to God's will and the world,"[20] perhaps
we could expand our literal translation by saying "has ceased with
regard to acts of sin." I have already expressed misgivings about the
possibility that Peter is suggesting that suffering for one's faith may
enable one to live without sinning. Can we make sense of this expression in terms of its context in Peter's letter and the larger context of
early Christian thought as found in the NT?

One may at least eliminate some options.[21]

1. Surely this text does not reflect a tradition in Second Temple Judaism whereby the suffering and death of martyrs reverses God's
judgment on Israel (e.g., 2 Macc 7:37-38; 4 Macc 1:11; 6:28-29; 9:23-24;
17:21-22; 1QS V 6-7; VIII 1-6; IX 4; 1 QSa I 3).[22] Not least of the
objections to this option is the fact that the readers have not died; they
are presently experiencing slander, ridicule and ostracism.

2. Neither does our text strike the same note as a similar sounding
Pauline text in Romans 6:7: "For whoever has died is freed from sin."
Paul is speaking of being liberated from the dominion of sin by being
united with Christ. Sin (*hamartia*) here refers to a power or force that
enslaves and the death Paul envisions is metaphorical. Baptism is the
evocative image employed to portray this new found freedom from the
flesh, here denoting fallen human nature, not the physical body. But
Peter is not speaking of this truth; he is addressing believers who are
literally suffering in the flesh, that is, in their mortal bodies.[23] While it

---

[19]Elliott, *1 Peter*, p. 715.

[20]Achtemeier, *1 Peter*, p. 280.

[21]I am indebted to Elliott for this section (*1 Peter*, pp. 715-18).

[22]But on this alleged parallel to the NT see Larry R. Helyer, *Exploring Jewish Literature of the
Second Temple Period* (Downers Grove, Ill.: InterVarsity Press, 2002), pp. 408-11.

[23]In this regard, note that Paul and Peter do not use the terms "flesh" (*sarx*) and "sin" (*hamartia*)

is true that the verb "to suffer" can have the meaning "to die" in Hebrews, that does not appear to be the case in 1 Peter 3:18, where Christ's suffering (*epathen*) is distinguished from his being "put to death" (*thanatōtheis*).[24]

3. Another suggestion is that innocent suffering does purify the flesh from sin. Several texts from the pseudepigraphic literature are sometimes cited in support of this (*1 En.* 67:9; *2 Bar.* 13:10; 78:6), along with Proverbs 20:30 (MT). But the passages from *1 Enoch* and *2 Baruch* are not really relevant because they deal with deserved, not undeserved, suffering, and the text from Proverbs refers to the notion that "suffering has a disciplining function and assists in the control of the flesh, which is prone to sinning."[25]

This latter idea of discipline probably points us in the right direction.[26] In both the OT and the NT, a significant number of texts underscore the value of suffering as an aid to spiritual maturity. As Elliott points out, Proverbs resonates with the idea that disciplinary suffering is a means to acquiring wisdom, and Peter either explicitly cites or alludes to Proverbs several times (1 Pet 2:17 and Prov 24:21; 1 Pet 3:6c and Prov 3:25; 1 Pet 4:8 and Prov 10:12; 1 Pet 4:18 and Prov 11:31; 1 Pet 5:5 and Prov 3:34).[27] In the NT, Hebrews provides the closest parallels to 1 Peter in this regard (Heb 5:8; 12:5-11).

But what precisely does "finished with sin" mean? Is it possible for the believer to achieve such an exalted state prior to glorification at the parousia? This probably presses the verb "finished" further than is warranted.[28] The "not yet" of redemptive history has not yet replaced the "now," a state described, in Pauline language, as accompanied by inward

---

in precisely the same sense.

[24]See further J. Kremer, "*paschō*," *EDNT* 3:51-52.

[25]Ibid.

[26]Elliot captures the meaning: "Our verse makes eminent sense in the light of this concept of the disciplining effect of suffering . . . suffering, especially innocent suffering, disciplines the physical body (*sarx*) by which sinning is carried out and thereby trains one to cease from sinning. As Christ's vicarious suffering has liberated believers from the proclivity to sin . . . so that they might live uprightly, . . . so now they are reminded that their own innocent suffering sustains this break with sinning and wrongdoing" (*1 Peter*, p. 717).

[27]Ibid., pp. 13-14.

[28]More literally translated as "has ceased" or "is done with," the verb is the perfect middle/passive indicative, third person singular of *pauō*.

groaning and hope for the ultimate victory (Rom 8:23-25, 30). Peter
was under no illusions about the spiritual condition of his readers; they
had a long way yet to go: "Rid yourselves, therefore, of all malice, and
all guile, insincerity, envy, and all slander. Like newborn infants, long
for the pure, spiritual milk, so that by it your may grow into salvation"
(1 Pet 2:1-2; cf. 1 Pet 2:11-12). Consequently, I think what Peter was
saying is that "those who suffer unjustly because of their faith in Christ
have demonstrated *that they are willing to be through, or done, with sin by
choosing obedience, even if it means suffering.*"[29]

**Suffering as a Christian does not justify retaliation.** This brings us to
Peter's hard saying about suffering for the name of Christ. The apostle
does not permit revenge and retaliation in response to undeserved suffering for the name of Christ; indeed, he clearly forbids it. One remembers Jesus' charge to Peter at Caesarea Philippi: "I will give you the
keys of the kingdom of heaven, and whatever you bind on earth will be
bound in heaven, and whatever you loose on earth will be loosed in
heaven" (Mt 16:19). The notion of binding and loosing is familiar from
rabbinic literature and means essentially forbidding and permitting.
And what Peter advocates is not his own best reflections on the situation. His teaching is clearly indebted to none other than the Master
himself. A quick perusal of the Sermon on the Mount verifies the
source of Peter's parenesis (see, e.g., Mt 5:10-12, 21-26, 38-48; 7:1-5).
The problem is that this runs against the grain of human nature, both
then and now.

Several questions vie for attention: Why are Christians forbidden to
retaliate? Is the principle of nonviolence a transcendent prohibition? In
other words, are believers ever justified in using force and violence in
order to alleviate undeserved suffering? The first question is more easily
answered. Peter's appeal to submission and his prohibition of resistance
and retaliation follow from the linkage he establishes between the
pattern of Christ's sufferings on behalf of his people and his people's
sufferings as a consequence of responding to Christ's sufferings. "Christ

---

[29]Jobes, *1 Peter*, p. 265, italics added. See also the discussion of Scot McKnight, *1 Peter* (Grand
Rapids: Zondervan, 1996), pp. 224-26, and the paraphrase of I. Howard Marshall, *1 Peter*
(IVPNTC 17; Downers Grove, Ill.: InterVarsity Press, 1991), p. 134.

also suffered for you, leaving you an example, so that you should follow in his steps" (1 Pet 2:21). Christ's example, as demonstrated during his passion, disallows returning abuse or threatening one's tormentors (1 Pet 2:23). But it goes much further than that: Christians must also "repay with a blessing" in order to "inherit a blessing" (1 Pet 3:9). As has often been observed, the positive form of the so-called Golden Rule embodies an unprecedented ethic in Second Temple Judaism. Not doing evil to those who wrong us is difficult; doing good to those who wrong us seems well-nigh impossible. Peter justifies his hard saying with a familiar refrain: "It is for this that you were called." At the level of exegesis, there is wide spread agreement on the substance of what Peter enjoins.

Disagreement quickly arises, however, when we turn to herme-neutics, that is, the question of significance: What does Peter's teaching mean today? Is the Petrine parenesis normative for all times and places? One can at least understand why the apostle clamped down on resis-tance and retaliation then. The Christian movement was small, isolated and extremely vulnerable. Taking on the abuse directly in a muscular manner would have invited catastrophic consequences. But what about later times and places?

William Wilberforce spearheaded an effort to abolish the inhuman slave trade in Britain (1807). He was able to accomplish this without a violent revolution. Unfortunately, the same cannot be said for other ef-forts to right wrongs. Examples quickly come to mind from American history, such as the Revolutionary War and the Civil War. World War II and the Holocaust provide a classic case study in this regard, forcing us to grapple with the hard issues of pacifism and just war theory.[30] More recently we have had to come to grips with ethnic cleansing in Bosnia, Darfur, Nigeria, Orissa (a state in India), Somalia and Indo-nesia, among others. These instances of persecution and undeserved

---

[30]For a concise treatment of this issue from a pacifist perspective, see Alan Kreider and John H. Yoder, "Christians and War," in *Eerdmans' Handbook to the History of Christianity* (Grand Rap-ids: Eerdmans, 1977), pp. 24-27. See also Richard B. Hays, *The Moral Vision of the New Testa-ment* (New York: HarperOne, 1996), pp. 313-46. For a concise defense of just war, see the *Catechism of the Catholic Church*, par. 2309, and J. Daryl Charles, *Between Pacifism and Jihad: Just War and Christian Tradition* (Downer Grove, Ill.: InterVarsity Press, 2005).

suffering—often involving large-scale massacres—require Christians who wish to submit to the authority of Scripture to confront some soul-searching questions. Can we take over Peter's pastoral counsel and apply it without qualification to these modern dilemmas? There are no easy answers, and a full-length discussion entails another book. Still, I feel obligated to at least offer some suggestions in this regard.

As a starting point, I draw a distinction between Peter's pastoral counsel to congregations under his apostolic care who were part of the Roman Empire and modern Christians living in nation states dealing with issues of persecution and ethnic cleansing. Only after Christianity became the recognized religion of the Roman Empire, in the wake of Constantine the Great during the fourth century, were Christian ecclesiastics in a position to influence national and international policy. And clearly they did that. Numerous instances may be cited in which the considerable power and influence of the church were brought to bear in order to alleviate persecution and unjust suffering.[31] Tragically, the record of the church is also deeply stained by disgraceful episodes of inflicting its own atrocities in the form of persecution and suffering on unbelievers and erring believers alike. The Crusades are the most egregious example, and this mentality has by no means vanished from Christendom. Furthermore, Christians have always tended to support and justify the actions of their own nation over against other nations. Without pursuing this further, I want to make the point that the context and situation have changed dramatically from Peter's time to our own and a simple one-to-one application is fraught with difficulties.[32]

However, much of what Peter enjoins has continuing relevance in situations where a small minority of believers lives in the midst of a larger society that is opposed to Christianity. One thinks, for example, of Christians living in Islamic states. Resistance and retaliation in such circumstances are ill-advised. More effective is the enactment of Peter's

---

[31]See, e.g., Rodney Stark, *The Victory of Reason* (New York: Random House, 2005), pp. 35-67, esp. pp. 63-67.

[32]See the thoughtful comments of Craig S. Keener, *Romans* (Eugene, Ore.: Cascade, 2009), pp. 155-56.

counsel to demonstrate high moral and ethical behavior that speaks for itself. Christian wives will still find Peter's advice helpful in dealing with non-Christian husbands. Admittedly, there may well be instances in which recourse to various legal and humanitarian agencies for protection are justified (something seldom or never available in the early years of Christianity).

What remains valid in Peter's counsel concerns Christian attitudes toward those who abuse and malign them. Love triumphs over hate; blessing trumps cursing; holiness not the desires of the flesh must be the controlling passion of our lives. This is contrary to human nature and requires supernatural assistance. No wonder Peter begins by reminding his readers of their new birth (1 Pet 1:3) and, consequently, the necessity to be obedient children, to be holy as God is holy, express "genuine mutual love" and "love one another deeply from the heart" (1 Pet 1:14-16, 22). They must "conduct themselves honorably among the Gentiles" (1 Pet 2:12), "accept the authority of every human institution" (1 Pet 2:13) and "have unity of spirit, sympathy, love for one another, a tender heart, and a humble mind" (1 Pet 3:8). And "above all," they must "maintain constant love for one another, for love covers a multitude of sins" (1 Pet 4:8).

In our pluralistic society, special-interest and political groups shrilly demand their rights. Christians belonging to these various groups are often indistinguishable from their non-Christian counterparts. Peter, however, urges that love be shown to all. "It is almost unbelievable that Peter never himself vilifies those pagans on account of the hostilities doled out to believers, nor urges his audience to vilify their antagonists. He casts no blame and never allows for an interpretation of pagans as evil on account of their stance over against Christians."[33] Peter offers no guarantees that persecutors will become partners in the grace of Christ. But his word to wives is applicable to the entire believing community: "they *may* be won over without a word . . . when they see the purity and reverence of your lives" (1 Pet 3:1-2, italics added; cf. 1 Cor 7:16). The testimony of bearing up in a Christ-like manner when undergoing suffering for his name should

---

[33]Green, *1 Peter*, p. 227.

never be underestimated.[34] We who call ourselves Christians need to call
a time out and seriously reevaluate our priorities.

## QUESTIONS FOR DISCUSSION

1. Is suffering or persecution for one's faith in Christ destined or
   inevitable? Why or why not?
2. Discuss the OT and Second Temple Judaism teaching on persecution because of one's religious faith.
3. Discuss whether Jesus, Paul and John agree with Peter on this
   topic.
4. Discuss the relationship between postconversion sin and suffering or persecution.
5. What role does suffering or persecution play in sanctification?
   Does it enable one to be entirely sanctified?
6. Is retaliation ever justified as a Christian response to persecution? Defend your answer.

## FOR FURTHER READING

In addition to commentaries and biblical theologies previously cited,
see the following special studies:

Beker, J. C. *Suffering and Hope: The Biblical Vision and the Human Predicament.*
   Grand Rapids: Erdmans, 1994.

Charles, J. Daryl. *Between Pacifism and Jihad: Just War and Christian Tradition.*
   Downers Grove, Ill.: InterVarsity Press, 2005.

Downing, F. G. "Pliny's Prosecution of Christians: Revelation and 1 Peter."
   *JSNT* 34 (1988): 105-23.

Hays, Richard B. *The Moral Vision of the New Testament.* New York: HarperOne, 1996.

Johnson, Luke Timothy. *The Writings of the New Testament: An Interpretation.*
   Philadelphia: Fortress, 1986.

Kruse, Colin C. "Persecution." *DNTB.* Downers Grove, Ill.: InterVarsity
   Press, 2000. Pp. 775-78.

---

[34]In this regard, the testimony of the Auca Indians who killed the missionaries Jim Elliot and
Nate Saint serves as a powerful illustration. See Steve and Marj Saint, *Beyond the Gates of
Splendor* (Oklahoma City: Bearing Fruit Communications, 2002) and the movie based on this
book, *End of the Spear* (2006).

Talbert, C. H. *Learning Through Suffering*: *The Educational Value of Suffering in the New Testament and in Its Milieu*. Collegeville, Minn.: Liturgical Press, 1991.

Webb, William J. "Suffering." *DLNTD*. Downers Grove, Ill.: InterVarsity Press, 1997. Pp. 1135-41.

# 10

---

# THE PEOPLE OF GOD

INTEGRAL TO PETER'S STRATEGY for guiding the Anatolian Christians in their response to persecution is addressing the pressing psychological and spiritual issue of self-identity. Being maligned and ridiculed erodes one's sense of self-worth. Being ostracized and marginalized by the primary social institutions, customs and citizens of the Greco-Roman world of Anatolia engenders fear and makes it next to impossible to acquire the highly prized value of honor. Its opposite, shame, was a stigma almost worse than death itself; indeed, some Romans and provincials committed suicide when forced to face shame cast on them by their opponents or community.[1] Viewed in this light, Peter's letter reflects the work of a virtuoso. Here is a masterful reconfiguring of self-image that transcends time and place. One might say he creates a gallery of paintings, each one portraying the new people of God, each one a "glittering image" requiring careful analysis and appreciation.[2]

## THE NEW ISRAEL

At the outset, Peter establishes an essential identity for his readers, an identity that in many ways comprehends all the other images employed, a sort of umbrella term. Surprisingly, the term "church" (*ekklēsia*), found frequently in Acts and the Pauline letters, occurs not

---

[1]See Miriam T. Griffin, "Suicide," *OCD*, p. 1453. On the importance of honor and shame in the first-century Mediterranean world, see D. A. deSilva, "Honor and Shame," *DNTB*, pp. 518-22.
[2]I borrowed this expression from a book by Susan Howatch, *Glittering Images* (London: Ballantine, 1995), though I am using it in a slightly different sense.

even once in 1 Peter.[3] According to Peter, the Anatolian believers constitute "the exiles of the Dispersion" (1 Pet 1:1). This expression recalls
the Jewish people, the descendents of the patriarchs, the children of
Israel, who were now scattered across the Roman Empire. This people,
bound by a solemn covenant to the one, true and living God were witnesses to this God and charged with being a light to the Gentiles (Is
41:8-10; 42:6-9; 43:8-21; 44:8; 45:4-7; 49:6). Peter's letter assumes that
all who respond to the gospel of Jesus Christ are now part of the Israel
of God (cf. Gal 6:16). But it is a new Israel, a regenerated Israel (Ezek
36:25-27), living under a new covenant (Jer 31:31-34) established
"with the precious blood of Christ, like that of a lamb without defect
or blemish" (1 Pet 1:19).[4]

The surprise in redemptive history is the inclusion of Gentiles into
this new covenant community, a turn of events in which Peter played a
decisive role (see Acts 10:1–11:26, 15:1-29). The bottom line is that
regardless of whether one was formerly Jewish or Gentile, responding
to God's grace in Christ results in a transfer into this new Israel of God.
This transfer can be likened to being "called . . . out of darkness into his
marvelous light" (1 Pet 2:9). It means that "once you were not a people,
but now you are God's people; once you had not received mercy, but
now you have received mercy" (1 Pet 2:10 citing Hos 2:23). As noted
earlier, the language of election Peter employs in his salutation ("chosen
and destined") harks back to the theophany on Mount Sinai and the
covenant-making ceremony (Ex 24). Like ancient Israel, the Anatolian
Christians have been "sprinkled with . . . blood," only in their case, and
making all the difference, it is "his" blood that accomplishes this remarkable transformation (1 Pet 1:2).

Peter thus fastens on the most important identity of the Anatolian
believers: they are now members of the new Israel, the new people of
God. This requires reflection. Given that the non-Christian Anatolians are heaping shame and dishonor on this small sect that refuses to

---

[3]"It is remarkable . . . that the author of 1 Peter does not speak about the *ekklēsia*, but instead
uses salvation-historical terminology." Reinhard Feldmeier, *The First Letter of Peter* (trans.
Peter H. Davids; Waco, Tex.: Baylor University Press, 2008), p. 140, n. 4.
[4]See W. S. Campbell, "Church as Israel, People of God," *DLNTD*, pp. 204-19.

conform to the old ways ("they malign you as evildoers" . . . "they are surprised that you no longer join them in the same excesses of dissipation, and so they blaspheme" [1 Pet 2:12; 3:16; 4:4]), the fact that Peter values this self-identity above all others is remarkable. This is so because Jews and Judaism were not highly regarded by many Gentile citizens of the empire.[5] The earliest followers of Jesus were all Jews and only after the breakout at Caesarea Maritima, in the person of Cornelius the centurion, was this ethnic barrier breached.[6] Soon thereafter, Gentiles began pouring into this new community, especially through the prodigious efforts of the Pauline mission to the Gentiles (Acts 13–14; 16–28). Throughout the era covered by the book of Acts (ca. A.D. 30-60), Christians were viewed by the Roman authorities as a sect of Judaism. Even the Jewish religious authorities in Jerusalem called them "the sect of the Nazarenes" (Acts 24:5). Consequently, the government and pagans in Anatolia probably made little distinction between Christians and Jews. Both were at best suspicious and at worst wicked. Why then would Peter deliberately emphasize such an identity, especially in terms of public relations?

The short answer is that he had no choice, nor would he have had it any other way. A historical connection with the Jewish people might be odious to some, but it is an irreplaceable given in terms of salvation history (see Rom 11:13-24). In spite of calumny and derision, "now for a little while," the Israel of God has a glorious destiny. Just like the Savior who was maligned, abused and threatened and who suffered in the flesh, so his people must follow in his steps. But beyond his suffering and their suffering lie eternal glory, an imperishable inheritance and an inexpressible joy. Like Moses, the Anatolian Christians must

---

[5]See J. L. Daniels, "Anti-Semitism in the Hellenistic-Roman Period," *JBL* 98 (1979): 45-65. Two works by Philo (*Flacc.* and *Embassy*) and a tract by Josephus (*C. Ap.*) demonstrate the virulent and vicious hatred of highly placed Roman citizens toward Jews. See further Larry R. Helyer, *Exploring Jewish Literature of the Second Temple Period* (Downers Grove, Ill.: InterVarsity Press, 2002), pp. 314, 347.

[6]See my earlier discussion of this event in chapter 4. The Samaritans were considered religious "half-breeds." In other words, their version of Judaism contained enough aberrations to justify no interaction with them (see Jn 4:9). In this regard, the conversion of many Samaritans before the conversions of Cornelius (Acts 8:4-17) and the Ethiopian eunuch, whose status is difficult to determine (Acts 8:26-39), are precursors to breaching the most formidable barrier, that separating Jews and Gentiles (Eph 2:14-16).

choose "rather to share ill-treatment with the people of God than enjoy the fleeting pleasures of sin. [They must consider] abuse suffered for Christ to be greater wealth than the treasures of Egypt, for he [Moses] was looking ahead to the reward" (Heb 11:25-26). The Anatolian believers must unashamedly wear the mantle of Israel.

## THE CHILDREN AND FAMILY OF GOD

Closely related to the notion of the Israel of God is the idea of belonging to God's family. Many passages in the OT bear this out (Ex 4:22; Jer 31:9; Hos 11:1). Peter is fond of familial language to describe this new relationship with God. As with physical families, one must be born into God's spiritual family (1 Pet 1:3). Heirs of well-to-do families in the Greco-Roman world had the prospect, after the death of their father, of receiving an inheritance. Christians are also promised an inheritance from their heavenly Father. Unlike their earthly counterparts, however, Christians have an eternal Father and, consequently, their inheritance is "imperishable, undefiled, and unfading" (1 Pet 1:4), more valuable than silver or gold (1 Pet 1:18).

Being "all in the family" carries with it filial responsibilities, analogous to what was expected and required in typical families of the empire. Household codes found in the writings of philosophers, moralists and statesmen put much emphasis on obligations incumbent on family members.[7] Chief among these obligations for both minor and adult children is honoring and obeying one's parents. Of course, the OT, especially the wisdom tradition, places great emphasis on filial responsibilities (e.g., Prov 1–9). Not surprisingly, Peter stresses precisely this duty in his pastoral letter. "Like obedient children, do not be conformed to the desires that you formerly had in ignorance" (1 Pet 1:14). They are to "live in reverent fear" because they invoke "as Father the one who judges all people" (1 Pet 1:17). Their "obedience to the truth" purifies their souls and enables them to "love one another deeply from the heart" (1 Pet 1:22).

Employing a striking metaphor in 1 Peter 2:2, Peter likens his

---

[7]See C. S. Keener, "Family and Household," *DNTB*, pp. 353-68.

Christian readers to "newborn infants." As such they are urged to "long for the pure, spiritual milk, so that by it you may grow into salvation." Paul also uses this metaphor of believers as "infants in Christ," but in a negative sense, chastising the Corinthians for their failure to grow up (1 Cor 3:1-2; see also Heb 5:11-14). Roman women of high standing preferred to employ nurses for breastfeeding. They also sought out well-educated nurses whose speech served as a good role model for their infants.[8] Probably few if any of Peter's readers fell into this social status, but I wonder if Peter is subtly encouraging his readers to accept the teaching role and authority of the elders who taught the Word of God in the house churches (1 Pet 5:5). One recalls that the apostle Paul likens himself and his missionary team to "a nurse tenderly caring for her own children" (1 Thess 2:7). At any rate, Peter continues his earlier motif of rebirth into the family of God with its incumbent expectations for proper behavior (1 Pet 1:3, 14, 17, 23).[9]

Peter thus reminds his readers of a scriptural truth: progress in spiritual growth requires deeply desiring the Word of God (e.g., Deut 8:3; Ps 19:7-14; 119:9-11).[10] Perhaps not coincidentally, Peter's command to lay aside "all guile" is matched by the requirement "to long for the pure, spiritual milk." The cognate Greek words for "guile" and "pure" are *dolos* and *adolos,* respectively. The relevance of Peter's remarks may lie in a particular situation confronting harassed believers. As a response to being maligned by their unbelieving, hostile neighbors, some of the Christians may have resorted to deceitful behavior in order to escape shameful treatment. Peter's parenesis addresses this failure to live up to biblical standards. Deeply desiring God's Word as a daily, dietary requirement remedies this behavioral deficiency and points the way toward "[growing] into salvation."

Peter exhorts the Anatolian Christians to "love the family [Gk *adelphotēs*] of believers" (1 Pet 2:17). This Greek word, used twice and only by Peter in the NT, is compounded from *delphus* with a resultant

---

[8]Ibid., p. 360.

[9]J. H. Elliott, *1 Peter: A New Translation with Introduction and Commentary* (AB 37B; New York: Doubleday, 2000), p. 405.

[10]"They should desire with the unrestrained intensity of a hungry nursing baby" (Feldmeier, *First Peter*, p. 126).

meaning "[born] from the same womb" and "could cover all the children of a family."[11] "Brothers" was widely used in the Mediterranean world for relatives and those belonging to the same guild or religious society. It was often applied metaphorically, especially "in addressing letters . . . [to a] fellow-official or a fellow-member of a society."[12] The term connoted a strong sense of solidarity shared by members of a subset within Greco-Roman society.

What sets Christian usage apart from its use in other groups is its linkage with *agapē*, the love of God, demonstrated by God's mercy in bringing about the new birth (1 Pet 1:3). Peter exhorts his readers: "Love one another deeply from the heart. . . . Above all, maintain constant love for one another, for love covers a multitude of sins" (1 Pet 1:22; 4:8). And the love here enjoined "involves willingness to share the fate of Jesus Christ even in a martyr's death" (1 Jn 3:16; Jn 15:13; cf. 1 Pet 2:21; 4:1, 12-19). Love (*agapē*) is the hallmark of Christian identity (Jn 13:35), expressed outwardly to fellow believers "with a kiss of love" (1 Pet 5:14). No surprise then that Peter addresses believers in his letter as "beloved" (*agapētoi*). In fact, Peter's letter may be outlined in light of this term. The central section of parenesis incorporating the household codes is prefaced by the direct address "beloved" (1 Pet 2:11). Then, as he draws his letter to a conclusion, perhaps anticipating an even more difficult phase of persecution for his readers, he once again prefaces his remarks with the direct address, "beloved" (1 Pet 4:12). This term is thus a fitting designation for people who have experienced God's love in an astounding way (1 Pet 1:3). They are the recipients of the most powerful act of love known to humankind, namely, the death of "the lamb without defect or blemish," the one who "committed no sin," the Lord Jesus Christ, on behalf of sinners (1 Pet 1:18-21; 2:21-25; 3:18-22). By divine grace they are now part of God's family. Responding to this life-transforming truth purifies the soul of sinners and makes it possible to express "genuine mutual love" (1 Pet 1:22; 3:8) and "a constant love" for fellow members of the family (1 Pet 4:8). As a gesture of this spiritual kinship, believers greet one another "with a kiss of love"

---

[11]W. Günther, "Brother," *NIDNTT* 1:255.
[12]Ibid.

(1 Pet 5:14). This kind of genuine love was unparalleled in the first century, and the same remains true in the twenty-first. This is the challenge of our day: demonstrate to a watching world that we really do "love the family of believers" (1 Pet 2:17).

Another distinctive way in which this strong sense of family solidarity expresses itself is in mutual service. As Peter phrases it, "Like good stewards of the manifold grace of God, serve one another with whatever gift each of you has received" (1 Pet 4:10). One surely hears echoes of the Upper Room Discourse and Peter's famous foot-washing experience. "Do you know what I have done to you? . . . I have set you an example, that you also should do as I have done to you. Very truly, I tell you, servants are not greater than their master, nor are messengers greater than the one who sent them. If you know these things, you are blessed if you do them" (Jn 13:12-17). This theme of humility recurs in Peter's brief letter (1 Pet 3:4, 8, 16) like a Mozartean motif and climaxes in 1 Peter 5:5-6: "And all of you must clothe yourselves with humility in your dealings with one another, for God opposes the proud, but gives grace to the humble. Humble yourselves therefore under the mighty hand of God, so that he may exalt you in due time."

Peter briefly mentions only two charisms (Gk. *charisma*, "a gift," "an endowment of God's grace") in his exhortation: speaking and serving (1 Pet 4:11). I am reminded of the earliest Jerusalem church and a crisis the apostles faced. Hellenistic widows complained of being neglected in the daily food distribution (Acts 6:1-6). The apostles considered this complaint and instituted the office of deacon in order to oversee the distribution. The appointment of deacons allowed the apostles "to devote [themselves] to prayer and to serving the word" (Acts 6:4). Similarly, Peter subsumes Christian ministry under the two fundamental activities of speaking the word of God and serving the needs of the saints. The Anatolian elders must exercise their oversight, whether speaking the word or serving the saints, as servant leaders and "examples to the flock" (1 Pet 5:3).

"Speaking the very words of God" probably involves the ministries of preaching and teaching, the two primary forms in which the word of God addresses human beings: *kērygma* ("proclamation") announces the good news of salvation in Christ and addresses unbelievers; *didachē* (from which we derive the English word *didactic*), denotes instruction, teaching and catechesis consisting of both creed (belief) and conduct (behavior), and is directed toward believers. Paranesis, moral and spiritual admonition, is the application of teaching to the all-important matter of personal and communal conduct. For Paul, Peter and John, the imperative of parenesis is always anchored in the indicative of the creed—believers ought to live lives that are consistent with the revealed truths of the gospel. As one example among many, Peter reminds his readers that if they invoke God as Father, then it follows that they must live in reverential fear (1 Pet 1:17).

In Ephesians, Paul distinguishes among apostles, prophets, evangelists, pastors and teachers (Eph 4:11), and in 1 Corinthians 12:8-11, 28-30, he enumerates two slightly different lists of grace gifts. Peter doubtless was familiar with such distinctions, but there was no need to discuss them further as there was in Paul's letter to the Corinthians, in which controversy swirled around their exercise. What Peter emphasizes is the seriousness with which one must view the task of speaking "the very words of God" and "the strength that God supplies" in order to serve the saints and thereby bring glory to God (1 Pet 4:11).

## THE NEW TEMPLE AND PRIESTHOOD OF GOD

Perhaps no image Peter employs has greater potential to elevate his readers' self-esteem than the notion of temple and priesthood. This is because, whether pagan or Jewish, a majority of people in the first century highly regarded priests and temples. In paganism, belonging to the priesthood was an exclusive privilege, eliciting prestige and entitling benefits.[13] In Second Temple Judaism, Jewish priests were generally held in high regard, with notable exceptions, and were the beneficiaries of considerable power and privilege. Even more than in paganism, membership in this select group was limited, in that only individuals belonging to families descended from the ancient Aaronides were eligible.[14] In the provinces of the empire, especially Ana-

---

[13]See J. A. North, "Priests (Greek and Roman)," *OCD*, pp. 1245-46.
[14]See L. D. Hurst and J. B. Green, "Priest, Priesthood," *DJG*, pp. 633-36.

tolia, cities competed with each other over the privilege and perks of building magnificent temples in honor of the divine Caesar or one of the pantheon of gods and goddesses sanctioned by Rome. The Second Temple was held in awe by a majority of Jews as the dwelling place of God. The Essenes (a separatist Jewish sect), while respecting the structure, were bitterly opposed to the Sadducees who controlled the complex and its considerable resources.[15] For most citizens and residents of the empire, however, it would have been considered most fortunate to belong to the restricted class of priests. For the Anatolian Christians, Peter's application of this imagery to them was both a morale booster and a moral challenge.

Peter's appeal to temple imagery occurs in the first main section of his letter in which he seeks to reconstruct his readers identity as the elect and holy people of God (1 Pet 1:14; 2:10). After depicting his readers as the children of God (1 Pet 1:14; 2:2), Peter suddenly switches imagery. Now, in direct address, he summons them to enter into their priestly ministry (1 Pet 2:4).[16] This section serves almost like an ordination service, setting the Anatolian believers apart for their priestly ministry. The temple in which they serve, however, radically departs from what might be expected: Peter spiritualizes the temple of God. There is no localized marble monument in which priestly ministrations take place; rather, the believers themselves are "a spiritual house."[17] In place of massive Herodian ashlars, such as girded and graced the Jerusalem temple, are "living stones" of flesh and blood who offer up "spiritual sacrifices." This is a theological masterstroke having a distinctly Pauline ring to it (Eph 2:19-22) and is but one more instance in which these two apostles, both of whom tradition locates in Rome at the end

---

[15]M. O. Wise, "Temple," *DJG*, pp. 813-16, and B. Chilton, P. W. Comfort and M. O. Wise, "Temple, Jewish," *DNTB*, pp. 1171-82.

[16]I follow the NRSV's rendering of the present participle *proserchomenoi* as an imperatival participle ("Come to him") rather than as an adverbial participle functioning in the indicative mood ("As you come") as in NIV, TNIV, NASB, ESV and HCSB. This is an admittedly rare usage but can be documented in the papyri. See H. E. Dana and Julius R. Manta, *A Manual Grammar of the Greek New Testament* (New York: Macmillan, 1955), p. 229, and Daniel B. Wallace, *Greek Grammar Beyond the Basics* (Grand Rapids: Zondervan, 1996), pp. 650-52.

[17]The Qumran community also saw themselves as a new, spiritual temple, a holy house, the true successors of the sons of Zadok (4Q174 1.1-19; 1QS 5.1-10; 8.4-6; 9.3-5; 1QpHab 12.1-3; CD iii.21-iv.3).

of their lives, display significant similarities of thought in their pastoral correspondence.

We have already considered the cornerstone Christology employed by Peter in this section. What interests us here is how this section contributes to Peter's view of the church. In the first place, there can be no mistaking where authority lies. Christ is both the focal point and the foundation of this spiritual house in Zion. He is the living stone who summons individuals to become part of this grand edifice. Through his resurrection, sinners are given "new birth into a living hope," and become "living stones" in a great "spiritual house."

Worth noting is Peter's democratization of the imagery of stones. While believers are not the cornerstone, they are, nonetheless, "living stones," by virtue of sharing in the spiritual life that flows from the "living stone." And as living stones they are also part of a holy priesthood. Notable for its absence is any notion of a hierarchical structure among the Anatolian house churches. That development belongs to a later stage in the history of the emerging church. We do have elders who exercise oversight and, though not mentioned, there were probably also deacons because this office goes back to the early Jerusalem church (Acts 6), and the Gentile churches established by Paul appointed deacons (Phil 1:1; 1 Tim 3:8, 10). In this regard, Peter's letter reflects a similar organizational and worship pattern as found in Paul's letters to the Corinthians (A.D. 55-56).[18]

Second, 1 Peter briefly sketches the type of ministry these Christian priests perform. The primary function and responsibility of priests, whether pagan or Jewish, involved offering proper, proscribed sacrifices. Both pagan and Jewish priests underwent considerable instruction and training in order to carry out this vital religious function. Peter's letter addresses this issue, but in a rather surprising way. He assumes that all believers are not only capable of offering "spiritual sacrifices acceptable to God" (1 Pet 2:5) but also are expected to do so. Thus no issues of genealogical or social status delimit who may or may not function in this holy priesthood. But what is mandatory is being "a

---

[18]"1 Peter allows that charismatic and institutional forms of leadership could exist side by side." K. N. Giles, "Church Order, Government," *DLNTD*, p. 224.

living stone"; that is, they must have experienced a new birth into the family of God through Christ. In this sense, there is a definite delimitation for priesthood. Furthermore, having been born into the family of God they must now make personal and corporate holiness their primary objective. They are to reflect the holiness of their heavenly Father and by so doing demonstrate their true credentials as "royal priests" (1 Pet 2:9). Once again, one cannot help but notice the similarity in thought to the apostle Paul, whose magisterial letter to the Romans transitions from teaching to parenesis with a summons to holiness couched in liturgical, priestly language: "I appeal to you therefore, brothers and sisters, by the mercies of God, to present your bodies as a living sacrifice, holy and acceptable to God, which is your spiritual worship" (Rom 12:1).

What are these "spiritual sacrifices" believers offer? The nearest Peter comes to answering this question occurs in his programmatic definition of believers as "a chosen race, a royal priesthood, a holy nation, God's own people" (1 Pet 2:9). This composite quotation pulling together snippets from Deuteronomy 7:6 and 10:15, Exodus 19:6 and Isaiah 61:6 concludes with a purpose clause: "in order that you may proclaim the mighty acts of him who called you out of darkness into his marvelous light" (1 Pet 2:9). Proclamation of God's saving acts constitutes the highest order of "spiritual sacrifices."

In what form might this proclamation take place? Comparing Peter's letter with 1 Corinthians, I infer that those who speak the words of God (1 Pet 4:11) focus on God's saving acts (1 Cor 12:8; 14:1, 24-25, 26, 29). As mentioned earlier, proclamation was of two basic types: evangelism and edification. Unbelievers are the assumed audience in the former and the people of God the latter. In the case of unbelievers, there are occasions when speaking the word of God takes on an apologetic thrust: "Always be ready to make your defense to anyone who demands from you an accounting for the hope that is in you" (1 Pet 3:15).[19] In a striking word picture, Peter portrays speaking the word of

---

[19]"When churches live out the gospel in accord with the admonitions in the various letters, the gospel will naturally become attractive to outsiders." Thomas R. Schreiner, *New Testament Theology: Magnifying God in Christ* (Grand Rapids: Baker, 2008), p. 748.

God to believers as supplying "spiritual milk" to newborn infants with a clearly stated objective: "so that by it you may grow into salvation" (1 Pet 2:2). Once again, parallels to Pauline literature abound (1 Cor 3:1-3; 14:20; 2 Cor 6:13; Gal 4:19; cf. Heb 5:13-14).

Serving also qualifies as a spiritual sacrifice (1 Pet 4:11). Just as pagan and Jewish priests engaged in a wide-ranging number of liturgical and nonliturgical service, so too do the new priests of the new people of God. The word for serving (*diakoneō*) covers a broad range of activities of a practical nature. One can envision a number of ways in which members of a harassed minority might extend a helping hand to brothers and sisters feeling the effects of economic and societal deprivation. Brothers and sisters in deep distress are vulnerable to the predations of the "roaring lion your adversary the devil" (1 Pet 5:8). Accordingly, Peter exhorts his readers: "be hospitable to one another without complaining" (1 Pet 4:9) and "above all, maintain constant love for one another" (1 Pet 4:8).

The practice of prayer occupies an important place among the spiritual disciplines of the early church. In fact, Peter urges his readers "to discipline yourselves for the sake of your prayers" (1 Pet 4:7). Most likely the plural refers not to private devotions but to regular prayers offered up during worship services in the house churches.[20] Certainly the content of such prayers featured the "praise and glory and honor [of] Jesus Christ" (cf. 1 Pet 1:7). We may also be quite sure the Anatolian believers regularly prayed for the emperor ("Honor the emperor," 1 Pet 2:17), as this was something Paul also insisted on in his churches (cf. 1 Tim 2:1-3).

In short, the notion of believers constituting a spiritual temple founded on Jesus Christ and simultaneously serving as royal priests offering up spiritual sacrifices is a major contribution of Petrine theology. Needless to say, it has played an enormous role in ecclesiastical self-understanding ever since. Unfortunately, division and conflict have wracked the catholic church in terms of the particulars of polity and liturgy.

---

[20]Elliott, *1 Peter*, p. 749.

## THE FLOCK OF GOD

The final glittering image in our mosaic derives from a motif indebted to Jesus' ministry and teaching (Mt 10:6; 15:24; Mk 6:34; Jn 10:1-18, 27). Peter likens his readers to "the flock of God" (1 Pet 5:2). Jesus himself did not originate the image but adapts a motif employed by OT prophets in order to depict the Lord's relationship to his covenant people. Thus, in Isaiah 40:11 we hear this majestic strain: "He [the Lord God] will feed his flock like a shepherd; he will gather the lambs in his arms, and carry them in his bosom, and gently lead the mother sheep." Zechariah assures his listeners that "the Lord of hosts cares for his flock, the house of Judah" (Zech 10:3). The hymnody of ancient Israel also resonates with this comforting theme (Pss 77:20; 78:52; 80:1; 95:7). Previously, I explored Peter's shepherd-king Christology. Now I turn to the flip side of this imagery: believers are likened to sheep who had formerly strayed but now "have returned to the shepherd and guardian of [their] souls" (1 Pet 2:25), the "chief shepherd" (1 Pet 5:4), the Lord Jesus Christ.

This image comes to the forefront as Peter concludes his pastoral letter. There is something fitting about this. Nothing could have been more deeply impressed on Peter's soul than the last interview with Jesus along the shore of Galilee (Jn 21:15-23). There Jesus reinstated Peter as the acknowledged leader of the movement. The threefold charge to "feed my lambs" (Jn 21:15), "tend my sheep" (Jn 21:16) and "feed my sheep" (Jn 21:17) was solemnly placed on his shoulders. He must be a pastor, a shepherd to God's flock, a heavy, unrelenting responsibility. The choice of sheep as a metaphor for believers is especially apt because sheep require constant attention and care. Dangers abound (1 Pet 1:14, 18; 2:1, 11-12; 3:14, 16; 4:12). Predators lurk (1 Pet 5:8). Spiritual sustenance is an ongoing necessity (1 Pet 2:2). Sheep tend to be fearful and skittish. And so do saints (1 Pet 3:6, 14).

So, as Peter wraps up his parenesis, he turns his attention to the elders who play such a vital role in the house churches. In view of the expected "fiery ordeal" (1 Pet 4:12-19), leadership issues are critical. Not pulling rank, Peter addresses his fellow elders: "Now as an elder myself . . . I exhort the elders among you to tend the flock of God that is in your charge, exercising the oversight" (1 Pet 5:1-2). One is reminded of the apostle Paul's farewell speech to the Ephesian elders, a speech resonating with the same notes sounded in Peter's letter: "Keep watch over yourselves and over all the flock, of which the Holy Spirit has made you overseers, to shepherd the church of God that he obtained with the blood of his own Son" (Acts 20:28). The Anatolian house churches, like the Pauline churches, have elders who were responsible for spiritual oversight. The book of Acts assumes that this was a regular feature of the Pauline mission (Acts 14:23; 20:17), and Paul's letters confirm this procedure (Phil 1:1; 1 Tim 3:1-7; Tit 1:5-9).[21] We wish Peter had provided more clues enabling us to infer the inner workings of this eldership. But his purpose is strictly focused on the attitudes and motives of the elders and he does so by means of a series of three contrastive approaches.

Table 10.1.

| Negative | Positive |
| --- | --- |
| Not under compulsion | Willingly, as God would have you do it |
| Not for sordid gain | Eagerly |
| Not lording it over those in your charge | Being an example to the flock |

First, what are we to make of Peter's appeal that they carry out their ministry "willingly" rather than "under compulsion"? What does that imply concerning the situation in the house churches? Given their precarious situation, the churches needed leaders whom they could trust and who would serve the group rather than themselves. The willing attitude is further defined: "as God would have you do it" (1 Pet 5:2). There must be conviction on the part of the elders that God has called them to serve in this capacity; a vague sense of responsibility "that someone must do it" is inadequate. A sense of call not compulsion is the proper motivation to serve.

As to purpose, several NT passages indicate that ministry for profit already plagued the early churches. Paul reminds Timothy that deacons

---

[21]J. Ramsey Michaels, *1 Peter* (WBC 47; Waco, Tex.: Word, 1988), p. 277, suggests that some of the Anatolian house churches had elders whereas others did not. This suggestion has not received much support.

must not be "greedy for money" and instructs Titus that bishops (lit., "overseers") must not "be greedy . . . for gain" (Tit 1:7). False teachers who imagined "that godliness is a means of gain" (1 Tim 6:5) and acted as "peddlers of God's word" (2 Cor 2:17) preyed on vulnerable house churches. Peter himself had earlier encountered a professed convert, Simon Magus, who sought to profit by the spiritual gift of healing (Acts 8:9-24). Even earlier, Peter confronted the hypocritical Ananias and Sapphira, a Christian couple pretending sacrificial generosity, all the while holding back a sum to assure their financial security (Acts 5:1-11). Second Peter rails against greedy false teachers who exploit the faithful "with deceptive words" (2 Pet 2:3). Instead of greed, elders must display eagerness for oversight and care of their flock.

The third contrast relates to the manner of exercising spiritual oversight and presents a stark contrast to the regnant culture. Greco-Roman society frequently featured highly dictatorial leadership styles ("You know that the rulers of the Gentiles lord it over them, and their great ones are tyrants over them," Mt 20:25). One gets a whiff of this roughshod approach in Paul's second letter to the Corinthians in which he sarcastically depicts the tactics of the false apostles: "For you put up with it when someone makes slaves of you, or preys upon you, or takes advantage of you, or puts on airs, or gives you a slap in the face. To my shame, I must say, we were too weak for that!" (2 Cor 11:20-21). Christian elders have a dramatically different pattern of leadership in which the role model is Jesus Christ, the chief shepherd. His style embodies self-giving love so powerfully demonstrated in the three christological passages earlier examined. It also insists that both leaders and the led "clothe [themselves] with humility in [their] dealings with one another" (1 Pet 5:5), a Christian virtue despised by Greco-Roman ethos. Once again the powerful lesson on humility acted out by the Master in the Upper Room informs this admonition to elders (Jn 13).

## CONCLUSION

Four glittering images portray the new people of God. Here is something to live, suffer and, if need be, die for. Nothing in the empire or in Anatolian history, religion and mythology can compare. The glory that will be revealed to those who endure a "little while" far surpasses any-thing imaginable. They will not regret their commitment to the chief shepherd. Peter's "short letter" of encouragement and testimony (1 Pet 5:12) sounds the same note as Paul's ringing affirmation: "I consider that the sufferings of this present time are not worth comparing with the glory about to be revealed to us" (Rom 8:18).

## SHARED CONVICTIONS

We are now in a position to identify some core concepts that give co-herence and shape to Peter's theology. These concepts are not immedi-ately obvious from a casual reading of 1 Peter, but after repeated reading and reflection, they emerge from the particulars of the letter. Not sur-prisingly, once recognized, they turn out not to be unique to Peter; they are part of a shared theological tradition in early Christianity. In short, they are the features that provide unity to the NT message.

*Redemptive history: The grand narrative.* I have occasionally pointed out how Peter's pastoral letter assumes a definite frame of reference: the Anatolian believers have, by a new birth, been swept up into an on-going story whose roots reach back into the OT. The narrative of Israel shapes their existence; they have been incorporated into this grand story and are now part of the new Israel of God.[22] As such they now greatly anticipate the long-prophesied glorious destiny of the people of God. Furthermore, the narrative of Jesus Christ has necessarily inter-sected their lives, for it is an essential subplot in the larger story of Israel. Indeed, without this all-important narrative, the larger narrative of Israel would never be realized.[23] This appears most clearly in Peter's opening comments. After his thanksgiving, reminding his readers of

---

[22]The overarching narrative is broader even than the story of Israel. As Joel Green reminds us:

the particular narratives related in the biblical books . . . participate in a more extensive, overarching narrative, or metanarrative. This is the story of God's purpose coming to fruition in the whole of God's history with us, from the creation of the world and hu-manity's falling away from God, through God's repeated attempts to restore his people, culminating in the coming of Jesus of Nazareth and reaching its full crescendo in the final revelation of Christ and the new creation. ("Narrative Theology," *DTIB*, p. 532)

[23]See Ben Witherington III, *The Indelible Image*, vol. 1: *The Individual Witnesses* (Downers Grove, Ill.: InterVarsity Press, 2009), pp. 174-203, for a discussion of the importance of under-standing the primary narratives in the NT.

their destiny, "the salvation of [their] souls" (1 Pet 1:3-9), Peter elaborates on this salvation. According to Peter, the prophets—and there can
be no doubt that he means the OT prophets—spoke about the grace of
God revealed in Christ (1 Pet 1:10). They were aware that the Messiah's career had two nodal points: suffering and glory, in that order (1
Pet 1:11). What remained unknown concerned the identity and timing
of these redemptive events (1 Pet 1:11), intriguing questions, so it would
seem, to angels as well (1 Pet 5:12). The prophets did, however, grasp
the eschatological setting of these events. "This salvation" was not
something they would witness; their messages were intended by the
Holy Spirit to encourage and motivate a future generation of believers
("you"). Note that Peter, in keeping with the NT, assumes that the
present generation of believers will witness the final consummation of
redemptive history (1 Pet 4:7; 5:4; cf. Acts 3:19-21).[24]

This last observation illustrates a hallmark of redemptive history as
reflected in NT thought. Peter's letter clearly displays the familiar
tension between the "now but not yet" character of redemptive history.
In the opening sentences, Peter establishes that the readers are already
partakers of "a living hope through the resurrection of Jesus Christ"
and "an inheritance that is imperishable" (1 Pet 1:3-4). But their present
"indescribable and glorious joy" (1 Pet 1:8) stands over against the
"praise and glory and honor when Jesus Christ is revealed" (1 Pet 1:7),
"the salvation of [their] souls" (1 Pet 1:9). In short, they have been saved,
are being saved and will be saved on the day Christ is revealed. As has
often been pointed out, Peter's thought, like that of other NT authors,
views salvation as unfolding in three tenses: past, present and future.
Thus the readers are reminded that they "were ransomed from the
futile ways inherited from [their] ancestors" (1 Pet 1:18) and have "purified [their] souls by . . . obedience to the truth" (1 Pet 1:22). The
present dimension of salvation comes into play when Peter reminds
them that they are living "during the time of [their] exile" (1 Pet 1:17),

---

[24]Once again, it is important to distinguish between what an apostle like Peter (or Paul) may
have thought about the timing of certain eschatological events and that which he affirmed as
part of the apostolic teaching. Like the rest of the NT, Peter does not set a date for the parousia.

and he exhorts them "to rid [themselves] . . . of all malice" and, "like newborn infants, [to] long for the pure, spiritual milk, so that by it [they] may grow into salvation" (1 Pet 2:1-2). Believers are now "living stones" in a "spiritual house" offering up "spiritual sacrifices" (1 Pet 2:4-5). But overshadowing their past and present, at crucial points in his exhortation, Peter holds out the hope of a glorious future (1 Pet 1:5, 7, 14; 2:12; 4:7, 13; 5:1, 4, 6, 10). This is his primary motivation for hanging tough and holding on. Looming above all else are these inspiring and comforting words: "And when the chief shepherd appears, you will win the crown of glory that never fades away" (1 Pet 5:4).

*Focal point.* Like Paul and John, Peter fastens his attention on the saving story of Jesus Christ. Since we have already examined Peter's Christology, I will not rehearse the findings here except to say that the three christological passages punctuating this letter leave no doubt as to the centrality of Christ and the cross for Peter's thought. These christological passages, though not identical to Paul's thought, display a number of correspondences, correspondences stemming from a shared reservoir of apostolic teaching. How could it be otherwise? The cross and resurrection transformed a dispirited band of Jesus' followers into fearless witnesses of his triumph over sin and death and his exaltation to the right hand of God (Acts 2:32-36; cf. 1 Pet 3:13-16). The risen Christ personally revealed himself to Saul of Tarsus (Gal 1:15-16), "formerly a blasphemer, a persecutor, and a man of violence" (1 Tim 1:13), and entrusted him with the same gospel (Gal 1:11-12; 2:6-10). No wonder then that the shadow of the cross, like a watermark, impresses itself on the contents of this letter. It is the focal point and thus shares common ground with the major NT witnesses, Jesus, Paul and John.[25]

*The human plight.* Peter's letter resonates with the same theological understanding of the human condition as depicted in Jesus, Paul and John.[26] Of these three witnesses, Peter's thought corresponds most closely to that of Paul. Many phrases may be appealed to demonstrating the affinity between the two leading apostles. This is not to say there is

---

[25]See further Larry R. Helyer, *The Witness of Jesus, Paul and John* (Downers Grove, Ill.: InterVarsity Press, 2008), pp. 384-89.
[26]Ibid., pp. 389-91.

dependence either way; each has his own distinctive witness in this regard.[27] On essentials, however, they are in agreement.

I briefly reprise several points of concord. Peter, like Paul, assumes an evil axis comprising the world, the flesh and the devil. Though not using the term *sarx* ("flesh") to describe the fallen nature as Paul does (e.g., "do not gratify the desires of the flesh" [*epithymian sarkos*], Gal 5:16), Peter can speak of "desires [epithymiais] that you formerly had in ignorance" (1 Pet 1:14). And whereas Paul urges the Roman Christians, "Do not be conformed to this world" (*mē syschēmatizesthe tō aiōni toutō*, Rom 12:2), Peter warns his readers: "do not be conformed [*syschēmatizomenoi*] to the desires [*epithymiais*] that you formerly had in ignorance." Paul's contrast of the old life with the new in Ephesians 2:1-3 establishes the same point in somewhat similar terminology as Peter in 1 Peter 1:14. Though Peter does not list the spiritual powers of darkness, as Paul does (Eph 6:12; Col 1:16; 2:10, 20), his third christological passage does mention Christ's proclamation "to the spirits in prison," perhaps a reference to the same spiritual beings Paul had in mind. And one must not forget Peter's warning about "your adversary the devil [who] prowls around, looking for someone to devour (1 Pet 5:8), echoing Paul's admonition to "put on the whole armor of God, so that you may be able to stand against the wiles of the devil" (Eph 6:11). The same general understanding of fallen humanity appears in the Johannine corpus: "The whole world lies under the power of the evil one" (1 Jn 5:19; cf. Jn 12:31). Peter, Paul and John share a common, conceptual understanding of the human predicament outside of Christ.

*The new covenant community.* Perhaps even more striking is the similarity of thought among Jesus, Peter, Paul and John in their understanding of the new people of God. Even though Peter never uses the term *ekklēsia* ("church") in his first letter, the number of shared conceptual images describing the church is noteworthy.[28] For example, Peter shares with Paul the notion of the people of God as a new Israel

---

[27]See Elliott, *1 Peter*, pp. 37-40, for a discussion of this issue.

[28]For that matter, only Matthew puts the word *ekklēsia* ("church") in Jesus' mouth ("I will build my church" Mt 16:18; 18:17). Many commentators take this as Matthean redaction, but good arguments may be advanced that Jesus may well have used the Aramaic equivalent, *qahal*. See Donald A. Hagner, *Matthew 14–28* (WBC 33B; Dallas: Word, 1995), pp. 465-66.

(1 Pet 1:1-2; 2:9; cf. Gal 3:29; 6:16), a new temple (1 Pet 2:5; cf. 1 Cor 3:16; 6:19; Eph 2:20-22) and being "in Christ" (1 Pet 3:16; 5:10, 14). Peter also shares with Paul the notion of the priesthood of believers (1 Pet 2:5, 9; cf. Rom 12:1; Phil 4:18; Eph 2:20-22). Like Jesus, Peter employs the imagery of believers as the flock of God (1 Pet 2:25; 5:2-3; cf. Jn 10; 21:16-17). Only Peter among the other NT witnesses mentions the charisms of the Spirit that Paul elaborates in Corinthians (1 Cor 12, 14) and Romans (Rom 12:6-8). Though Peter does not explicitly refer to a new covenant, his employment of covenantal terminology conveys a mindset congenial to the apostle Paul's understanding of the new covenant in Christ (cf. 2 Cor 3:6; Gal 4:22-26 with 1 Pet 1:2-15; 2:4-10; 4:17).[29]

*Eschatology.* The eschatology of 1 Peter displays the familiar contours of NT eschatological belief generally. That which immediately strikes the reader is the pronounced sense of imminence. "The end of all things is near" (1 Pet 4:7).[30] One hears a familiar chord often struck by Paul ("For the present form of this world is passing away" [1 Cor 7:31]; "the night is far gone, the day is near" [Rom 13:12]). This same note of imminence appears in the Johannine corpus, even though it is overshadowed by a pronounced realized eschatology. Consider these Johannine sayings: "Children, it is the last hour! As you have heard that antichrist is coming, so now many antichrists have come. From this we know that it is the last hour" (1 Jn 2:18). "I am coming soon" (Rev 3:11). "See, I am coming like a thief! Blessed is the one who stays awake and is clothed" (Rev 16:15). "See, I am coming soon. . . . Surely I am coming soon" (Rev 22:12, 20). Imminence is a hallmark of early Christian proclamation.

The verdict is clear: Peter's message and theology cohere with that of the major NT witnesses, and this unity of thought is a bulwark that safeguards the church as it sails into the troubled waters of the twenty-first century.

---

[29]For a more detailed discussion of the differences and similarities, see Paul J. Achtemeier, *1 Peter: A Commentary on First Peter* (ed. Eldon J. Epp; Hermeneia; Minneapolis: Fortress, 1996), pp. 15-19, and Elliott, *1 Peter*, pp. 37-40.

[30]"The explicit reference to the imminent end shows that the author of 1 Peter basically still holds firmly to the earliest Christian expectation of a speedy end to the world." Feldmeier, *First Peter*, p. 217.

## QUESTIONS FOR DISCUSSION

1. How important is self-image for Christian discipleship?

2. How does 1 Peter's reimaging of Christian identity relate to the emphasis on self-esteem in modern (mostly North American) Christianity?

3. Why was it important in 1 Peter to link Christians with the people of Israel? Is this necessary today?

4. Why is the family imagery in 1 Peter so important for modern Christianity?

5. What contribution do the temple and priesthood metaphors make toward understanding the nature of the church?

6. How relevant are the passages on communal worship (1 Pet 4:10-11) and pastoral leadership (1 Pet 5:1-5) for modern Christianity?

7. Evaluate the case for a fundamental theological unity of Petrine thought with that of Jesus, Paul and John.

## FOR FURTHER READING

In addition to commentaries and theologies previously cited, see the following:

Campbell, W. S. "Church as Israel, People of God." *DLNTD*. Downers Grove, Ill.: InterVarsity Press, 1997. Pp. 204-19.

Lim, D. S. "Evangelism in the Early Church." *DLNTD*. Downers Grove, Ill.: InterVarsity Press, 1997. Pp. 353-59.

Matera, Frank J. *New Testament Theology: Exploring Diversity and Unity.* Louisville: Westminster John Knox, 2007. Pp. 373-79.

Schreiner, Thomas R. *New Testament Theology: Magnifying God in Christ.* Grand Rapids: Baker, 2008. Pp. 743-48.

Thielman, Frank. *Theology of the New Testament: A Canonical and Synthetic Approach.* Grand Rapids: Zondervan, 2005. Pp. 572-83.

# 11

## 2 PETER

*Introductory Questions*

*No NT document had a longer or rougher
struggle to win acceptance than 2 Peter.*

J. N. D. KELLY

*Second Peter is sometimes considered the one real
embarrassment in the New Testament Canon.*

FRANK THIELMAN

THIS LETTER, AT FACE VALUE, claims to be from Simeon Peter (2 Pet
1:1) and addresses a theological and ethical crisis in unspecified house
churches. Though nowhere does the author identify the readers, the
reference to this being "the second letter I am writing to you" (2 Pet 3:1)
suggests that the first letter was 1 Peter and the addressees are the same
Anatolian believers from the provinces mentioned in 1 Peter 1:1.
Modern scholarship for the most part rejects this traditional understanding of 2 Peter.[1]

---

[1]"In short, the majority of scholars reject it as a genuine work of the apostle Peter, in spite of its
own claims, and regard it as a later pseudepigraphon." Donald Guthrie, *New Testament Introduction* (3rd rev. ed.; Downers Grove, Ill.: InterVarsity Press, 1970), p. 814.

## Contents and Genre

What immediately strikes the reader of 2 Peter is the sudden transition from an affirming, encouraging tone (2 Pet 1:3-21) to a sharply argumentative, threatening one (2 Pet 2:1-22), concluding with an exhortatory, encouraging word (2 Pet 3:1-18). The central section castigates false teachers for their "destructive opinions" (2 Pet 2:1) and, at the center of this controversy, lies a blatant denial of a cardinal doctrine of the earliest church, namely, the return of Jesus Christ (2 Pet 2:16-21; 3:1-10). Coupled with this eschatological deviation is a disturbing moral and ethical defection: "They have left the straight road and have gone astray" (2 Pet 2:15). Either as a cause or result of this deviancy, "they . . . even deny the Master who bought them" (2 Pet 2:1). Once again, theology and ethics are inextricably intertwined in 2 Peter.[2] Believers are exhorted to "be all the more eager to confirm your call and election" in order to enter "into the eternal kingdom of our Lord and Savior Jesus Christ" (2 Pet 1:10-11). Indeed, the letter is framed by a twofold exhortation: "make every effort" (2 Pet 1:5; 3:14 TNIV). Thus both Christian creed and conduct are under assault and our author confronts the crisis head on.

But parenesis and polemic are not the only moods projected by this pastoral letter. The implied author is aware that his days on this earth are numbered (2 Pet 1:14). Mindful of this impending reality, he expresses a deep concern for the spiritual well-being of his readers, exhorts them to be "established in the truth that has come to you" (2 Pet 1:12) and commits himself to "make every effort so that after my departure you may be able at any time to recall these things" (2 Pet 1:15). There is a certain pathos and poignancy about this letter that gives it the feel of a last testament, a literary genre appearing in both the OT and in extracanonical Jewish literature. In the NT, there is an even closer parallel in 2 Timothy. "In both cases the legacy and a sort of last will and testament of a great apostle are being passed on."[3] This literary

---

[2] A point untiringly made by Ben Witherington III. See, e.g., *The Indelible Image* (2 vols.; Downers Grove, Ill.: InterVarsity Press, 2009), 1:13-24.

[3] Ibid., 1:774. In fairness, however, I must point out that Witherington assumes that both 2 Timothy and 2 Peter were written by close disciples after the death of the respective apostles.

feature figures prominently in the debate over authorship.

Add characteristics of apocalyptic literature and you have the makings of a remarkably diverse document despite its brevity. Permeating the content of the letter is an assumed apocalyptic worldview of pervasive evil ("the corruption that is in the world because of lust," 2 Pet 1:4) traced back to a primeval angelic rebellion (2 Pet 2:4). A vivid sense of living "in the last days" (2 Pet 3:3) and robust hope while "waiting for and hastening the coming of the day of God" (2 Pet 3:12) punctuate the parenesis. Culminating this day of God is nothing short of a total renovation of the cosmos, a "new heavens and a new earth" (2 Pet 3:13). This apocalyptic substratum will be an essential part of our inquiry into the theology of this diverse document.

## Authorship

Even though the implied author is Simeon Peter, many modern scholars doubt that he is the real author. How then should the theology of 2 Peter be understood and presented? I think it helpful at the outset to lay out briefly the primary options.

1. The standard historical-critical approach of the nineteenth and early twentieth century viewed 2 Peter as a pseudepigraphon (a work falsely claiming to be written by a revered figure from the past). Based on stylistic, linguistic and historical arguments, scholars assigned this testamentary letter to the second century A.D., written by an anonymous Christian who wished to invoke the memory (and perhaps some traditions) of Peter in order to confront the onslaught of Gnosticism on the churches. Accordingly, 2 Peter was reckoned the latest NT document. Typically, scholars holding this view regarded the content as falling short of apostolic standards and displaying "early Catholicism." This latter term designates a period in which expectation of an imminent parousia has faded and a concern for institutional viability and consolidation of doctrinal consensus takes center stage. The upshot typically resulted in 2 Peter being neglected if not denigrated for its "inferior" theology. [4]

---

[4]A classic statement of this position is found in Ernst Käsemann, "An Apologia for Primitive Christian Eschatology," in *Essays in New Testament Themes* (London: SCM, 1964), pp. 179-85,

2. A less extreme variation is the notion that the document dates to the end of the first century or the very beginning of the second. The opponents attacked are not identified with the fully developed Gnosticism of the second century but rather to a libertine movement appearing in the last third of the first century. This view makes it more likely that the author did have some access to genuine Petrine traditions.[5]

3. This latter variation can be further tweaked to constitute a third approach, in which, after Peter's death, one of his disciples invokes his authority and traditions in order to stave off the inroads of libertines and naysayers of Jesus' return.[6] Pseudepigraphy is understood to be an acceptable literary device, by no means viewed as fraudulent or deceptive, since the readers are aware of and tacitly consent to what is going on. Adherents appeal to the literary convention of testaments whereby respected figures from the past purportedly pass along their last instructions to the current generation. The OT, Second Temple Judaism and the world of Hellenism afford numerous literary examples of this genre. On this understanding, 2 Peter may be placed in the decades after Peter's martyrdom (ca. A.D. 64-65) but before the second century.

4. Finally, one may resist the consensus and maintain that Peter is not only the implied author but also the real author. Taking the letter at face value, a majority of conservative scholars still locate this letter shortly before Peter's death in Rome and understand it as a follow-up letter to the Anatolian house churches addressed in 1 Peter.[7] The many

---

193, and idem, "Paul and Early Catholicism," in *New Testament Questions of Today* (Philadelphia: Fortress, 1969), pp. 236-37. See also Werner Kümmel, *Introduction to the New Testament* (trans. Howard Clark Kee; rev. ed.; Nashville: Abingdon, 1975), pp. 430-34, and J. C. Beker, "Peter, Second Letter of," *IDB* 3:767-69. Ralph P. Martin offers a careful critique of Käsemann's view in *New Testament Theology: The Theology of the Letters of James, Peter and Jude* (New York: Cambridge University Press, 1994), pp. 148-51.

[5]On this approach, see Frank J. Matera, *New Testament Theology: Exploring Diversity and Unity* (Louisville: Westminster John Knox, 2007), pp. 385-87.

[6]See, e.g., Richard J. Bauckham, *Jude, 2 Peter* (WBC 50; Dallas: Word, 1983), pp. 158-64, and Witherington, *Indelible Image*, 1:775-79. Witherington even suggests that the disciple was Linus, traditionally reckoned as the successor of Peter as bishop of Rome and mentioned in 2 Timothy 4:21 as a Roman believer who sends his greetings to Timothy. On Linus, see F. W. Gingrich, "Linus," *IDB* 3:136.

[7]Gary M. Burge, Lynn H. Cohick and Gene L. Green assert: "No compelling arguments have been forwarded against the authenticity of 2 Peter, and doubts that have arisen have reasonable

stylistic and linguistic differences between 1 and 2 Peter are often reconciled by positing different amanuenses. Silvanus assisted Peter in
composing 1 Peter, and an unknown amanuensis, though not mentioned in the letter itself, possessing a flair for rather flamboyant, florid
prose, assisted with 2 Peter. Or, one might even assume that Peter was
fully capable of writing the prose of both letters and did so addressing
quite different situations requiring different vocabulary and style. Peter
may even be incorporating some of the style and vocabulary of his opponents. Such a supposition appeals to Paul's letter to the Colossians,
in which, assuming genuineness, he does something similar.

So, what is my view and approach? In spite of the fact that a growing
number of evangelical NT scholars are now espousing some form of
pseudepigraphy along the lines of the second or third alternatives mentioned above, I still incline to the traditional view that Peter is the real
author. Perhaps he used an amanuensis, perhaps not. As I argued in my
discussion of the authorship of 1 Peter, I think we sell short Peter's
ability to write cultured Hellenistic Greek simply because he was a
Galilean fisherman. Though quite different in style and tone, 2 Peter
has more similarities to 1 Peter than does any other NT document.
Since I accept both letters as genuine, the simplest and most obvious
relationship between the two is that 2 Peter is indeed "the second letter"
referred to in 2 Peter 3:1. It follows, then, that the readership of both
letters is essentially the same, namely, Anatolian Christians of the
eastern provinces. As already indicated above, 2 Timothy and 2 Peter
share certain features that characterize a well-known literary genre
called testament. This may reflect a kind of cross-pollination between
these two apostolic leaders, just the sort of thing one would expect, if
the traditional view that places Paul and Peter in Rome near the end of
their lives is correct.

---

explanations. We should consider this an authentic work of Peter since the accused has not been
found guilty." *The New Testament in Antiquity* (Grand Rapids: Zondervan, 2009), pp. 405-6.
Also defending authenticity are Thomas R. Schreiner, *1, 2 Peter, Jude* (NAC; Nashville: Broadman & Holman, 2003), pp. 259-77; Norman Hillyer, *1 and 2 Peter, Jude* (NIBC; Peabody,
Mass.: Hendrickson, 1992), pp. 1-2; 9-11; Donald Guthrie, *New Testament Introduction* (3rd
ed., rev., Downers Grove, Ill.: InterVarsity Press, 1970), pp. 820-48, and Douglas J. Moo, *2
Peter and Jude* (NIVAC; Grand Rapids: Zondervan, 1996), pp. 21-26. Moo, however, is uncertain whether 2 Peter is addressed to the same location as 1 Peter (p. 25).

In what follows I summarize the four main arguments against the genuineness of 2 Peter and offer a brief rejoinder to each.[8]

***Lack of external attestation in the early church fathers.*** Surprisingly, given the relatively early attestation for 1 Peter, the earliest reference to 2 Peter by name occurs in Origen (A.D. 182-251) during the third century. Although Origen is aware that some doubted its genuineness, he quotes it six times, famously remarking that "even Peter blows on the twin trumpets of his own Epistles" (Origen, *Hom. in Josh.* 7.1). According to Werner Kümmel, nowhere do the well-known second-century apologists Irenaeus, Tertullian, Cyprian and Clement of Alexandria mention 2 Peter.[9] However, Donald Guthrie reviews the same evidence and comes to a different conclusion.[10] Guthrie assumes that when Eusebius (ca. 265-339) says Clement of Alexandria wrote a commentary on all the Catholic Epistles, this included 2 Peter, since Eusebius also acknowledges the widespread acceptance of 2 Peter in his day (*Hist. eccl.* 6.14.1). Kümmel's assumption that 2 Peter was excluded from Clement's commentary seems arbitrary. According to Guthrie, "there are one or two faint allusions in Irenaeus' writings," and less convincing examples of possible citations may be adduced from Theophilus of Antioch, Aristides, Polycarp and Justin Martyr.[11] Michael Kruger is even more confident that Justin Martyr, Irenaeus, Clement of Alexandria, *The Apocalypse of Peter* and *1 Clement* cite or allude to 2 Peter.[12]

Although an early listing of canonical works appearing in the so-called Muratorian Fragment does not mention 2 Peter, it does mention several spurious documents, like the *Epistle to the Laodiceans* and the *Epistle to the Alexandrians*, calling them "forgeries." Because five other NT books that eventually did achieve canonical status (including 1 Peter) are also omitted, the most that can be said is that, on the basis of this document, the status of 2 Peter is uncertain.[13]

---

[8]I am indebted to the analysis of Michael J. Kruger, "The Authenticity of 2 Peter," *JETS* 42/4 (December 1999): 643-70, and Schreiner, *1, 2 Peter, Jude,* pp. 255-76.

[9]Kümmel, *Introduction to the New Testament,* p. 433.

[10]Guthrie, *New Testament Introduction,* pp. 814-20.

[11]Ibid.

[12]Kruger, "Authenticity of 2 Peter," pp. 652-55.

[13]The Muratorian Canon is "a codex containing a list of twenty-two NT books accepted by the churches at the time it was composed. It is named after L. A. Muratori, who discovered it in

Both 1 and 2 Peter appear in one of our earliest surviving Greek MSS, Bodmer papyrus (p72), dating to the third century. The great uncial (script written in large capital letters) MSS, Codex Sinaiticus (fourth century), Codex Vaticanus (fourth century) and Codex Alexandrinus (fifth century), all contain 2 Peter. Eusebius acknowledges that 2 Peter "appeared useful to many" and "was studiously read with the other Scriptures" (*Hist. eccl.* 3.3), even if he personally had reservations about its authenticity. Eusebius places 2 Peter along with James, Jude and 2 and 3 John in the category called the antilegomena ("disputed books") but, significantly, not in the group of spurious books like *Apocalypse of Peter* (*Hist. eccl.* 3.25.3). Jerome (ca. 347-420), with his exceptional linguistic skills, doubtless played a key role in the widespread acknowledgment of 2 Peter as authentic.[14] The councils of Laodicea, Hippo and Carthage in the fourth century secured a place for 2 Peter in the canon.

While the textual evidence and external attestation may not be as early as one might wish, what exists is not inconsequential. How likely is it that early church fathers, who apparently took pains to exclude spurious works and whose fluency in Greek far exceeds that of modern scholars for whom it is a reading language only, were hoodwinked into admitting 2 Peter into the canon or, knowing the true circumstances of its composition, were nonetheless unconcerned with what today would be labeled a "pious fraud"?

*The issue of pseudepigraphy.* This raises an important issue in regard to 2 Peter. If Peter is spurious, what bearing does that have on its canonical status? In the heyday of theological liberalism, a determination of pseudepigraphy often led to a negative evaluation of the document as a whole and to its virtual neglect. More often today, NT scholars assume that pseudepigraphy in the ancient world was not plagiarism but a recognized and accepted invocation of a highly respected au-

---

1740. Scholars disagree on whether the list goes back to A.D. 200 or 400." Arthur G. Patzia and Anthony J. Petrotta, *Pocket Dictionary of Biblical Studies* (Downers Grove, Ill.: InterVarsity Press, 2002), p. 82.

[14]Jerome says, "It is rejected by the majority because in style it is incompatible with the former [letter of 1 Peter]" (*Vir. ill.*, 1; translation by Kümmel, *Introduction to the New Testament*, p. 434, n. 11). However, he accepted 2 Peter as canonical and accounted for the linguistic differences by assuming a different amanuensis.

thority from the past in order to encourage, warn and strengthen believers in the present. Thus the tradition embodied in a particular pseudepigraphon is indebted to the apostle placed under attribution. For the most part, in this new perspective, there has been a welcome rehabilitation of NT documents deemed to be pseudepigraphic (such as the Pastorals, Ephesians and Jude).

A benign view of pseudepigraphy, however, is problematic. The evidence such as we have points in a different direction. In fact, the NT itself provides a starting point, in which we learn that Paul warned the Thessalonians not to be taken in by a letter purportedly written by him (2 Thess 2:2). Three times he indicates to his different readers the distinguishing marks of his personal, handwritten greetings (Gal 6:11; Col 4:18; 2; Thess 3:17; cf. Rom 16:22).[15]

We know of at least two church leaders who rejected as forgeries works falsely claiming apostolic authorship. Tertullian (fl. ca. A.D. 196-212) disciplined the author of the *Acts of Paul and Thecla* on the charge of "augmenting Paul's fame from his own store." The testimony of Serapion, bishop of Antioch in Syria, is especially telling: "We receive both Peter and the other apostles as Christ, but the writings which falsely bear their names (ψευδεπίγραφα) we reject."

This is difficult to square with the approach of most modern scholars who dismiss pseudepigraphy as not being an integrity issue. For example, Richard Bauckham states, "The pseudepigraphal device is therefore not a fraudulent means of claiming apostolic authority, but embodies a claim to be a faithful mediator of the apostolic message."[16] But J. A. T. Robinson weighs in with a quite different assessment: "If we ask what is the evidence for orthodox epistles being composed in the name of the apostles within a generation or two of their lifetime, and for this being an acceptable literary convention within the church, the answer is nil."[17] L. R. Donelson, after writing a monograph on this issue, concludes: "No one

---

[15]I am mindful that a number of NT scholars consider Colossians pseudepigraphic.

[16]*Jude, 2 Peter* (WBC 50; Waco, Tex.: Word, 1983), pp. 161-62. Similarly, Glenn W. Barker, William L. Lane and J. Ramsey Michaels, *The New Testament Speaks* (New York: Harper & Row, 1969), p. 352; Ralph P. Martin, *New Testament Foundations* (2 vols.; Grand Rapids: Eerdmans, 1978), pp. 383-88, and *Theology of Peter*, pp. 145-46.

[17]J. A. T. Robinson, *Redating the New Testament* (Philadelphia: Westminster, 1976), p. 187.

ever seems to have accepted a document as religiously and philosophically prescriptive which was known to be forged. I do not know of a single example."[18] The reader should know that a majority of evangelical scholars still argue for the genuineness of 2 Peter.[19] In my opinion, the stress in the NT on speaking the truth, being honest and transparent in all one's dealings, is incompatible with the notion of pseudepigraphy, even as qualified by Bauckham, as an acceptable procedure in the propagation and promotion of the Christian message.[20]

*Stylistic and literary objections to the genuineness of 2 Peter.* But what does the internal evidence of the letter demonstrate? Are there features that cast decisive doubt on Petrine authorship? A majority of modern scholars are confident the same author could not have written both 1 and 2 Peter. In their view, "the style, outlook, and concerns of the two letters are too disparate for a common authorship."[21]

But stylistic and literary objections are quite subjective. Taking into account the different occasion and purpose of the respective epistles and the small amount of text on which to draw conclusions, one is advised to be more cautious.[22] What we do not know is whether and to what extent an amanuensis was used in both 1 and 2 Peter. What is clearly stated in 2 Peter is the identification of the author as "Simeon Peter, a servant and apostle of Jesus Christ" (2 Pet 1:1). This must be the starting point in any credible investigation of authorship. Is there anything in the style and content of 2 Peter that rules out Petrine au-

---

[18]*Pseudepigraphy and Ethical Argument in the Pastoral Epistles* (HUT 22; Tübingen: Mohr-Siebeck, 1986), p. 11.

[19]See the extensive discussion of this issue in Guthrie, *New Testament Introduction*, pp. 814-48. Most recently, Burge, Cohick and Green assert: "No compelling arguments have been forwarded against the authenticity of 2 Peter, and doubts that have arisen have reasonable explanations. We should consider this an authentic work of Peter since the accused has not been found guilty" (*The New Testament in Antiquity*, pp. 405-6).

[20]I think Moo is right: "The 'have-your-cake-and-eat-it-too' theory of a canonical pseudepigraphon does not seem to be an alternative" (*2 Peter and Jude*, p. 24).

[21]Donald Senior, ed., *The Catholic Study Bible* (New York: Oxford University Press, 1990), p. RG 559. Kümmel leaves no room for doubt: "The conceptual world and the rhetorical language are so strongly influenced by Hellenism as to rule out Peter definitely, nor could it have been written by one of his helpers or pupils under instructions from Peter. Not even at some time after the death of the apostle" (*Introduction to the New Testament*, pp. 431-32).

[22]"Analysis of style lacks a scientific foundation when we are dealing with just a few pages." Schreiner, *1, 2 Peter, Jude*, p. 265.

thorship? The fact is that 2 Peter has more similarities to 1 Peter than any other NT writing.[23] This is downplayed by those who are convinced 2 Peter is a pseudepigraphon. Furthermore, the claim that the Hellenistic character of the epistle counts against Petrine authorship is overstated. Peter's long association with and ministry among Gentiles, especially in Rome, would necessitate familiarity and facility with conventions, expressions and idioms of the day.[24]

*The relationship between Jude and 2 Peter.* A major argument against genuineness concerns the close similarities to Jude. It is often claimed that 2 Peter borrows from Jude, and this is hard to square with the notion of an apostle borrowing from an obscure figure in the church. Indeed, most hold that Jude is also a pseudepigraphon, making the evidence of borrowing even more decisive against Petrine authorship.

A couple of points should be noted. The direction of borrowing between these two epistles is not as clear-cut as often maintained.[25] A good case can still be argued for the other direction.[26] Some scholars hold that both works independently draw on a common source. In any case, the fact or direction of borrowing does not disqualify Peter as the author of this letter.[27] Why should it be thought historically improbable for Peter to make use of Jude in his pastoral response to the challenge of false teachers if he found the material useful? Are apostles required to be original? Remember, apostles were not constrained by the copyright laws of our modern age. In short, this argument lacks the weight its proponents assign to it.

## Conclusion

I permit 2 Peter a place at the table in my discussion of Petrine the-

---

[23]See Kruger, "Authenticity of 2 Peter," pp. 659-61, for the evidence.

[24]"Modern day evangelists and writers commonly follow the same procedure." Schreiner, *1, 2 Peter, Jude*, p. 267.

[25]For a helpful discussion and a chart showing the parallels, see Schreiner, *1, 2 Peter, Jude*, pp. 415-19.

[26]"If I were forced to the wall, I would probably opt for the theory that has Jude borrowing from Peter." Moo, *2 Peter, Jude*, p. 18.

[27]"The bare use of Jude does not in itself exclude Petrine authorship," writes Guthrie, *New Testament Introduction*, p. 824.

ology.[28] It is understood, of course, that it affords only a very modest glimpse into the theological thought of this apostle, conditioned as it is by the urgent pastoral circumstances prompting its composition. So I now turn to the theological message embedded in the epistle. I think you will agree that the truths Peter communicates are worthy of deep reflection, even if "you know them already and are established in the truth that has come to you" (2 Pet 1:12).

## QUESTIONS FOR DISCUSSION

1. Why is the question of the genuineness of 2 Peter important?
2. What is the evidence for 2 Peter as a testament, and do you find it persuasive?
3. Which argument against authenticity do you think is the strongest? Which is the weakest?
4. Which argument for authenticity is the strongest? Which is the weakest?
5. In your opinion, which way does the cumulative evidence point in terms of authorship?
6. What appears to be the purpose of 2 Peter?

## FOR FURTHER STUDY

Bauckham, Richard J. *Jude, 2 Peter.* WBC 50. Dallas: Word, 1983. Pp. 158-64.*
———. "2 Peter." *DLNTD.* Downers Grove, Ill.: InterVarsity Press, 1997. Pp. 924-25.*
Burge, Gary M., Lynn H. Cohick and Gene L. Green. *The New Testament in Antiquity.* Grand Rapids: Zondervan, 2009. Pp. 405-6.
Carson, Donald A., and Douglas J. Moo. *An Introduction to the New Testament.* 2nd ed. Grand Rapids: Zondervan, 2005.
Guthrie, Donald. *New Testament Introduction.* 3rd rev. ed. Downers Grove, Ill.: InterVarsity Press, 1970. Pp. 814-48.
Kruger, Michael J. "The Authenticity of 2 Peter." *JETS* 42 (December 1999): 643-70.

---

[28]For a good example of an evangelical scholar who likewise treats 1 and 2 Peter as genuine and includes the sermons in the book of Acts as reflecting Petrine theology, see Paul A. Himes, "Peter and the Prophetic Word: The Theology of Prophecy Traced Through Peter's Sermons and Epistles," *BBR* 21/2 (2011): 227-44.

Kümmel, Werner Georg. *Introduction to the New Testament*. Translated by
    Howard Clark Kee. Rev. ed. Nashville: Abingdon, 1973. Pp. 430-34.*
Moo, Douglas J. *2 Peter, Jude*. NIVAC. Grand Rapids: Zondervan, 1996. Pp.
    21-26.
Schreiner, Thomas R. *1, 2 Peter, Jude*. NAC. Nashville: Broadman & Holman,
    2003. Pp. 259-77.


*Author holds that 2 Peter is a pseudepigraphon.

# 12

---

# THEOLOGICAL
# THEMES IN 2 PETER

◊

WHAT IS STRIKING ABOUT 2 PETER is its christocentric focus.[1] Once we grasp the occasion prompting the epistle, such an emphasis makes sense. The false teachers who have infiltrated the house churches are "ineffective and unfruitful in the knowledge of our Lord Jesus Christ" (2 Pet 1:8) and "deny the Master who bought them" (2 Pet 2:1). In response to this defection, Peter counters with a sustained polemic against their errors, both doctrinal and moral, and focuses on the centrality of Christ as the key to a salvation both "already but not yet."

## CHRISTOLOGY

Second Peter displays an extraordinarily high Christology. In his salutation, Peter attaches to Jesus Christ the title "our God and Savior Jesus Christ" (2 Pet 1:1).[2] Immediately thereafter, in his blessing on the readers, he follows suit with the quintessential NT affirmation of faith, "Jesus our Lord" (2 Pet 1:2). God, Savior and Lord are juxtaposed with Jesus Christ, all in the same immediate context. Herein lays the heart of the NT gospel.[3]

---

[1]C. C. Ryrie says, "Petrine theology is fundamentally Christological." See *Biblical Theology of the New Testament* (Chicago: Moody Press, 1959), p. 269.

[2]"Käsemann's claim that the Christology is inferior is a stunning mistake, for there are convincing grounds for claiming that Jesus Christ is called God himself in 1:2." Thomas R. Schreiner, *1, 2 Peter, Jude* (NAC; Nashville: Broadman & Holman, 2003), p. 267.

[3]Frank J. Matera says "the initial verses of this testament (1:3-4) summarize the essential content of the gospel Peter has handed down to them." *New Testament Theology: Exploring Diversity and Unity* (Louisville: Westminster John Knox, 2007), p. 385.

But does 2 Peter 1:1 call Jesus God, or does it refer to God (the Father) *and* the Savior Jesus Christ, especially given the immediately following verse, in which there is mention of "God *and* of Jesus our Lord" (2 Pet 1:2, italics added)? There are both strong grammatical and contextual grounds for assuming that Peter refers to Jesus Christ as both God and Savior.[4] This could be appealed to as evidence of the late date of 2 Peter, when a high Christology appears in the postapostolic fathers. But strong arguments can be marshaled for a high Christology in Paul, well in advance of the admittedly high Christology of John at the end of the first century.[5] In my opinion, Frank Matera is correct when he asserts that "this is one of the few instances in the New Testament where Jesus is called God. Other instances are John 1:1; 20:28; Rom. 9:5; Titus 2:13; Heb. 1:8-9."[6]

Here in table format is a listing of the christological titles in 2 Peter:

**Table 12.1.**

| Christological Title | Probable Reference to Christ | Scriptural Reference |
|---|---|---|
| Jesus Christ | | 2 Peter 1:1 |
| Our God and Savior Jesus Christ | | 2 Peter 1:1 |
| Our Lord Jesus Christ | | 2 Peter 1:8 |
| Our Lord and Savior Jesus Christ | | 2 Peter 1:11 |
| Our Lord Jesus Christ | | 2 Peter 1:14 |
| Our Lord Jesus Christ | | 2 Peter 1:16 |
| My Son, my Beloved | | 2 Peter 1:17 |
| | The morning star | 2 Peter 1:19 |
| The Master | | 2 Peter 2:1 |
| | The Lord | 2 Peter 2:9 |

---

[4]This is an instance of the so-called Granville Sharp rule. Essentially, this grammatical rule states that "when two nouns are connected by καί and the article precedes only the first noun, there is a close connection between the two. That connection always indicates at least some sort of *unity.*" Daniel B. Wallace, *Greek Grammar Beyond the Basics* (Grand Rapids: Zondervan, 1996), p. 270, italics in original. See his entire discussion of this rule in pp. 270-90. J. Neyrey, *2 Peter, Jude* (AB 37C; Garden City, N.Y.: Doubleday, 1993), pp. 147-48, denies that 2 Peter 1:1 is a reference to Jesus as God, but Richard J. Bauckham, *Jude, 2 Peter* (WBC 50. Dallas: Word, 1983), pp. 168-69, argues for the identification. See also Murray Harris, *Jesus as God: The New Testament Use of Theos in Reference to Jesus* (Grand Rapids: Baker, 1992).

[5]In defense of Paul's high Christology, see Larry R. Helyer, *The Witness of Jesus, Paul and John* (Downers Grove, Ill.: InterVarsity Press, 2008), pp. 273-89.

[6]*New Testament Theology*, p. 385, n. 27.

| Christological Title | Probable Reference to Christ | Scriptural Reference |
|---|---|---|
| | The Lord | 2 Peter 2:11 |
| Our Lord and Savior Jesus Christ | | 2 Peter 2:20 |
| The Lord and Savior | | 2 Peter 3:2 |
| | The Lord | 2 Peter 3:8 |
| | The Lord | 2 Peter 3:9 |
| | (Day of) the Lord | 2 Peter 3:10 |
| Our Lord | | 2 Peter 3:15 |
| Our Lord and Savior Jesus Christ | | 2 Peter 3:18 |

No other NT author uses the full title "our Lord and Savior Jesus Christ." Paul has one instance that is very close: "expecting a Savior, the Lord Jesus Christ" (Phil 3:20), and Jude has "to the only God our Savior, through Jesus Christ our Lord" (Jude 25), but in this latter case, God the Father and Jesus Christ are distinguished. Peter's use of the full title joins together the deity of Christ and his soteriological significance: He is both Lord and Savior. Herein lay the fatal flaw of the false teachers' view. They are "shortsighted and blind" when it comes to "the knowledge of our Lord Jesus Christ" (2 Pet 1:8-9). They fail to realize that it was Christ's "divine power" that enables them to "escape from the corruption that is in the world . . . and . . . become participants of the divine nature" (2 Pet 1:3-4).

Peter underscores the full deity of Jesus Christ in a section aptly styled as "Peter's final words," having the feel of a testamentary deposition (2 Pet 1:12–2:3). He recounts his extraordinary experience on the mount of transfiguration when God the Father's voice conveyed this endorsement of Jesus: "This is my Son, my Beloved, with whom I am well pleased" (2 Pet 1:17).[7] Peter's understanding of Jesus' Sonship far transcends the metaphorical, adoptive sonship of ancient Israelite kings in relation to Yahweh (cf. 2 Sam 7:14; Ps 2:7).[8] That he revered Jesus as the Messiah

---

[7]In talmudic literature the divine voice is called the *bat qol* (lit., "daughter of a voice," i.e., an echo of God's voice, sometimes conceived of as an angel who speaks). The sages did not, however, value such experiences above the Torah, nor did they expect that any such revelations would add to what Torah already revealed. This may reflect rabbinic Judaism's rejection of Christian claims about Jesus and his teaching (e.g., Heb 1:1-2).

[8]There is some evidence that "my Beloved" was already a messianic title in early Judaism. For example, in the "Similitudes of Enoch" (*1 En.* 32-71), the title "my Chosen One" is used along-

is clear; but more profoundly, he also believed that Jesus is God's unique Son, who is coming again in glory just as he appeared years ago on the mount of transfiguration. The radiant glory that emanated from Jesus on that occasion dramatically declared his divine nature ("And he was transfigured before them, and his clothes became dazzling white," Mk 9:2b-3). Notice how Peter emphasizes that "we had been eyewitnesses of his majesty" (2 Pet 1:16). This dazzling display was then capped by a divine investiture: "For he received honor and glory from God the Father when that voice was conveyed to him by the Majestic Glory" (2 Pet 1:17). Peter believes that Jesus shares in the glory and majesty of God the Father. In short, Jesus possesses a divine nature.

Notice the several references to "the Lord" in Peter's letter. It is difficult to know with certainty, in a given passage, whether Peter is referring to God the Father or to Jesus Christ. It may be that he is deliberately ambiguous and assumes that what applies to one applies to the other. At any rate, he shows no reticence in ascribing to Jesus Christ the exalted title "Lord." Along with other NT writers, he identifies Jesus with the exalted Yahweh of the OT, most often translated as "LORD" in English versions. In a very real sense, then, the LORD of the OT manifests himself in the person of Jesus Christ and the great day of the Lord, announced by the OT prophets, is the day of the Lord Jesus Christ.

Two further titles in 2 Peter deserve brief mention. Second Peter 1:19 urges the readers to hold fast to the prophetic testimony witnessing to the return of Jesus Christ in glory. They are exhorted to do so "until the day dawns and the morning star rises in your hearts." Is the "morning star" a messianic reference? Almost certainly it is. Appealing to another eyewitness to the transfiguration, I cite the apostle John, who twice makes reference to a "morning star" (Rev 2:28; 22:16) in his apocalypse. The latter reference is a direct word from the risen Lord: "It is I, Jesus, who sent my angel to you with this testimony for the churches. I am the root and the descendant of David, the bright

---

side "the Righteous One" and "Son of Man" in reference to an expected messianic figure. This is very close to "my Beloved." The title does not occur in the Dead Sea Scrolls, but Paul seems to use "the Beloved" as a messianic title in Ephesians 1:6 (cf. Col 1:13), a usage perhaps owing to his Pharisaic heritage. See further Ben Witherington III, *The Indelible Image* (2 vols.; Downers Grove, Ill.: InterVarsity Press, 2009), 1:788-89.

morning star" (Rev 22:16). The planet Venus, appearing in the eastern sky just before sunrise, serves as a stirring symbol of the new age inaugurated by Jesus Christ.[9] Perhaps also Peter's reference to the *rising* of the morning star alludes to the famous fourth oracle of Balaam: "A star shall come out of Jacob; a scepter shall *rise* out of Israel" (Num 24:17b, italics added).[10] This text, referring to the rise of the Davidic dynasty in its original setting, was given a messianic interpretation in some circles of Second Temple Judaism.[11] The eschatology of 2 Peter, focusing on a brand new age, is well served by this christological word picture.

The other singular title Peter uses is "the Master" (2 Pet 2:1). A master (*despotēs*) is "one who has legal control and authority over persons, such as subjects or slaves."[12] Here is another way of stating the lordship of Jesus Christ over all his people against the backdrop of the social institution of slavery, recalling Peter's earlier instructions to Christian slaves concerning their earthly masters in 1 Peter 2:18. Jesus is the Master because he "bought them" (2 Pet 2:1). Once again the almost seamless connection between Christology and soteriology is evident.

## God

Second Peter displays a characteristically Jewish view of God. The prescript offers a prayer for the readers and in so doing draws attention to God as the source of all grace and peace and a God who reveals himself and is thus accessible (2 Pet 1:2). Though not elaborated, the rest of the letter (e.g., 2 Pet 1:17-18), in harmony with the NT, makes clear that God reveals himself supremely in the Lord Jesus Christ. The opening parenesis identifies God's divine power as the source of all that is needed for godly living.[13]

---

[9]For the OT and intertestamental background of this figure, see A. E. Hill, "Morning," *ISBE* 3:413.

[10]So also Witherington, *Indelible Image*, 1:790.

[11]See, e.g., *T. Jud.* 24.1-6; CD vii.20; 1Q28b v.27-28; 1QM xi.4-9; 4Q175 1.9-13. In addition, all four targums on the Pentateuch interpret this text messianically.

[12]BAGD, p. 220. According to Thayer, *despotēs* denotes "absolute ownership and uncontrolled power" (*Greek-English Lexicon of the New Testament* [trans., rev. and enl. by Joseph Henry Thayer, 1889; repr. ed.; Grand Rapids: Eerdmans, 1978], p. 1265).

[13]"Life and godliness" is probably a hendiadys (the use of two nouns or verbs to express a single

*God as Father.* To a much greater degree than in the OT, God reveals himself as a heavenly Father during the climactic events of
redemptive history, centering on Jesus of Nazareth.[14] Peter selects an
instance, germane to his rebuttal of the false teachers' denial of the
parousia, namely, the transfiguration. There "God the Father" dramatically reveals to the inner three, Peter, James and John, that Jesus of
Nazareth is far more than a Davidic Messiah or a prophet like John the
Baptist, Elijah or Jeremiah; he is the unique Son of God, the "Beloved."[15]
The Father both proclaims and showcases Jesus' essential divine nature:
"[Jesus] received honor and glory from God the Father" (2 Pet 1:17). As
Jesus was "transfigured" and "his clothes became dazzling white" (Mk
9:2-3), the "Majestic Glory" (2 Pet 1:17) "overshadowed them" (Mk
9:6). This episode recalls Israel's exodus from Egypt and God's self-
revelation on Mount Sinai (Ex 16:10; 19:9; 24:15-18; 33:9-10; 34:5;
40:34-38). Once again, on another "holy mountain," (2 Pet 1:18), God
the Father's voice booms forth from the glory cloud. This episode was
not "a cleverly devised myth" (2 Pet 1:16), says Peter, for "we ourselves
heard this voice came from heaven" (2 Pet 1:18). Herein lies the essential message of the divine voice: the beloved Son reveals the Father:
"listen to him!" (Mk 9:7; cf. Ex 19:9). The apostle John echoes Peter's
testimony: "Whoever has seen me has seen the Father" (Jn 14:9 cf. Jn
10:30; 17:11, 21). Peter concludes this section by insisting that God the
Father's self-revelation through his beloved Son on the mount of transfiguration is not an apostolic invention; rather, it fully confirms the
"prophetic message" (2 Pet 1:19).

*God as judge and deliverer.* God the Father is also a judge and has
already sentenced and punished certain disobedient figures in the historic past, before their final judgment at the great white throne (Rev
20:11-15). Thus judgment, like salvation, bears an "already but not
yet" character. In this Peter agrees with both Paul and John (Rom
1:18; Jn 3:18). He lists four instances of divine judgment in history as
recorded in the Scriptures: the angels who sinned, the flood of Noah,

---

idea) for "godly living."

[14]On this, see further Helyer, *Witness of Jesus, Paul and John*, pp. 153-56, 158-59.

[15]See the earlier discussion of this episode in chapter 2, "Peter in the Gospels."

Sodom and Gomorrah and the false prophet Balaam (2 Pet 2:4-6, 15-16), each of which serves to warn the audience about the dire consequences of succumbing to the false teachers' enticements to enjoy the forbidden fruits of libertinism. This ominous recital, however, is portrayed against the backdrop of God's gracious deliverance of the righteous: Noah (and seven others) and Lot. In short, God the Father is both a judging and saving God. The false teachers gravely err by denying the former.

1. The angels who sinned are probably the "sons of God" (Gen 6:2) and the sin was cohabitation with human women, a transgression of a divinely imposed boundary between the angelic and human realms. I have earlier connected these beings with "the spirits in prison" mentioned by Peter in 1 Peter 3:19-20. In his second letter, Peter explicitly describes their punishment: "cast them into hell and committed . . . to chains of deepest darkness to be kept *until the judgment*" (2 Pet 2:4, italics added). The false teachers are put on notice: their "destruction," like that of the fallen angels, "is not asleep" (2 Pet 2:3). The Greek word translated as "cast . . . into hell" in the NRSV is the verb *tartaroō*, literally, "to send to Tartarus," the deepest region of the underworld and fearsome prison of the Titans of Greek mythology (see Hes. *Theog.* 119). The Hebrew Bible probably refers to something similar when it speaks of the lowest depths of Sheol or the Pit (Ps 88:6; Prov 9:18). The intent is to deliver a wake-up call to the false teachers by warning them of the dire consequences of maligning the way of truth and of transgressing the sexual boundaries imposed on followers of Jesus (Mt 5:17-32; 19:3-12).

2. The second instance Peter cites is the great flood in the days of Noah. As the book of Genesis narrates, the ancient world was swept away and the ungodly perished (Gen 6–8). I remind the reader that, in his first letter, Peter also utilizes the flood of Noah in his great christological passage setting forth Christ's victory over the rebellious spirits at his exaltation to the right hand of God the Father (1 Pet 3:19, 23). He will return to the flood story in 2 Peter 3 when he addresses the crisis generated by a denial of the parousia. The cosmic scope of this divine judgment is a sobering reality, a fact duly impressed on the addressees.

3. The third episode directly bears on the conduct of the false teachers. Sodom and Gomorrah were reduced to ashes (Gen 19) and its inhabitants described as "ungodly." The context of Genesis 19 implies, and Second Temple Jewish traditions amplify, that the overriding sin of these miscreants was sexual aberration. Like the ancient cities, the false teachers follow "licentious ways," "indulge their flesh in depraved lust" and "have eyes full of adultery, insatiable for sin" (2 Pet 2:2, 10, 14). The fate of Sodom and Gomorrah "is coming to the ungodly" (2 Pet 2:6), and there is no doubt who is intended!

Peter piggybacks on the account of Sodom and Gomorrah by appealing to one more biblical story, the story of Lot, "a righteous man." Drawing on Second Temple traditions that portray Lot in considerably more favorable light than a face value reading of Genesis 19 suggests,[16] he uses Lot as a paradigm for beleaguered believers in the house churches. Just as Lot was "tormented in his righteous soul" by the lawless deeds of his compatriots, so the Anatolian believers must wrestle with and resist the inroads of licentious behavior, all the while trusting in the certain and unsparing judgment eventually coming on the prevaricators of truth and the perpetrators of vice.

4. Finally, Peter reminds his readers about the infamous false prophet Balaam (Num 22:7, 21-35). The false teachers, like that accursed man (Josh 13:22), "have left the straight road and have gone astray" and have "loved the wages of doing wrong" (2 Pet 2:15). Given his description of these interlopers, it is not likely he holds out much hope for any of them repenting; they seem to be irretrievably doomed (2 Pet 2:20-22). However, we should never discount the fact that the Lord is "not wanting any to perish, but all to come to repentance" (2 Pet 3:9). Repentance is possible until death closes the door (see Heb 9:27). One is reminded of that great moment on Mount Sinai when the Lord passes before Moses and proclaims: "The LORD, the LORD, a God merciful and gracious, slow to anger, and abounding in steadfast love and faithfulness, keeping steadfast love for the thousandth generation, forgiving iniquity and transgression and sin, yet by no means clearing the guilty"

---

[16]See Larry R. Helyer, *Exploring Jewish Literature of the Second Temple Period* (Downers Grove, Ill.: InterVarsity Press, 2002), p. 133.

(Ex 34:6-7). There the mercy and justice of God embrace. What vexes Peter is the false teachers' willful denial of the latter, hence his vitriolic polemic. Peter reminds his readers that the Lord "is patient with you," but he also "is not slow about his promise" (1 Pet 3:9). In essence, Peter echoes the apostle Paul: "For we will all stand before the judgment seat of God" (Rom 14:10).

*God as creator.* God the Father almighty is creator of all things as celebrated in the OT (see Pss 19; 33:6-7; 104; Is 40). Second Peter 3:5-7 juxtaposes the beginning and end of redemptive history to good effect. Since the false teachers are denying the parousia and its accompanying day of judgment (2 Pet 3:3-7) and rationalizing their rejection by trotting out what sounds like a party slogan—"all things continue as they were from the beginnings of creation!" (2 Pet 3:4)—Peter counters by forcing them to face a dilemma: How can you accept the doctrine of creation without also accepting the doctrine of eschatological consummation?[17] Such inconsistency diminishes the power of God that brought all things into existence by the mere word of his mouth (2 Pet 3:5). Peter's allusion to Genesis 1 and Psalm 33:6 is unmistakable. Furthermore, Peter reminds them, the "world of that time" was utterly destroyed by a mere word of God through the deluge (2 Pet 3:6), alluding to Genesis 6–8 and the great flood of Noah. Finally, the self-same word of God has decreed that the present heavens and earth exist until a final, cosmic judgment by fire, after which God will create "new heavens and a new earth" (2 Pet 3:12-13), echoing the soaring cadence of Isaiah 65–66. In sum, Peter's response to the false teachers' denial of the parousia amounts to this: the word of God created all things, sustains all things and will terminate all things. By dismissing or diluting the sovereignty, providence and justice of God, the false teachers betray a seriously deficient theology. Peter sets the record straight: God is the blessed controller of all things. A worldview that denies God's intervention and judgment in history is flatly in error, then and now.

---

[17]Witherington also wonders how they made sense of the incarnation; see *Indelible Image*, 1:797.

## THE HOLY SPIRIT AND HOLY SCRIPTURE

There is but one reference to the Holy Spirit in 2 Peter, highlighting the Spirit's role in the origins of scriptural prophecy (2 Pet 1:21). Too much should not be made of this scarcity, since the focus of this brief letter lies in a bitter dispute over ethics and eschatology, at the heart of which lies a defective Christology. What Peter does say about the Spirit, however, is important and deserves careful attention.[18]

Immediately after Peter's eyewitness (2 Pet 1:16) and "earwitness" ("we ourselves heard this voice," 2 Pet 1:18) testimony to the Father's declaration of Jesus' divine status, he concludes that "we have the prophetic message more fully confirmed" (2 Pet 1:19). The "prophetic message," at the least, alludes to passages from the OT prophets describing the day of the Lord,[19] and may well include the entire OT.[20] He then urges his readers to "be attentive" to this prophetic message and trust it fully. The reason for Peter's utmost confidence in this prophetic word is grounded in its source. Note carefully: just as the heavenly voice of God the Father was "conveyed" to the inner three ("we ourselves") on the mount of transfiguration, so prophets (men and women) in the OT were "moved" by the Holy Spirit to speak from God.[21] Both verbs are in the passive voice, underscoring Peter's insistence that no prophecy of Scripture was "a matter of one's own interpretation" or "by human will." Most likely this "private interpretation" (KJV) or "one's own interpretation" (HCSB) refers not to readers and exegetes of the scriptural text, such as the false teachers Peter refutes, but to the initial

---

[18]We noted earlier that 1 Peter also has few references to the Holy Spirit, but what does occur is significant and implies a much more fully developed pneumatology than one might infer only on the basis of either letter.

[19]"Some think that Peter might have in mind the entire Old Testament or even Old and New Testament prophecy. But the context suggests rather that he refers specifically to Old Testament prophecies about the kingdom to be established by the Messiah at the end of history." Douglas J. Moo, *2 Peter and Jude* (NIVAC; Grand Rapids: Zondervan, 1996), p. 75.

[20]"All the known instances of the Greek phrase *ton prophētikon logon* point to its being synonymous with the term "Scriptures" (Bauckham, *2 Peter*, p. 224).

[21]The NRSV disguises the fact that the key verbs, "conveyed" and "moved," are just different tenses of the same Greek word, *pherō*, meaning "to bear, to carry." In the former instance, Peter uses the aorist tense, the usual tense of historical narration, to depict an action viewed in its entirety; in the latter, he employs the historical present tense in order to emphasize the ongoing nature of this "being carried along" by the Holy Spirit.

recipients of the revelation, the prophets themselves.[22] Human beings were thus the recipients of a divine message from God the Father and were assisted in the reception, recital and recording of this message "by the Holy Spirit." A more forceful endorsement of the trustworthy nature of scriptural prophecy could scarcely be penned.

A close examination of the way Peter appeals to Scripture in both his letters leaves no doubt that he was convinced it was, in its entirety, the inspired, trustworthy Word of God. For example, he affirms that God's judgment on the false teachers was already "pronounced against them long ago" (2 Pet 2:3), by which he surely means passages found in the Prophets condemning false prophets (see, e.g., Jer 23; Ezek 34). Furthermore, his recital of specific instances of divine judgment and deliverance in the past (2 Pet 2:4-10) reinforces the certainty of the false teachers' destiny, an outcome guaranteed only by the veracity of the scriptural witness. His blistering attack on the false teachers in 2 Peter 2 is interspersed with a direct reference to the story of Balaam (Num 21:7, 21-35) from the Pentateuch and a citation from the Wisdom tradition (Prov 26:11). Finally, as he directly addresses the denial of the parousia, he prefaces his remarks by appealing to "the words spoken in the past by the holy prophets" (2 Pet 3:2) and concludes by appealing to God's promise to create "new heavens and a new earth," as found in Isaiah 65–66.[23]

Peter's reliance on the truthfulness of Scripture is hardly an isolated instance; the same conviction repeatedly surfaces throughout the NT (see, e.g, Jn 10:35; 16:13; Rom 1:1; 15:4; 1 Cor 9:10; 10:6, 11; 2 Tim 3:16: Heb 1:1; Jas 1:22-23; 2:8). The historic Christian church continues to maintain this conviction: "The authority of the Holy Scripture, for which it ought to be believed and obeyed, dependeth not upon the testimony of any man or church, but wholly upon God (who is truth itself), the author thereof; and therefore it is to be received because it is the

---

[22]Bauckham, *2 Peter*, pp. 77-79. But see Schreiner, *1, 2 Peter, Jude*, p. 323, for good arguments in favor of the view that Peter is attacking the false teachers' errant interpretation of OT prophetic passages.

[23]Note also the allusion to Psalm 90:4, which belongs to the third major division of the Hebrew Bible, the Writings.

Word of God."[24] As the Reformers never tired of affirming, Scripture is self-authenticating.[25]

There is one more matter to be considered in regard to the doctrine of Scripture. As he wraps up his letter, Peter appeals to the witness of his fellow apostle, "our beloved brother Paul" (2 Pet 3:15) and "all his letters" (2 Pet 3:16). On the main points of contention between Peter and the false teachers, involving Christology, ethics and eschatology, Paul is a powerful ally supporting Peter's apostolic teaching. Assuming a date of writing for 2 Peter sometime between A.D. 64 and 68, some of Paul's letters written to various congregations stretching from Anatolia (Galatians) to Rome had already been in circulation for between ten (1 and 2 Corinthians) to fourteen years (1 and 2 Thessalonians), with Paul's letter to the Romans having been penned perhaps seven years earlier. One cannot rule out that several other prison letters, Philippians, Colossians and Ephesians, dating to the late 50s or early 60s, were also widely circulating at this time.[26] The degree of mobility and communication between the network of Christian house churches throughout the eastern Mediterranean is often underestimated—in this regard, a careful reading of Romans 16 is enlightening. To borrow a phrase from the book of Acts, "this was not done in a corner" (Acts 26:26).

It is Peter's remarkable inclusion of Paul's letters with "the other scriptures" (2 Pet 3:16) that attracts our attention. At face value, Peter assumes that Paul's letters were already acknowledged as sacred Scripture, long before the church officially declared them canonical in the fourth century A.D. This should not, however, occasion surprise, given that Paul's earliest surviving letters, the Thessalonian correspondence, convey unmistakable apostolic authority. Paul does not offer suggestions; he delivers ultimatums (1 Thess 5:27; 2 Thess 3:14)!

---

[24]*The Westminster Confession of Faith*, 1.4. See further G. W. Bromiley, "Scripture, Authority of," *ISBE* 4:362-63.

[25]See further Moo, *2 Peter and Jude*, pp. 86-89.

[26]Though not impossible, the Pastorals (ca. A.D. 62-64) were probably not widely known and read as yet. As George Eldon Ladd reminds us, "there is no need to think that the author was familiar with a collection of Pauline writings, only that he was familiar with some of them." *A Theology of the New Testament* (Donald A. Hagner ed.; rev. ed.; Grand Rapids: Eerdmans, 1993), p. 653.

## SOTERIOLOGY

Peter's soteriology reflects aspects not vetted in his first missive. The reason for this difference lies, to a considerable extent, in the occasion prompting the letter. False teachers are infesting the house churches and apparently making inroads. Peter counterattacks, probably employing some of the false teachers' language and concepts, either by reinvesting them with orthodox understandings or refuting them on the basis of apostolic tradition. Let us see how this plays out.

What is striking about Peter's depiction of salvation is his heavy accent on cognition. A key word group is deployed in order to stress the importance of intellectually and volitionally comprehending God's saving plan in Christ. Two nouns, *epignōsis* and *gnōsis*, rendered consistently as "knowledge" in the NRSV, serve as shorthand for salvation.[27] "The knowledge of God and Jesus our Lord" (2 Pet 1:2; cf. 2 Pet 1:8; 2:20; 3:18) amounts to being "participants of the divine nature" (2 Pet 1:4) and "entry into the eternal kingdom of our Lord and Savior Jesus Christ" (2 Pet 1:11). Correlatively, Peter untiringly appeals to his audience to know, remember, recall and be attentive to certain revealed facts in salvation history and apostolic teaching, all the while reminding them and refreshing their memories concerning these things (2 Pet 1:8-9, 12-13, 15, 19; 3:1-3, 8, 17).

This heavy emphasis on knowledge constituted an important argument supporting the claim of earlier scholars that 2 Peter dates from the heyday of Gnosticism in the second century A.D. For them, 2 Peter was an anti-Gnostic tract, written in the guise of a testament of "the historical Peter." Modern research and discovery have, by and large, laid this contention to rest. Second Peter shows no awareness of distinctive Gnostic features. The emphasis on knowledge is hardly such an indicator.[28] One need go no further than the OT to realize that 2 Peter's emphasis on knowledge is comfortably at home in the milieu of the Hebrew Scriptures and tradition. The Pentateuch, Wisdom tradition (especially Psalms and Proverbs) and Hebrew Prophets con-

---

[27]In order to bring out the emphatic nature of *epignōsis* with its prefixed preposition, the KJV renders the word as "true knowledge" and NET has "rich knowledge"

[28]For further evidence against a Gnostic background for 2 Peter, see Ladd, *Theology*, pp. 650-52.

stantly refer to knowing God and walking in the knowledge of his will."[29] What is particularly relevant for our study of 2 Peter is the observation that in the OT "knowledge is insight into the will of God in command and blessing. It is primarily acknowledgement and obedient or grateful submission to what is known."[30] This usage clearly carries over into the NT and fits admirably in the context of 2 Peter. "The theoretical element is present . . . yet it is assumed that Christian knowledge carries with it a corresponding manner of life."[31] The Jewish setting of 2 Peter is validated by the discovery and publication of the Qumran documents, in which it is abundantly clear that knowledge and salvation may be closely linked without the need to suppose any underlying Gnostic substratum.

The most obvious background to Peter's stress on knowledge, however, derives from the Master who was himself fully immersed in the Hebrew Scriptures. In fact, several leading NT scholars identify Jesus as a Jewish sage.[32] Without falling prey to reductionism (he was much more than a Jewish sage) or subscribing to all the details of their reconstructions, I readily agree that the Synoptic Gospels and the Gospel of John offer abundant evidence testifying to the influence of Jewish Wisdom on the teaching and self-perception of Jesus of Nazareth. In fact, in Matthew 11:28-30, Matthew identifies Jesus with OT Wisdom (cf. Prov 11:1, 16; 9:5; Sir 51:23-27; 24:19).[33] The Johannine declaration of Jesus, "If you continue in my word, you are truly my disciples; and you will know the truth, and the truth will make you free" (Jn 8:31-32), is precisely Peter's point in his second letter (2 Pet 2:19-22).

Peter makes clear that salvation is a gift. In the prescript, he addresses his readers as those "who have received a faith as precious as ours" (2 Pet 1:1). He goes on to speak of divine power that "has given us everything needed for life and godliness" (2 Pet 1:3). The familiar

---

[29]The Hebrew word "yāda⁽" "expresses a multitude of shades of knowledge gained by the senses." See Jack P. Lewis, "yāda⁽," *TWOT* 1:366.

[30]Rudolf Bultmann, "*Ginōskō*," *TDNT* 1:704-5.

[31]Ibid., 1:707.

[32]See especially, Witherington, *Indelible Image*, 1:73-74, 78-84, passim.

[33]On the importance of Wisdom Christology, see Helyer, *Exploring Jewish Literature*, pp. 101-2, 109.

contours of Pauline theology emphasizing salvation by grace through faith are readily visible (cf. Eph 2:8-9).

Salvation in 2 Peter possesses a distinct polarity in at least two dimensions; that is, in both material and temporal terms, there are two contrasting aspects to salvation. Materially, salvation may be viewed, on the one hand, as an escape from the world—a deliverance from corruption (2 Pet 1:4). On the other hand, salvation consists of participating in the divine nature. Temporally, and in step with the consistent NT witness, salvation may be viewed as "now, but not yet." Each of these needs further elaboration.

Second Peter, as indicated earlier, assumes an apocalyptic worldview in which free moral agents are enmeshed in a fallen, corrupt world system, enthralled by their own sinful inclinations and oppressed by supernatural, evil beings under the command of a quintessentially evil being, "your adversary the devil" (1 Pet 5:8). This frame for viewing the human plight is a shared feature of all NT literature.[34] Against this somber backdrop, Peter's confident assertion that such a desperate plight may be overcome is good news indeed: "His divine power has given us everything needed for life and godliness" (2 Pet 1:3). These "precious and very great promises" involve an escape from the fallen world system lying under God's condemnation and ultimate destruction (2 Pet 3:11-12). Nothing explicit is said in this context about the role of the cross in effecting this rescue, as was the case in 1 Peter. Here Peter encapsulates the message of the cross in the shorthand expression "knowledge of God and of Jesus our Lord." The reason for this should probably be attributed to Peter's polemical purpose; namely, to attack the bold claims of the false teachers to possess special, liberating knowledge (2 Pet 2:19). Peter sarcastically styles their substitute knowledge as "destructive opinions" (2 Pet 2:1), "deceptive words" (2 Pet 2:3) and "bombastic nonsense" (2 Pet 2:18). Bundled in Peter's use of the word *knowledge* then is a shared understanding between himself and his audience: the knowledge of the Lord Jesus Christ involves the message of the cross and this is confirmed by the fact that Peter re-

---

[34]See Helyer, *Witness of Jesus, Paul and John*, pp. 389-91.

peatedly refers to Jesus as "Savior" (2 Pet 1:1; 2:20; 3:2, 18). Furthermore, in 2 Peter 2:1, he speaks of "the Master who bought them," an obvious allusion to the redemptive work of Christ on the cross (cf. 1 Pet 1:18-21; 3:18; 4:1). As Peter concludes his letter, he urges his readers "to be found by him at peace, without spot or blemish" (2 Pet 3:14). Although the "by him" is a bit ambiguous as to whether it refers to God the Father or to Jesus, the text recalls the motif of the imitation of Christ whereby believers are called to share in Christ's holiness, a reality made possible only through "the precious blood of Christ" (1 Pet 1:19). In short, we should not read 2 Peter as if it reflects a much later version of Christianity in which the cross no longer plays a central role.[35] The larger context of Petrine teaching may be safely assumed in this letter.

The mysterious expression "participants of the divine nature" (2 Pet 1:4) has generated considerable controversy. Does this text mean that believers become metamorphosed into divine beings, somewhat like Mormon theology maintains? Less extreme, may we agree with Eastern Orthodox theology that, in a very real sense, believers may acquire certain divine qualities of a transitive nature, that is, attributes in which there is common ground between God and humanity, such as goodness, righteousness, mercy and faithfulness? The technical term for this is *theosis*. Or, does Peter simply mean that believers experience a spiritual union with the Godhead? The short answer to the first option is no. The second option, if carefully qualified, is possible, and none of the major Christian traditions deny the third.

The major branches of Christianity, Eastern Orthodoxy, Roman Catholicism and Protestantism, essentially agree that salvation involves union with the Godhead. The Johannine witness here is decisive: "As you, Father, are in me and I am in you, may they also be in us . . . I in them and you in me, that they may become completely one" (Jn 17:21, 23). "And I will ask the Father, and he will give you another Advocate, to be with you forever. . . . But the Advocate, the Holy Spirit, whom the Father will send in my name, will teach you everything, and remind

---

[35]As Ernst Käsemann argued in *Essays on New Testament Themes* (London: SCM, 1964), pp. 169-95.

There is no scriptural evidence that the enormous gap between God and humanity may ever be closed. This flies in the face of too many unambiguous texts (Deut 6:4; Num 23:19; Job 9:32; Is 55:9; Hos 11:9; Jn 1:18; Rom 3:30; 11:33-36; 1 Cor 8:6; Eph 4:4-6). Thus the classical Mormon view, which is essentially apotheosis, the elevation of a person to the status of a god, may be rejected out of hand. The Eastern Orthodox view has more to commend it. We should first note that Christians in the Roman, Orthodox and Protestant traditions all agree that salvation is progressive, an ongoing process in which believers become more and more "consecrated to the Lord in true purity of life" by the indwelling of Christ through the Holy Spirit.[a]

Eastern Christianity places great emphasis on the mystical union between believer and the Godhead. In a real sense, the believer participates in the divine life, insofar as this is possible for created beings. A primary purpose of the incarnation and atonement was the incorporation of humanity into the divine. In the words of Athanasius, "God became man so that man might become god."[b] Note carefully that Athanasius, the great champion of the Nicene Creed, uses lower-case "god," for he was well aware that human beings could never become like God in his transcendent essence (e.g., self-existence, omnipotence, omnipresence and omniscience). Irenaeus held a similar position: "the Word of God, our Lord Jesus Christ, who did, through his transcendent love, become what we are, that He might bring us to be even what He is Himself."[c] Eastern Orthodox soteriology involves three stages: purification, illumination and theosis. Theosis is essentially likeness to and union with God, itself a three-stage process, beginning with the early struggles of the Christian life, continuing with growth in the knowledge of God and finally completed at the resurrection. In general, this scheme is foundational to the Roman and Protestant traditions as well.

Among Protestants, Wesleyans and other Holiness movements have most insistently stressed the concept of sharing in the divine nature as a stated goal of Christian living. In this regard, John Wesley's emphasis on "entire sanctification" comes to mind. While non-Wesleyans may quibble about the appropriateness of this particular formulation, the call to personal and corporate holiness is a shared goal of all Christians.[d] Peter says we should "make every effort" to actualize our participation in the divine nature. With this there should be no quarrel or equivocation.

[a]John Calvin, *Institutes of the Christian Religion*, 3.3.14; 3.14.9. See further K. Bockmuehl, "Sanctification," *NDT*, pp. 613-16.
[b]*On the Incarnation Against Apollinaris* 54:3 (PG 25:192B).
[c]*Against Heresies*, 5, preface.
[d]See the reservations of J. I. Packer, "Holy Spirit," *NDT*, pp. 318-19.

you of all that I have said to you" (Jn 14:16, 26). The distinctly Pauline formulation "in Christ" (e.g., Rom 8:10; Gal 2:19-20; Col 1:27) seems to me to be essentially the same idea, even if Paul does not emphasize the Johannine reciprocity of mutual indwelling.[36] What is denied in all three branches of Christendom is any notion of absorption into the being of God, a deification or transformation into deity. These are Hellenistic, pagan concepts, quite at odds with what Peter is portraying.[37] Union with Christ, so prominent in Pauline letters, is no doubt what Peter has in mind here. The similarity to Paul's thought is better grasped when we note that Peter says believers are "participants [Gk *koinōnoi*, lit., "sharers"] of the divine nature" (2 Pet 1:4). "It is not a believer's private possession, but it is something that they share together with other believers."[38]

Furthermore, the major streams of Christianity teach that growth in grace is incumbent on those who profess faith in Christ. This is a major

[36]See further M. A. Seifrid, "In Christ," *DPL*, pp. 433-36.
[37]See Moo, *2 Peter, Jude*, p. 52.
[38]Witherington, *Indelible Image*, 1:781.

burden of Peter's parenesis in 2 Peter 1:5-11.[39] This process of growth is predicated on two essential movements: escape from one realm and entrance into another. More specifically, one must "escape from the corruption that is in the world," in order to share in the divine nature (2 Pet 1:4).[40] One cannot miss the correlation with the Pauline language of transfer and incorporation. Paul often speaks of two existential possibilities: one is either "in Adam" or "in Christ." To be in the former is death; to be in the latter is life (Rom 5:12-21; 1 Cor 15:21-23, 45-49; Eph 2:1-6). In 2 Peter we read Peter's equivalent of this theological reality.

## REDEMPTIVE HISTORY AND SALVATION

Functioning just below the surface of Peter's parenesis is a presupposition governing the entire discourse: Peter holds to a "now but not yet" understanding of salvation.[41] Personal salvation, like redemptive history, unfolds in stages. When one commits to Jesus Christ as Savior and Lord, a journey of faith begins. In Peter's words, the Christian life begins when one has "received a faith" anchored "in the knowledge of God and of Jesus our Lord" (2 Pet 1:1-2), enabling one "to escape from the corruption" and "become participants of the divine nature" (2 Pet 1:4). This initial phase of salvation is the equivalent in Johannine terms to the new birth, and to dying and rising with Christ in Pauline terminology.

Conversion must be followed by the hard, gritty task of becoming sanctified or holy, an impossible undertaking apart from the enabling and encouraging of the Holy Spirit. The goal of sanctification is to be

---

[39]"Whereas in Greco-Roman thought participating in the divine nature meant things ranging from immortality even to apotheosis and entering the Elysian Fields, here it has an ethical dimension: participating in the holiness of God and thereby being enabled to act ethically" (ibid.).

[40]The participle *apophugontes* is aorist active. Typically, an aorist participle depicts an action prior to the action denoted by the finite verb. In other words, sharing in the divine nature depends on a decisive break with the corruption in the world. There must be a genuine conversion experience that liberates from the slavery of the fallen world.

[41]Some passages in this letter speak of a "now" experience with the Lord (2 Pet 1:1-3, 12) whereas others imply a "not yet" experience on the eschatological horizon (2 Pet 3:10-14). It is this tension between the "now but not yet" that aligns Peter's soteriology and eschatology with what is so evident in 1 Peter and in Paul and John. The taproot for this way of conceptualizing salvation goes back to Jesus, who in turn draws on the earlier scheme of redemptive history portrayed in the OT. In short, this is a master key to the interpretation of the entire Bible.

completely conformed to the moral and ethical image of Christ, exhibiting the graces and virtues that flow effortlessly from his inner being.
In theological terms, the end point of the Christian journey is glorification (see Rom 8:28-30). Peter refers to this end point as "entry into
the eternal kingdom of our Lord and Savior Jesus Christ" (2 Pet 1:11)
and describes it as a place "where righteousness is at home" (2 Pet 3:13).

In order to ensure arrival at that destination serious effort must be
expended. This is the burden of Peter's earnest exhortation in 2 Peter
1:5-11, in which one supports faith by cultivating Christian virtues (2
Pet 1:5-7): goodness, knowledge, self-control, endurance, mutual affection and, as a crowning virtue, self-denying, self-giving love.[42] This
entails "leading lives of holiness and godliness" (2 Pet 3:11) and striving
to be "without spot or blemish" (2 Pet 3:14). Through this process, says
Peter, we "confirm [our] call and election," that is, we validate our
passport and finally gain entrance into the promised land, the "new
heavens and a new earth" (2 Pet 3:13), wherein at last we experience
the full dimensions of "peace" (2 Pet 3:14), Peter's vision of glorification. "To him be the glory both now and to the day of eternity.
Amen" (2 Pet 3:18).

## Questions for Discussion

1.  What evidence is there that the theology of 2 Peter is con-
    tingent on the circumstances prompting its composition?

2.  What appears to be the fundamental error against which Peter
    contends?

3.  Does 2 Peter view Jesus Christ as truly God? Defend your
    answer.

4.  Summarize the contribution each title of Christ in 2 Peter
    makes to an overall understanding of this letter's Christology.

5.  How does 2 Peter illustrate the common, NT view of salvation
    as "now but not yet"?

6.  What is the most important factor determining the doctrine of
    God in 2 Peter?

---

[42]Note that Paul also reckons love as the supreme, overarching virtue of Christian character (1
Cor 13:8, 13; Col 3:14).

7. Discuss the contribution of 2 Peter to the doctrine of the inspiration and authority of Scripture.

## For Further Reading

Guthrie, Donald. *New Testament Theology*. Downers Grove, Ill.: InterVarsity Press, 1981. Pp. 147-48, 300, 341, 977-78.

Ladd, George Eldon. *A Theology of the New Testament*. Edited and revised by Donald A. Hagner. Grand Rapids: Eerdmans, 1993. Pp. 652-53.

Morris, Leon. *New Testament Theology*. Grand Rapids: Zondervan, 1986. Pp. 322-23.

Ryrie, C. C. *Biblical Theology of the New Testament*. Chicago: Moody Press, 1959. Pp. 269-89.

Schreiner, Thomas R. *New Testament Theology: Magnifying God in Christ*. Grand Rapids: Baker, 2008. Pp. 406-11.

Witherington, Ben, III. *The Indelible Image*. Vol. 1: *The Individual Witnesses*. Downers Grove, Ill.: InterVarsity Press, 2009. Pp. 340-47.

# 13

# THE CHARACTER AND DESTINY
# OF THE FALSE TEACHERS

THE MOST OBVIOUS PURPOSE OF 2 PETER is to refute the errors of unidentified false teachers who have infiltrated unspecified house churches. The taproot of the errant teaching involves a denial of Christ (2 Pet 2:1). This denial seems to be both ethical and theological; conduct and creed are under attack and Peter is at pains to refute this deviation from orthopraxy and orthodoxy. Clearly, the false teachers' lifestyle is at odds with the way of life taught by Christ and the apostles (2 Pet 2:2-3, 10-22); just as clearly, they deny that Christ is going to return at "the day of the Lord" (2 Pet 3:10), punish evildoers, bring to an end the present world order and usher in a new one. In so doing, they delete a key component of Christian hope. In response, Peter counterattacks on two fronts:

- He issues a dire warning aimed at those claiming to have "the knowledge of our Lord and Savior Jesus Christ," while making mockery of his moral standards (2 Pet 1:16; 2:20).

- He rebuts their willfully ignorant arguments denying the parousia, final judgment and the new creation (2 Pet 3:3-13).

So much seems clear. But can more be teased out by carefully examining Peter's polemical rhetoric?

## SETTING THE TABLE

In the opening (2 Pet 1:3-11), Peter anticipates his main blast against the false teachers in 2 Peter 2 and 3 by first establishing the credibility of apostolic teaching on the parousia. In much the same way, the apostle Paul approaches the "Colossian heresy" by first laying the groundwork in an appeal to a common confession of faith (Col 1:15-20).

## Exposing the Pretenders

Several features of Peter's polemic against the false teachers invite closer inspection. Just as at Pentecost (Acts 2:16-21), so now, as his earthly life nears its close, he sees the end times unmistakably unfolding, as foretold. Of course, the most relevant feature of those end times, in this context, has to do with the prediction of false teachers secretly bringing in "destructive opinions" (2 Pet 2:1). Not only was their rise predicted; so also was their certain condemnation and destruction (2 Pet 2:3). To what is he referring? Is he once again drawing on OT prophetic passages? If so, which ones?

*Jeremiah and the false prophets.* Jeremiah struggled mightily against the false prophets of his day. Like an odd man out, a solitary voice crying in the wilderness, only he announced impending judgment on disobedient Judah. Arrayed against him was the vocal majority who confidently proclaimed, "You shall not see the sword, nor shall you have famine, but I will give you true peace in this place" (Jer 14:13). With utter contempt the false prophets flung in his face this challenge: "Where is the word of the LORD? Let it come!" (Jer 17:15). They tried vainly to silence his dissenting voice: "Come, let us make plots against Jeremiah . . . let us bring charges against him" (Jer 18:18). In response, Jeremiah unleashes a stinging indictment against the false prophets. Listen carefully to his critique of their lifestyle and teaching: "Their course has been evil, and their might is not right. Both prophet and priest are ungodly; even in my house I have found their wickedness, says the LORD. . . . they commit adultery and walk in lies; they strengthen the hands of evildoers, so that no one turns from wickedness; all of them have become like Sodom to me, and its inhabitants like Gomorrah" (Jer 23:10-11, 14). Jeremiah leaves no doubt about their ultimate destiny: "for I will bring disaster upon

them in the year of their punishment, says the LORD" (Jer 23:12).[1]
One hears echoes of this impassioned rhetoric in Peter's polemic
against the false teachers troubling his house churches. Nor is one left
in the dark about the fate of the false teachers: "Their condemnation,
pronounced against them long ago, has not been idle, and their destruction is not asleep" (2 Pet 2:3).

*Jesus and the religious leaders of his day.* There is, however, another
prophetic voice to be reckoned with. Many thought Jesus of Nazareth
was Jeremiah come back from the dead (Mt 16:14). Like Jeremiah
before him, Jesus unleashed a devastating critique on the religious
leaders of his own day. Against the Pharisees and their scribes he
leveled these charges: "They love to have the place of honor at banquets
and the best seats in the synagogues" (Mt 23:6; cf. 2 Pet 2:13); they
"lock people out of the kingdom of heaven," "do not go in [themselves]"
and "when others are going in, [they] stop them" (Mt 23:13; cf. 2 Pet
2:2, 14, 18); they are "blind guides" (Mt 23:16; cf. 2 Pet 2:12, 19), "blind
fools" (Mt 23:17; cf. 2 Pet 2:16), "full of greed and self-indulgence" (Mt
23:25; cf. 2 Pet 2:3, 10, 14, 18-19), "full of hypocrisy and lawlessness"
(Mt 23:28; cf. 2 Pet 2:21-22), who will not "escape being sentenced to
hell" (Mt 23:33; cf. 2 Pet 2:12-13, 17). Jesus bluntly refutes the Sad-
ducean denial of bodily resurrection: "You are wrong, because you
know neither the scriptures nor the power of God" (Mt 22:29). Jesus'
critique of the Sadducees is especially relevant because they, like the
false teachers of Peter's time (2 Pet 3:3-7), deny divine, eschatological
intervention. The chief priests fare no better (Mt 27:41-43, 62-63).

That brings me to an important observation: Jesus prophesied the
rise of false teachers within the nascent church. Thus the most obvious prophecy to which Peter is indebted derives directly from the
Master with indirect indebtedness to Jeremiah. At the end of his
earthly ministry, Jesus warned his disciples about the danger of false
teachers leading many astray before his glorious parousia (Mk
13:21-23 and pars.).[2]

---

[1]One hears a similar condemnation of false prophets in Ezekiel 13. As is the case with Jeremiah,
there are a number of significant links between the ministry of Ezekiel and Jesus.
[2]Interpretation of the Olivet Discourse is fraught with many difficulties, but most commenta-

The last days have begun and deceivers are already at work. Neither deception nor deviation ceases until the parousia.[3] The operative watchword remains effective until the Lord returns: "Be alert, I have already told you everything" (Mk 13:23). False teachers will arise because the Master has so predicted; therefore, believers should be neither panicked nor perplexed. What is important is to recognize what is afoot and to take appropriate steps. They must be alert to the modus operandi of these interlopers and forcefully resist their insidious inroads. The first step Peter executes with unsparing invective.

## PETER'S POLEMIC AGAINST THE FALSE TEACHERS

Peter opens his defense of the parousia (2 Pet 3:2) by appealing to three authoritative witnesses (cf. Deut 19:15): the holy prophets, the Lord and Savior and the apostles (cf. Eccles 4:12). This appeal to apostolic tradition rooted in Scripture once again points to a basic conflict in this letter. It is not likely the false teachers rejected the Scriptures or Jesus Christ per se. What is at stake is apostolic authority; the teachers deny the apostolic interpretation of the OT prophets and the dominical sayings about the parousia. Notice how this issue surfaces throughout the letter. God has given "very great promises" (2 Pet 1:4), and anyone lacking these "is shortsighted and blind" (2 Pet 1:9). Peter is compelled "to keep on reminding" his readers "of these things" because they are "the truth *that has come to you*" (2 Pet 1:12, italics added) and insists that "we [the apostles] did not follow cleverly devised myths when we [the apostles] *made known to you* the power and

---

tors are agreed there are two focal points: the lead-up to the Jewish War (A.D. 66-73) and the lead-up to Jesus' parousia. I agree with those commentators who see a close connection between the two. In keeping with a feature of OT prophecy, Jesus juxtaposes a near, historical judgment, the fall of Jerusalem, with a far, end-of-history judgment, the parousia. Fluidity between the two moments, perhaps even a collapsing of one into the other, characterizes the discourse. Peter deals with this "problem of perspective" in 2 Peter 3. The best OT example occurs in the prophecy of Joel—recall that Peter uses Joel 2 as his primary text on the day of Pentecost in Acts 2. Joel predicts a disastrous plague of locusts, and his poetic description of these locusts shades imperceptibly into a description of the day of the Lord, also under the figure of a grotesque locust plague. In fact, Joel seemingly uses the expression "day of the Lord" to refer to both the historical judgment lying just on the horizon and a more distant eschatological judgment, beyond the horizon, at some undetermined time. Both the historical and eschatological judgments, however, are depicted as "near."

[3]See further Douglas J. Moo, *2 Peter and Jude* (NIVAC; Grand Rapids: Zondervan, 1996), p. 92.

coming of our Lord Jesus Christ" (2 Pet 1:16, italics added).

He continues by narrating the transfiguration, an event witnessed by three apostles and which more fully confirms the prophetic message (2 Pet 1:19). The readers should attend to this prophetic message until it is fulfilled when "the day dawns," that is, the parousia. He then follows this with a solemn reminder that no prophecy of Scripture "is a matter of one's own interpretation" (2 Pet 1:20), a phrase almost certainly responding to an accusation by the false teachers. In other words, the false teachers charge that the apostles concocted the parousia from their own imaginations. On the contrary, Peter affirms that the scriptural prophecies concerning the coming of the Lord in glory arose under the impulse and enabling of the Holy Spirit, the same Holy Spirit who informs the apostles' interpretation of these passages.

This then leads into his warning against the false teachers and their "destructive opinions" who, according to the Scriptures, will arise among God's people in the last days (cf. Dan 12:10). Scriptural case studies dramatically illustrate the reality of inevitable divine judgment on evildoers: "They have left the straight road and have gone astray" (2 Pet 2:15) and "[turned] back from the holy commandment *that was passed on to them*" (2 Pet 2:21, italics added). In short, they have rejected apostolic teaching as authoritative. Not surprisingly, they are "bold and willful, they are not afraid to slander the glorious ones" (2 Pet 2:10).[4]

Peter is not caught off guard by this blatant denial of the parousia. In fact, he reminds his readers that such was already predicted: "in the last days scoffers will come, scoffing and indulging their own lusts and saying, 'Where is the promise of his coming? For ever since our ancestors died, all things continue as they were from the beginning of creation!'" (2 Pet 3:3-4). Two things should be noted here. First, we have a proposition disguised as a question. The proposition amounts

---

[4]The precise identity of the "glorious ones" is not immediately clear. A comparison, however, with Jude 8-10 suggests that they are angelic beings. The background of this accusation apparently stems from the pseudepigraphal work *Assumption of Moses*, in which Michael the archangel refrains from using abusive language towards Satan during a dispute over the body of Moses. This dispute does not appear in any extant MSS. The earliest existing MS breaks off suddenly, and presumably the episode in question occurred in that lost portion. See Larry R. Helyer, *Exploring Jewish Literature of the Second Temple Period* (Downers Grove, Ill.: InterVarsity Press, 2002), pp. 139-46.

to this: there is no coming (parousia). Second, this proposition is supported by an appeal to empirical evidence, namely, the non-occurrence of the parousia. The assumption of the uniformity of nature is the bottom line argument of the teachers. The initial question, then, amounts to a conclusion derived from a major premise and an assumed minor premise. The false teachers' argument may be laid out as follows:

Major Premise: The created order operates uniformly.

Minor Premise: The Christian doctrine of the parousia violates this principle of uniformity.

Conclusion: The doctrine of the parousia is not part of the created order (it is a myth).

Peter denies their starting point. He has already narrated some dramatic examples of divine intervention in the form of judgment in 2 Peter 2. In 2 Peter 3 he draws attention to three major discontinuities in the created order (note once again the threefold witness): creation itself, worldwide judgment by water (Noah's flood) and the final, worldwide judgment by fire. These testify to the reality of divine intervention in a world that normally operates uniformly. The emphasis is on the dynamic, all-powerful word of God. By his word God brought the heavens and earth into existence, and by that word God "the world of that time was deluged," and "by the same word" God will destroy the present word with fire on "the day of judgment and destruction of the godless" (2 Pet 3:5-7). In short, the parousia is quite in keeping with God's mighty acts in salvation history. The false teachers' theology is vitiated at its core: their view of God and his works is woefully deficient.

I backtrack for a moment. Second Peter 3:4 puts into the mouths of the false teachers what they view as a knock-down argument against the parousia: "For ever since our ancestors died, all things continue as they were from the beginning of creation!" The word translated "ancestors" in the NRSV, *pateres*, is translated as "fathers" in the NIV, ESV, NEB, REB and HCSB. The difference is rather important. If one translates as "fathers," then perhaps the false teachers are appealing to the fact that an earlier generation of Christian leaders has passed away and still Jesus has not returned. On this understanding, the "fathers" are the apostles and the first generation that saw the Lord or had contact with those who did. This is often the meaning assumed by those who date the letter to the end of the first century or the beginning of the second. It would be one of those subtle hints that the author is not Simon Peter but someone writing in his name after his death. This understanding of the fathers is linked to two other groups mentioned in 2 Peter 3:2, namely, "the holy prophets" and "your apostles." Critical scholarship usually identifies these as two groups that were active in the early church but now long since absent from the stage of history ("spoken in the past").

Before we jump to this conclusion, however, the following factors should be taken into account. The term *pateres* "never refers to the first generations of Christians in the New Testament, but it always refers to the patriarchs of the Old Testament."[5] This is its most likely meaning in 2 Peter 3:2 because the false teachers do not appeal to the fact that things continue as they always do from the time of Jesus' ministry, but from the beginning of creation, a more forceful argument for uniformity than a mere two or three generations. Furthermore, whereas the reference to "holy prophets" in 2 Peter 3:2 could refer to NT prophets, more likely it means the OT prophets. Peter has already had occasion to speak of OT prophets indirectly in 2 Peter 1:19-21 and of false OT prophets in 2 Peter 2:1 (cf. 2 Pet 3:15-16), nor should we overlook 1 Peter 1:10, where he speaks of "the prophets who prophesied of the grace that was to be yours." The same basic notion appears in Hebrews 1:1: "Long ago God spoke to our ancestors in many and various ways by the prophets, but in these last days he has spoken to us by a Son." To this we add Romans 1:2, where Paul says the gospel was "promised beforehand through his prophets in the holy scriptures" (cf. Eph 2:20; Jas 5:10). The similar contextual settings involving divine revelation through the OT prophets in Hebrews 1, 1 Peter 1 and Romans 1 suggests a similar understanding of the term "prophets" here in 2 Peter 3 as well.

The mention of "your apostles" is more difficult. Ben Witherington

---

[5]Thomas R. Schreiner, *1, 2 Peter, Jude* (NAC 37; Nashville: Broadman & Holman, 2003), p. 373. He lists the approximately forty passages where the term in the plural occurs.

claims that "it reflects the editorial work of the one who assembled these apostolic traditions from Peter and Jude. Our editor is not claiming to be an apostle, much less the chief Jewish apostle, Peter."[6] However, Richard Bauckham, who also doubts that Peter himself wrote 2 Peter, holds that the apostles in question are those who initially proclaimed the gospel to the readers.[7] This latter view makes good sense in the context. To read into this statement an inference that the author did not view himself as an apostle goes beyond what is warranted.[8] Here is the bottom line: Peter is addressing a defection of faith in the parousia near the end of his life, and he does so by appealing to the authority of Scripture, the teaching of the Lord Jesus Christ (summarized in the singular idea of "the commandment") and his apostles who spoke the word to the readers. We know the names of at least two of their apostles: "Simeon Peter, a servant and apostle of Jesus Christ" (2 Pet 1:1) and "our beloved brother Paul" (2 Pet 3:15).

## PROFILING THE FALSE PROPHETS

Peter's rebuttal of the false teaching allows us to infer some of the beliefs of the false teachers (mirror reading). Though this is hardly an exact science, one can reasonably ferret out the main lines of deviation.

Fundamentally, the dispute centers on whether Jesus Christ will intervene in history and require each individual to give account for his or her deeds. In addition, there is the question of the cosmos itself. Is it indestructible and eternal, or is it doomed to destruction and replacement by a new world order following Christ's return? That the false teachers deny the parousia and the destruction of the cosmos is clear, but their precise teaching and the worldview informing it is not. Scholars have cast a wide net over the various streams of thought emanating from the Greco-Roman world of the first century, and, not surprisingly, differing reconstructions have emerged.

---

[6]*Indelible Image*, 1:778. See also J. N. D. Kelly, *A Commentary on the Epistles of Peter and Jude* (Grand Rapids: Baker, 1981), p. 354: "it inadvertently betrays that the writer belongs to an age when the apostles have been elevated to a venerated group who mediate Christ's teaching authoritatively to the whole Church."

[7]*Jude, 2 Peter* (WBC 50. Dallas: Word, 1983), p. 287.

[8]See also Moo, *2 Peter and Jude*, pp. 164-65.

For me the decisive question is: Do these teachers consider themselves Christians? Peter introduces them as false teachers who bring in
destructive opinions. They are described as the prophesied counterparts of the false prophets who "arose among the people" (2 Pet 2:1).
This implies that they have access to and participate in the worship of
believers in Christ (cf. 2 Pet 2:13; Jude 2). This does not neatly fit a
pagan hypothesis. More likely they still see themselves as Christians
but have been greatly influenced by pagan thinking.

*2 Peter and Jude.* At this point, I glance at a long-standing issue that
bears on our study. What is the relationship between 2 Peter and Jude?
The reason for bringing it up now is that these two letters share a remarkable amount of common material and appear to address common
opponents. A majority of scholars favor the view that 2 Peter borrows
from and adapts material from Jude. Without going into a long discussion of this issue, let me state my position.[9] Most likely 2 Peter does
borrow from Jude, but this is by no means certain.[10] I also think both
letters respond to false teachers who are very similar in both stance
and style.[11]

What is helpful is paying close attention to how Peter's argument is
similar to but also differs from Jude's at certain critical points. A point
of common agreement has to do precisely with this matter of where the
false teachers are operating. Both letters assume, if not explicitly state,
that they are in the midst of the house churches. For example, in Jude
12 we read, "These are blemishes on your love-feasts, while they feast
with you without fear, feeding themselves." Similarly, Peter describes
their reveling "while they feast with you" (2 Pet 2:13). The love feast
was held in conjunction with the Lord's Supper, and the latter was
barred to unbelievers (see *Did.* 9.5). Perhaps the decisive piece of information about the false teachers' background is the warning that "it
would have been better for them never to have known the way of righteousness than, *after knowing it*, to turn back from the holy commandment that was passed on to them" (2 Pet 2:21, italics added). For

---

[9]See further my earlier discussion of this issue in chapter 11.
[10]Moo, *2 Peter and Jude*, pp. 120-22, and Bauckham, *Jude, 2 Peter*, p. 141.
[11]Moo, *2 Peter and Jude*, pp. 18-19.

this reason, any hypothesis identifying them as essentially non-Christians seems unlikely. Rather, we are dealing with a group deviating from apostolic authority and teaching at certain key points, which appears to be the nub of the dispute.

***The Gnostic hypothesis.*** According to a widely held view among scholars of the nineteenth and twentieth centuries, the antagonists are adherents of an early form of Gnosticism that eventually crystallizes into several distinct streams during the second century A.D. Underlying this position is the assumption that there is "substantial indirect evidence" to support the contention that already in the last third of the first century, various forms of teaching that would later become full-blown Gnosticism were "in the air," and this is what alarms the author and prompts his counterattack.[12] Irenaeus, in the mid-second century, traces this deviant doctrine, ironically, back to another Simon, Simon Magus, whom we meet in the book of Acts (Acts 9:9-24). This was the standard view of the church fathers. In several NT writings, dating from the last third to the end of the first century, many scholars think they catch a whiff of a malignant teaching displaying affinities to Gnosticism (e.g., Colossians, 1 and 2 Timothy, Gospel of John, 1 John).

Bauckham rejects this view and claims that "this identification, as recent scholarship has recognized, is insecure."[13] He rightly points out that the only two clear features attributed to the opponents involve a denial of the parousia and a pronounced moral laxity. His bottom line is this: a Gnostic hypothesis has no basis because the text itself lacks any indication of cosmic dualism, a distinguishing feature of Gnosticism.[14] He is correct that there is no explicit evidence of cosmic dualism in 2 Peter. In reply, however, such an observation counts more against dating 2 Peter to the second century A.D., when full-blown Gnosticism with its cosmic dualism comes to light, than against the hypothesis of an earlier form of Gnosticism. Bauckham dates 2 Peter to the end of the first century, and so his claim loses some of its force. Cosmic du-

---

[12]See further D. M. Scholer, "Gnostics, Gnosticism," *DLNTD*, pp. 400-412, esp. pp. 402-6. The direct quotes are on p. 403.

[13]"2 Peter," *DLNTD*, p. 925.

[14]Bauckham, *Jude, 2 Peter*, pp. 154-56.

alism may not have been a regular feature of the early Gnostic movements surfacing in the last third of the first century.

At any rate, the opening gambit reads like a response to a Gnostic-
tinged philosophy. In place of esoteric knowledge, a true knowledge of
God that enables believers to escape from the corruption of this world
and become participants of the divine nature (2 Pet 1:3-11) is proclaimed. This passage, widely recognized as one of the most Helle-
nistic-sounding passages in the NT,[15] may borrow the language of the
errant teaching but infuses it with apostolic, orthodox meaning (much
as Paul does in Colossians). Peter's full-scale assault on the false teachers
indicts them for "licentious ways" (2 Pet 2:2), "greed" and "deceptive
words" (2 Pet 2:3), "depraved lust," "despis[ing] authority" (2 Pet 2:10),
"slander[ing] the glorious ones" (2 Pet 2:10), "bombastic nonsense" (2
Pet 2:18) and promising freedom but being themselves "slaves of corruption" (2 Pet 2:19). As J. Ramsey Michaels points out, "These features agree remarkably with certain traditions surrounding the earliest
attested form of Gnosticism. This was Simonian Gnosticism, which
claimed Simon Magus as its founder."[16]

***Epicureans or scoffers.*** Over against the Gnostic hypothesis, Jerome
Neyrey argues that "the opponents were either Epicureans, who rejected traditional theodicy, or 'scoffers' (Apikoros) who espoused a
similar deviant theology."[17] He collates a number of sources illustrating
the widespread influence of this teaching in both Christian and Jewish
sources. He then shows how the polemic in 2 Peter makes good sense
in light of this assumed background. Here is a summary of his position:

When the template of Epicurean doctrine about theodicy is placed
over 2 Peter, we are able to discern the contours of the commonplace
arguments, both denying the judgment of God and affirming it. But as
we noted above, the same antitheodicy argument can be found in Jewish
and Greek sources without the specific attribution to Epicurus. Hence

---

[15]Ibid., p. 926.
[16]"Peter, Second Epistle of," *ISBE* 3:818. J. C. Beker claims "the kergyma of the Gnostics per-
colates at times through the abusive language of the author" ("Peter, Second Letter of," *IDB*
3:769). However, he identifies the particular strain of Gnosticism as Marcionite and locates 2
Peter ca. A.D. 150.
[17]Jerome H. Neyrey, *2 Peter, Jude* (AB 37C; New York: Doubleday, 1993), p. 122.

it remains a probable argument that the opponents of 2 Peter voice a doctrine usually associated with "atheists" such as Epicureans. . . . But the materials discussed above clearly indicate that we look to popular skepticism about God's judgment as the background of the polemic in 2 Peter and not gnosticism or some other thought world.

Bauckham essentially accepts Neyrey's hypothesis, with an important caveat. He rightly locates the false teachers within the house churches.[18] As I have already indicated, a movement considering itself Christian is a much more likely candidate than a species of unvarnished paganism. In short, the false teachers, perhaps disillusioned by the non-occurrence of the parousia, may have fallen prey to popular skepticism picked up from the Epicurean "atheists." This is a plausible explanation for what is going on in the background of 2 Peter.

However, the Epicurean hypothesis is not without difficulty. The charge of moral libertinism leveled against the false teachers does not comport well with classical Epicureanism or its continuation in the Roman age as exemplified in the thought of Lucretius. Contrary to popular understanding, neither Epicurus nor Lucretius encouraged abandonment of oneself to sensual pleasure. Pleasure was indeed the ideal, but unbridled indulgence usually leads not to pleasure but pain. What Epicurus sought was maximal pleasure, that is, a state of repose, consisting of both physical rest and relaxation and psychological freedom from worry. Since fear disrupts repose, and, according to Epicurus, the two primary sources of fear are death and divine judgment, denial of divine intervention is a necessary condition in order to achieve this state.[19] This much makes sense of Peter's polemic. But the point I want to make is this: the kind of moral anarchy described in 2 Peter would hardly qualify as repose. The false teachers are likened to "irrational animals, mere creatures of instinct" counting it "a pleasure to revel in the daytime," "reveling in their dissipation," having "eyes full of adultery, insatiable for sin," "heart[s] trained in greed," having "licentious desires of the flesh" and winding up "en-

---

[18]Bauckham, *Jude, 2 Peter,* p. 155.

[19]A brief summary of Epicureanism may be found in W. T. Jones, *A History of Western Philosophy,* 2 vols. (New York: Harcourt, Brace & World, 1952), 1:260-61.

tangled and overpowered" by their desires. This is a far cry from the
Epicurean ideal of simple frugality! Now, to be sure, Neyrey and
Bauckham do not argue that the false teaching advocated classical
Epicureanism; rather, it reflects various and sundry ideas picked up
from popular paganism, among which was the Epicurean denial of
divine providence and judgment.

But where is the evidence that such was the case? At this point, both
scholars resort to an unstated assumption: this must have been what
happened given the nice fit with the rhetoric of 2 Peter. In other words,
2 Peter is the smoking gun for this hypothesis. I call attention to the
fact that Neyrey and Bauckham reject the proto-Gnostic view because
they find no evidence of cosmic dualism in 2 Peter and other first-
century sources. They criticize adherents of this view for assuming that
there was nevertheless an early form of Gnosticism in which cosmic
dualism was not yet present. In point of fact, both positions share a
common shortcoming: they cannot demonstrate that their hypothesis
covers all the bases.

## CONCLUSION

A final decision on this matter is difficult. Each hypothesis has difficulty accounting for all the evidence as it may be gleaned from 2 Peter.[20]
Perhaps the best procedure is to leave it as an open question. We can,
nonetheless, still engage in a fruitful examination of Peter's defense of
the parousia, which is the aim of the next chapter.

## FATE OF THE FALSE TEACHERS

Before doing so, however, I draw attention to Peter's dire warning directed at the false teachers. This affords some material that throws
light on his understanding of divine judgment, both in history and at
the end of history. He narrates three examples of God's historical
judgment on evildoers, interspersed with two examples of deliverance
for the righteous (2 Pet 2:4-10). These examples carry eschatological
implications. That is, these events from primeval and historical times

---

[20]"The descriptions are so vague that they . . . fit almost any group who combined skepticism
about future judgment with an immoral lifestyle." Moo, *2 Peter and Jude*, p. 20.

are precursors of eschatological judgment and salvation; the beginning foreshadows the end.

Thus the sinning angels are incarcerated until the day of judgment (2 Pet 2:4), but their story is not over yet; they must face the music and stand trial. Though not explicitly stated here, the pre-flood generation must also have their day in court. Finally, attention is drawn to the historical judgment on Sodom and Gomorrah, concluding with these sobering words: "an example of what is coming to the ungodly" (2 Pet 2:6). Noah and Lot, by contrast, presage the Lord's deliverance of his people in the eschatological travails accompanying the parousia and thus encourage the faithful to persevere in hope. In this regard, one notes the similar idea expressed by the apostle Paul in 2 Thessalonians 1:5-10.

### THE NATURE OF FINAL JUDGMENT

So what does Peter believe about the nature of final punishment? That evildoers will be punished is certain; the specific form it takes is less so. In 2 Peter 2:3, he pairs the terms "condemnation" (*krima*) and "destruction" (*apōleia*), noting that the former "has not been idle" and the latter "is not asleep." Thus the divine judge's verdict (*krima*) against the false teachers consists of destruction (*apōleia*).[21] Does this destruction amount to annihilation or to a state of unending punishment? In the immediately following verse, he begins listing three instances of divine judgment, the first of which is the case of the sinning angels.

Following a tradition that closely parallels *1 Enoch*, if not alluding to that source itself (*1 En.* 10:4; 13:1-2; 14:4-7), Peter says that God "cast them into hell and committed them to chains of deepest darkness to be kept until the judgment" (2 Pet 2:4).[22] And what will happen at "the judgment"? *First Enoch* 10:5-6 consigns Azazel, the ringleader of the angelic rebellion, to the fire. But this is not the whole story. "For instance, the composite *1 Enoch* variously describes the wicked as pun-

---

[21]A. Kretzer notes that "the entire eschatological scenery and tension in 2 Peter is characterized by this word (6 occurrences): deceivers as well as deceived are on the way to ruin, not least of all because of their false interpretation of Scripture" (2 Pet 3:16). "*apollumi*," *EDNT* 1:136.

[22]Or "pits." See textual note in NRSV.

ished with torment for ever (22:11), as an eternal spectacle for the righteous (27:3), yet *also* destroyed for ever (91:19)."[23]

In light of this, the next example, Sodom and Gomorrah, is instructive. God turned these cities into ashes and "condemned them to extinction" (*katastrophē*) as an example "of what is coming to the ungodly" (2 Pet 2:6). The analogy seems to imply annihilation, but one must be careful not to read more than is warranted into the passage. The text compares the destruction (*phthora*) of "mere creatures of instinct" with the false teachers, likened to "irrational animals," who will also be "destroyed" (*phtharēsontai*, 2 Pet 2:12). Once again, this suggests annihilation. But we learn that "the deepest darkness has been reserved" for the false teachers (2 Pet 2:17), a destiny more in keeping with the notion of some type of ongoing existence. Perhaps this only means they are incarcerated until the final judgment at which time they are annihilated in the fire, as in *1 Enoch*. After all, 2 Peter 3 speaks of the present world being "reserved for fire, being kept until the day of judgment and destruction of the godless" (2 Pet 3:7). Peter seems to parallel the destruction of the present heavens and earth with the destruction of the godless. One could argue that since the former destruction is annihilation, so is the latter. As we will see shortly, however, there are objections to the notion that the present universe is annihilated, and thus the analogy may not be precise. At any rate, on the basis of 2 Peter, annihilation of the wicked is at least a possible interpretation.

But in light of Peter's religious background which option seems most likely? Unfortunately, as already indicated by *1 Enoch*, Second Temple Judaism does not speak with one voice on this subject. One may find texts supporting both options. It is fair to say, however, that the majority view conceives of final punishment as an unending experience. What would carry decisive weight in this question, however, is the view of the Master.[24] According to Jesus, the respective outcomes of the righteous and the wicked are commensurate in terms of duration and

---

[23]P. S. Johnston, "Hell," *NDBT*, p. 543.
[24]See Larry R. Helyer, *The Witness of Jesus, Paul and John* (Downers Grove, Ill.: InterVarsity Press, 2008), pp. 156-57.

radically disparate in terms of experience. Jesus' view, as derived from
the Gospels, seems to endorse the notion that the wicked suffer everlasting punishment: "And these will go away into eternal punishment,
but the righteous into eternal life" (Mt 25:46), a position generally
comparable to that exhibited in *1 Enoch* (*1 En.* 10:13) and *Jubilees*.

Advocates of both annihilation and eternal punishment appeal to
Paul. This is so because Paul speaks of "eternal destruction" for those
"who do not obey the gospel" (2 Thess 1:8-9) and immediately thereafter describes this as being "separated from the presence of the Lord
and from the glory of his might" (2 Thess 1:9), a description more in
keeping with eternal punishment than annihilation. In short, his letters
exhibit the same ambiguity and tension in this regard as do the letters
of Peter. Given Paul's Pharisaic background, however, and the fairly
clear position of Jesus, I would think he held to some type of everlasting
punishment (see Rom 2:7-9). With John there is little doubt, especially
if one accepts Johannine authorship of Revelation. "And the devil who
had deceived them was thrown into the lake of fire and sulfur, where
the beast and the false prophet were, and they will be tormented day
and night forever and ever . . . and anyone whose name was not found
written in the book of life was thrown into the lake of fire" (Rev 20:10,
15; 21:8).

The majority opinion in Christian theology stands in favor of interpreting this to mean eternal punishment. Whether the language of everlasting fire and burning should be taken literally, however, is debatable. Most modern interpreters take this as a metaphorical expression
for an intense, emotional form of suffering. Clearly, Jesus' primary emphasis is on exclusion from God's presence, and with this Peter, Paul (2
Thess 1:9), and John (Rev 22:15) agree. Perhaps this is the best place to
leave it.

## Questions for Discussion

1. Which background do you think best fits the false teachers of
   2 Peter? Are there other possible options?

2. What seems to be the heart of the dispute between Peter and
   the false teachers? Is this a disputed issue in our own day?

3. Are the false teachers professing Christians or not? Defend your answer.

4. What light do OT passages dealing with false prophets throw on the rhetoric of 2 Peter?

5. What is the nature and extent of final judgment according to 2 Peter?

## For Further Reading

Bauckham, Richard J. *Jude, 2 Peter*. WBC 50. Waco: Word, 1983.

Ladd, George Eldon. *A Theology of the New Testament*. Rev. ed. Grand Rapids: Eerdmans, 1993.

Marshall, I. Howard. *New Testament Theology: Many Witnesses, One Gospel*. Downers Grove, Ill.: InterVarsity Press, 2004.

Matera, Frank J. *New Testament Theology: Exploring Diversity and Unity*. Louisville: Westminster John Knox, 2007.

Moo, Douglas. *2 Peter and Jude*. NIVAC. Grand Rapids: Zondervan, 1996.

Morris, Leon. *New Testament Theology*. Grand Rapids: Zondervan, 1986.

Schreiner, Thomas R. *1, 2 Peter, Jude*. NAC 37. Nashville: Broadman & Holman, 2003.

———. *New Testament Theology: Magnifying God in Christ*. Grand Rapids: Baker, 2008.

Thielman, Frank. *Theology of the New Testament: A Canonical and Synthetic Approach*. Grand Rapids: Zondervan, 2005.

Witherington, Ben, III. *The Indelible Image*. Vol. 1: *The Individual Witnesses*. Downers Grove, Ill.: InterVarsity Press, 2009.

# 14

## ESCHATOLOGY OF 2 PETER

THIS CHAPTER SUMMARIZES the eschatological beliefs that are either assumed or explicitly asserted in 2 Peter. Since I have already touched on Peter's understanding of final judgment in connection with the fate of the false teachers in the preceding chapter, I will not repeat that material here.

### PERSONAL ESCHATOLOGY: LIFE AFTER DEATH

Peter's reference to his approaching death in 2 Peter 1 affords a brief glimpse into his view of personal eschatology, that is, life after death. By using the expression "as long as I am in this body" (2 Pet 1:13), Peter echoes Pauline terminology.[1] In 2 Corinthians 5, Paul sketches the three possible states of existence for a believer. One's present, mortal life may be described as living "in this tent" (*skēnei*, 2 Cor 5:2, 4), equivalent to "[living] in the flesh" (Phil 1:22, 24) or "in the body." At death, "the earthly tent we live in is destroyed" or "taken . . . off" (2 Cor 5:1, 3) and one becomes "unclothed" or "naked" (2 Cor 5:3-4), the same condition Paul describes as departing this life and being with Christ (Phil 1:23). The final state is having "a building from God, a house not made with hands, eternal in the heavens" (2 Cor 5:1), also described as being "further clothed, so that what is mortal may be swallowed up by life" (2 Cor 5:4). This is the spiritual body described by Paul in 1 Corinthians 15:42-53.[2] Most likely, Peter held a similar view (1 Pet 3:18-

---

[1]The TNIV renders this more literally, "as long as I live in the tent [*skēnōmati*] of this body."
[2]See further Larry R. Helyer, *The Witness of Jesus, Paul and John* (Downers Grove, Ill.: InterVarsity Press, 2008), pp. 297-300.

19), chiming in with that of Jesus (Mt 10:28; 22:23-33) and John (Rev 6:9-11; 20:4).

## COSMIC ESCHATOLOGY

Most of the eschatological content of 2 Peter is cosmic in scope. Two focal points dominate the discussion: the parousia and the new creation.

*Peter's defense of the parousia.* In his opening exhortation, Peter assures the readers that if they confirm their call and election, they "will never stumble" or be denied "entry into the eternal kingdom" (2 Pet 1:10-11). This "entry" is yet future and apparently correlates with Jesus' return in power and glory, a doctrine denied by the false teachers.[3]

The apostle's response to their denial is somewhat surprising. I would have expected him to cite the words of Jesus, perhaps from the Olivet Discourse or related sayings about the parousia scattered throughout the Gospels. Instead, he appeals to the moment when Jesus was transfigured (Mk 9:2; Mt 17:1), an event in which he, along with James and John, were eyewitnesses and which he now interprets as a preview of "the power and coming of our Lord Jesus Christ" (2 Pet 1:16). Rather than being a misplaced postresurrection appearance,[4] the transfiguration was a moment of revelation, an epiphany, disclosing Jesus' divine nature. Though none of the Synoptic Gospels explicitly states that the transfiguration is a dress rehearsal for the parousia, the immediately preceding context supplies two dominical sayings filled with eschatological content. The first speaks of the Son of Man coming in glory with the holy angels to "repay everyone for what has been done" (Mt 16:27; Mk 8:38). Luke expands this so that Jesus comes "in his glory and the glory of the Father and of the holy angels" (Lk 9:26). The

---

[3]A typological understanding of redemptive history underlies much NT theology. The great pattern of exodus, wilderness wanderings and entry into the Promised Land, as sketched in the OT books Exodus through Joshua is recapitulated in the life of Christ and his church in the NT. Just as Jesus' life and ministry recapitulates key moments in the life of Israel, so also the experience of an individual believer. Thus at baptism one crosses the Red Sea, so to speak (cf. 1 Cor 10) and begins the long journey to Zion. The wilderness wanderings represent the ongoing struggle with the world, the flesh and the devil. Entry into the Promised Land is what Simeon calls "entry into the eternal kingdom." It is the culmination of the long trek to the heavenly Mount Zion, in Paul's theological language, glorification (Rom 8:28-30).

[4]As argued by R. H. Bultmann, *History of the Synoptic Tradition* (New York: Harper, 1968), pp. 209, 259-61, 423-33.

second is the intriguing saying about some of those standing in Jesus' immediate presence who "will not taste death before they see the Son of Man coming in his kingdom" (Mt 16:28; Mk 9:1; Lk 9:27). "Six days later" (Mt 17:1; Mk 9:2),[5] Peter, James and John do indeed experience a foretaste of the glory of the coming Son of Man.[6] Like an earlier prophet named Simeon (Lk 2:25-35), Simeon Peter may now rest in peace, because his eyes "have seen the glory of the coming of the Lord."

The apostle denies that this episode is a "cleverly devised myth," almost surely quoting the false teachers' derisive dismissal of the tradition. On the contrary, the apostolic, eyewitness testimony "on the holy mountain" powerfully confirms the "prophetic message." Thus, in accordance with OT precedent, he appeals to two independent witnesses, in order that the matter may be established (Deut 19:15; cf. 2 Cor 13:1; 1 Tim 5:19). This, of course, raises the question: What "prophetic message" did he have in mind? The most obvious candidate is Daniel 7:13-14. Here in a visionary account is a description of an individual who appears human yet possesses divine attributes.[7] Jesus dramatically identifies himself as this person before the high priest and Sanhedrin at his trial: "Are you the Messiah, the Son of the Blessed One? Jesus said, I am; and 'you will see the Son of Man seated at the right hand of the Power,' and 'coming with the clouds of heaven'" (Mk 14:61-62 par.).[8] The false teachers have seriously erred. Ironically, the high priest clearly understood what Jesus was claiming: "You have heard this blasphemy!" (Mk 14:64).

Psalm 110, one of the so-called Royal Psalms (see also Pss 18, 20, 21, 45, 72, 89, 101, 110, 132, 144), is another good candidate: "The LORD says to my lord, 'Sit at my right hand until I make your enemies

---

[5]Luke 9:23 has "Now about eight days after these sayings."

[6]Peter H. Davids calls the transfiguration "a proleptic glorification of Jesus" ("2 Peter," *NDBT*, p. 350). Douglas J. Moo comments, "Put simply, the Transfiguration reveals Jesus as the glorious King, and Peter was there to see it" (*2 Peter and Jude* [NIVAC; Grand Rapids: Zondervan, 1996], p. 75).

[7]These are as follows: (1) He arrives on the scene "coming with the clouds of heaven." (2) He has unrestricted and immediate access to the throne of God. (3) He accepts worship from all "peoples, nations, and languages." (4) He exercises universal sovereignty. (5) He is an everlasting person.

[8]See further Larry R. Helyer, *Yesterday, Today, and Forever: The Continuing Relevance of the Old Testament* (2nd ed.; Salem, Wis.: Sheffield, 2004), pp. 307-10.

your footstool' " (Ps 110:1).[9] Jesus appealed to this text (Mk 12:35-37) in order to challenge the scribes' conception of the messiah in narrowly nationalistic terms. "David himself calls him Lord; so how can he be his son?" (Mk 12:37). The mystery of the divine nature of Jesus was, understandably, beyond the disciples' complete comprehension until after the resurrection (Mk 4:41). Significantly, Psalm 110 highlights the absolute sovereignty and judgment entrusted to this mighty monarch, the very things the false teachers have conveniently ignored about the work of Christ. Psalm 110 appears several times in the NT as a key OT text supporting the resurrection, exaltation and heavenly reign of Jesus Christ (Acts 2:34-35; 1 Cor 15:25; Eph 1:20), in fact, there are no fewer than seven quotations or allusions to Psalm 110:1 in the book of Hebrews (Heb 1:3, 13; 4:14; 7:26; 8:1; 10:12-13).[10]

The hymnody of ancient Israel occasionally gives voice to motifs stemming from Canaanite traditions. For example, several references to Yahweh (the Lord) riding in his chariot on the winds and clouds occur. This motif is borrowed (and disinfected!) from the depiction of the Canaanite storm god Baal riding his chariot on the storm clouds. Listen to a classic example: "Sing to God, sing praises to his name; lift up a song to him who rides upon the clouds—his name is the LORD—be exultant before him . . . O rider in the heavens, the ancient heavens; listen, he sends out his voice, his mighty voice" (Ps 68:4, 33; cf. Ps 18:6-15; 97:1-3; 104:3; Nahum 1:3; Is 19:1). Note especially the mention of the Lord's voice, a feature of great importance in the transfiguration narrative. In short, the transfiguration was a theophany (cf. Ex 19), an epiphany and a preview of the parousia. Peter's eyewitness testimony confirms what the prophets foretold: the Lord will come on the clouds and establish his undisputed rule over all peoples. Evildoers are put on notice: a day of reckoning is looming—false teachers beware!

The divine voice reveals another aspect of the transfiguration: "This is my Son, my Beloved, with whom I am well pleased" (2 Pet 1:17).

---

[9]On the royal psalms see ibid., pp. 178-81.
[10]"It would be hard to exaggerate the importance of Psalm 110:1 for the christological reflections of the early church." Ben Witherington III, *The Indelible Image* (2 vols.; Downers Grove, Ill.: InterVarsity Press, 2009), 1:410.

Consider the close similarity in wording between this pronouncement and the Lord's summons to Abraham: "Take your son the beloved one, whom having loved" (Gen 22:2 LXX, author's translation). Suddenly, a new screen opens. Is it possible he alludes to the near sacrifice of Isaac, the so-called *aqedah* (Heb "binding")? A typological link between the binding of Isaac and the transfiguration of Christ is relevant if we remember the placement of this event in Jesus' ministry. Shortly after coming down from the mountain, Jesus reveals the fate awaiting the Son of Man in Jerusalem during the festival of Passover (Mk 9:30-32; Mt 17:22-23; Lk 9:43-45). Humiliation precedes exaltation. Furthermore, the conclusion of the story of the binding of Isaac promises that Abraham's offspring would be "as numerous as the stars of heaven and as the sand that is on the seashore" (Gen 22:17-18). So too, at the parousia, the elect are gathered "from the four winds, from one end of heaven to the other" (Mt 24:31), and they "inherit the kingdom prepared for [them] from the foundation of the world" (Mt 25:34). The Abraham cycle concludes with this declaration: "Abraham gave all he had to Isaac" (Gen 25:5). Believers, being "participants of the divine nature" (2 Pet 1:4), are also "heirs of the gracious gift of life" (1 Pet 3:7), indeed, heirs of "an inheritance that is imperishable, undefiled, and unfading, kept in heaven" (1 Pet 1:4). In Paul's words, believers are "heirs of God, and joint heirs with Christ" (Rom 8:17). A typological reading of Scripture results in a richly textured theology.

One further link merits mention, the so-called Servant Songs of Isaiah (Is 42:1-9; 49:1-6; 50:4-9; 52:13–53:12). For example, in the first song, the Lord refers to an unnamed individual as "my servant, whom I uphold, my chosen, in whom my soul delights; I have put my spirit upon him" (Is 42:1). The similarity in wording to the divine voice on the mount of transfiguration is striking. Then, in the fourth song (Is 52:13–53:12), the prophet traces the servant's descent from being "exalted and lifted up" (Is 52:13) to being "crushed for our iniquities" (Is 53:5) and "cut off from the land of the living" (Is 53:8). At the nadir, the song dramatically reverses direction and soars to a triumphant climax with the servant being allotted "a portion with the great, and . . . [dividing] the spoil with the strong" (Is 53:12). A predetermined pattern emerges: humiliation precedes exaltation. The career of Christ is a seamless robe; one cannot dismember one part without marring the whole. The parousia is thus essential and brings the saving story full circle. For this reason, the false teachers' denial of the parousia is not trivial; it amounts to lacking a proper "wedding robe" (Mt 22:12) and banishment from the marriage supper of the Lamb (Rev 19:6-9).

*Explanation for the delay of the parousia.* If the first part of Peter's defense of the parousia concerns the principle of divine intervention in history, the second addresses the undeniable delay. How does Peter account for the fact that Jesus has not yet returned?

His argument has two prongs, the first of which is that God's time is not our time. Peter is the first Christian we know who makes use of Psalm 90:4 in order to explain the delay of the parousia; he will not be the last. Psalm 90 begins with an eloquent testimony to the eternity and creative power of God and focuses primarily on the notion of accountability to this awesome God, his certain judgment of sinners and the relative brevity of human life. The appeal of the psalm is for transient human beings to come to their senses and recognize the eternal God and his claims on their fleeting lives. Peter fastens, however, on one verse because of its aptness in answering the skeptical denial of the parousia: "For a thousand years in your sight are like yesterday when it is past, or like a watch in the night" (Ps 90:4). He paraphrases the verse and sets up a statement of equivalence from the eternal God's perspective: "with the Lord one day is like a thousand years, and a thousand years are like one day" (2 Pet 3:8). Because God is outside time whereas humans are enmeshed within it, our perspective can never be the same as God's.[11] Consequently, God's unfolding plan cannot be adequately measured by our puny perceptions of what counts as a "long" or "short" time. This is not to say that Peter projects the parousia into a far distant future. One still detects the early Christian sense of imminence in this letter. After all, he addresses his readers by urging them to wait for and hasten the coming of the day of God (2 Pet 3:12), an exhortation making little sense if he did not think it might happen in their lifetime. Still, in harmony with the

---

[11]"Put simply, mortals cannot understand divine chronometry." Jerome H. Neyrey, *2 Peter, Jude* (AB 37C; New York: Doubleday, 1993), p. 238.

Master and the other apostles, Peter refuses to set a date. Instead, he denies that delay falsifies the parousia; rather, delay demands patience.

*Millennialism in 2 Peter.* But is there more to it than that? Does Peter allude to a prophetic calendar already known to his readers? Is there a passing reference to a millennial scheme in which the six days of creation in Genesis 1 are taken as six, successive, one-thousand-year periods climaxed by a glorious thousand-year reign in Jerusalem? The suggestion should not be dismissed out of hand, given "several instances of temporally delimited periods of divine rule" in noncanonical Jewish literature (*1 En.* 91:12-17; 93; *2 En.* 32:3-33:1; *2 Esd.* 5:1-7:35; *2 Bar.* 29, 39-40, 73), one of which, *1 Enoch*, antedates 2 Peter by at least two centuries.[12] In addition to this, we have the apostle John's testimony in the Apocalypse, depicting a millennial reign of Christ on the earth (Rev 20:1-6). We also know that postapostolic writings evidence millenarian views as witnessed in the *Epistle of Barnabas*, Justin Martyr and Irenaeus, among others.[13] But if the text alludes to the millennium, how does it fit the context? Does Peter assume that he and his readers are now in the sixth thousand-year period, the one climaxed by the parousia and ushering in the great millennial finale? If so, perhaps his point is that there is still some way to go and therefore doubts about the parousia are unfounded.[14] I doubt that this so, because it reads too

---

[12]J. W. Montgomery, "Millennium," *ISBE* 3:357. See also Larry R. Helyer, "The Necessity, Problems and Promise of Second Temple Judaism for Discussions of New Testament Eschatology," *JETS* 47 (2004): 597-615.

[13]For example, here is an excerpt from the *Epistle of Barnabas* 15:

> "And God made in six days the works of His hands, and made an end on the seventh day, and rested on it, and sanctified it." Attend, my children, to the meaning of this expression, "He finished in six days." This implieth that the Lord will finish all things in six thousand years, for a day is with Him a thousand years. And He Himself testifieth, saying, "Behold, to-day will be as a thousand years." Therefore, my children, in six days, that is, in six thousand years, all things will be finished. "And He rested on the seventh day." This meaneth: when His Son, coming [again], shall destroy the time of the wicked man, and judge the ungodly, and change the sun, and the moon, and the stars, then shall He truly rest on the seventh day.

See also Justin, *Dial.* 81; Irenaeus, *Haer.* 5.23.2; 5.28.3.

[14]Thomas R. Schreiner misses the point when he says that "Peter would then have been saying that the day of judgment lasts one thousand years, which is a rather strange notion" (*1, 2 Peter, Jude* [NAC 37; Nashville: Broadman & Holman, 2003], p. 380). Rather, Peter would be implying that the present age, the sixth one-thousand-year period, had nearly run its course and the millenial age was at hand.

much into the text. While he may have harbored millennial ideas, that does not seem to be what he is referring to here. Rather, he insists that doubts about the truthfulness of the parousia based on its delay are unfounded. Human beings must not superimpose their sense of time on that of the almighty God who inhabits eternity (Is 57:15).

On the assumption that Peter is writing this letter sometime around Nero's pogrom of A.D. 64, more than thirty years have now elapsed since Jesus ascended and began his heavenly session at the right hand of the Father. During his earthly ministry, Jesus predicted that the Son of Man would return in glory and establish his kingdom on earth. Some of his sayings could easily have been understood as placing his triumphant return within the lifespan of the disciples themselves (Mk 9:1 pars.; Mt 10:23; Mk 13:30 pars.). Clearly, the apostles Paul (1 Thess 4:15, 17; 5:4-11; 1 Cor 7:29-31; Rom 13:11-12; Phil 4:5) and James (Jas 5:8) spoke as if they expected the parousia during their lifetime, to which we should add 1 Peter 4:7: "The end of all things is near." But now the first generation of believers is passing away. How can Christians continue to adhere to a teaching that flies in the face of an undeniable fact? He has not returned.

At this point, it must be admitted that a later dating of 2 Peter has some force.[15] After all, on a dating of about A.D. 64, Peter, Paul and John would still be living and, although James the son of Zebedee (Acts 12:2) and James the half brother of Jesus (Josephus, *Ant.* 20.9.1) had by then suffered martyrdom, many of the first generation were still alive (1 Cor 15:6). The argument that 2 Peter reflects a time when that first generation exists in memory only must be given its full due. In reply, however, as I have previously argued, the primary objection of the scoffers is not that Jesus has failed to return since the founding fathers of the church have died; rather, the parousia and final judgment contradict an established principle of uniformity going back to the beginning of creation itself. While the scoffers may also have appealed to the lapse of time since Calvary, this is not what is explicitly stated in the rebuttal of their beliefs. It seems plausible that a delay of thirty or more

---

[15]A point also acknowledged by Moo, *2 Peter and Jude*, p. 167.

years could cause some concern and gnawing doubt. But would adding another twenty to thirty years to the assumed life setting of this document make the false teachers' case more credible?

Peter's second reply to the scoffers highlights another attribute of God, a very personal one. God is merciful and patient. He delays the parousia in order to grant space for repentance. God is "not wanting any to perish, but all to come to repentance" (2 Pet 3:9). In short, Jesus' delay is a stay of execution. Unquestionably, those of us living in the twenty-first century are grateful for the long delay! It has allowed us to be twice-born creatures (1 Pet 1:3) and enter the eternal kingdom. But precisely here the mystery of divine sovereignty and human freedom intersect. Like the conundrums of time-eternity and transcendence-immanence, the sovereignty-freedom paradox proves problematic. I resist resolving the dilemma by distinguishing between "desiring" and "decreeing" as two aspects of God's will, such that God decrees who will be saved, all the while desiring those not so elected to be saved.[16] I urge that our text be taken at face value: God desires the salvation of all, makes it available for all and by no means passes over any who are excluded on the basis of a hidden decree forged in eternity past. Paul affirms that God "desires everyone to be saved and to come to the knowledge of the truth" (1 Tim 2:4), and John joins the chorus when he affirms that "Jesus Christ the righteous . . . is the atoning sacrifice for our sins, and not for ours only but also for the sins of the whole world" (1 Jn 2:2).

*Parousia and morning star.* I conclude our discussion of the parousia by returning to Peter's reference to the dawning of a new day and the rising of the morning star (2 Pet 1:19). I earlier called attention to the possible allusion to Numbers 24:17 ("a star shall come out of Jacob") and its probable connection with the planet Venus. John of Patmos

---

[16]Which is precisely what Schreiner argues in *1, 2 Peter, Jude*, pp. 381-82, with appeal also to John Piper, "Are There Two Wills of God?" in *Still Sovereign* (Grand Rapids: Baker, 2000), pp. 419-32. Schreiner observes: "Many object that a desire that is not decreed is nonsense and theological double-talk. I would reply that such a view is rooted in biblical exegesis, that the Scriptures themselves, if accepted as a harmonious whole, compel us to make such distinctions [and] . . . such exegesis is not a rationalistic expedient but an acknowledgment of the mystery and depths of God's revelation" (*1, 2 Peter, Jude*, p. 82).

picks up on this as a fitting symbol for Christ and the new creation (Rev 2:28; 22:16). What is of special interest in the letter, however, is not so much the public dimension of this event but its personal, inward nature. We probably have another instance of the "now, but not yet" character of NT eschatology generally. Already, believers are equipped with a sort of spiritual compass, pointing them in the right direction, in spite of the surrounding darkness and uncertainties of the present world. Shining through the confusion is the morning star, orienting believers to that which is truly eternal. In Pauline terms this is the equivalent of "Christ in you, the hope of glory" (Col 1:27).

*The new heavens and new earth.* I remind the reader that 2 Peter is heavily colored by an apocalyptic worldview. Accordingly, the present world order languishes in corruption and condemnation. In spite of this grim reality, God graciously promises believers a way of escape. Not until 2 Peter 3, however, are we offered a few tantalizing glimpses of the new world order prepared for those who currently wait for it with eager longing and hope (2 Pet 3:12; cf. Rom 8:18-25). The new heavens and new earth (2 Pet 3:13) seem equivalent to what Peter calls "the eternal kingdom" in his opening exhortation (2 Pet 1:11). The "not yet" character of this kingdom follows from the shift to the future tense, "will be richly provided for you" (2 Pet 1:11). The verb employed, "to provide" (*epichorēgeō*), may carry the connotations of Greco-Roman culture in which a wealthy benefactor bestows a generous gift as an act of public service to the citizens of his city.[17] The passive voice implies that it is God the Father, acting as a generous benefactor, who extravagantly grants gifts to all the citizens of the eternal kingdom.[18] We now examine more closely at the nature of the divine benefactions.

Some of what Peter has in mind may be inferred by appealing to the witness of the apostle John in his Apocalypse. John's highly figurative description of the New Jerusalem portrays features flowing from God the Father's generous benefaction: incalculably precious things like immediate

---

[17]See the suggestion of DBAG, pp. 386-87.

[18]This is probably an instance of the "divine passive," whereby pious Jews referred to God indirectly and not by name in order not to "make wrongful use of the name of the LORD your God" (Ex 20:7).

access to God's throne and the Lamb; immortality, absence of all pain, sickness, suffering and evil; perpetual light, beauty, security, fellowship, happiness and worship (Rev 21–22). Much of what John describes of the New Jerusalem is an adaptation of Isaiah's famous visions of Jerusalem's restoration (Is 54:11-14) and the new heavens and a new earth (Is 65:17-25; 66:22-23), along with Ezekiel's vision of the new temple in a restored land (Ezek 40–48). These canonical, apocalyptic visions are reworked and adapted to become part of Second Temple Judaism's diverse menu portraying eschatological hope, as may be seen in a number of Second Temple writings (e.g., Tob 13:16-17; *2 Esd.* 7:28-44; *2 Bar.* 32:1-4), of which the NT is an important part and 2 Peter a textbook example. Alluding to several visions from Isaiah (Is 13:10; 24:21-23; 34:4; 65:17; 66:22-23), Peter asks his readers "what sort of persons" they ought to be in light of this incredible "out with the old, in with the new" bequest (2 Pet 3:11). Clients have obligations to their patrons, and the obligation of Christian clients to their heavenly patron is beyond reckoning.

*The day of the Lord and the day of God.* We now arrive at Peter's climactic insight into God's saving purpose for the entire creation, a breathtaking panorama of the wrap-up of redemptive history (2 Pet 3:10-13). Before us lies a theological and moral vision of God's plan that causes the scoffers' pitiful agenda to pale in comparison. The first thing to note about this passage is the conjunction of two days, the day of the Lord and the day of God. Does the former initiate and prepare the way for the latter? Or are these two days simply two aspects of the same period?

Echoing the warnings of the Master (Mt 24:43; Lk 12:39; cf. Mk 13:32-33, 37), Peter reminds his readers that "the day of the Lord will come like a thief," once again sounding the note of imminence. Jesus' use of the expression "day of the Lord" derives from the OT prophets. Starting with Amos of Tekoa (mid-eighth century b.c.), the Hebrew prophets begin painting a picture of God's climactic intervention into human history to render justice to all and establish everlasting peace and righteousness (Amos 5:18-20; 9:11-15).[19] In my mind's eye, I visu-

---

[19]On this see Helyer, *Yesterday, Today and Forever*, pp. 294-302; *Witness of Jesus, Paul and John*, pp. 128-30.

alize Michelangelo's magnificent painting of the last judgment, with its clearly demarcated panels and scenes, a helpful analogy, I think, when reflecting on this topic. The prophets who follow Amos add more paint strokes to a massive canvas that eventually depicts the grand culmination of God's kingdom in all its finality and glory. Amos focuses primarily, though not exclusively, on the judgment panel of this monumental masterpiece whereas others, such as Isaiah and Ezekiel, while also filling in more details in the judgment panel (e.g., Is 2:10-22; 13:6-13; 27; Ezek 38–39), make major contributions to the panel showcasing God's reward for the righteous (Is 2:1-4; 4:2-6; 65:17-25; Ezek 40–48). Remember, the day of the Lord is like a coin with two sides: a day of blessing and a day of blasting; the side you experience depends entirely on your relationship to the Lord.

The expression "day of God," by contrast, occurs only here (2 Pet 3:12). In John's Apocalypse, however, in a context describing the battle of Armageddon, we have a close parallel: "These are demonic spirits, performing signs, who go abroad to the kings of the whole world, to assemble them for battle on the great day of God the Almighty" (Rev 16:14). Also, in the book of Job, after listing a variety of ways in which God exercises his judgment on sinners during their lifetime, the author describes sinners as carried off in the day of God's wrath (Job 20:28). On the basis of these few texts, it appears that the day of the Lord and the day of God both refer to the same general time period. Furthermore, the many OT passages prophesying about the day of the Lord make abundantly clear that it is an extended period of time during which many different things transpire.[20]

Borrowing Hellenistic language about the nature of reality and its composition, Peter depicts the end of the age as dissolution by fire. The fundamental elements holding everything together melt. It should be noted that nowhere in the OT is this specific notion entertained; it probably owes its appearance in Scripture to the Hellenistic world.[21]

---

[20]See further Helyer, *Yesterday, Today and Forever*, p. 298.

[21]Neyrey notes that "Greek ears would hear this material in terms of the Stoic doctrine of 'conflagration' (*ekpyrōsis*) and 'regeneration' (*paliggenesia*)" (*2 Peter, Jude*, p. 241). For a helpful overview of the Hellenistic background here, see W. T. Jones, *A History of Western Philosophy*, 2 vols. (New York: Harcourt, 1952), 1:32-65, 266-72.

*Annihilation or renovation.* At face value, this seems to describe the annihilation of the present order. But is this what Peter means? Could he not be depicting renovation by fire? It is hard to be sure, and good arguments can be advanced for either alternative. Some passages in the OT suggest that the earth (Ps 104:5; Eccl 1:4) and the moon (Ps 89:37) will last forever, but such texts are not in eschatological contexts and therefore may be referring only to the world as it exists during this present age. But if we assume the everlasting nature of the created order, perhaps renovation, not annihilation, is intended. In other words, the new earth is new, not in a strictly chronological and compositional sense but a qualitative sense, a reconfiguration of the same essential elements. One might compare the apostle John's vision of the new heavens and new earth (Rev 21:1-8). He says nothing about the heavens being set ablaze, passing away with a loud noise, and the elements being dissolved and melted with fire (2 Pet 3:10), perhaps because he is transfixed by a glorious sight: a new heaven and a new earth suddenly appear and the holy city, the New Jerusalem, dramatically descends to the earth (Rev 21:1-2). Admittedly, this is an argument from silence and too much weight should not be placed on it. At any rate, the Greek word John employs for "new" is *kainos*, connoting not so much the notion of newness with respect to time (a notion generally connoted by the Greek word *neos*) but newness in regard to quality, "like brand new."

So what are we to make of this graphic depiction of the dissolution of the old order and the appearance of a new one? Is there any evidence or argument tipping the scales one way or the other? A key question might well be: Is there some inherent reason why God must annihilate the present world order and recreate a new one? Perhaps sin has so invaded the fabric and DNA of our present world order that there is no other recourse than a new beginning. Some may object that I am being overly literal in so speaking of sin. Sin should not be concretized in the actual "stuff" of our world but viewed merely as an essentially mental and volitional aspect of human behavior that can of course radically affect our physical bodies and the physical environment. To be sure, the OT traditions (Prov 4:23; Jer 17:9) and the teaching of Jesus (Mk 7:20-23) require us to locate the wellsprings of sinful behavior in the

heart or mind. But does this recognition exclude a much more tangible, corporeal dimension and presence to sin? Do not the "thorns
and thistles" of Genesis 3 intimate that the physical environment is
affected by sin? Is not death a tragic consequence of disobedience (Gen
2:17; 3:19; 5:5-30)? Perhaps we can even broaden this to include the
predatory cycle in the animal kingdom, tingeing it "red in tooth and
claw" and leaving most of us with a queasy stomach. What about
deadly viruses, possessing almost preternatural abilities to morph and
mutate, frustrating medical researchers who can never quite corner
and eradicate them? And do we seriously entertain the notion that the
new earth will be racked by earthquakes, volcanoes, hurricanes, tor-
nados and floods?

I take this one step further. What about the apostle Paul's grand
defense of the bodily resurrection of believers predicated on the bodily
resurrection of Jesus? What is this resurrection body he describes as
imperishable, glorious, powerful and spiritual (1 Cor 15:42-45)? There
is both continuity and discontinuity. But is it of a different kind of
"substance" than the former, physical body? I cannot say for sure, but I
think there must be some continuity if we are to maintain the physi-
cality of Jesus' resurrection body. After all, he could be recognized and
touched, and he could eat and converse with his disciples (Jn 20:26-29;
13-14, esp. 15-23). Consequently, I incline to the view that the new
creation is a radically new reconfiguration of the essential elements
God spoke into existence at the dawn of the first creation. However, I
should be quite content if it turns out that he speaks into existence a
new kind of "stuff." At any rate, whether by annihilation or renovation,
the Lord's judgment on the cosmos constitutes the end of redemptive
history and the fulfillment of the prophetic word.

A couple of subsidiary questions require further reflection. What,
for example, does Peter mean when he says that "the earth and everything that is done on it will be disclosed" (2 Pet 3:10)? According to the
textual footnote in the NRSV, "Other ancient authorities read *will be
burned up.*" The *United Bible Society Greek New Testament* assigns a D
reading (a very high degree of doubt as to the correct variant) to its

preference for *heurethēsetai* ("will be found or discovered").[22] The majority variant *katakaēsetai* ("will be burned up") fits naturally in the immediate context, but the more difficult and earlier reading is *heurethēsetai*. But if the latter, what does "will be disclosed" mean in this context?

Perhaps the "discovery" should be understood in judicial terms, a kind of pretrial deposition, disclosing damning evidence of wrongdoing. This fits retrospectively with Peter's emphatic warnings about God's judgment on the false teachers and any who should succumb to their aberrations. He may also be alluding to sayings of the Master warning about hidden deeds and words being brought out into the light on the day of judgment (Lk 12:36; Mt 7:21-23), a notion also appearing in Paul (Rom 2:3-5; 14:10; 1 Cor 3:10-15; 2 Cor 5:10) and John (1 Jn 4:17; Rev 20:11-15). On this understanding, the day of the Lord conjoins a destruction of the old order with an individual judgment. The point is this: Let no one think they can sneak into the eternal kingdom by suppressing evidence; the judgment seat of Christ involves full disclosure!

***The eternal state.*** There is one more matter of considerable importance. Many Christians labor under a misunderstanding about their ultimate destiny. They conceive of their eternal state in ethereal (otherworldly) terms situated in a celestial city "up there somewhere." The truth is our final destination is on a new earth. In short, "heaven" comes down and does more than "fill my soul;" it takes up residence on this planet and fills the whole world with God's glory. The apostle John provides the most detailed description about the new earth in his apocalypse, although his focus rests largely on the centerpiece, the New Jerusalem (Rev 21–22). Though conveyed with metaphors and figures of speech, his vision concerns something real and tangible.

The theological importance of this datum should not be lost. In the beginning, God created the earth as the special abode of his special creation, that creature alone among all other creatures uniquely bearing his own image (Gen 1:26-27). Here on earth the great drama of salvation history unfolds. Our first parents were charged with filling the

---

[22]Bruce M. Metzger, *A Textual Commentary on the Greek New Testament* (3rd ed.; New York: United Bible Societies, 1971), pp. 705-6.

earth, subduing it and having dominion over it (Gen 1:28-30). The context of the commission conveys the notion of responsibility: human beings are installed as vice-regents and stewards who must care for and protect the good earth. Obviously, we have failed, a failure rooted in spiritual rebellion against our creator.

But God is patient and his mercy endures forever. God is love (1 Jn 4:8, 16) and so, exhibiting a measure of love beyond all comparison and comprehension (Eph 3:18-19), he sent his only Son into our world who died for the sins of the whole world (Jn 3:16; 1 Jn 2:2). Re-creation begins when rebels are reconciled to God, by faith in the crucified one, and start their journey toward a new creation (2 Cor 5:16-21). This process takes place in stages, the last being the liberation of the entire planet from the malign effects of sin (Rom 8:18-25). The original creation, described as "very good" (Gen 1:31), is destined to be dissolved; in its place comes forth a new creation that is perfect. It is also material. Gnostic eschatology has no place in orthodox Christian theology. God made us with material bodies to live in a material world. So it was and so it shall be for all eternity.[23] This is where Peter concludes his apology. He lifts the eyes of his readers to the final destination, the finished product, the grand finale of redemptive history.

Let the full impact sink in: the new world order is a place "where righteousness is at home" (2 Pet 3:13). Righteousness triumphs over unrighteousness. As Peter says in his first letter, "Christ . . . suffered for sins once for all, the righteous for the unrighteous, in order to bring you to God" (1 Pet 3:18). Paul agrees: "so by the one man's obedience the many will be made righteous" (Rom 5:19). John chimes in: "we have an advocate with the Father, Jesus Christ the righteous; and he is the atoning sacrifice for our sins, and not for ours only but also for the sins of the whole world. . . . If we confess our sins, he who is faithful and just [righteous] will forgive us our sins and cleanse us from all unrighteousness. . . . Everyone who does what is right is righteous, just as he is righteous" (1 Jn 2:1-2; 1:9; 3:7). The long-held prophetic promise of a world in which peace and righteousness reign is not a pipe dream (see

---

[23]See James Oliver Buswell, *A Systematic Theology of the Christian Religion*, 2 vols. (Grand Rapids: Zondervan, 1963), 2:511-38, for a good discussion of the new heavens and new earth.

Is 1:26b; 11:5; 62:1-12); it is a reality in which holiness and godliness is the norm and the whole earth is full of God's glory (Is 6:3).

The present problem of moral pollution and the inevitable physical pollution accompanying it resolves itself in a climactic act of divine intervention. Presently, believers are in a strenuous process of growth in the knowledge of our Lord Jesus Christ (2 Pet 1:3-8). We have not yet arrived (Phil 3:12), but when the day of the Lord does occur, this process of growing in the grace and knowledge of our Lord and Savior Jesus Christ (2 Pet 3:18) accelerates to its omega point. Conformed to the image of Christ (Rom 8:29-30) by the same power that raised him from the dead (1 Pet 1:3-5), we are suddenly thrust into a new world "without spot or blemish" (2 Pet 3:14), the final triumph of grace.

## QUESTIONS FOR DISCUSSION

1. Are you convinced Peter shared the same essential view of life after death as Jesus, Paul and John? Why or why not?

2. Why was the transfiguration so important to Peter's argument against the false teachers?

3. Discuss the various suggested backgrounds that throw light on the transfiguration. Are there any other backgrounds that might be relevant?

4. Do you agree with the author of this textbook that typological interpretation plays an important role in understanding the overall message of Scripture? Why or why not?

5. In your view, does Peter hold to annihilation of the present heavens and earth, or does he envision a complete renovation? What difference does this distinction make?

6. Why is it that many Christians hold an unbiblical view of the eternal state? Why is this an important issue?

## FOR FURTHER READING

See the suggested sources from the previous chapter.

# 15

## THE REST OF THE STORY

### Tradition

*He was known throughout the world, even in the western countries, and his memory among the Romans is still more alive today than the memory of all those who lived before him.*

EUSEBIUS

*Buried at Rome in the Vatican near the triumphal way he is venerated by the whole world.*

JEROME

NO STUDY OF THE LIFE AND THOUGHT of the apostle Peter can be complete without taking into account the enormous influence he has exercised over the imagination and piety of Christians through the centuries. Those of us in the Protestant tradition, "the separated brethren," are sometimes reluctant to engage this dimension of Peter's life, but I want to pay tribute to his unquestioned influence and legacy. To this end, I survey briefly some of the varied extrabiblical traditions that cast some light, however dim, on the prince of the apostles.[1]

---

[1]"The New Testament information about Peter leaves a number of gaps in the account. Later Christian tradition fills out many of the missing details." Pheme Perkins, *Peter: Apostle for the Whole Church* (Columbia: University of South Carolina Press, 1994), p. 131.

## Peter in the Postapostolic Fathers

1. One of the earliest postapostolic writings is a letter written by Clement of Rome to the Corinthians and dated to about A.D. 96.[2] This locates it close in time to the Apocalypse of John. Interestingly, the Corinthian church, as evidenced by this pastoral letter, displays the same factiousness Paul had dealt with earlier (*1 Clem.* 1:1; cf. 1 Cor 1–4). Clement diplomatically praises the Corinthians for their renowned faith, hospitality and piety (*1 Clem.* 1:2–2:8) before suddenly shifting gears and addressing the schism directly (*1 Clem.* 3:1-4), an approach resembling that of the apostle Paul (cf. 1 Cor 1:3-17).

After illustrating how jealousy and envy wreaked havoc in the lives of OT figures like Cain, Jacob, Joseph, Moses, Aaron and Miriam, Dathan and Abiram and Saul (*1 Clem.* 4:1-13), Clement fast forwards to the apostolic era:

> Because of jealousy and envy the greatest and most righteous pillars were persecuted, and fought to the death. Let us set before our eyes the good apostles. There was Peter, who, because of unrighteous jealousy, endured not one or two but many trials, and thus having given his testimony went to his appointed place of glory. Because of jealousy and strife Paul by his example pointed out the way to the prize for patient endurance. (*1 Clem.* 5:2-5)[3]

This text, written some thirty years after 1 and 2 Peter, mentions both apostles, their trials and their martyrdoms. It does not explicitly say they were together at Rome or that they died at the same time and were buried there. However, the immediate context of the letter implies that Peter and Paul were in Rome at some unspecified time and that both suffered martyrdom during the reign of Nero: "To these men who

---

[2]For a careful investigation of the letter and its relevance for our discussion, see Oscar Cullmann, *Peter: Disciple—Apostle—Martyr* (trans. Floyd V. Filson; 2nd ed.; Philadelphia: Westminster, 1953), pp. 89-109; Daniel Wm. O'Connor, *Peter in Rome: The Literary, Liturgical and Archaeological Evidence* (New York: Columbia University Press, 1969), pp. 70-86.

[3]*The Apostolic Fathers* (2nd ed.; ed. J. B. Lightfoot, J. R. Harmer and Michael W. Holmes; Grand Rapids: Baker, 1992), p. 35. The text goes on to elaborate on Paul's sufferings and his ministering to "the farthest limits of the West," presumably referring to Spain though some dispute this (O'Connor, *Peter in Rome*, pp. 82-83).

lived holy lives there was joined a vast multitude of the elect who, having suffered many torments and tortures because of jealousy, set an illustrious example among us" (*1 Clem.* 6:1). The only known period in which such large-scale martyrdom occurred in the first century was the brief but bloody persecution under Nero.[4]

The mention of "unrighteous jealousy" and "many trials" is tantalizing, but the only other sources that elaborate on this stem from apocryphal legends. Some of these will be considered in the next chapter. As we have seen in our study of 1 Peter, the apostle addresses readers who "have had to suffer various trials" (1 Pet 1:6). At the least, we may infer that Peter spoke from firsthand experience of suffering for the name of Christ.

Reading between the lines, one might suggest a parallel to the apostle Paul based on Paul's letter to the Philippians: "Some proclaim Christ from envy and rivalry . . . out of selfish ambition, not sincerely but intending to increase my suffering in my imprisonment" (Phil 1:15-17). Since Peter championed Paul's law-free gospel, he may also have encountered bitter Jewish Christian opposition. Is it going too far to suggest that some of these opponents informed on Peter's whereabouts and were indirectly involved in his arrest and martyrdom? Tacitus tells us that after Nero fastened the guilt for the great fire at Rome on the Christians, "an arrest was first made of all who pleaded guilty; then, *upon their information*, an immense multitude was convicted" (*Ann.* 15.44.12-14, italics added). Perhaps something like this

---

[4]Here is Cullmann's verdict on the testimony of *1 Clement*:

> We conclude . . . with the highest probability , that Peter suffered martyrdom at Rome about the time of the Neronian persecution, while divisions existed in the church there. Peter and Paul, therefore, became martyrs at about the same time, not necessarily on the same day, but probably in the same period of persecution, which may have covered a more or less extended period. Concerning Peter, First Clement does not permit us to say whether he also carried on a real activity in Rome as a missionary or church leader. Just as little can we learn from this text when he came to Rome. (*Peter*, p. 109)

O'Connor's conclusion is even more nuanced:

> It is most probable that Clement believed, on the basis of written or oral tradition or both, that Peter and Paul (in that order) died at about the same time in Rome during the persecution under Nero. Clement neither states nor implies any more than this. There is not even a hint of: 1) when Peter came to Rome and how long he stayed, 2) what relationship he had to the Roman Church, 3) the manner of his death or where he was buried. (*Peter in Rome*, p. 86)

was the occasion for Peter's trials and martyrdom.[5]

2. Another probable early witness to the presence of both Peter and Paul in Rome comes from Ignatius, bishop of Antioch. Ignatius was arrested and sent to Rome for public execution. En route, he wrote seven pastoral letters to important church centers. Among those was one sent ahead to Rome in anticipation of his arrival. The letter dates to around A.D. 110.

Ignatius implores the Roman Christians not to seek his release but allow him to "be food for the wild beasts" (Ign. *Rom.* 4.1). In this context, he then says, "I do not give you orders like Peter and Paul: they were apostles, I am a convict; they were free, but I am even now still a slave. But if I suffer, I will be a freedman of Jesus Christ, and will rise up free in him. In the meantime, as a prisoner I am learning to desire nothing" (Ign. *Rom.* 4.3). The text does not say explicitly that Peter and Paul had ever been in Rome, but this seems implied given that Ignatius is writing to the Roman Christians and mentions both apostles by name. Some scholars, however, suggest that Ignatius is not referring to Peter and Paul's actual apostolic presence but to their eminent position as apostles or to their respective epistles (e.g., 1 Peter and Romans).[6] This seems unlikely to me, especially since none of the other letters of Ignatius invoke Peter and Paul's authority and 1 Peter was sent *from* not *to* Rome.[7] Oscar Cullmann puts considerable weight on the expression "give you orders." He thinks it likely that this refers to a personal

---

[5]Cullmann suggests that the reason Acts does not mention this is because "the Christians who had caused the death of other Christians did not offer an edifying example for others. Moreover, it is possible that the abrupt ending to The Book of Acts may be explained in this way" (*Peter*, p. 104).

[6]See, e.g., Perkins, *Peter*, p. 139.

[7]See the careful examination of the text and scholarly objections to citing it as evidence that Peter and Paul were ever in Rome in O'Connor, *Peter in Rome*, pp. 18-22. O'Connor cautiously concludes:

It is learned indirectly from the other letters of Ignatius and directly from Romans 4:3 [Ign. *Rom.* 4.3] that by the end of the first decade of the second century there was a tradition known even in Asia Minor that Peter and Paul had been to Rome and that they had enjoyed some position of authority in that church. There is, however, no *explicit* reference in the letter to the Romans that Peter or Paul or both had lived or were martyred in Rome nor that they founded the Church there. There is no hint whatsoever that either apostle served as bishop of Rome. (p. 22, italics in original)

presence of the apostles in Rome.[8] Ignatius's desire to be a "freedman of Jesus Christ" and to "rise up free in him" appears to allude to a shared destiny of martyrdom and ascension to heaven with the apostles. Cullmann infers that Ignatius is "conscious that he has something in common with them. This is not the apostolic office, but probably the martyrdom in Rome."[9] But not all would agree.[10]

3. Be that as it may, by the end of the second century, the tradition is firmly entrenched that Peter and Paul were martyred in Rome "about the same time" and monuments of some sort ("trophies") commemorated their deaths. For example, Eusebius cites Caius, a contemporary of Zephyrinus, bishop of Rome (A.D. 199-217), and Dionysius, bishop of Corinth (ca. A.D. 170) to this effect:

> "But I can show," says he [Caius], "the trophies of the apostles. For if you will go to the Vatican, or to the Ostian road, you will find the trophies of those who have laid the foundation of this church. And that both suffered martyrdom about the same time, Dionysius bishop of Corinth bears the following testimony, in his discourse addressed to the Romans. 'Thus, likewise you, by means of this admonition, have mingled the flourishing seed that had been planted by Peter and Paul at Rome and Corinth. For both of these having planted us at Corinth, likewise instructed us; and having in like manner taught in Italy, they suffered martyrdom about the same time.'"[11]

Worth noting is the supporting testimony that Peter ministered at Corinth, although the claim that Peter and Paul planted the church at Rome is wrong, as may be verified by Paul's letter to the Romans, written between A.D. 55 and 58, in which he clearly indicates that he had not yet even visited the church, much less founded it (Rom 1:11-13; 15:20-24).

4. To this testimony should be added a few direct statements from church fathers. Irenaeus (ca. A.D. 180) affirms that "Peter and Paul

---

[8]Cullmann, *Peter,* p. 111.

[9]Ibid.

[10]O'Connor says "it is not possible . . . to find in Romans 4:3 [Ign. *Rom.* 4.3] a reference to Peter's death in Rome that is sufficiently explicit to be presented as evidence" (*Peter in Rome,* p. 87).

[11]*Hist. eccl.* 2.25.

were preaching at Rome, and laying the foundations of the Church. After their departure, Mark, the disciple and interpreter of Peter, did also hand down to us in writing what had been preached by Peter."[12] Note that Irenaeus repeats the claim that these two apostles founded the church at Rome. The Latin father Tertullian (ca. A.D. 208), reminding his readers of the leading churches where the apostles labored, says this about the Roman church: "from which there comes even into our own hands the very authority (of apostles themselves). How happy is its church, on which apostles poured forth all their doctrine along with their blood! Where Peter endures a passion like his Lord's! Where Paul wins his crown in a death like John's!"[13] As to Peter's manner of death Tertullian adds, "In Rome Nero was the first who stained with blood the rising faith. Then is Peter girt by another, when he is made fast to the cross."[14] Tertullian also mentions in passing that Peter "baptized in the Tiber," the main river running through Rome.[15] Patristic sources tend to expand the earliest written traditions of the first and early second centuries; historians tend to be skeptical of these additions, attributing them to inferences and pious invention rather than sober fact.

5. By the time Eusebius writes his magnum opus just before A.D. 300, Peter's post-NT career is summarized as follows: "Peter appears to have preached through Pontus, Galatia, Bithynia, Cappadocia and Asia, to the Jews that were scattered abroad; who also, finally coming to Rome, was crucified with his head downward, having requested of himself to suffer in this way,"[16] to which he adds, "after the martyrdom of Paul and Peter, Linus was the first that received the episcopate at Rome."[17] Shortly thereafter he appends: "Linus, whom he [Paul] mentioned in his Second Epistle to Timothy as his companion at Rome, has

---

[12]*Haer.* 3.1.
[13]*Praescr.* 36. Similarly, *Marc.* 4.5. Or are we misunderstanding Dionysius, Irenaeus and Tertullian? Did they mean that Peter and Paul established the Roman church on a true apostolic foundation, not that they were the first to evangelize and organize house churches? In light of Paul's discussion in 1 Corinthians 3:10-15, however, this suggestion seems unlikely.
[14]*Scorp.* 15.
[15]*Bapt.* 4.
[16]*Hist. eccl.* 3.1.
[17]Ibid., 3.2.

been before shown to have been the first after Peter, that obtained the episcopate at Rome. Clement also, who was appointed the third bishop of this church, is proved by him to have been a fellow-labourer and fellow-soldier with him."[18]

6. But Eusebius is not the first to claim Peter as the first bishop of Rome; such claims already appear in the second century. For example, Irenaeus introduces his famous succession list of the bishops of Rome by appealing to

> that tradition derived from the apostles, of the very great, the very an-
> cient, and universally known Church founded and organized at Rome
> by the two most glorious apostles, Peter and Paul; For it is a matter of
> necessity that every Church should agree with this Church, on account
> of its preeminent authority, that is, the faithful everywhere, inasmuch as
> the apostolical tradition has been preserved continuously by those
> [faithful men] who exist everywhere. (*Haer.* 3.3.3)

7. Tertullian apparently connects Jesus' declaration "you are Peter" (Mt 16:18) to the primacy of Rome. In his attack on heretics like Marcion, Apelles, Valentinus and others, he asks rhetorically: "Was anything withheld from the knowledge of Peter, who is called 'the rock on which the church should be built,' who also obtained 'the keys of the kingdom of heaven,' with the power of 'loosing and binding in heaven and on earth?'"[19] Later in the same work, he confronts the heretics with this challenge:

> Let them produce the original records of their churches; let them unfold
> the roll of their bishops, running down in due succession from the be-
> ginning in such a manner that [that first bishop of theirs] shall be able
> to show for his ordainer and predecessor some one of the apostles or of
> apostolic men,—a man, moreover, who continued steadfast with the
> apostles. For this is the manner in which the apostolic churches transmit
> their registers: as the church of Smyrna, which records that Polycarp
> was placed therein by John; as also the church of Rome, which makes
> Clement to have been ordained in like manner by Peter. In exactly the
> same way the other churches likewise exhibit (their several worthies),

[18]Ibid., 3.4.
[19]*Praescr.* 22.

whom, as having been appointed to their episcopal places by apostles, they regard as transmitters of the apostolic seed. Let the heretics contrive something of the same kind.[20]

In the above excerpt, however, Tertullian appears to view the Roman bishop as *primus inter pares* ("first among equals"). Likewise, Cyprian (ca. 200-258), bishop of Carthage (North Africa), strongly argues for the primacy of Peter among the apostles, at the same time "demanding his rights as a bishop be respected, ceding his authority to no-one, not even the bishop of Rome."[21] I include an excerpt from one of his writings (251):

> The Lord says to Peter: "I say to you," he says, "that you are Peter, and upon this rock I will build my Church, and the gates of hell will not overcome it. And to you I will give the keys of the kingdom of heaven; and whatever things you bind on earth shall be bound also in heaven, and whatever you loose on earth, they shall be loosed also in heaven" [Mt 16:18-19]. . . . On him [Peter] he builds the Church, and to him he gives the command to feed the sheep [Jn 21:17], and although he assigns a like power to all the apostles, yet he founded a single chair [*cathedra*], and he established by his own authority a source and an intrinsic reason for that unity. Indeed, the others were also what Peter was [i.e., apostles], but a primacy is given to Peter, whereby it is made clear that there is but one Church and one chair. So too, all [the apostles] are shepherds, and the flock is shown to be one, fed by all the apostles in single-minded accord. If someone does not hold fast to this unity of Peter, can he imagine that he still holds the faith? If he [should] desert the chair of Peter upon whom the Church was built, can he still be confident that he is in the Church? (*Unit. eccl.* 4)

By the time of Jerome (ca. 347-420), the tradition affirms that Peter had been the bishop of Antioch, ministered in Anatolia, went to Rome in the second year of Claudius to oppose Simon Magus, was bishop of Rome for twenty-five years, was crucified head down and was buried at the Vatican (*Vir. ill.* 1). Some of this appears to be inferred from the NT, such as the Antioch bishopric (see Gal 2:11) and

---

[20]Ibid., 32.
[21]G. L. Bray, "Cyprian," *NDT*, p. 184.

the Anatolian ministry (1 Pet 1:1). The confrontation with Simon
Magus and the notion that Peter was crucified upside down first appear
in apocryphal works of the second and third centuries.

8. Pope Julius I (340) provides the earliest, unequivocal, written affirmation of Rome's supremacy over all other churches. In a letter to the
Eastern bishops in defense of Athanasius, he even claims jurisdiction
over the bishops of Antioch and Alexandria. "Men write first to us, and
it is here that justice is dispensed."[22] Leo the Great (440-461), the first
true pope in the modern sense of the term, exemplifies this consolidation of authority in that he was the unquestioned head of Christendom, nominating all bishops to their office and staunchly upholding
both the primacy of Peter and his successors in Rome. A sermon he
preached on the occasion of his birthday and the anniversary of his elevation to the pontificate underscores the point, and at the Council of
Chalcedon (451) he exercises the leading role in all its proceedings.[23]

## VARIOUS PETRINE TRADITIONS

I conclude our survey of the traditions about Peter with various recorded incidents relating to his life and ministry:

- Clement of Alexandria tells us that Jesus baptized Peter and Peter in
  turn baptized his brother Andrew (*Hypotyposes* 5 as cited by Eusebius, *Hist. eccl.* xx).

- Clement informs us that Peter's wife did not merely accompany him
  on his apostolic journeys but functioned as a collaborator (*Strom.*
  3.53.3).

- Clement also explains why James the Just was chosen as the first
  bishop of Jerusalem rather than Peter: "Peter, and James, and John
  after the ascension of our Saviour, though they had been preferred by
  our Lord, did not contend for the honour, but chose James the Just as
  bishop of Jerusalem" (*Institutions* 6 cited by Eusebius, *Hist. eccl.* 2.1.3).

- A fascinating tradition found in Origen claims that Simon was one
  of the two Emmaus disciples (Lk 24:13-35) (*Cels.* 2.62, 68; *Hom. Jer.*

---

[22]*Epistle of Julius to Antioch*, 100.22.
[23]"Sermon III," *ANF* 12.

20). One wonders if this tradition arose in an attempt to account for the very early tradition that Jesus appeared first to Cephas (1 Cor 15:5) even though the Gospels are silent about this appearance.

## VENERATION OF PETER

During the third century, veneration of the apostle Peter proliferates. By the time of Emperor Constantine, in the early fourth century, a basilica marks the place of Peter's martyrdom and his grave site is venerated in a vault below the apse. Graffiti scratched on the walls record prayers offered to Peter by pilgrims.[24] Recall Peter's house at Capernaum, where graffiti mentioning Peter's name were also found.[25] The enormous expense and effort required to construct the Constantinian basilica on that particular site strongly suggests that it was owing to a desire to build it precisely over the site of Peter's grave. Over the succeeding centuries, a number of renovations, repairs and alterations were necessitated during which two distinct floor levels were placed above the Constantinian floor. Finally, Pope Julius II decided to demolish the Constantinian basilica and launched a 120-year project (1535-1655) to build in its place the grand edifice known as St. Peter's Basilica.

I insert at this point the testimony of liturgical sources. In A.D. 354, a secretary of Pope Damascus, Furius Dionysius Filocalus, issued a liturgical calendar which included a section called *Depositio Martyrium* ("burial of martyrs"). The following notation for June 29 appears: *Petri in catacumbas et Pauli Ostense, Tusco et Basso consulibus* ("Peter in the catacombs, Paul on the Highway to Ostia, in the consulship of Tuscus and Bassus").[26] Although the catacombs are not located on Vatican hill and

---

[24]See O'Connor, *Peter in Rome*, pp. 180-82. For photographs of the graffiti, see John Evangelist Walsh, *The Bones of St. Peter* (New York: Doubleday, 1982), photographs 23, 24, 26, 27.

[25]Excavators found graffiti mentioning Peter dating to the second century. A rectangular house dubbed Peter's house seems clearly to have functioned as a place of Christian worship ( a *domus ecclesia*) in the fourth century. This was replaced by an octagonal church dated to the fifth century. See Jack Finegan, *The Archaeology of the New Testament: The Life of Jesus and the Beginning of the Early Church* (rev. ed.; Princeton: Princeton University Press, 1992). See also the following website for excellent background information and photographs: www.bibarch.com/ArchaeologicalSites/Capernaum.htm.

[26]Translation by Cullmann, *Peter*, p. 125. The consulate of Tuscus and Bassus fell in A.D. 258. No date is given for the martyrdom of Peter and Paul.

June 29 is probably not the exact day of Peter and Paul's martyrdom, the Roman church continues to memorialize their deaths on this day.[27]

Modern archaeological excavations below the basilica, beginning in 1939, have once again exposed the Constantinian Aedicula (small shrine).[28] In 1942 Pope Pius XII announced that the "trophies" mentioned by Gaius had been identified, and he followed this up on December 23, 1950, with an assertion that "the grave of the Prince of the Apostles has been found."[29] But then on June 26, 1968, Pope Paul VI stunned the world with his announcement that Peter's bones had been discovered and identified. The following day, in a brief ceremony presided over by the pope, the bones, placed in boxes of heavy plastic, were reinterred in the ancient grave site where they remain to this day in a "floodlit glassed-in repository."[30] This latter claim, however, has proven to be a hard sell in the scholarly community, and the jury is still out. Most scholars (even a few Roman Catholic scholars) are not convinced.

What is historically verifiable is that the primacy of Rome gradually acquired acceptance and for a thousand years no one in Christendom seriously questioned it. What is especially noteworthy is the fact that none of the four great Eastern churches, Antioch, Alexandria, Constantinople and especially Jerusalem, ever challenged Rome's assertion to supremacy. By the fifth century, bishops consulted the bishop of Rome for rulings in matters of faith and polity, and he in turn issued decrees having the force of law. No doubt the importance of Rome as the capital city of the empire played a major role in the ascendance of the bishop of Rome. But not to be discounted is the early and persistent tradition linking Peter the Rock to the magnificent Basilica of Saint Peter standing resplendently in Rome. Today, Benedict XVI sits on the

---

[27]See Cullmann's discussion of the historical problems surrounding this source, including an alleged transfer of Peter's bones from Vatican hill to the catacombs and then back to the Vatican (ibid., pp. 125-32).

[28]For details, see Margherita Guarducci, *The Tomb of Saint Peter* (London: George G. Harrap, 1960), idem, *The Primacy of Rome: Documents, Reflections, Proofs* (trans. Michael J. Miller: San Francisco: Ignatius, 2003), and O'Connor, *Peter in Rome*. For an informative, lively narrative of the excavations and the ensuing controversy, see Walsh, *Bones of St. Peter*.

[29]Cited from Cullmann, *Peter*, p. 138.

[30]Walsh, *Bones of St. Peter*, p. 129.

chair of Saint Peter as the 265th pope.[31]

But with regard to Peter himself, what can confidently be claimed about the traditions surrounding the later years of the apostle Peter? Here is the succinct verdict of O'Connor:

> In summary, it appears *more plausible than not* that 1) Peter did reside in Rome at some time during his lifetime, most probably near the end of his life. 2) He was martyred there as a member of the Christian religion. 3) He was remembered in the traditions of the church and in the erection of a simple monument near the place where he died. 4) His body was never recovered for burial by the Christian group which later, when relics became of great importance for apologetic reasons, came to believe that what originally had marked the general area of this death also indicated the precise placement of his grave.[32]

I think Peter would be content with O'Connor's summary; his focus was not on the "earthly life" (1 Pet 4:2) but on the "inheritance that is imperishable, undefiled, and unfading, kept in heaven" (1 Pet 1:4). The great concern of his heart after his "departure" (2 Pet 1:15) was not that believers stand in awe at a tangible trophy but recall the Lord's "precious and very great promises" whereby they "become participants of the divine nature" (2 Pet 1:4). His concluding word is the most hopeful message one could ever embrace. "In accordance with his promise, we wait for new heavens and a new earth" (2 Pet 3:13). "To him be the glory both now and to the day of eternity. Amen" (2 Pet 3:18).

## QUESTIONS FOR DISCUSSION

1. What evidence does Clement's letter to the Corinthians add to our understanding of the last years of Peter's life?
2. What do you make of the claims of Ignatius with regard to the

---

[31]I take this opportunity to encourage my fellow evangelicals to read some of Benedict XVI's books. Three that I have found helpful are *Jesus of Nazareth* (New York: Doubleday, 2007); *Saint Paul* (San Francisco: Ignatius, 2009); *Credo for Today: What Christians Believe* (San Francisco: Ignatius, 2009). May he, like Peter, faithfully "tend the flock of God that is in [his] charge" and "win the crown of glory that never fades away" (1 Pet 5:2, 4).

[32]O'Connor, *Peter in Rome*, p. 209. Ralph P. Martin's evaluation of the archaeological evidence echoes that of O'Connor: "The maximum conclusion to be drawn from these Vatican excavations is that Peter's memorial was cherished near the spot where he died. His body was never recovered—therefore all talk of Peter's bones is chimerical" ("Peter," *ISBE*, pp. 806-7).

status and authority of Peter at the beginning of the second century?

3. How do you account for the extraordinary influence of the Roman church and the importance of apostolic succession during the second and third centuries?

4. Why was the fourth century so decisive in establishing Petrine and Roman authority in the church?

5. Evaluate the veracity of the claim that the grave and bones of Peter have been discovered in the crypt below the Basilica of Saint Peter.

6. What is your assessment of the postapostolic traditions concerning Peter's later years?

## FOR FURTHER READING

Cullmann, Oscar. *Peter: Disciple—Apostle—Martyr.* Philadelphia: Westminster, 1953. Pp. 132-52.

Grant, Michael. *Saint Peter.* New York: Scribner, 1994. Pp. 152-58.

Guarducci, Margherita. *The Tomb of Saint Peter.* London: George G. Harrap, 1960.

————. *The Primacy of the Church of Rome: Documents, Reflections, Proofs.* Translated by Michael J. Miller. San Francisco: Ignatius, 2003.

O'Connor, Daniel Wm. *Peter in Rome: The Literary, Liturgical and Archaeological Evidence.* New York: Columbia University Press, 1969.

Perkins, Pheme. *Peter: Apostle for the Whole Church.* Columbia: University of South Carolina Press, 1994. Pp. 168-81.

Walsh, John Evangelist. *The Bones of St. Peter.* New York: Doubleday, 1982.

# 16

––––

# THE REST OF THE STORY

*Legends About Peter*

VENERATION OF PETER BEGINS to appear in the second century. As evidence of this, I rapidly review several works attributed to Peter but clearly falling into the category of pseudepigrapha, that is, works falsely ascribed to Peter. The sheer fact that more such works were attributed to Peter than any other apostle speaks for itself. The provenance of these various works is notoriously difficult, so no attempt will be made to place them in a strictly chronological sequence.

### *The Apocalypse of Peter*
Perhaps the earliest of our Petrine pseudepigrapha is the *Apocalypse of Peter*, generally dated to the first half of the second century.[1] If Richard Bauckham is correct that the work should be placed during the Bar Kochba revolt (A.D. 132-135), then it is Palestinian in provenance.[2] At any rate, the *Apocalypse* is noteworthy as "our earliest extant Christian document that describes Heaven and Hell."[3]

The introductory line informs us that Peter received a revelation concerning the second coming and resurrection. As he ponders its meaning, an opportunity presents itself to inquire further on the Mount of Olives. The disciples ask Jesus, "What are the signs of your coming

---

[1]J. K. Elliott claims "it must have been in existence before A.D. 150." *The Apocryphal New Testament* (Oxford: Clarendon, 1993), p. 593.

[2]Richard J. Bauckham, "The Two Fig Tree Parables in the 'Apocalypse of Peter,'" *JBL* 104 (1985): 269-87.

[3]Elliott, *Apocryphal New Testament*, p. 595.

and of the end of the world?" (*Apoc. Pet.* 1. 11; cf. Mk 13:1-5). After a condensed version of the Olivet Discourse, Jesus tells the parable of the fig tree. Peter then asks the Lord to explain its meaning: "Interpret the fig-tree to me: how can we understand it?" (*Apoc. Pet.* 2.20). In keeping with the canonical Gospels, the apocalypse portrays Peter as the spokesman for the other apostles. The explanation of the parable is primarily from Luke 13:6-9, with interesting additions drawn from Revelation 11 and Revelation 13. Especially interesting is the apparent identification of the two witnesses in Revelation 11 with Enoch and Elijah (*Apoc. Pet.* 2.21).

Then the Lord shows the apostles the fate of the unrighteous, which caused all of them, the Lord included, to weep (*Apoc. Pet.* 3). This prompts Peter to make the following observation: "It were better for them if they had not been created." In response, Peter receives a stinging rebuke: "Peter, why do you say that not to have been created were better for them? You resist God" (*Apoc. Pet.* 3.22). The *Apocalypse* thus adds another episode to those occasions in the Gospels when Peter is censured. Nor should we overlook the similarity to Peter's words in his second epistle about the fate of the false teachers: "For it would have been better for them never to have known the way of righteousness than, after knowing it, to turn back from the holy commandment that was passed on to them" (2 Pet 2:21). The saying in the apocalypse more closely resembles one found in *2 Esdras*: "It would have been better for us not to be here than to come here and live in ungodliness and to suffer and not understand why" (*2 Esd.* 4:12; cf. *2 Esd.* 5:35; 7:63).

Most of the *Apocalypse of Peter* consists of a lengthy and gruesome depiction of tortures meted out to the unrighteous at the final judgment and a short description of the blessedness of the righteous. At the end of the work, however, the Lord directly addresses Peter and commissions him:

> Go forth therefore and go to the city of the west and enter into the vineyard which I shall tell you of, in order that by the sufferings of the Son who is without sin the deeds of corruption may be sanctified. As for you, you are chosen according to the promise which I have given you. Spread my gospel throughout all the world in peace. Verily men shall

rejoice; my words shall be the source of hope and of life, and suddenly shall the world be ravished. (*Apoc. Pet.* 14)

Several items are of interest. (1) The city of the west must surely be Rome, thus adding to the early testimony concerning Peter's presence there. (2) The reference to the Son who is without sin (1 Pet 2:22; 3:18) and the efficacy of his sufferings for sanctification reminds one of 1 Peter 4:1: "Since therefore Christ suffered in the flesh, arm yourselves also with the same intention (for whoever has suffered in the flesh has finished with sin)." (3) The commission to spread the gospel to the entire world implies an itinerant ministry for Peter as confirmed by Paul's letters, 1 Peter and early church tradition. (4) The reference to hope and life picks up a leading motif in 1 Peter (1 Pet 1:3-11). (5) The metaphor of the world being ravished may allude to Peter's graphic portrayal of the dissolution of the heavens and earth on the day of God in his second epistle (2 Pet 3:10-13). (6) Finally, the apocalypse begins with a reference to Peter's vision of Christ's second coming and resurrection, two leading themes of both 1 and 2 Peter (1 Pet 1:3, 5, 11, 13, 21; 3:18, 22; 4:5, 7, 13; 5:1, 4, 10; 2 Pet 1:16-19; 3:3-15). There can be little doubt that the *Apocalypse of Peter* is indebted to both canonical epistles.

### The Preaching of Peter

Dating close in time to the *Apocalypse of Peter* are fragments of a work titled the *Preaching of Peter* (*Pre. Pet.*) that appears only in patristic sources. We know of it from brief citations in Clement of Alexandria and possible allusions in Origen, Gregory of Nazianus and John of Damascus.[4] What is interesting is that Clement appears to accept this work as genuine. Origen, however, possessing good linguistic skills, had his doubts. Eusebius rejects it as not genuine (*Hist. eccl.* 3.3.1). The contents, given their fragmentary nature as brief citations, make it impossible to describe its original content. The most that can be said is that it argued for "the superiority of Christian monotheism."[5]

Based on these brief extracts, a couple of observations are in order.

---

[4]See ibid., pp. 20-21, and Edgar Hennecke, *New Testament Apocrypha* (ed. Wilhelm Schneemelcher; trans. R. McL. Wilson; 2 vols.; Philadelphia: Westminster, 1964), 2:94-98.

[5]Elliott, *Apocryphal New Testament*, p. 20.

First, the author articulates a Logos Christology and this obviously strikes a chord with Clement of Alexandria. Worth noting is the fact that Alexandria, Egypt, was also the home of Philo the Jew whose doctrine of the Logos was probably known in educated Alexandrian circles and provides a possible source for its appearance in *Preaching of Peter*. More likely, however, the Logos Christology derives directly from the Johannine Logos tradition and only secondarily from Philo.

On this assumption, may we go further and hypothesize that the *Preaching of Peter* is genuine and that the Logos Christology reflects cross-fertilization with John, Peter's fellow "pillar" apostle and lifelong family friend? Almost certainly not, and for the following reasons:

- The external attestation for this work as noted above is weak.

- Its vocabulary and phrasing are decidedly non-Petrine.

- The teaching in this work strikes a quite different note from the canonical writings; in particular, no Logos doctrine appears in 1 and 2 Peter, the Gospel of Mark or the Petrine speeches in Acts.[6]

In my opinion, Origen's doubts were well-founded and Eusebius's verdict, though harsh, is not far from the mark. In a blanket rejection of works supposedly composed by the apostles, which includes the *Preaching of Peter* (*Hist. eccl.* 3.3.), Eusebius says:

> the character of the style itself is very different from that of the apostles, and the sentiments, and the purport of those things that are advanced in them, deviating as far as possible from sound orthodoxy, evidently proves they are the fictions of heretical men; whence they are to be ranked not only among the spurious writings, but are to be rejected as altogether absurd and impious. (*Hist. eccl.* 3.25)

### The Gospel of Peter

Two surviving Greek fragments from Akhmim, Egypt, dating to the eighth century, confirm the existence of a gospel attributed to Peter and mentioned by Origen (*Comm. Matt.* 10.17) and Eusebius (*Hist. eccl.* 3.3.2; 6.12). Most scholars date the original composition to the

---

[6]This is an argument from silence and cannot bear too much weight.

second half of the second century, though some date it as early as the mid-first century.[7] Two tiny Greek fragments of this work exist (*P. Oxy.* 2949), dated to the late second or early third century. Justin Martyr (ca. 150) and Melito of Sardis (d. ca. 180) very likely make use of the *Gospel of Peter*,[8] and the *Didascalia* (third century) refers to a resurrection scene in the house of Levi, which likely follows the break in the Akhmim fragment.

The Akhmim fragment begins abruptly with Jesus' trial before Pilate and Herod. Here is the narrative flow:

- Herod refuses to wash his hands (thus taking full responsibility for Jesus' execution) and orders that Jesus be crucified.

- Joseph, said to be a friend of both Pilate and the Lord, requests Jesus' body.

- Jesus is abused and mocked by the Jews, is crucified and dies.

- At the ninth hour, when the spikes are removed from the Lord's hands, there is an earthquake and darkness followed by sunshine at which the Jews rejoice. The Jews give the body of Jesus to Joseph, who buries it in his own sepulcher.

- The Jews lament the evil they have done and fear impending judgment on Jerusalem. The disciples go into hiding and mourn.

- The religious leaders request and obtain a seal and guard (apparently Jewish) for the tomb lest the disciples steal the body and claim that Jesus rose from the dead. Petronius the centurion is charged with this detail.

- Early on the Lord's day, while it was still dark, two men (angels) appear to the guards; the stone sealing the sepulcher rolls back of its own accord, and the two men enter.

---

[7]For the former dating, see Elliott, *Apocryphal New Testament*, p. 150. For the latter, see Paul Allen Mirecki, "Peter, Gospel of," *ABD* 5:278-81. J. D. Crossan's contention that the *Gospel of Peter* is not only an independent witness to the passion of Christ but a source for the four canonical Gospels (*Four Other Gospels* [Minneapolis: Winston, 1985], pp. 125-81) has garnered little scholarly support. See Raymond E. Brown's response, "The Gospel of Peter and Canonical Gospel Authority," *NTS* 33 (1987): 321-43.

[8]R. J. Bauckham, "Gospels (Apocrypha)," *DJG*, p. 288.

- Petronius and the guards see three men emerge from the tomb, two of them supporting the third. As they ascend to heaven, the heads of the two men reach heaven, but that of the third, the Lord, reaches beyond the heavens. A voice from heaven inquires, "Have you preached to those who sleep?" A heavenly voice replies, "Yes" (*Gos. Pet.* 41-42).

- When another man (angel) enters the tomb, the centurion and guards flee to Pilate and report what happened. Pilate reminds the Jews that he is not responsible, and they beseech him to keep everything quiet.

- Mary Magdalene and two other women come to the sepulcher to perform burial rites. They discover the stone rolled away and a young man sitting in the middle of the sepulcher. He asks them what they seek and proclaims that Jesus has risen. They flee in fright.

- The twelve disciples mourn and return to their own homes. Peter, Andrew and Levi set off to fish. Unfortunately, the fragment breaks off in mid-sentence. Based on the *Didascalia*, the text must have gone on to record an appearance of the Lord to Levi.

Obviously, this gospel tells us little about Peter himself in that he is mentioned only once. However, Peter is identified as the narrator (*Gos. Pet.* 60). Thus the gospel purports to be Peter's retelling of Christ's passion and so invites the question whether it, like the Gospel of Mark, should be traced back to Peter. A close reading of the text lends little support for such a conjecture since, for the most part, this gospel is indebted to the canonical Gospels.

- From Matthew comes the washing of hands, sealing the tomb and bribing the soldiers.

- From all three Synoptics comes the dividing of Jesus' clothes.

- From Luke comes the episode of the thief on the cross and the involvement of Herod.

- From John comes the dating of Jesus' death, and from Luke and John come details about breaking the legs.

- From Matthew and Mark come the cry of dereliction, though differently worded.

- From all three Synoptics comes the rending of the temple veil.

- The appearance of Jesus to the women comes primarily from Mark.

- From Mark comes the fleeing of the women in fright.

- A careful comparison thus shows that the *Gospel of Peter* is primarily dependent on the Gospel of Mark and Matthew's special material.[9]

Furthermore, the special additions of the *Gospel of Peter* reflect polemical and theological interests that are not compatible with what we know of Peter's thought from the canonical sources. For example, only here do we learn of Herod's leading role in Jesus' death. It also seems that the execution and burial squads are entirely Jewish. This appears to be part of an agenda that squarely fastens the blame for Jesus' death on the Jewish leaders under Herod. The canonical Gospels, Acts (Acts 2:23; 4:27) and Paul's letters (1 Thess 2:14-16) do hold the Jewish leaders and Jerusalem Jews responsible for Jesus' execution but not so one-sidedly (cf. Acts 4:23, 28) as we read here. The *Gospel of Peter* reflects the rising tide of anti-Judaic sentiment that clearly appears in postapostolic Christian writings.

What is particularly striking about this gospel's portrayal of Jesus' death is the notice that "he held his peace as (if) he felt no pain" (*Gos. Pet.* 4).[10] This has fueled suspicion that we are dealing with a Docetic or even Gnostic text.[11] At the least, the passage lends itself to a Docetic interpretation of Christ's person. Thus, contrary to John's Gospel (Jn 19:32), the *Gospel of Peter* says that the legs of the repentant thief were not broken and the reason was to prolong his agony on account of his belief in Jesus (*Gos. Pet.* 14). This adds further to the negative portrayal of Jews in this gospel.

---

[9]Bauckham concludes: "It seems then that the *Gospel of Peter* drew primarily on Mark's Gospel and on Matthew's special source, independently of Matthew's Gospel" (ibid.).

[10]Elliott, *Apocryphal New Testament*, p. 155.

[11]Pheme Perkins, however, notes that it "makes no attempt to negate the death of Jesus. Indeed, the narrative suggests that Jesus felt pain and torment even though he may have appeared not to (*Gos. Pet.* 4)" (*Peter: Apostle for the Whole Church* [Columbia: University of South Carolina Press, 1994], p. 136).

The *Gospel of Peter* heightens the miraculous nature of Jesus' resurrection going well beyond the canonical Gospels, which, by comparison, are quite restrained. A pronounced anti-Jewish polemic surfaces in the postresurrection narrative. In spite of being eyewitnesses of Jesus' resurrection, the Jewish elders conspire to hush up what happened: "'For it is better for us,' they said, 'to make ourselves guilty of the great sin before God than to fall into the hand of the people of the Jews and be stoned'" (*Gos. Pet.* 48). This is a clear instance of reliance on and embellishment of Matthew's special material (Mt 28:11-15).

The heavenly question asking whether the Lord has "preached to those who sleep" almost certainly alludes to the celebrated passages in 1 Peter 3:19 and 1 Peter 4:6. At the least, we have an early witness to the *descensus ad inferos* interpretation of these verses, an interpretation clearly at odds with the view that Christ preached to the pre-flood generation of Noah.

There are several other instances of divergence from the canonical Gospels: no reference to Peter's denial; the apostles are suspected of wanting to burn the temple; no reference to an Easter Sunday appearance to the disciples; only those hostile to Jesus experience a vision of the resurrection.

Eusebius's account of a letter by Serapion, bishop of Antioch (190-212), to the church at Rhossos in Cilicia confirms our suspicions about this gospel. There we learn that Serapion had previously granted permission for the church to use the *Gospel of Peter* in its services, but when he examined the document more closely, he discovered "the heresy of Marcianus" and "many things superadded to the sound faith of our Saviour." Serapion identifies the heretical teachers as members of a sect called the "Docetae" (*Hist. eccl.* 6.12). According to Eusebius, Serapion wrote a treatise refuting the false teachings of this gospel. Presumably, he also banned its use in the church.

### The Acts of Peter

This work, thought to emanate from either Rome or Asia Minor, dates to the end of the second century.[12] Most scholars acknowledge citations

---

[12]For background and text, see Hennecke, *New Testament Apocrypha*, 2:259-322; Elliott, *Apoc-*

from it in Clement of Alexandria (ca. 150-215), Origen (185-254) and the *Didascalia* (third century), suggesting that it was considered authoritative. In the fourth century, however, Eusebius declares it, along with two other allegedly Petrine works, noncanonical: "As to that work, however, which is ascribed to him called 'the Acts,' and the 'Gospel according to Peter,' and that called 'The Preaching and the Revelations of Peter,' we know nothing of their being handed down as Catholic writings" (*Hist. eccl.* 3.3.2).

Several features deserve mention:

1. Peter is portrayed as a prodigious miracle worker in keeping with his portrayal in the book of Acts (Acts 3:1-10; 5:1-16; 9:32-42). Two short miracle stories that probably circulated independently before being incorporated into the *Acts of Peter* dramatically illustrate the point.

In the first, believers question how it is that Peter can heal so many and yet his own daughter suffers from paralysis. So that they might believe in God's power, Peter invokes God's healing power and she is instantly restored. But then he immediately rescinds the healing and she reverts to her former helpless condition, causing anguish for the believers. Peter explains his seeming callousness as a blessing in disguise; God is preventing her from being sexually violated. Clearly, the circles in which this story originated highly valued celibacy. Some see here indications of the rigorous wing of Gnosticism, but this is not a necessary conclusion. More likely we are in touch with an ascetic piety similar to that later appearing in the monastic movement.

The second, the gardener's daughter, makes the same point but in a highly ironic manner. A gardener, with a virgin daughter, asks Peter to pray for her. He does, and the girl immediately dies. The distraught father beseeches Peter to heal his daughter. Peter obliges, but some time later a professed believer runs off with the daughter and they were never seen again.

The theological perspective on sex in both works hardly reflects that of the historical Peter. From the NT it is clear that Peter highly valued marriage, as one would expect given his Judaic heritage. Chastity, not celibacy, is his prescription for the perennial problem of sexuality (1 Pet 2:11; 3:1-2, 7; 4:3; 2 Pet 1:4, 6; 2:2, 14, 18). The image of Peter as an ascetic who championed celibacy is an alien imposition.

2. The centerpiece of the *Acts of Peter* is Peter's confrontation with Simon Magus in Rome. Here is a tradition that carries forward and embellishes Luke's account in Acts 8. After the apostle Paul departs for his Spanish mission (*Acts Pet.* 3), Simon Magus comes on the scene claiming to be "the great power of God" (*Acts Pet.* 4; cf. Acts 8:10). By wonders and deception Simon undermines the faith of many and acquires a growing following. A few faithful believers fast and pray even as God prepares Peter for this moment, said to be "after twelve years had passed" (*Acts Pet.* 5), presumably after the confrontation between Peter and Simon narrated in Acts 8.[13] Here is a summary of what happens:

- Peter undertakes a sea voyage from Caesarea to Rome, similar to Paul's (Acts 27:1–28:15). The steersman is converted through Peter's witness.

- On arriving in Rome, Peter learns of the serious inroads Simon has already made and addresses the wavering believers, calling for repentance and complete trust in Christ as savior. Those who do so urge Peter to confront Simon.

- Peter goes to the house where Simon was staying and "calls him out." By means of a talking dog and the repentance of a backslider, Marcellus, Simon's host, Peter regains the initiative.

- Peter performs another miracle, bringing a dead fish to life, further strengthening Marcellus's faith; Marcellus then throws Simon out of his house. Many more lapsed believers repent and return to full faith in Jesus.

---

[13]Though linked by some to Acts 12:17: "Then he left and went to another place." That is, after leading the Jesus movement in Palestine for twelve years, Peter then began evangelizing and teaching in the Diaspora. With this reckoning one is barely able to squeeze in the tradition that Peter had been bishop of Rome for twenty-five years before his martyrdom (A.D. 30 + 12 = 42; 42 + 25 = A.D. 67). There are a number of objections to this proposal, however. See Oscar Cullmann, *Peter: Disciple—Apostle—Martyr* (trans. Floyd V. Filson; 2nd ed.; Philadelphia: Westminster, 1953), pp. 37-39.

- By means of a seven-month-old child who speaks in a "manly voice," Peter conveys to Simon his punishment: he will be rendered speechless.

- Following more visions, miracles and teaching, Peter finally confronts Simon in a public forum before the emperor, senators and a great crowd. After testifying to Christ, Peter raises three men from the dead and exposes Simon as a fraud.

- Simon tries to regain his influence by publicly ascending to God. As he soars over Rome, Peter prays that God would cast him down and break his leg in three places. When this happens, Simon is thoroughly discredited and taken to Aricia, where he dies of his injuries.

This portion of *Acts of Peter* is an amalgam of various sources. Here and there one detects faint echoes of phrases in the book of Acts and 2 Peter (e.g, Acts 1:24; 2:11, 47; 3:9, 12, 17; 5:11, 16; 8:1, 10; 15:8; 17:30; 19:22; 20:25, 29, 38; 2 Pet 1:18; 2:16). Worth noting is a citation from the Suffering Servant song of Isaiah 53 in Peter's preaching (*Acts Pet.* 7.20; cf. Is 53:4). This may reflect an awareness of or indebtedness to 1 Peter, given that no other NT epistle, other than Romans (Rom 10:16), directly quotes from Isaiah 53.[14] There may be another echo from 1 Peter when Peter rejects the crowd's cry to burn Simon Magus alive: "We have learned not to recompense evil for evil, but we have learned to love our enemies and to pray for those who persecute us" (*Acts Pet.* 28; cf. 1 Pet 3:9; but Rom 12:17; 1 Thess 5:15; Mt 5:44 are possible candidates as well). Also, *Acts of Peter* several times emphasizes Peter's role as an eyewitness, which reminds us of 2 Peter 1:16 (cf. 1 Pet 5:1).

What stands out in *Acts of Peter* is the elevation of the apostle to a bigger-than-life stature, adorned with fable-like touches. The fable of the speaking dog reminds us of Balaam's donkey (Num 22:22-35), and it may be more than coincidence that 2 Peter 2:15-16 likens the false teachers to Balaam, who "was rebuked for his own transgression; a speechless donkey spoke with a human voice and restrained the prophet's madness." In this respect, *Acts of Peter* reflects some of the

---

[14]It should be noted, the Pauline citation from Isaiah 53 is not appealing to the sufferings of Christ as in 1 Peter, but rather, to the lack of response to the gospel message.

features that appear in popular, Hellenistic romances of the period.[15]

3. The last portion of *Acts of Peter*, relating his martyrdom, probably circulated independently but is now subjoined to the larger complex. The circumstances of Peter's martyrdom are as follows:

- Agrippa becomes enraged when Peter's preaching on chastity results in Agrippa's concubines refusing his sexual advances.

- Albinus, whose wife, Xanthippe, also converts and refuses sexual relations, joins with Agrippa in a plot to assassinate Peter.

- The believers warn Peter to flee the city. However, as he exits the gate, he encounters Christ, who has come to Rome "to be crucified again."

- Peter understands this as foreshadowing his own death, so he re-enters the city and is subsequently arrested. He requests to be crucified upside down and, while on the cross, allegorically interprets what this means.

- After his death, Peter appears to Marcellus and rebukes him for wasting funds on his corpse. Nero, angry that he missed the opportunity to torture Peter, intends to persecute all the believers Peter had instructed. A vision, however, warns him against this and he relents.

The most memorable scene in this section is the moment when Peter, fleeing from Rome, sees the Lord entering the city and asks him, "Lord, where are you going?" (*Quo vadis, Domine*). Henryk Sienkiewicx wrote a historical novel called *Quo Vadis*, which was later made into a Hollywood movie (1951) starring Robert Taylor as Peter. The novel and movie both include this scene from the *Acts of Peter*. A painting by Annibale Carraci depicts the tradition, and both the Church of Quo Vadis, near the Catacombs of Saint Callistus, and the Basilica of Saint Sebastian contain a stone which is said to preserve Jesus' footprints. Probably the most well-known painting of Peter's crucifixion upside down is by Caravaggio (1600) and is now located in the chapel of the Santa Maria del Popolo in Rome.

---

[15]"The genre of the apocryphal Acts is frequently described as a Christian adaptation of the popular novel." Perkins, *Peter*, pp. 140-41.

But how reliable is the tradition? Was Peter crucified upside down? One would not necessarily infer this from reading John 21:18-19. However, there is evidence that occasionally Roman soldiers did crucify people in various positions just to satisfy their sadistic impulses, so the notion itself is not implausible.[16] Furthermore, if the tradition is unhistorical, why was it invented? No certain answers are forthcoming. In my opinion, it is at least possible the tradition is genuine.

### The Acts of Peter and the Twelve Apostles

Most scholars date *The Acts of Peter and the Twelve Apostles* to the second century.[17] This charming story, narrated from Peter's point of view, is set just after the crucifixion. Here are the salient points:

- Peter and the apostles, covenanting among themselves, vow to fulfill the Lord's commission to them. They set off on a sea voyage, accomplished in just a day and night, and arrive at a town called Habitation.

- There they meet a pearl merchant named Lithargoel who is Christ in disguise. But the merchant does not have the pearl in his possession; rather, he invites the apostles and the poor—the rich disdain the merchant—to journey to his city where they may acquire it. But they are forewarned: there are many dangers and perils on the way and they must live lives of utter simplicity if they would arrive successfully.

- Peter has a vision of this city and tells his companions. They set out with joy and, following the merchant's advice, arrive in the city where they meet a physician, who is once again really Christ (*Acts Pet. 12 Apos.* 9.8-15).

- Christ reveals himself to Peter and the Eleven, and they worship him.

- Christ commissions the apostles to return to Habitation and engage in a healing ministry of both body and soul. The former is to convince the poor that the apostles possess the power "to heal the illnesses of the heart also" (*Acts Pet. 12 Apos.* 6.11).

- Christ warns the apostles to beware of the wealthy in the congregations.

---

[16]See, e.g., Seneca, *Dial.* 6; Josephus, *J.W.* 5.449-51; Y. Yadin, "Pesher Nahum (4QpNahum) Reconsidered," *Israel Exploration Journal* 21 (1971): 1-12; (1973): 18-22.

[17]Douglas M. Parrott and R. McL. Wilson, "The Acts of Peter and the Twelve Apostles," *NHL*, p. 265; Douglas M. Parrott, "Peter and the Twelve Apostles, The Acts of," *ABD* 5:265-66.

There are a number of allegorical features in the story. For example, the city called Habitation, said to mean "Foundation [and] endurance" (*Acts Pet. 12 Apos.* 6.2), clearly represents the inhabited world. The name Lithargoel, "the slender rock," seems to pick up on the Petrine image of Christ as the rejected stone that becomes the chief cornerstone (1 Pet 2:4-8). The portrayal of the soul has a clear allegorical cast to it, as does the imagery of the pearl, the latter recalling the parable of the pearl of great value (Mt 13:45-46). The poor and the rich function allegorically in the story, and so does the healing imagery.

Two episodes in this work, recalling events in the canonical Gospels, deserve mention. In the first, after successfully making the journey to the city by renouncing all worldly comforts, the apostles meet Lithargoel disguised as a physician. Peter asks him for directions to the home of Lithargoel, who tells them to rest a while and return; then he will reveal the location. When they return, Lithargoel stuns Peter by calling him by name:

> And Peter was frightened, for how did he know that his name was Peter? Peter responded to the Savior, "How do you know me, for you called my name?" Lithargoel answered, "I want to ask you who gave the name Peter to you?" He said to him, "It was Jesus Christ, the son of the living God. He gave this name to me." He answered and said, "It is I! Recognize me, Peter." He loosed his garment, which clothed him—the one into which he had changed himself because of us—revealing to us in truth that it was he. (*Acts Pet. 12 Apos.* 9)

This recognition scene seems to fuse the Gospel of John's account of Peter's initial call (Jn 1:41-42) with Peter's confession of faith at Caesarea Philippi (Mt 16:16-18) and the postresurrection account of the disciples at Emmaus (Lk 24:28-35; cf. Mt 28:17). The mention of the Savior's garment "into which he had changed himself because of us" sounds very Docetic or even Gnostic. This tractate, found among the Nag Hammadi corpus, seems to move us further on a trajectory away from a relatively benign ascetic Christianity, as seen in the *Apocalypse of Peter* and the *Acts of Peter*, toward a more serious deviation from orthodox faith. Pheme Perkins is probably correct, however, in her observation that the work "contains no peculiarly Gnostic features."[18]

A second episode also seems indebted to the Gospel of John. After the Savior commissions the apostles to go back to Habitation and give to the poor what they need to live, Peter is perplexed. How will they be able to supply such great need? In John's Gospel, Jesus once asks Philip, "'Where are we to buy bread for these people to eat?' He said this to test him, for he himself knew what he was going to do" (Jn 6:5-6). But one also recalls the Upper Room Discourse in John's Gospel (Jn 13–16) in which Simon Peter, Thomas and Philip, deeply troubled, ask a series of questions. Simon first asks, "Lord, are you going to wash my feet?" and then later inquires, "Lord, who is it?" and "Lord, where are you going?" (Jn 13:6, 25, 36). Thomas asks, "How can we know the way?" (Jn 14:5), and Philip completes the queries with this request, "Lord, show us the Father, and we will be satisfied" (Jn 14:8). In response to Peter's request in *Acts of Peter and the Twelve Apostles*, Jesus chides Peter: "O Peter, it was necessary that you understand the parable that I told you! Do you not understand that my name, which you teach, surpasses all riches, and the wisdom of God surpasses gold, and silver, and precious stones?" (*Acts Pet. 12 Apos.* 10).

At this point, Peter is afraid to reply lest he further embarrass himself. Instead, he turns to John and says, "You talk this time" (*Acts Pet. 12 Apos.* 11). So John straightforwardly asks the Savior, "How then will we know how to heal bodies as you have told us?" (*Acts Pet. 12 Apos.* 11). Jesus replies, surprisingly, "Rightly have you spoken, John, for I know that the physicians of this world heal what belongs to the world. The physicians of souls, however, heal the heart" (*Acts Pet. 12 Apos.* 11). Jesus then tells the apostles to heal the body first in order that those healed may believe and be healed in the heart. What are we to make of Jesus' different response to Peter and John over essentially the same question? Are we glimpsing an underlying rivalry between Johannine and Petrine communities—somewhat like what existed years earlier in Corinth? This probably reads too much into the text. At the least, the *Acts of Peter and the Twelve Apostles* demonstrates a light touch which is entertaining for the reader. This too probably reflects the influence of popular romances.

---

[18]Perkins, *Peter*, p. 145.

## THE GNOSTIC PETER

A quite unflattering account of Peter is found in the Gnostic *Gospel According to Mary*.[19] In the surviving fragments, Peter asks Mary (Magdalene) to share with them what the Lord has revealed to her, and she proceeds to do so. Most scholars think that the missing four pages depict a heavenly journey in which the soul encounters hostile heavenly powers (in keeping with Gnostic thought). At any rate, at the conclusion of her revelation, Andrew expresses skepticism about its content, and Peter agrees. He then asks, "Did he [Jesus] really speak privately with a woman and not openly to us? Are we to turn about and all listen to her? Did he prefer her to us?" (*Gos. Mary* 17). Listen to Mary's response and Levi's surprising rebuke of Peter:

> Then Mary wept and said to Peter, "My brother Peter, what do you think? Do you think that I thought this up myself in my heart, or that I am lying about the Saviour?" Levi answered and said to Peter, "Peter, you have always been hot-tempered. Now I see you contending against the woman like the adversaries. But if the Savior made her worthy, who are you indeed to reject her? Surely the Savior knows her very well. That is why he loved her more than us. Rather let us be ashamed and put on the perfect man, and separate as he commanded us and preach the gospel, not laying down any other rule or other law beyond what the Savior said." (*Gos. Mary* 18)

An even more misogynist attitude on the part of Peter appears in logion 114 from the *Gospel of Thomas*: "Simon Peter said to them, 'Let Mary leave us, for women are not worthy of life.'"[20] These last two passages clearly reflect certain Gnostic attitudes and not that of the apostle Peter. For example, the sentiments are hardly compatible with Peter's pastoral admonition to husbands in 1 Peter 3:7 ("heirs with you of the gracious gift of life," TNIV).

There is a discernible trajectory in this later literature away from reliance on the Gospel tradition toward more adventuresome embellishment and creativity, almost all of which may safely be dismissed as

---

[19]For background, see Douglas M. Parrott, "The Gospel of Mary (BG 8052, 1)," in *NHL*, p. 471, and Hennecke, *New Testament Apocrypha*, 2:340-44.
[20]Thomas O. Lambdin, trans., "The Gospel of Thomas," *NHL*, p. 130.

having no historical foundation.[21] It may be that here and there a genuine tradition has survived, but one is well advised to err on the side of caution and treat these with a grain of salt.

## QUESTIONS FOR DISCUSSION

1. Why are there so many postbiblical writings attributed to the apostle Peter?
2. What contribution, if any, does the *Apocalypse of Peter* make to reconstructing Peter's life and thought? What is your opinion as to the independence of this work with regard to the canonical epistles attributed to Peter?
3. What traditions about Peter reappear in the *Preaching of Peter*? Are there any new traditions?
4. Discuss whether the *Gospel of Peter* adds any genuine traditions about Peter.
5. Discuss the reliability of the traditions involving Peter and Simon Magus.
6. Discuss the reliability of the tradition that Peter was crucified upside down.
7. Do you agree with the author of this textbook that the traditions about Peter in the pseudepigrapha are largely legend? Why or why not?
8. What trends are discernible as one moves from earlier to later traditions in this material?

## FOR FURTHER STUDY

In addition to the sources listed in the previous chapter, see the following specialized sources:

Elliott, J. K. *The Apocryphal New Testament*. Oxford: Clarendon, 1993.

Hennecke, Edgar. *New Testament Apocrypha*. Edited by Wilhelm Schneemelcher. Translated by R. McL. Wilson. 2 vols. Philadelphia: Westminster, 1964.

---

[21]Jerome's assessment seems justified: "The books, of which one is entitled his Acts, another his Gospel, a third his Preaching, a fourth his Revelation, a fifth his 'Judgment' are rejected as apocryphal" (*Vir. ill.* 1). The book Jerome calls "Judgment" has apparently been lost.

# 17

## THE REST OF THE STORY

*Peter's Legacy*

IT IS A LONG WAY FROM the Sea of Galilee to the see of Rome. Even discounting many of the legendary details that appear in the later traditions about this man, one must still marvel at what God accomplished through a Galilean fisherman who became a fisher of men.

### PETER: PASTOR AND PRACTICAL THEOLOGIAN OF THE EARLIEST CHURCH

Peter's exercise of the keys of the kingdom played a crucial role in the transformation of a small, persecuted, Jewish sect into a universal faith that now numbers more than two billion souls. There is hardly any ethnic, linguistic group on the planet that does not have at least a few adherents. It is instructive to remember that Peter's part in this cosmic mission began with a painful admission: "Go away from me, Lord, for I am a sinful man!" (Lk 5:8). Repentance and rebirth, not self-reliance, connect one to divine resources beyond human reckoning (1 Pet 1:3-5, 22-25; 2:2; 2 Pet 1:1-4). Though not without difficulties and doubts, Peter accepted the Savior's summons and set out to "follow in his steps" (1 Pet 2:21). A vast host has followed in his wake.

Perhaps no figure from the earliest years of what became Christianity is more approachable and endearing than Peter. There is something about Peter that resonates in the soul of most Christians whether ancient or modern. We who are attempting to follow in the footsteps of Jesus sense that in Peter we have a fellow traveler. Paul often seems to live on a different plane than we do; Peter closes the gap and is more accessible.

No image, symbol or metaphor in history has equaled the transformative power of the cross of Christ, and no single adjective better describes Peter's practical theology than cruciform. In this Peter and Paul share a common commitment and legacy. To be sure, in Paul's letters, the cross of Christ functions more as the instrumental means whereby sinners die to sin and rise to new life in Christ (see Rom 6:1-11; Gal 6:14), whereas in 1 Peter it serves as a paradigm for discipleship (1 Pet 2:21). But too much should not be made of this functional distinction because, at the end of the day, both apostles ground God's grace in Christ's death on the cross on behalf of sinners (see Rom 3:24-25; 2 Cor 5:19; 1 Pet 1:19-20; 2:24; 3:18; 2 Pet 2:1).

A key theological issue surfacing in both Petrine epistles concerns Christian discipleship. As professor Henry Jones (Sean Connery) said to his son Indiana Jones (Harrison Ford): "My son, we're pilgrims in an unholy land."[1] In short, how does one live as an alien in a foreign land (1 Pet 1:1; 2:11)? Does one withdraw from the "futile ways" (1 Pet 1:18) and "the corruption that is in the world" (2 Pet 1:4) and live in a Christian ghetto? Or does one assimilate into the cultural mainstream? Interestingly, one can find verses here and there in Peter's letters to defend either alternative because Peter does not prescribe a precise formula. What he offers are parameters and reminders. These should be carefully heeded or the result is spiritual shipwreck: "Do not use your freedom as a pretext for evil" (1 Pet 2:16; cf. 2 Pet 2:19). But he does not urge Christian isolationism. He encourages Christians to be law-abiding, engaged citizens whose moral and ethical character is beyond reproach: "Conduct yourselves honorably among the Gentiles, . . . so that they may see your honorable deeds and glorify God when he comes to judge" (1 Pet 2:12). This delicate balancing act requires discernment and grace, something Peter believes Christians who truly want to walk in the footsteps of the Master can rely on: "His divine power has given us everything needed for life and godliness, through the knowledge of him who called us by

---

[1]The context was a Nazi book burning in Berlin (*Indiana Jones and the Last Crusade*).

his own glory and goodness" (2 Pet 1:3; cf. 1 Pet 5:10). Predictably, this
sounds very much like what "our beloved brother Paul wrote to you" (1
Cor 1:9; Eph 4:1; 1 Thess 2:12; 2 Tim 1:9).

Peter's theology tends to focus on the nitty-gritty issues of family
and workplace. To be sure, there are huge cultural differences between
then and now, but underlying his Spirit-inspired pastoral parenesis, one
finds a remarkable paradigm for Christian living in any time and place.
Once again, the shadow of the cross falls over Peter's specific directives.
Not least of Peter's contributions in this area are his sensitive and sen-
sible directives for husbands and wives and especially his helpful
guidance for those in mixed marriages (believer with unbeliever). A
majority of such marriages, then and now, involve a believing wife and
an unbelieving husband. The power of a gentle and quiet spirit as a
witness to Christ is sometimes derided as chauvinistic and sexist and
often dismissed as capitulation. But when it is sincerely practiced, the
results speak for themselves. Furthermore, a gentle and quiet spirit is
not a gender-specific admonition; it is a powerful paradigm for both
genders, since it is the path trod by the Suffering Servant who invites
each believer to follow in his steps (1 Pet 3:4, 7; cf. 1 Pet 2:23).

The difficulty with Peter's theology of the cross is not in comprehending it but rather the danger of domesticating and diluting it.
Therein lies a challenge for every serious reader: to recover the meaning
and power of the cross in one's own life. Here in a nutshell is Peter's
cross-centered message: By the cross and its correlative sequel, the resurrection, we have been given "a new birth" (1 Pet 1:3). By means of "the
precious blood of Christ" (1 Pet 1:19) we are enabled to "come to him, a
living stone" (1 Pet 2:4) and enter into our "royal priesthood" (1 Pet 2:9)
and serve "like living stones . . . [in] a spiritual house" (1 Pet 2:5) and
"offer spiritual sacrifices acceptable to God through Jesus Christ" (1 Pet
2:5). To this end, it is essential that personal and nationalistic agendas—
especially Americanism—give way to something more transcendent
and divine and infinitely more satisfying, nothing short of "a living
hope," an "imperishable, undefiled, and unfading" inheritance (1 Pet
1:3-4), "eternal glory in Christ" (1 Pet 5:10), a participation in the divine
nature (2 Pet 1:4) and a "new heavens and a new earth, where right-

eousness is at home" (2 Pet 3:13). In short, will we join Peter and follow Christ on the Via Dolorosa that leads to the Via Gloria?

In retrospect, we once again wonder why only two canonical letters, both disputed, especially the second, are attributed to the prince of the apostles. Then again, we remind ourselves that the Master himself chose not to leave behind a written legacy, only accounts written by apostles and disciples of apostles. Still, what we have from Peter is a priceless treasure. In Peter's two letters, the Gospel of Mark and the reported deeds and sayings of Peter in Acts, we hear the voice of one who physically walked and talked with the Master for three years and then communed with him spiritually for at least another thirty years. These were years in which a few living stones led by "the Rock" began rising into a great "spiritual house" founded on "a cornerstone chosen and precious" and a little flock shepherded by Pastor Peter multiplied into a great flock. Spreading the good news from Jerusalem to Rome, Peter was a point person for the Great Commission, especially among the Jews. Above all, he was a pastor with a compassionate heart and an undying passion for his Savior.

## PETER AND NT THEOLOGY

In conclusion, here is my list of the top ten contributions of the apostle Peter to NT theology:

- Peter is supremely a theologian of the cross.

- Peter is a theologian of the new birth through faith in Christ.

- Peter, like his apostolic cohorts, champions a high Christology.

- Peter is a theologian of redemptive history anchored in the story of Israel.

- Peter contributes the fullest exposition of suffering for the name of Christ.

- Peter's theology demonstrates a profound understanding of the human condition.

- Peter sees the grace of God as the source and sustenance of all Christian discipleship.

- Peter strenuously defends apostolic teaching as inspired, authoritative and normative.
- Peter's theology is both culturally engaged and cosmically oriented.
- Peter's theology stands under the shadow of the parousia.
- Peter's theology is supremely a theology of hope.

The last-named item may in fact be Peter's most relevant contribution in the twenty-first century. Church historians claim that in absolute numbers the twentieth century tallied more martyrs for Christ than any previous century, and the twenty-first century is already on pace to eclipse that grim record.[2] Added to that are ominous signs that all is not well with our world. As we move ever closer to the day of dissolution (2 Pet 3:12), Peter's concluding word drowns out all voices of doom and despair: "In accordance with his promise, we wait for new heavens and a new earth" (2 Pet 3:13). "To him be the glory both now and to the day of eternity. Amen" (2 Pet 3:18).

## QUESTIONS FOR DISCUSSION

1. Do you agree that Peter seems more accessible than Paul? Why or why not?
2. Discuss Peter's contribution to the challenge of living as an alien in a foreign land.
3. What contribution does Peter make to problems of gender and grace?
4. What would you add to my list of the top ten contributions of Peter to NT theology?
5. At the end of the day, does Peter deserve a place at the table with Paul and John?

## FOR FURTHER STUDY

Chester, Andrew, and Ralph P. Martin. *The Theology of the Letters of James, Peter and Jude.* Cambridge: Cambridge University Press, 1994. Pp. 65-86, 87-133.

---

[2]See, e.g., Robert Royal, *The Catholic Martyrs of the Twentieth Century: A Comprehensive World History* (New York: Crossroad, 2000).

Cullmann, Oscar. *Peter: Disciple—Apostle—Martyr.* Translated by Floyd V. Filson. Philadelphia: Westminster, 1953. Pp. 65-69.

Davids, P. H. "2 Peter." *NDBT.* Downers Grove, Ill.: InterVarsity Press, 2000. Pp. 350-51.

Ericson, Norman R. "Peter, First, Theology of." *EDBT.* Grand Rapids: Baker, 1996. Pp. 604-6.

———. "Peter, Second, Theology of." *EDBT.* Grand Rapids: Baker, 1996. Pp. 606-7.

Green, G. L. "1 Peter." *NDBT.* Downers Grove, Ill.: InterVarsity Press, 2000. Pp. 346-49.

Grant, Michael. *Saint Peter.* New York: Scribner, 1994. Pp. 159-67.

Marshall, I. Howard. *New Testament Theology: Many Witnesses, One Gospel.* Downers Grove, Ill.: InterVarsity Press, 2004. Pp. 648-58, 674-79.

Matera, Frank J. *New Testament Theology: Exploring Diversity and Unity.* Louisville: Westminster John Knox, 2007. Pp. 372-92.

Perkins, Pheme. *Peter: Apostle for the Whole Church.* Columbia: University of South Carolina Press, 1994. Pp. 183-86.

Thielman, Frank. *Theology of the New Testament: A Canonical and Synthetic Approach.* Grand Rapids: Zondervan, 2005. Pp. 522-35, 569-84.

# Name Index

*Page numbers in bold refer to bibliographic entries.*

# Subject Index

# Scripture Index